Survey of Commercial Insurance

Survey of Commercial Insurance

Edited by

Arthur L. Flitner, CPCU, ARM, AIC, AU

2nd Edition • 2nd Printing

The Institutes
720 Providence Road, Suite 100
Malvern, Pennsylvania 19355-3433

2nd Edition • 2nd Printing • June 2015

Library of Congress Control Number: 2014948608

ISBN 978-0-89463-799-5

Foreword

The Institutes are the trusted leader in delivering proven knowledge solutions that drive powerful business results for the risk management and property-casualty insurance industry. For more than 100 years, The Institutes have been meeting the industry's changing professional development needs with customer-driven products and services.

In conjunction with industry experts and members of the academic community, our Knowledge Resources Department develops our course and program content, including Institutes study materials. Practical and technical knowledge gained from Institutes courses enhances qualifications, improves performance, and contributes to professional growth—all of which drive results.

The Institutes' proven knowledge helps individuals and organizations achieve powerful results with a variety of flexible, customer-focused options:

Recognized Credentials—The Institutes offer an unmatched range of widely recognized and industry-respected specialty credentials. The Institutes' Chartered Property Casualty Underwriter (CPCU) professional designation is designed to provide a broad understanding of the property-casualty insurance industry. Depending on professional needs, CPCU students may select either a commercial insurance focus or a personal risk management and insurance focus and may choose from a variety of electives.

In addition, The Institutes offer certificate or designation programs in a variety of disciplines, including these:

- Claims
- Commercial underwriting
- Fidelity and surety bonding
- General insurance
- Insurance accounting and finance
- Insurance information technology
- Insurance production and agency management
- Insurance regulation and compliance
- Management
- Marine insurance
- Personal insurance
- Premium auditing
- Quality insurance services
- Reinsurance
- Risk management
- Surplus lines

Ethics—Ethical behavior is crucial to preserving not only the trust on which insurance transactions are based, but also the public's trust in our industry as a whole. All Institutes designations now have an ethics requirement, which is delivered online and free of charge. The ethics requirement content is designed specifically for insurance practitioners and uses insurance-based case studies to outline an ethical framework. More information is available in the Programs section of our Web site, www.TheInstitutes.org.

Flexible Online Learning—The Institutes have an unmatched variety of technical insurance content covering topics from accounting to underwriting, which we now deliver through hundreds of online courses. These cost-effective self-study courses are a convenient way to fill gaps in technical knowledge in a matter of hours without ever leaving the office.

Continuing Education—A majority of The Institutes' courses are filed for CE credit in most states. We also deliver quality, affordable, online CE courses quickly and conveniently through CEU. Visit www.CEU.com to learn more. CEU is powered by The Institutes.

College Credits—Most Institutes courses carry college credit recommendations from the American Council on Education. A variety of courses also qualify for credits toward certain associate, bachelor's, and master's degrees at several prestigious colleges and universities. More information is available in the Student Services section of our Web site, www.TheInstitutes.org.

Custom Applications—The Institutes collaborate with corporate customers to utilize our trusted course content and flexible delivery options in developing customized solutions that help them achieve their unique organizational goals.

Insightful Analysis—Our Insurance Research Council (IRC) division conducts public policy research on important contemporary issues in property-casualty insurance and risk management. Visit www.ircweb.org to learn more or purchase its most recent studies.

The Institutes look forward to serving the risk management and property-casualty insurance industry for another 100 years. We welcome comments from our students and course leaders; your feedback helps us continue to improve the quality of our study materials.

Peter L. Miller, CPCU
President and CEO
The Institutes

Preface

Survey of Commercial Insurance is the assigned textbook for CPCU 557, Survey of Commercial Insurance, in The Institutes' Chartered Property Casualty Underwriter (CPCU) designation program. This text provides learners with a broad understanding of the property and liability loss exposures faced by most organizations, and the corresponding types of commercial insurance that can be used for covering those loss exposures.

Assignments 1 through 10 examine the major types of commercial insurance, including commercial property, business income, commercial crime, equipment breakdown, inland and ocean marine, general liability, commercial auto, workers compensation, and businessowners. Assignment 11 concludes the text by discussing several specialty coverages, including excess and umbrella liability, professional liability, management liability, environmental, aircraft, cyber risk, terrorism, and surety.

The Institutes are grateful to the insurance professionals, course leaders, and course sponsors who provided guidance and review during the planning of this text. Their assistance helped to ensure that the text is accurate and reflects current industry practices.

For more information about The Institutes' programs, please call our Customer Service Department at (800) 644-2101, email us at CustomerService@TheInstitutes.org, or visit our website at www.TheInstitutes.org.

Mary Ann Cook

Arthur L. Flitner

Contributors

The Institutes acknowledge with deep appreciation the contributions made to the content of this text by the following persons:

Richard Berthelsen, JD, CPCU, AIC, ARM, AU, ARe, MBA

Pamela J. Brooks, MBA, CPCU, AAM, AIM, AIS

Douglas Froggatt

Contents

1

Commercial Property Insurance, Part I

Educational Objectives

After learning the content of this assignment, you should be able to:

▷ Describe commercial property insurance in terms of these elements:

- The major categories of loss exposures that can be covered
- The components of a commercial property coverage part

▷ Determine whether a described item of property qualifies as Covered Property under one or more of these categories in the Building and Personal Property Coverage Form:

- Building
- Your Business Personal Property
- Personal Property of Others

▷ Determine which of the additional coverages and coverage extensions of the Building and Personal Property Coverage Form (BPP) apply to a described loss.

▷ Determine whether the cause of a described loss is a covered cause of loss under either the Causes of Loss—Basic Form or the Causes of Loss—Broad Form.

▷ Determine whether the cause of a described loss is a Covered Cause of Loss under the Causes of Loss—Special Form.

▷ Apply the Limits of Insurance and Deductible provisions of the Building and Personal Property Coverage Form to a described loss.

Commercial Property Insurance, Part I

OVERVIEW OF COMMERCIAL PROPERTY INSURANCE

Almost all businesses, including not-for-profit and governmental organizations, face potentially devastating losses associated with commercial property ownership. Purchase of a commercial package policy's commercial property coverage is one method businesses may use to transfer the risks associated with such potential losses.

Commercial property loss exposures may be analyzed according to three components:

- Types of property
- Causes of loss to property
- Financial consequences of property losses

The commercial property coverage part is a common example of insurance policy provisions that cover commercial property loss exposures.

Commercial Property Loss Exposures

The three components used to analyze property loss exposures allow for identification of the exposures in specific terms. For example, they may refer to a building exposure (type of property), a windstorm exposure (cause of loss), or a loss of business income exposure (financial consequence). Similarly, they could identify a property loss exposure in terms of two or even all three of these elements, such as a building fire exposure or loss of business income resulting from breakdown of a production machine.

Types of Property

Property is any item with value. Individuals, families, and organizations own and use property, depend on it as a source of income or services, and rely on its value. Property can decline in value—or even become worthless—if it is lost, damaged, or destroyed. Any item of property can be classified as either **real property (realty)** or **personal property**.

Examples of real property, in addition to land, are buildings, driveways, sidewalks, underground piping, and radio transmission towers. Property that is permanently attached to a structure, such as built-in appliances or paneling,

Real property (realty)
Tangible property consisting of land, all structures permanently attached to the land, and whatever is growing on the land.

Personal property
All tangible or intangible property that is not real property.

is also generally considered part of the structure. For example, most buildings also include plumbing, wiring, and heating and air conditioning equipment. Similarly, a high-rise building usually has elevators and may have specially designed platforms, hoists, and tracks used by window washers. Such equipment is considered part of the building.

All property that is not real property is personal property. Examples of personal property include vehicles, merchandise, furniture, tools, clothing, and oil while being transported through an underground pipeline. For insurance purposes, personal property falls into these classifications:

- Contents—Property insurance policies typically use the term "personal property" to refer to the contents of a building (for example, office furniture, machinery and equipment, and stock such as completed products in inventory), rather than "contents," because the property often is covered even when it is not literally contained in the building. Policies generally use the term "business personal property" to refer to the contents of a commercial building. Contents also include personal property of others that is in the insured's care, custody, or control; this property is covered by the Personal Property of Others provision in commercial property coverage forms.

- Property in transit—Most businesses ship property to others (such as merchandise) or receive property from others (such as raw materials or supplies). Property in transit can be transported by a variety of means, for any length of time, and over various distances on the owner's own vehicles or by a transportation company. A commercial property policy may provide some coverage for property in transit, but it is often inadequate for insureds with significant transit exposures. A firm that needs broader coverage for property in transit can purchase separate cargo insurance.

- Property in the possession of others—In many situations, an organization may place its property in the temporary possession of others for processing, cleaning, repairing, adjusting, storing, exhibiting, or selling. Because the probability of loss at the temporary location could differ greatly from the probability of loss at the owner's location, building and contents insurance policies usually provide only a nominal amount of insurance for property at other locations. Like property in transit, property in the possession of others can be insured for its full value under specialized policies designed for that purpose.

- "Floating" property—Many businesses own property that normally does not remain at a fixed work site or that is in transit between work sites (for example, a wedding photographer's cameras and a building contractor's tools and mobile equipment). Such property is often referred to as "floating" property. Insurance for floating property is available under specialized inland marine policies called "floaters."

Causes of Loss to Property

The potential causes of loss to property are another important aspect of property loss exposures. A cause of loss (for example, fire or vandalism) adversely affects property and leaves it in an altered state. Some causes of loss do not alter the property itself but do affect a person's ability to possess or use the property. For example, property lost or stolen may still be used, but not by its rightful owner.

Buildings and personal property are subject to many potential causes of loss. For most insureds, fire is the cause of loss that poses the greatest risk of a large or even total property loss. Windstorms, such as hurricanes and tornadoes; flood; earthquake; terrorism; and war also pose potentially catastrophic exposures for insurers and insureds.

Financial Consequences of Property Losses

Financial consequences are the third and final important aspect of property loss exposures. The adverse financial consequences of a property loss may include a reduction in the value of the property, lost income, and/or extra expenses.

When a property loss occurs, the property's value is reduced. This reduction in value can be measured in different ways. Property that must be replaced has no remaining worth, unless some salvageable items can be sold. If the property can be repaired or restored, the reduction in value can be measured by the cost of the repair or restoration. For example, if a fence worth $7,000 is damaged by a falling tree and the fence owner has to pay $2,000 to have the damage repaired, the fence owner has incurred a partial loss that reduces the value of the fence by $2,000.

A business may lose income as a result of a property loss. When property is damaged, income might be lost because the property cannot be used until it is repaired, restored, or replaced. For example, when a business suffers a serious fire, it might have to close until repairs to the building are made and personal property is replaced. The resulting loss of income occurs over time. As another example, the owner of a rental property faces rental income loss if the property is damaged and temporarily unavailable for rent. The owner would probably continue to incur some expenses, such as mortgage payments and taxes, but would not receive the rent that helped pay those expenses.

For a business to determine the extent of a property loss exposure, it must consider the extra expenses that the loss of the property would require. When property is damaged, the property itself declines in value, and the owner or other affected party suffers a corresponding loss. In addition, the owner or other user of that property might incur extra expenses in acquiring a temporary substitute or in temporarily maintaining the damaged property in a usable condition. For example, when a store's premises are damaged, the owners might have to rent temporary space at considerably greater expense than their normal rent.

Components of a Commercial Property Coverage Part

Commercial property loss exposures can be insured under a **commercial property coverage part**, which consists of five components:

- Commercial property declarations
- One or more commercial property coverage forms
- One or more causes of loss forms
- Commercial Property Conditions
- Any applicable endorsements

Commercial property coverage part

Commercial package policy (CPP) coverage component that provides a broad range of coverages to "middle-market" or larger firms to insure buildings and business personal property.

Commercial package policy (CPP)

Policy that covers two or more lines of business by combining ISO's commercial lines coverage parts.

Monoline policy

Policy that covers only one line of business.

Package modification factors

Factors that are applied to the regular policy premiums for certain coverage parts of a CPP that includes both property and liability coverages, resulting in premium discounts for those coverage parts.

Commercial property declarations page

A required commercial property coverage part component that provides basic information about the policyholder and the insurance provided.

The commercial property coverage part is a component of the **commercial package policy (CPP)** program of Insurance Services Office, Inc. (ISO). A commercial property coverage part can be one of the two or more coverage parts included in a CPP. It can also be the single coverage part included in a **monoline policy** under ISO procedures.

An important element of the CPP program is the package discount the insured may receive. The premium for a CPP is initially determined as if each coverage part were being issued as a monoline policy. If a CPP includes both property coverage and liability coverage, the premiums for certain coverage parts are multiplied by **package modification factors**, resulting in premium discounts. These discounts are justified by the greater efficiency of issuing a single package policy instead of several monoline policies.

Commercial Property Declarations

A **commercial property declarations page** contains information that pertains specifically to property insurance:

- A description of the property insured
- The kinds and amounts of coverage provided and the covered causes of loss (basic, broad, or special)
- A list of mortgagees, if any
- The deductible amount
- A list of the property coverage forms and endorsements attached to the policy
- The applicable coinsurance percentage(s)
- Any optional coverages

Supplemental declarations can be added as needed on a separate page. For example, if an insured fast-food franchise cannot list all of its locations on the declarations page, it may add a supplemental schedule to show them.

Commercial Property Coverage Forms

The CPP program includes several different **commercial property coverage forms**. A commercial property coverage form typically contains these elements:

- Insuring agreement
- Delineation of the property covered and not covered
- Additional coverages and coverage extensions
- Provisions and definitions that apply only to that coverage form

A commercial property coverage part often includes more than one commercial property coverage form. Typically, one coverage form insures the insured's buildings and/or personal property, and another coverage form insures business income and/or extra expense.

A commonly used commercial property coverage form is the Building and Personal Property Coverage Form, also referred to as the BPP, which can be used to insure buildings, business personal property of the insured, and personal property of others in the insured's custody. Additional personal property coverage forms are available for insuring buildings and/or personal property in several special situations, such as buildings under construction, condominium association property, and condominium commercial unit owners' property. Commercial property coverage forms are also available for insuring loss of business income and/or extra expense.

Commercial property coverage form

A commercial property coverage part component that can be any of several commercial property forms containing an insuring agreement and related provisions.

Causes of Loss Forms

The three types of **causes of loss forms**—Basic, Broad, and Special—allow the insured to select, or the underwriter to offer, a range of covered perils.

A commercial property coverage part may contain more than one causes of loss form. One causes of loss form (such as the Special Form) may apply to buildings, while another (such as the Broad Form) may apply to personal property.

The commercial property declarations indicate which form applies to each type of property at each location. It is generally the underwriter's reluctance to provide the broader coverages for certain types of property that results in the use of different causes of loss forms in the same policy. Such instances are infrequent, however.

Causes of loss form

A required component of the commercial property coverage part that specifies perils covered.

Commercial Property Conditions

The **Commercial Property Conditions** are a required component of the commercial property coverage part that contains conditions applicable to all commercial property coverage forms. They are printed as a separate form and apply to all coverage forms included in a commercial property coverage part unless a coverage form contains a condition to the contrary. Like the

Commercial Property Conditions

A required component of the commercial property coverage part that contains conditions applicable to all commercial property coverage forms.

Common Policy Conditions, the Commercial Property Conditions do not require reiteration in each coverage form.

Endorsements

Many endorsements are available to tailor commercial property coverage to meet the specialized needs of particular insureds or to eliminate exposures that underwriters are not willing to insure.

BPP COVERED PROPERTY

The main insuring agreement of the Building and Personal Property Coverage Form (BPP) states that the insurer will pay for direct physical loss of or damage to Covered Property at the described premises caused by or resulting from any Covered Cause of Loss. Determining whether property qualifies as Covered Property is therefore an essential step in deciding whether the BPP covers a loss.

The BPP can cover any combination of three broad categories of property:

* Building
* Your Business Personal Property
* Personal Property of Others

Coverage can be provided on any combination of these categories. The insured's selection of categories is indicated on the commercial property declarations page by entering a limit of insurance for each chosen category of covered property.

If there is no entry for one of the categories of covered property (for example, Building), then no coverage applies to that category, even if the insured owns property fitting that category. The Property Not Covered section of the BPP specifies property that is not covered and therefore works in tandem with the Covered Property section to describe what property is covered by the BPP.

Categories of Covered Property

Understanding how the BPP defines each of the three categories of Covered Property is essential to determining whether it covers a particular loss.

Building

The policy covers buildings or structures listed and described in the declarations.

The BPP's definition of Building also includes these elements:

* Completed additions to covered buildings
* Fixtures (including outdoor fixtures)

- Permanently installed machinery and equipment
- Personal property owned by the insured and used to maintain or service the building or its premises (for example, fire extinguishing equipment; outdoor furniture; floor coverings; and equipment for refrigeration, ventilation, cooking, dishwashing, or laundering)

In addition, if they are not otherwise insured, the building description covers additions, alterations, or repairs in progress, including materials, equipment, and supplies used in connection with such work. However, such materials, equipment, and supplies are covered only if they are located within 100 feet of the described premises.

Fixtures are items attached to a building or to the land, usually in such a way that they cannot easily be removed, such as plumbing and electrical fixtures. Outdoor fixtures include items outside the building but attached to the land, such as light poles and flagpoles.

Fixtures are real property. The term "fixtures" is broad enough to include fences and outdoor signs, but coverage for these items is specifically excluded or limited.

Your Business Personal Property

Your Business Personal Property covers personal property owned by the insured and used in the insured's business. Except for an extension that provides limited coverage for property while away from the insured premises, coverage applies only when the property is located in or on the described Building or in the open (or in a vehicle) within 100 feet of the building or structure or within 100 feet of the described premises, whichever distance is greater.

Your Business Personal Property includes furniture and fixtures, machinery and equipment, stock, and all other personal property owned by the insured and used in the insured's business, except those items excluded under the Property Not Covered section.

The form defines stock as "merchandise held in storage or for sale, raw materials and in-process or finished goods, including supplies used in their packing or shipping." Your Business Personal Property also includes labor, materials, or services furnished by the insured on personal property of others.

The insured's interest in improvements and betterments is also insured as Your Business Personal Property, even though improvements and betterments are actually a part of the building and are technically real property. For example, a restaurant that rents space in a commercial building might install elaborate wall and ceiling treatments that could not be removed when the lease is terminated.

It is common for some commercial tenants to spend $1 million or more upgrading their premises. It is important to consider the insurable value of improvements and betterments when setting the amount of insurance that a tenant should carry; ignoring improvements and betterments can result in severe underinsurance difficulties when a loss occurs.

Your Business Personal Property also includes leased personal property for which the named insured has a contractual responsibility to procure coverage. An example of such property is phone or computer equipment leased by the insured under an agreement requiring the insured to purchase insurance on the equipment.

Personal Property of Others

This coverage is designed to protect the insured against loss of or damage to the personal property of others while such property is in the custody of the insured. It is an important coverage for businesses (bailees) that have customers' property in their custody, such as laundries, dry cleaners, appliance repair shops, and furniture upholstery shops.

The BPP covers such property only while it is in the insured's care, custody, or control and in or on the building described in the declarations or within 100 feet of the building or structure or within 100 feet of the described premises, whichever distance is greater. Coverage applies regardless of whether the insured is legally responsible for the damage.

Even if the insured does not buy coverage for personal property of others (as indicated by an amount of insurance being shown for that category on the declarations page), the BPP still provides a coverage extension for personal property of others, which is limited to $2,500 at each insured location.

Property Not Covered

The BPP's Property Not Covered section lists several classes of property or kinds of property losses that do not qualify as covered property. Therefore, the Covered Property section and the Property Not Covered section must be read together when determining whether a specific kind of property is insured.

There are several reasons for excluding some kinds of property from coverage:

- Some kinds of property, such as smuggled goods being held for sale, are illegal to insure.
- Some property may be much less susceptible to loss by most of the perils insured against. Examples include building foundations below the lowest basement floor or the surface of the ground, retaining walls that are not part of a building, and underground pipes.
- Some kinds of property are excluded because they can be insured more advantageously under other forms. For example, insurers generally prefer to cover money, securities, automobiles, and aircraft under other policies.

By endorsement, insurance can be made available for almost all of the items listed in the Property Not Covered section. Only contraband or property in the course of illegal transportation or trade is totally uninsurable.

Property otherwise insured is not totally excluded. The BPP covers such property, but only in excess of the other insurance.

For example, assume that a computer system valued at $150,000 is insured under the general category of business personal property in a BPP and is also insured for $100,000 under a separate electronic data processing (EDP) equipment policy issued by a different insurer. If the computer system is totally destroyed by fire, a cause of loss insured under both policies, the insurer that issued the EDP policy must pay its limit ($100,000). The insurer that issued the BPP would then pay the difference between the limit of the EDP policy and the amount of loss otherwise payable under the BPP.

Marketing Tip—Typically, property is excluded from a policy because it is considered uninsurable (such as land and water) or because the loss exposures require careful underwriting (such as bridges, piers, wharves, or docks) beyond that which is contemplated by a standard form. Additionally, under the BPP, items such as foundations or pilings and underground pipes and flues are excluded from building and personal property coverage to reduce the amount of insurance needed to satisfy the coinsurance clause.

Coverage for some excluded items can be added back to the BPP, although doing so increases the amount of insurance needed (and therefore the coinsurance required). Producers can endorse the policy to provide coverage for those items and should help the insured determine the need for coverage. Even though the probability of loss to items such as excavations, foundations below ground, and underground pipes is very low, they are susceptible to serious loss from such perils as explosion and water damage. Should a loss occur, the insured will appreciate the coverage.

Exceptions provide coverage under certain circumstances for some types of property not covered. For example, animals are not covered unless they are owned by others and boarded by the insured or held as stock, as in a pet shop. Similarly, some coverage is provided for vehicles or self-propelled machines.

Apply Your Knowledge

A business owns an office building and insures it under a BPP covering only the Building as defined in the policy. Would equipment that the business owns and uses to clean and maintain the building be Covered Property under its BPP?

Feedback: Yes, the equipment would be Covered Property under the BPP, because the definition of Building includes personal property owned by the insured and used to maintain or service the building or its premises.

A business owns a building insured under a BPP, with coverage indicated for the Building and Your Business Personal Property as defined in the policy. Would merchandise that the business owns and displays at a trade show held in a different city qualify as Covered Property under its BPP?

Feedback: No. The insured's merchandise meets the BPP's definition of stock, and stock is one of the types of property listed under Your Business Personal Property. However, while located in another city, the merchandise does not meet the requirement that the property must be located in or on the described building or in the open (or in a vehicle) within 100 feet of the insured's building or the described premises.

Therefore, the merchandise is not Covered Property while located at the trade show. (However, a coverage extenson in a later section of the BPP provides limited coverage for this loss exposure.)

BPP ADDITIONAL COVERAGES AND COVERAGE EXTENSIONS

The Building and Personal Property Coverage Form, also referred to as the BPP, includes additional coverages and coverage extensions that provide several enhancements of its basic coverage.

The BPP provides several supplemental coverages in addition to the basic coverages for buildings, the insured's business personal property, and the property of others. These supplemental coverages are described under two subheadings: Additional Coverages and Coverage Extensions. See the exhibit "BPP Additional Coverages and Coverage Extensions: Special Limits."

BPP Additional Coverages and Coverage Extensions: Special Limits

All of the BPP's additional coverages and coverage extensions, except Preservation of Property, are subject to special dollar limits. In many cases, these limits result in insufficient coverage. For example, the limit for the Pollutant Cleanup and Removal additional coverage is $10,000 per policy year. Because losses related to pollutant cleanup can be extensive, this limit often proves inadequate for policyholders. Similarly, the Electronic Data additional coverage limit is $2,500 per policy year, a limit that does not adequately address the potentially catastrophic effects of losses related to electronic data.

The limits for many of the BPP's additional coverages and coverage extensions can be increased by showing a higher limit in the declarations, adding an appropriate coverage endorsement, or buying another type of policy to supplement the BPP. However, many insurers will not provide higher limits under the BPP for the Pollutant Cleanup and Removal or the Electronic Data additional coverages.

[DA07809]

Additional Coverages

These are the six additional coverages in the BPP:

- Debris Removal
- Preservation of Property
- Fire Department Service Charge
- Pollutant Cleanup and Removal
- Increased Cost of Construction
- Electronic Data

Debris Removal

Following a loss, large amounts of debris may remain on the premises, and the cost of removing the debris may be substantial. The Debris Removal additional coverage covers the cost of removing debris of covered property resulting from a covered cause of loss during the policy period. It would not, for example, pay to remove the debris resulting from a flood if flood is not a covered cause of loss or to remove the debris of the insured's licensed automobiles, because they are not covered property.

In some cases, the cost to remove debris of property that is not covered property is also covered. For example, the cost to remove debris of a neighboring building that a windstorm blew onto the insured's premises would be covered.

The Debris Removal additional coverage includes the cost to clean up pollution at the insured's premises caused by an insured peril. For example, if a building is shown as covered property, the cost to clean up debris from a fire that causes the release of toxic chemicals onto the floor of the insured's building would be covered. However, the Debris Removal provision does not apply to costs for cleanup or removal of pollutants from land or water. Limited coverage for these costs is available under the provisions of another additional coverage. No coverage is provided for cleanup of off-premises pollution even when it results from a covered loss.

Preservation of Property

It is sometimes necessary to move covered property to another location to protect it. The Preservation of Property additional coverage extends the policy to protect covered property while it is being moved and for up to thirty days at the new location. This coverage is broader than the normal coverage under the policy. It protects against "any direct physical loss or damage" and is not limited to either the covered causes of loss or locations stipulated in the coverage form. The protection provided under this additional coverage is subject to the limits of insurance stated in the declarations. Consequently, the additional coverage provides no protection if the applicable limit of insurance is exhausted by payment for the physical loss.

Fire Department Service Charge

In some localities, the fire department may make a charge for its services in controlling or extinguishing a fire. The Fire Department Service Charge additional coverage pays fire department charges up to the specified limit at each location if they are required by local ordinance or are assumed by contract before the loss occurs.

Pollutant Cleanup and Removal

The Pollutant Cleanup and Removal additional coverage provides limited coverage for the cleanup and removal of pollutants from land or water at the described premises. This additional coverage pays the insured's expenses to extract pollutants from land or water at the described premises if the release, discharge, dispersal, seepage, migration, or escape of the pollutants is the result of a covered cause of loss that occurs during the policy period.

Increased Cost of Construction

The Ordinance or Law exclusion contained in the causes of loss forms that can be attached to the BPP excludes the increased cost to comply with ordinances or laws regulating the repair, rebuilding, or replacement of covered buildings. The Increased Cost of Construction additional coverage provides a small amount of insurance to cover this loss exposure. The amount of insurance is equal to 5 percent of the amount of insurance or $10,000, whichever is less. It is paid in addition to the policy limit. This additional coverage applies only if the Replacement Cost optional coverage has been selected.

The Increased Cost of Construction additional coverage provides no coverage for these items:

- Loss to any undamaged portion of the building that an ordinance or law does not permit to remain in use
- The cost to demolish the undamaged portion of the structure and remove its debris

Electronic Data

Because of businesses' growing dependence on electronic data and the widespread belief that the exposure could better be treated by other forms of insurance, the BPP excludes electronic data in most instances except as provided by the Electronic Data additional coverage. This additional coverage is subject to a limit that is too low to provide meaningful coverage for most businesses and is the most that the insurer will pay per policy year, regardless of the number of occurrences or locations covered. All electronic data damage is deemed to have been sustained in the policy year that an occurrence began, even if the damage continues or results in additional loss or damage in a subsequent policy year.

Coverage Extensions

The BPP coverage extensions apply only if at least 80 percent coinsurance or a value reporting period symbol is shown in the declarations. The amounts payable under the coverage extensions are payable in addition to the overall limits of insurance stated in the declarations, subject to the special limits that apply to the coverage extensions. These are the six BPP coverage extensions:

- Newly Acquired or Constructed Property
- Personal Effects and Property of Others
- Valuable Papers and Records (Other Than Electronic Data)
- Property Off-Premises
- Outdoor Property
- Non-Owned Detached Trailers
- Business Personal Property Temporarily in Portable Storage Units

Newly Acquired or Constructed Property

If the policy covers a building, the Newly Acquired or Constructed Property extension provides automatic coverage for a new building being constructed at the premises described in the declarations. Automatic coverage is also provided for newly acquired buildings at other locations, provided the purpose of the newly acquired building is similar to the use of the building described in the declarations or the newly acquired building will be used as a warehouse. The coverage extension states a maximum amount of coverage that applies to each building.

If the policy covers business personal property, the extension also provides automatic coverage for these types of property:

- Business personal property at any newly acquired location other than fairs, trade shows, or exhibitions
- Business personal property located at newly constructed or acquired buildings at the location described in the declarations

A stated amount of coverage applies to loss of business personal property at each building.

The coverage for buildings and business personal property provided by this extension is temporary. It terminates automatically at the earliest of three dates:

- The expiration date of the policy
- Thirty days after the acquisition of the new location or the start of construction of the new building
- The date the insured notifies the insurer of the new location or new building

Personal Effects and Property of Others

The Personal Effects and Property of Others extension provides a limited amount of coverage for personal effects (such as a coat or jewelry) owned by an individual insured or a partner, a member, an officer, a manager, or an employee of the insured while on the premises described in the declarations. Personal effects are not covered for loss by theft. The extension also covers property of others in the care, custody, or control of the insured.

Valuable Papers and Records (Other Than Electronic Data)

Valuable papers and records (such as records of accounts receivable, mailing lists, legal documents, medical records, specifications, and drawings) are covered as business personal property, but only for the cost of blank records plus the labor to transcribe or copy duplicate information. This extension does not apply to electronic data; previous versions of the BPP did cover the cost of reconstructing electronic data.

Property Off-Premises

The Property Off-Premises extension provides coverage for covered property while it is away from the described premises. In addition to property temporarily at locations that the insured does not own, lease, or operate, the extension also covers property in storage at a location leased after the inception of the current policy and property at any fair, trade show, or exhibition. This extension does not apply to property in or on a vehicle or in the custody of the insured's salespersons unless the property in custody is at a fair, trade show, or exhibition.

Outdoor Property

The Outdoor Property extension covers loss to outdoor fences; radio and television antennas (including satellite dishes); and trees, shrubs, and plants in most instances. Unlike the other coverage extensions, the Outdoor Property extension has its own list of covered causes of loss. It covers only loss by fire, lightning, explosion, riot or civil commotion, and aircraft. Some of the more likely causes of loss to outdoor property—windstorm, vehicles, and vandalism—are not covered.

Non-Owned Detached Trailers

Insureds frequently lease trailers to expand office space or to provide additional storage or work areas at their own premises. The Non-Owned Detached Trailers extension permits the insured to extend Your Business Personal Property to include such trailers. The trailer must be used in the insured's business and be in the insured's care, custody, or control at the described premises. Moreover, the insured must have a contractual responsibility to pay for loss or damage to the trailer.

The coverage does not apply while the trailer is attached to any motor vehicle or motorized conveyance, whether or not it is in motion. Nor does it apply during hitching or unhitching operations or when a trailer becomes accidentally unhitched from a motor vehicle or conveyance.

Business Personal Property Temporarily in Portable Storage Units

This coverage extension provides temporary insurance for business personal property while stored in a portable storage unit, which could include either a unit specifically designed for this purpose or a detached trailer or semitrailer. For the contents of the unit to be covered, the unit must be located within 100 feet of the building or structure described in the declarations or within 100 feet of the described premises, whichever distance is greater.

The coverage is truly limited to temporary storage: coverage ends ninety days after the property is placed in the unit. Moreover, the coverage does not apply if the unit has been in use at the described premises for more than ninety days. Unless a higher limit is shown in the declarations, $10,000 is the most that the insurer will pay for business personal property under this extension, regardless of the number of units in use.

Apply Your Knowledge

A business insures its building under a BPP that has 80 percent coinsurance. As the business grows, it acquires another building for use as a distribution warehouse. Two weeks after the insured acquires the building, a lightning strike on the warehouse premises damages the building and an outdoor security fence. At the time of the lightning strike, the insured has not reported the new building to the insurer. Identify the coverage extensions that would apply to this loss.

Feedback: The Newly Acquired or Constructed Property and the Outdoor Property coverage extensions would apply to this loss. The Newly Acquired or Constructed Property coverage extension applies because the purpose of the business's newly acquired building was for it to be used as a warehouse and because the business acquired the warehouse less than thirty days before the loss. The Outdoor Property coverage extension applies to the loss because lightning is a covered cause of loss and the outdoor fence is specifically covered.

Fire damages a business's office complex, which is covered under a BPP. The blaze destroys one of the complex's two buildings, which the business intends to rebuild. The cost of rebuilding the destroyed building will be increased because of building code changes that have taken place since it was constructed. The other building sustained only minor damage, but fire-damaged covered property will need to be hauled away before repairs can begin. Identify the additional coverages that would apply to this loss.

Feedback: The Increased Cost of Construction and the Debris Removal additional coverages would apply to this loss. The Increased Cost of Construction additional coverage applies because it provides coverage for the increased cost to comply with ordinances or laws regulating the repair, rebuilding, or replacement of covered buildings. The Debris Removal additional coverage applies because it covers the cost of removing debris of covered property resulting from a covered cause of loss during the policy period.

CAUSES OF LOSS—BASIC FORM AND BROAD FORM

The perils covered in an Insurance Services Office, Inc. (ISO) commercial property policy are specified in any of three causes of loss forms.

The Causes of Loss—Basic Form (CP 10 10) and the Causes of Loss—Broad Form (CP 10 20), two of the three causes of loss forms available for use in the ISO commercial property coverage part, are nearly identical. The coverage provided by the third causes of loss form, the Causes of Loss—Special Form (CP 10 30), differs from the other two forms. This discussion focuses on three sections of the Basic Form and the Broad Form, noting instances where the two forms diverge:

- Covered Causes of Loss
- Exclusions
- Additional Coverages

Covered Causes of Loss

The Basic Form and the Broad Form both explicitly name the policy's covered causes of loss. This is known as a "named perils" approach. The Broad Form covers all of the perils covered in the Basic Form but also includes three additional perils that the Basic Form does not cover. Although the Broad Form is slightly more expensive than the Basic Form, most insureds choose it over the Basic Form. See the exhibit "Covered Causes of Loss in the Basic Form and Broad Form."

Exclusions

Both forms contain several exclusions that further define or limit the covered causes of loss. See the exhibit "Anti-Concurrent Causation Wording."

Covered Causes of Loss in the Basic Form and Broad Form

Covered Cause of Loss	Description
Fire	For most insureds, fire is the peril that poses the greatest risk of a large or total property loss.
Lightning	Lightning is a naturally occurring electrical discharge between clouds or between a cloud and the earth.
Explosion	The explosion peril includes the explosion of gases or fuel in a furnace or flue (called "combustion explosion" or "furnace explosion").
Windstorm or hail	Hurricanes and tornadoes are both examples of windstorms, although less severe windstorms can cause property damage and also fall within the coverage. Damage by rain, snow, sand, or dust to the interior of a building or to property inside the building is not covered unless the building first sustains exterior damage by wind, and the rain, snow, sand, or dust enters through the damaged part of the building. Does not include hail damage to lawns, trees, shrubs, or plants that are part of a vegetated roof.
Smoke	For smoke damage to be covered, it must be sudden and accidental. No coverage exists for damage by smoke from industrial operations or agricultural smudging (the intentional production of smoke to protect crops from frost damage).
Aircraft or vehicles	Damage caused by aircraft must result from actual physical contact with the aircraft or objects falling from it. Vehicle damage must result from accidental physical contact with a vehicle or an object thrown by the vehicle (such as a pebble propelled by a truck's tire). There is no coverage for damage caused by vehicles owned by the insured or operated in the insured's business.
Riot or civil commotion	In most states, a riot is defined by law as a violent public disturbance by three or more persons. However, the riot or civil commotion peril includes acts by striking workers while occupying the insured premises as well as looting occurring at the time and place of a riot or civil commotion.
Vandalism	Vandalism means the willful and malicious damage to or destruction of property. Although the vandalism peril does not cover loss by theft, it does cover damage to the building caused by the entry or exit of burglars.
Sprinkler leakage	Sprinkler leakage means the escape of any substance (water, carbon dioxide, or any other extinguishing agent) from an automatic fire protection or extinguishing system. The collapse of a tank constituting a part of such a system is covered, as is the cost of repairing damage to the system if the damage results in the sprinkler leakage or if the damage is caused by freezing. The cost to tear out and replace any part of the building or structure to repair damage to the automatic sprinkler system is also covered.
Sinkhole collapse	Sinkholes result from underground water dissolving limestone or dolomite and creating an empty space or cavern under the ground. When the roof of the cavern gets too close to the ground surface, the surface collapses, causing damage to buildings or other property located over or near the resulting sinkhole. This peril insures resulting damage to covered property (buildings or business personal property), but not the cost of filling the sinkhole. Loss caused by the collapse of land into man-made underground cavities, such as mineshafts, is not covered by this peril.
Volcanic action	The volcanic action peril covers damage caused by lava flow, ash, dust, particulate matter, airborne volcanic blast, or airborne shock waves resulting from a volcanic eruption. The earthquake damage that often accompanies a volcanic eruption is excluded by one of the exclusions discussed subsequently. Because such losses may occur over a relatively long period of time, both forms stipulate that all eruptions that occur within any 168-hour period are considered a single occurrence and are thus subject to only one deductible and policy limit.
Falling objects (Broad Form only)	The coverage for falling objects does not include damage to personal property in the open or to damage inside a building unless the roof or an outside wall is first damaged by the falling object.
Weight of ice, snow, or sleet (Broad Form only)	Does not cover damage to personal property in the open, or to lawns, trees, shrubs, or plants that are part of a vegetated roof.
Water damage (Broad Form only)	Despite its name, the water damage peril is not intended to cover flooding, rainfall, sewer backup, and similar causes of water damage. Instead, it is limited to covering loss caused by water or steam leakage resulting from the breaking apart or cracking of a plumbing, heating, air conditioning, or other system or appliance that is located on the described premises. If the building is covered property, the form also covers the cost to tear out and replace any part of the building to repair damage to the appliance or system that leaked. The water damage peril is subject to several exclusions, including the cost to repair any defect that caused the loss or damage and the cost to repair any gradual damage that occurs over a period of fourteen days or more.

Anti-Concurrent Causation Wording

The introductory language to the first group of eight exclusions provides that losses caused directly or indirectly by any of those perils are not covered, even if another covered cause contributed to the loss, regardless of the sequence in which the causes of events occur, unless the exclusion specifically provides otherwise. This wording was developed to eliminate claims based on the concurrent causation doctrine and is therefore referred to as "anti-concurrent causation wording." The concurrent causation doctrine holds that a loss is covered when caused by two or more independent, concurrent perils if only one of the perils is covered—even if the other peril or perils are clearly excluded.

[DA07825]

Ordinance or Law

To promote public welfare and safety, municipalities enact and regularly upgrade the building codes that set the standards for new construction or significant remodeling. For example, a building code might require that new buildings in a certain area be fire resistive. If an existing building in that area does not comply with the code and sustains damage by fire or another peril, the building code may require that its restoration meet the standards for new buildings. In some cases, a building ordinance or law may require that a partially damaged building be totally demolished, changing what would have been a partial loss to a total loss. The Ordinance or Law exclusion eliminates coverage for consequential losses that result from the enforcement of building ordinances or laws. Some coverage for this exposure is provided by the Increased Cost of Construction additional coverage. Broader coverage for the excluded losses can be provided by an endorsement for an additional premium.

Earth Movement

Coverage is not provided for damage caused by earth movement other than sinkhole collapse. Earth movement includes earthquake, landslide, mine subsidence, and similar movements. The exclusion does not apply to damage by fire or explosion caused by earth movement. Earthquake coverage can be added for an additional premium.

Governmental Action

Seizure or destruction of property by governmental action is not covered. This exclusion does not apply to the destruction of property by governmental order to stop the spread of a covered fire.

Nuclear Hazard

Loss caused by nuclear reaction, radiation, or radioactive contamination is excluded. However, the exclusion does not apply to loss by fire resulting from these causes.

Utility Services

Loss caused by power failure or failure of another utility service is excluded if the failure originates away from the described premises. For example, if electrical power to the described premises is interrupted because of lightning damage to an overhead power line situated away from the described premises, the exclusion will eliminate coverage for any loss caused by the resulting power failure.

The exclusion also applies if the utility failure originates at the described premises, but only if the failure involves equipment that supplies utility service to the described premises from a source away from the described premises. For example, if lightning takes out an overhead power line on the described premises, the exclusion will apply to any loss caused by the resulting power failure.

The exclusion does not apply to loss from a covered peril resulting from power failure. If, for example, loss of electrical power causes a natural gas leak that results in an explosion (a covered cause of loss), the Utility Services exclusion would not apply to the damage caused by the explosion.

War and Military Action

The War and Military Action exclusion eliminates coverage for loss caused by war, revolution, insurrection, or similar actions. The current insurance industry consensus is that the War and Military Action exclusion does not apply to acts of terrorism, such as the terrorist attacks of September 11, 2001. Instead, insurers attach separate terrorism exclusion endorsements unless the insured purchases terrorism coverage.

Water

Flood-related loss is difficult to insure because of the potential for a large and concentrated loss. Insurers therefore exclude flood losses from commercial property forms.

The Water exclusion eliminates coverage for damage caused by these:

- Flood, surface water, tides, waves (including tidal wave and tsunami), tides, tidal water, overflow of a body of water, or spray from any of these
- Mudslide or mudflow
- Backing up of sewers, drains, or sumps
- Underground water pressing on or flowing or seeping through foundations, walls, floors, basements, doors, windows, or other openings

The exclusion does not apply to damage by fire, explosion, or sprinkler leakage caused by any of the foregoing. The Water exclusion applies regardless of whether the loss event results in widespread damage or affects a substantial area.

"Fungus," Wet Rot, Dry Rot, and Bacteria

In recent years, mold claims have disrupted the homeowners insurance markets in some states and posed a similar problem for commercial property insurance. To mitigate this problem, ISO added a "Fungus," Wet Rot, Dry Rot, and Bacteria exclusion to the commercial property causes of loss forms. Fungus is defined to include mold or mildew and any mycotoxins, spores, scents, or by-products produced or released by fungi.

The exclusion does not apply when the fungus, wet rot, dry rot, and bacteria result from fire or lightning, but it is one of the exclusions subject to the anti-concurrent causation wording.

In addition to the foregoing exclusion, each of the causes of loss forms contains an additional coverage titled Limited Coverage for "Fungus," Wet Rot, Dry Rot, and Bacteria, which provides a modest amount of insurance for such losses.

Other Exclusions Skip

The Basic Form and the Broad Form also contain a set of exclusions that are not subject to the anti-concurrent causation wording. These exclusions eliminate coverage for loss or damage caused by any of these:

- Electrical, magnetic, or electromagnetic energy that damages or otherwise interferes with any electrical or electronic wires or devices, including devices, appliances, systems, or networks using cellular or satellite technology. However, if a fire results, the resulting fire damage is covered.
- Rupture or bursting of water pipes, unless caused by a covered cause of loss. This exclusion does not apply to sprinkler leakage and is included only in the Basic Form.
- Leakage of water or steam from any part of an appliance or system containing water or steam (other than an automatic sprinkler system), unless caused by a covered cause of loss.
- Explosion of steam boilers, steam pipes, steam turbines, or steam engines owned by, leased to, or operated by the insured. However, if such an explosion causes a fire or a combustion explosion, the damage caused by fire or combustion explosion is covered.
- Mechanical breakdown, including rupture or bursting caused by centrifugal force.
- Loss resulting from the neglect of the insured to use all reasonable means to save and preserve property at and after the time of loss. This exclusion reinforces the insured's duty to protect covered property after a loss.

Finally, several additional exclusions apply only to certain commercial property coverage forms, such as ones that provide business income and extra expense coverage. These exclusions do not apply to the Building and Personal Property Coverage Form, also referred to as the BPP.

Additional Coverages

The Basic Form and the Broad Form both provide an additional coverage titled Limited Coverage for "Fungus," Wet Rot, Dry Rot, and Bacteria. The additional coverage is limited in dollar amount ($15,000 in the aggregate for any one twelve-month policy period) and scope of coverage.

The Broad Form also provides an additional coverage for collapse. Under this additional coverage, the insurer agrees to pay for loss resulting from collapse of a building or any part of a building if the collapse is caused by one or more of these:

- Any of the covered causes of loss.
- Hidden decay, unless such decay is known to an insured before the collapse occurs.
- Hidden insect or vermin damage, unless such damage is known to an insured before the collapse occurs.
- Weight of people or personal property.
- Weight of rain that collects on a roof.
- Use of defective materials or construction methods if the abrupt collapse occurs during the course of construction. (Collapse of a completed building caused by defective materials or construction is covered only if it is caused in part by any of the causes of loss listed here.)

Collapse is specifically and narrowly defined. It means an abrupt falling down or caving in of a building or part of a building that, as a result, can no longer be occupied for its intended purpose. It does not include a building that is in danger of falling down or caving in, nor one that is standing but shows evidence of cracking, bulging, sagging, bending, leaning, settling, shrinking, or expanding. A part of a building that is standing is not considered to be in a state of collapse even if it has separated from another part of the building.

The additional coverage for collapse also covers loss to property caused by the collapse of personal property inside a building (such as storage racks in a warehouse) if the collapse is a result of one of the causes listed previously.

Apply Your Knowledge

Assuming that each of these losses involved covered property, indicate whether each loss would be covered by the Broad Form:

Leaking natural gas accumulated in the insured's storage room and exploded.

Feedback: This loss would be covered under the Broad Form's explosion peril.

Vandals break several windows in the insured building.

Feedback: This loss would be covered under the Broad Form's vandalism peril.

A tree branch falls and damages the roof of the insured's store.

Feedback: This loss would be covered under the Broad Form's falling objects peril.

An earthquake damages an insured building.

Feedback: The loss would not be covered under the Broad Form, because earthquake is not a covered cause of loss (and is excluded by the Earth Movement exclusion).

CAUSES OF LOSS—SPECIAL FORM

Because it is the broadest option for covered causes of loss, the Insurance Services Office, Inc. (ISO) commercial property policy's Causes of Loss— Special Form is the most frequently selected of the three causes of loss forms.

The Causes of Loss—Special Form (CP 10 30) states that it covers "direct physical loss unless the loss is excluded or limited in this policy," instead of listing the perils covered. Moreover, the loss or damage must be accidental and unforeseen by the insured in order to be covered. The Special Form is designed to cover any loss that would be covered by the Basic and Broad Forms. In addition, the Special Form covers perils that are not specified in the Basic and Broad Forms.

The Special Form offers these advantages to the insured:

*   Certain causes of loss that are omitted or excluded under the Broad Form are not excluded—and are therefore covered—under the Special Form. Most significantly, the Special Form covers theft of covered property under a wide variety of circumstances, subject to some exclusions and limitations. The Basic and Broad Forms cover theft by looting at the time of a riot or civil commotion, but in no other circumstances.
*   By covering direct physical losses other than those that are specifically excluded, the Special Form covers losses that the insured might not have anticipated.
*   The Special Form shifts the "burden of proof" from the insured to the insurer. Under a named perils form, such as the Basic or Broad Form, the insured must prove that the loss was caused by a covered cause. Under the Special Form, an accidental loss to covered property is presumed to be covered unless the insurer can prove that it was caused by an excluded peril.

Exclusions and Limitations

The Special Form contains most of the exclusions of the Basic and Broad Forms, including many (but not all) of the limitations expressed in the descriptions of the basic and broad covered causes of loss. In those instances in which the Special Form does not contain an exclusion or a limitation equivalent to any of those contained in the Basic and Broad Forms, it provides broader coverage, as in these examples:

- The vehicle peril in both the Basic and Broad Forms excludes loss or damage caused by or resulting from vehicles owned by the named insured or operated in the course of the named insured's business. The Special Form, in contrast, does not contain such an exclusion. For example, the Special Form covers loss or damage to an insured building when an employee accidentally drives a truck owned by the insured into the building's garage wall.

- The windstorm peril in the Basic and Broad Forms excludes damage to the interior of a building by rain, snow, sleet, ice, sand, or dust, unless the roof or walls of the building are first damaged by a Covered Cause of Loss. The Special Form contains the same exclusion, but with an additional exception—the Special Form exclusion does not apply if loss results from the melting of ice, sleet, or snow on the building or structure. Therefore, unlike the Basic and Broad Forms, the Special Form covers water damage that occurs when water backs up under roof shingles because roof gutters are clogged with ice, a phenomenon known as ice damming.

Exclusions and Limitations Unique to the Special Form

Because the Special Form covers more causes of loss than the Broad Form, it contains some exclusions and limitations that are not needed in the Broad Form. The Special Form covers any risks of loss other than those that are specifically excluded. Thus, many difficult-to-insure perils that are not covered under the Basic and Broad Forms (because they are not named as covered causes of loss in those forms) must be specifically excluded in the Special Form. Examples of perils that the Special Form specifically excludes are these:

- Wear and tear
- Rust, corrosion, decay, deterioration, or hidden or latent defect
- Smog
- Settling, cracking, shrinking, or expansion
- Infestations and waste products of insects, birds, rodents, or other animals
- Mechanical breakdown
- Dampness or dryness of atmosphere, changes or extremes in temperatures, or marring or scratching (applicable to personal property only)

However, the insurer will pay losses caused by a "specified cause of loss" that results from the excluded peril. The Special Form defines "specified causes of loss" to include all of the causes of loss insured under the Broad Form. However, if one of these excluded causes of loss results in a"specified cause of loss," the insurer will pay for the loss caused by the resulting "specified cause of loss."

The Special Form also excludes loss caused by these:

- Weather conditions that contribute to other excluded causes of loss. If, for example, covered property is damaged by flood waters that were driven in part by high winds, the flood damage will not be covered even though windstorm is not otherwise excluded.

- Acts or decisions, including the failure to act or decide, of any person, group, organization, or governmental body. Thus, for example, if flooding occurs because municipal authorities fail to take proper flood control measures, the flood exclusion cannot be overcome by the insured's claim that the municipality's failure to act was the cause of the loss.

- Faulty or inadequate planning, zoning, surveying, siting, design, specifications, workmanship, repair, construction, renovation, remodeling, grading, compaction, materials, or maintenance.

If one of these excluded causes of loss results in a Covered Cause of Loss, the insurer will pay the loss resulting from the covered cause. For example, the failure of a city's fire department to take necessary measures might allow a fire to spread and burn down several row houses adjoining the insured's building. Even though the fire department's failure to act contributed to the destruction of the adjoining row houses, they were destroyed by fire, a Covered Cause of Loss. Thus, fire damage to the insured's building would be covered.

The Loss or Damage to Products exclusion eliminates coverage for damage to merchandise, goods, or other products resulting from production errors, such as adding wrong ingredients or measuring ingredients incorrectly. Many insurers believe that damage to products resulting from errors in the production process is a business risk that should not be insurable under commercial property policies. However, the exclusion specifically does not apply to loss or damage caused by a Covered Cause of Loss that results from an error or omission in the production process. If, for example, an error in the production process results in an explosion, the explosion damage will be covered.

Another noteworthy exclusion that is unique to the Special Form eliminates coverage for the release, discharge, or dispersal of pollutants. However, the exclusion does not apply to any release of pollutants caused by any of the specified causes of loss, nor does it apply to glass damaged by chemicals applied to the glass.

Loss to these kinds of property is covered only if it is caused by specified causes of loss:

- Valuable papers and records
- Animals, and then only in the event of their death

- Fragile articles if broken, such as glassware, statuary, marble, chinaware, and porcelain (but not including building glass and containers of property held for sale)
- Builders' machinery and equipment owned or held by the insured unless on or within 100 feet of the described premises

Another exclusion unique to the Special Form concerns trees, shrubs, plants, and lawns that are part of a vegetated roof. Covered property under the Building and Personal Property Coverage Form (BPP) includes trees, shrubs, plants, and lawns that are part of a vegetated roof.

Consequently, the BPP covers such items without application of the per item and per occurrence limits and the restricted specified perils that apply to other trees, shrubs, and plants under the BPP's Outdoor Property coverage extension. However, the Special Form excludes these causes of loss to trees, shrubs, plants, or lawns that are part of a vegetated roof:

1. Dampness or dryness of atmosphere or of soil supporting the vegetation;
2. Changes in or extremes of temperature;
3. Disease;
4. Frost or hail; or
5. Rain, snow, ice or sleet[1]

The excluded perils are either commercially uninsurable or would require a significant additional premium to insure. It is noteworthy that the Special Form covers trees, shrubs, plants, and lawns that are part of a vegetated roof against loss by windstorm as well as any other causes of loss that are not specifically excluded.

Theft-Related Exclusions and Limitations

The Special Form does not contain an absolute exclusion of theft, and thus it covers any theft of covered property that is not specifically excluded. Several theft-related exclusions and limitations define the scope of theft coverage under the Special Form.

The Special Form excludes dishonest or criminal acts (including theft) of the insured or of partners, members, officers, managers, directors, or employees of the insured, but the exclusion does not apply to acts of destruction by employees. For example, if Fred vandalizes his employer's property in response to being demoted, the vandalism damage is covered. If, however, Fred steals money from his employer, this dishonest act is subject to the exclusion. Losses resulting from the excluded types of dishonest acts can be covered under separate crime coverage forms.

The Special Form also excludes the voluntary surrendering of property as the result of a fraudulent scheme or trickery. If, for example, a thief posing as an honest customer tricks the insured's salesperson into voluntarily allowing the thief to remove merchandise from the insured's store, the resulting theft loss will not be covered. Similarly, the Special Form excludes loss of property transferred outside the described premises on the basis of unauthorized instructions.

Loss by theft of construction materials not attached as part of the building is excluded unless the materials are held for sale by the named insured. Moreover, the Special Form excludes loss of property that is simply missing without explanation or that is evidenced only by an inventory shortage.

The Special Form imposes special limits on theft loss of certain kinds of property that are especially attractive to thieves, such as furs, jewelry, precious metals, and tickets. Such property can be insured for higher limits under separate crime or inland marine forms.

A theft exclusion endorsement can be attached to the policy to eliminate theft coverage entirely when the underwriter feels that the risk is unacceptable or when the insured wants to reduce the policy premium.

Additional Coverages and Coverage Extensions

The Special Form includes the same additional coverages for collapse and fungus as the Broad Form. It also contains three coverage extensions that insure certain losses not otherwise covered.

The Property in Transit extension provides up to $5,000 of additional protection for loss to the insured's property in transit. The property must be in or on a motor vehicle owned, leased, or operated by the insured and cannot be in the custody of the insured's sales personnel. It covers only those losses that occur within the coverage territory.

The transit extension does not provide special form coverage. The perils insured against are fire, lightning, explosion, windstorm, hail, riot, civil commotion, vandalism, upset or overturn of the conveying vehicle, collision of the conveying vehicle with another vehicle or an object other than the roadbed, and theft. The coverage for theft is limited to theft of an entire bale, case, or package by forced entry into a securely locked body or compartment of the vehicle, evidenced by marks of the forced entry.

Because the transit extension has a low coverage limit and restricted covered perils, insureds who have property in transit should consider covering such property under an inland marine or ocean marine policy.

The Water Damage, Other Liquids, Powder or Molten Material Damage extension covers the cost to tear out and replace any part of a building necessary to repair an appliance or a system from which water or another liquid—or even powder fire-extinguishing agents or molten materials—has escaped. The extension does not pay for the repair of any defect that resulted in the leakage. It does pay for repairs to fire extinguishing equipment if the damage results in the discharge of any substance from an automatic fire protection system or is directly caused by freezing.

The Glass extension covers the expenses of installing temporary glass plates or boarding up openings when repair or replacement of damaged glass has been delayed. The insurer will also pay for the cost to clear obstructions (but not window displays) that prevent replacement of the glass. While the Basic, Broad, and Special Forms all insure glass breakage by a Covered Cause of Loss, only the Special Form includes this Glass coverage extension.

Apply Your Knowledge

A soft-drink producer is insured under the Building and Personal Property Coverage Form, also referred to as the BPP, with Special Form coverage. A mistake during the production process for one of its diet sodas causes too much artificial sweetener to be added to a large quantity of the beverage, forcing the soft drink producer to dispose of the entire batch. Would the cause of this loss be covered under the soft-drink producer's Special Form?

Feedback: No, the cause of the loss would not be covered under the soft-drink producer's Special Form, because the Loss or Damage to Products exclusion eliminates coverage for damage to merchandise, goods, or other products resulting from production errors, such as adding wrong ingredients or measuring ingredients incorrectly.

An office building is insured under the BPP with Special Form coverage. Firefighters' efforts to extinguish a fire caused extensive water damage to the insured building. In addition, several windows were broken by the intense heat of the fire. Would the cause of these losses be covered under the Special Form? Additionally, would the Special Form cover the cost of boarding up the windows?

Feedback: Yes, the Special Form would cover the cause of this loss, which was fire, because the Special Form does not exclude fire or any of the consequences of the fire.

BPP LIMITS OF INSURANCE AND DEDUCTIBLE

The dollar amount that the insurer is obligated to pay for a loss covered under the Building and Personal Property Coverage Form, also referred to as the BPP, is largely determined by the Limits of Insurance and Deductible provisions of the BPP.

The BPP's Limits of Insurance section contains provisions explaining how the insurer will apply the limit(s) of insurance to covered losses. The amount that the insurer will pay for a covered loss is also affected by the BPP's Deductible provision, which provides the rules for applying the deductible shown in the declarations.

Limits of Insurance

The Insurance Services Office, Inc. (ISO) BPP's Limits of Insurance section states that the most the insurer is obligated to pay for a loss in any one occurrence is the applicable limit of insurance shown in the declarations. Total commercial property losses are rare, and the forms contain other limitations that reduce the amount the insurer pays. Therefore, the amount that the insurer pays for a loss covered under the BPP is generally less than the applicable limit of insurance. However, payments under all of the BPP's coverage extensions and under most of the additional coverages are paid in addition to the limit of insurance, which makes it possible for the total payment for one loss to exceed the limit of insurance.

A BPP can be subject to one or more limits, which can be either specific or blanket limits. When specific limits are used, the declarations show separate limits of insurance for each covered building and for personal property at each location. For example, a BPP's declarations could show these limits for the insured location:

- $1,000,000 for a Building
- $800,000 for Your Business Personal Property
- $50,000 for Personal Property of Others

A blanket limit is the alternative to specific limits. A blanket limit can apply one amount of insurance to all property covered by the policy. If the property described in the previous example was insured on a blanket basis, then the declarations would state that $1,850,000 blanket coverage is available on the Building, Your Business Personal Property, and Personal Property of Others at the address.

Property at different locations can also be covered on a blanket basis, in which case one limit of insurance can apply to all covered property at all locations. Alternatively, one blanket limit could apply to all of the insured's buildings (at one or more locations) and another blanket limit could apply to all the insured's business personal property (at one or more locations).

Deductible

An insurer is not obligated to pay anything to the insured unless the loss exceeds the deductible shown in the policy declarations. The limit of insurance then applies to the loss in excess of the deductible. That is, the deductible is subtracted from the loss, not from the limit of insurance. For example, under a policy that has a $100,000 limit on a building and a $1,000 deductible, an insurer's payment would be calculated as shown:

Amount of Loss	Insurer's Payment
$500	No payment (loss is less than deductible)
$100,000	$99,000 ($100,000 − $1,000 deductible)
$110,000	$100,000 ($110,000 − $1,000 deductible exceeds limit of insurance)

Unless a BPP is written for a single blanket limit, it typically covers two or more categories of property (such as two buildings, or a building and business personal property) with a separate limit applying to each category. How the deductible applies in such situations is determined by this passage in the Deductible provision:

> When the occurrence involves loss to more than one item of Covered Property and separate Limits of Insurance apply, the losses will not be combined in determining application of the Deductible. But the deductible will be applied only once per occurrence.

For example, a BPP covers five buildings at one location, each building is insured for a separate limit, and a $5,000 deductible applies. A windstorm (one occurrence) causes less than $5,000 damage to each of the buildings, but the combined total is $10,000 of damage. As stated in the Deductible provision, the losses will not be combined for purposes of applying the deductible. Therefore, because the insurer is not obligated to pay anything to the insured unless the loss on at least one building exceeds the deductible, the insurer will pay nothing for this loss.

If, instead, the amount of loss on one of the buildings is $6,000, the insurer will pay the $1,000 amount of loss on this building that exceeds the $5,000 deductible. And, because the deductible has now been applied (and "the deductible will be applied only once per occurrence"), the insurer will also pay the amount of loss on each of the other buildings even if it does not exceed the deductible amount.

If the Coinsurance condition or the Agreed Value optional coverage applies, the amount of the loss is first reduced by any penalty imposed by those provisions before applying the deductible.

Under ISO *Commercial Lines Manual* (CLM) rules, the standard deductible is $500. This may be reduced to $250 for an additional premium or increased to a higher amount that reduces the premium. A $1,000 or $5,000 deductible is common for middle-market insureds. The savings for higher deductibles are seldom attractive to smaller firms, but underwriters tend to prefer higher deductibles because they save the insurer the expense of handling small claims. In some cases, an underwriter may require a higher deductible before agreeing to provide coverage for an insured with frequent small losses.

Apply Your Knowledge

The owners of a restaurant are insured under a BPP coverage form that covers their building for a $400,000 limit and their business personal property for a $200,000 limit. The policy has a $1,000 deductible. A covered cause of loss results in $100,000 worth of damage to the building and a $50,000 loss of business personal property. Assuming that no coinsurance penalty applies, apply the policy's limits and deductible to this loss to determine the amount payable.

Feedback: In accordance with the Deductible provision, the $1,000 deductible is subtracted from the building loss before applying the building limit: $100,000 – $1,000 = $99,000. Because this amount is less than the $400,000 building limit, the insurer will pay $99,000 for the building loss. Because the deductible applies only once per occurrence and has already been applied to the building loss, it does not apply to the business personal property loss. Moreover, the business personal property loss does not exceed the applicable $200,000 limit. Therefore, the insurer will pay the $50,000 business personal property loss in full. The insurer's total payment will be calculated as $99,000 + $50,000 = $149,000.

A business office is insured under a BPP coverage form that specifies a $2 million limit of insurance on the office building and a $900,000 limit of insurance on business personal property at the building's address. The policy has a $5,000 deductible. A covered cause of loss results in $2.2 million worth of damage to the building and a $300,000 loss of business personal property. Two shrubs are destroyed, resulting in a $500 loss fully covered by the BPP coverage form's Outdoor Property coverage extension. Assuming that no coinsurance penalty applies, apply the policy's limits and deductible to this loss to determine the amount payable.

Feedback: The $5,000 deductible is subtracted from the amount of the building loss before applying the building limit: $2,200,000 – $5,000 = $2,195,000. Because this amount exceeds the applicable limit of insurance, the insurer will pay the full $2 million limit of insurance for the building loss. The deductible applies only once per occurrence and has already been applied to the building loss; therefore, it does not apply to the business personal property loss. Moreover, because the business personal property loss does not exceed the applicable $900,000 limit of insurance, the insurer will pay the $300,000 business personal property loss in full. Finally, the $500 payment for the shrubs under the Outdoor Property coverage extension is payable in addition to the limits of insurance. Therefore, the insurer will pay a total of $2,300,500, calculated as $2,000,000 + $300,000 + $500.

SUMMARY

Three important aspects of commercial property loss exposures are the types of property that might be exposed to loss, damage, or destruction; the causes of loss that might result in property being lost, damaged, or destroyed; and the financial consequences of a property loss. Many of the basic property coverages an organization needs are commonly provided under a commercial property coverage part, which consists of commercial property declarations, one or more commercial property coverage forms, one or more causes of loss forms, Commercial Property Conditions, and any applicable endorsements.

The BPP can be used to insure buildings; business personal property of the named insured; and personal property of others in the named insured's care, custody, or control. With only minor exceptions, property is covered only while located on or within 100 feet of the building or structure or within 100 feet of the described premises, whichever distance is greater. The Property Not Covered section lists the various types of property that are not covered by the BPP. However, most types of property not covered can be insured by adding optional coverage endorsements to the BPP.

The BPP's additional coverages and coverage extensions cover loss exposures that would not otherwise be covered by the BPP's basic coverages. However, in some cases, the special limits that apply to these supplemental coverages are inadequate for many businesses. The limits stated in the form can often be increased by showing a higher limit in the declarations, adding an appropriate coverage endorsement, or buying another type of policy to supplement the BPP.

The perils covered in an ISO commercial property coverage part are specified in any of three causes of loss forms. The Causes of Loss—Basic Form and the Causes of Loss—Broad Form include nearly all of the same covered perils, but the Broad Form covers three additional perils, including collapse. This additional coverage makes the Broad Form the choice of most insureds over the Basic Form.

The most frequently selected of the three causes of loss forms, the Causes of Loss—Special Form is designed to cover any loss that would be covered by the Basic and Broad Forms. In addition, the Special Form provides coverages not found in the Basic and Broad Forms.

The Special Form offers several advantages to the insured, including coverage for certain causes of loss that are omitted or excluded under the Broad Form, coverage for losses the insured might not have anticipated, and the placement of the "burden of proof" on the insurer as opposed to the insured.

Under the ISO BPP, the most the insurer is obligated to pay for loss in any one occurrence is the applicable limit of insurance shown in the declarations. The insurer is not obligated to pay anything to the insured unless the loss exceeds the deductible; the limit of insurance then applies to the loss in excess of the deductible.

ASSIGNMENT NOTE

1. Includes copyrighted material of Insurance Services Office, Inc., with its permission. Copyright, Insurance Services Office, Inc., 2011.

2

Commercial Property Insurance, Part II

Educational Objectives

After learning the content of this assignment, you should be able to:

▷ Explain how each of the Loss Conditions and Additional Conditions affects coverage under the Building and Personal Property Coverage Form.

▷ Explain how each of the following optional coverages described in the BPP modifies the basic coverage of the BPP:

- Agreed Value

- Inflation Guard

- Replacement Cost

- Extension of Replacement Cost to Personal Property of Others

▷ Summarize each of the Commercial Property Conditions.

▷ Explain how each of the conditions contained in the Common Policy Conditions affects coverage under a commercial property coverage part.

▷ Explain how each of these documents modifies the Building and Personal Property Coverage Form:

- Ordinance or Law Coverage endorsement

- Spoilage Coverage endorsement

- Flood Coverage endorsement

- Earthquake and Volcanic Eruption Coverage endorsement

- Peak Season Limit of Insurance endorsement

- Value Reporting Form

▷ Identify the factors that affect commercial property insurance premiums.

▷ Given a case, determine whether, and for what amount, a described loss would be covered by a commercial property coverage part that includes the Building and Personal Property Coverage Form and any of the three causes of loss forms.

▶▷

Commercial Property Insurance, Part II

2

BPP LOSS CONDITIONS AND ADDITIONAL CONDITIONS

The Building and Personal Property Coverage Form, also referred to as the BPP, requires both the insurer and the insured to perform certain duties and follow certain procedures in connection with any claim made under the BPP.

The Loss Conditions section of the BPP stipulates the duties of the insured and the insurer after a loss has occurred and establishes procedures for adjusting claims. It also includes an explanation of methods for establishing the value of damaged property. The BPP's Additional Conditions deal with coinsurance and the interests of a mortgageholder (mortgagee).

Abandonment

The Abandonment condition prohibits the insured from abandoning damaged property to the insurer for repair or disposal. Although the Loss Payment condition permits the insurer, at its option, to take all or any part of damaged property at an agreed or appraised value, the Abandonment condition clarifies that making arrangements for the repair or disposal of covered property is the insured's responsibility, unless the insurer chooses to exercise its option under the Loss Payment condition.

Appraisal

The Appraisal condition establishes a method for the insurer and the insured to resolve disputes about the insured property's value or amount of loss. It does not apply to policy coverage disputes. If the insured and the insurer cannot agree on the value of the property or the amount of loss, either party may issue a written demand for an appraisal. When either party demands an appraisal, the appraisal process described in the BPP must be followed.

Duties in the Event of Loss or Damage

The BPP imposes several duties on the insured when a loss occurs. If the insured fails to perform any of them, the insurer may not have to pay for the loss. When a loss occurs, the insured must take several actions:

- Notify the police if the loss appears to have resulted from a violation of law, such as vandalism, arson, or theft.
- Give the insurer prompt notice of the loss, including a description of the property damaged. Prompt notice is generally held to mean as soon as feasible under the circumstances.
- Provide information as to how, when, and where the loss occurred.
- Take all reasonable steps to protect the property from further loss.
- At the insurer's request, furnish the insurer with inventories of the damaged and undamaged property and permit the insurer to inspect the property and records.
- Submit to examination under oath regarding any matter related to the loss.
- Cooperate with the insurer in the adjustment of the loss.
- Send a signed, sworn **proof of loss** to the insurer within sixty days after the insurer's request for one.

Proof of loss

A statement of facts about a loss for which the insured is making a claim.

Loss Payment

If loss or damage is covered, the insurer has four loss payment options:

- Pay the amount of the loss or damage
- Pay the cost of repairing or replacing the damaged property (does not include any increased cost attributable to enforcement of ordinances or laws regulating the construction, use, or repair of the property)
- Take over all or any part of the property and pay its agreed or appraised value
- Repair, rebuild, or replace the damaged property with other property of like kind and quality

Insurers seldom exercise the last option because it may cause the insurer to become a guarantor of the repaired or replaced property. If the repaired or replaced property proves to be unsatisfactory, the insurer might be required to make it satisfactory, even if the cost of doing so exceeds the applicable limit of insurance.

The Loss Payment clause also states that regardless of the value of the loss, the insurer will pay no more than the insured's financial interest in the covered property.

The insurer is required to notify the insured of its intent either to pay the claim or to deny payment within thirty days after receipt of a satisfactory proof of loss. The insurer may, for example, deny payment because of lack of coverage under the policy or failure of the insured to comply with one or more of the policy conditions. Actual payment is due within thirty days after the parties have agreed on the amount of loss or an appraisal has been completed.

Recovered Property

If either the insurer or the insured recovers property, such as stolen merchandise, for which the insurer has paid a loss, the party that makes the recovery is obligated to promptly notify the other party. The insured has the option of taking the recovered property and refunding the loss payment to the insurer. The insurer would then pay the cost of recovering the property and the cost, if any, of repairing it. If the insured elects not to take the recovered property, the insurer may dispose of the property as it sees fit.

Vacancy

If the building where a loss occurs has been vacant for more than sixty consecutive days before the loss occurs, the insurer will not pay if the loss is caused by vandalism, sprinkler leakage (unless the sprinkler system was protected against freezing), breakage of building glass, water damage, theft, or attempted theft. If any other covered peril causes the loss, loss payment will be reduced by 15 percent.

The vacancy conditions apply differently for a building's tenant than for its owner or general lessee. A general lessee is an entity that leases the entire building and subleases portions of the building to others. In the case of a tenant, a vacant "building" means the unit or suite rented or leased to the tenant. A building is vacant when it does not contain enough business personal property to conduct customary operations.

If the policy covers a building owner or general lessee, "building" means the entire building, and it is considered vacant unless at least 31 percent of its total square footage is rented to a lessee or sublessee and is used by that party to conduct its customary operations or by the building owner to conduct its customary operations. Buildings under construction or renovation are not considered to be vacant.

Because of the differing definitions for tenants and building owners, when the building does not meet the 31 percent standard, the loss payment to the building owner may be reduced or eliminated, but a tenant may be able to collect in full. Similarly, if the building meets the 31 percent standard, the building owner may have full coverage, but a tenant may be penalized when its premises do not contain enough business personal property to conduct the tenant's customary operations.

Valuation

The Valuation condition sets forth rules for establishing the value of insured property. Subject to the exceptions summarized in the exhibit, the insured property is valued at its **actual cash value (ACV)**. ACV valuation can be changed to replacement cost valuation by activating the BPP's optional coverages for replacement cost, which are printed in the BPP. See the exhibit "BPP Valuation Provisions."

Actual cash value (ACV)

Cost to replace property with new property of like kind and quality less depreciation.

BPP Valuation Provisions

Property Type	Valuation Basis
Property other than that specifically listed	Actual cash value
Building damage of $2,500 or less	Replacement cost except for awnings, floor coverings, appliances, and outdoor equipment or furniture
Stock sold but not delivered	Selling price less discounts and unincurred costs
Glass	Replacement cost for safety glazing if required by law
Improvements and betterments:	
(a) replaced by other than the insured	Not covered
(b) replaced by insured	Actual cash value
(c) not replaced	Percentage of cost based on remaining life of lease
Valuable papers and records (excluding electronic data)	Cost of blank media and cost of transcription or copying ($2,500 coverage extension to replace or restore lost information)
Electronic data	(Covered only under additional coverage with a $2,500 annual aggregate limit)
If replaced	Cost to replace or restore electronic data that have been destroyed or corrupted by a covered cause of loss
If not replaced	Cost to replace the media with blank media of substantially identical type

[DA02466]

Coinsurance

The Coinsurance condition requires the insured to carry insurance equal to at least a specified percentage of the covered property's ACV (or replacement cost, if that optional valuation approach is in effect). The coinsurance percentage is shown in the declarations. If the amount of insurance carried is equal to or greater than the required percentage, the insurer will pay covered losses in full (subject to any applicable deductible) up to the limit of insurance. If the amount of insurance carried is less than the required percentage, loss payments are reduced proportionately.

If the amount of insurance carried does not meet the coinsurance requirement, the amount the insurer will pay (subject always to the limit of insurance) is calculated by this formula:

$$\text{Loss payment} = \left(\frac{\text{Amount of insurance carried}}{\text{Amount of insurance required}} \times \text{Loss} \right) - \text{Deductible}$$

The amount of insurance required is the property's ACV (or replacement cost, if that option has been chosen) immediately before the loss occurred multiplied by the coinsurance percentage. The deductible is subtracted after the coinsurance penalty has been calculated. The example in the exhibit illustrates this calculation. See the exhibit "Coinsurance Example."

Coinsurance Example

ACV of covered building at time of loss	$200,000
Limit of insurance	$140,000
Coinsurance percentage	80%
Amount of loss	$40,000
Deductible	$500

Amount of insurance required = 0.80 × $200,000 = $160,000

$$\text{Loss payment} = \left(\frac{140,000}{160,000} \times \$40,000 \right)$$

$$= \left(0.875 \times 40,000 \right) - 500$$

$$= 35,000 - 500$$

$$= 34,500$$

If the amount of insurance carried had been $160,000 or more, the insurer would have paid $39,500, the amount of loss less the deductible.

[DA02468]

Mortgageholder

If a mortgageholder (such as a bank that has made a mortgage loan to the named insured) is shown in the declarations, the insurer is obligated to include the mortgageholder in any payment for loss to the mortgaged property. In practice, the loss payment check or draft is usually made payable jointly to the insured and all mortgageholders so that they can agree on the division of the payment. In most cases, the loss payment is used to repair or rebuild the mortgaged property, and the mortgages continue in force as before.

Any act or default of the insured does not impair the rights of the mortgageholder, provided the mortgageholder pays any premium due that the insured has not paid, submits a proof of loss if requested, and has notified the insurer of any change in ownership, occupancy, or substantial increase in risk of which the mortgageholder is aware. Consequently, the insurer is sometimes obligated to make a loss payment to the mortgageholder even though it has denied coverage, for example, to an insured who has committed arson. In such cases, the insurer, at its option, can take either of these actions:

- Take over the rights of the mortgageholder to the extent of such payment and collect the amount of payment from the insured
- Pay off the outstanding balance of the mortgage and take over all of the rights of the mortgageholder

If the insurer cancels the policy because the insured failed to pay the premium or if the insurer does not renew the policy for any reason, it must notify the mortgageholder ten days before the termination of coverage. If the insurer cancels the policy for any reason other than nonpayment of premium, it must give thirty days' advance notice to the mortgageholder. If the insurer fails to give the required notice to the mortgageholder, the policy remains in force for the protection of the mortgageholder even though it may not provide any protection for the insured.

BPP: OPTIONAL COVERAGES

The Optional Coverages section of the BPP contains provisions for four optional coverages:

- Agreed Value
- Inflation Guard
- Replacement Cost
- Extension of Replacement Cost to Personal Property of Others

The optional coverages apply only when an appropriate notation is made on the declarations page. Agreed Value, Inflation Guard, and Replacement Cost may be used for buildings only, personal property only, or both buildings and personal property.

Agreed Value optional coverage

Optional coverage that suspends the Coinsurance condition if the insured carries the amount of insurance agreed to by the insurer and insured.

Agreed Value

To activate the **Agreed Value optional coverage**, an amount is entered under the Agreed Value heading in the declarations for each category of property (building, personal property, or both) to which the option applies. This option enables the insured to remove the uncertainty as to whether the amount of insurance carried complies with the Coinsurance condition. With the option in force, the insurer and the insured have agreed in advance that the amount stated in the declarations—the agreed value—is adequate for coinsurance purposes. Because most losses are partial, insureds are often tempted to underinsure, knowing they will not suffer a coinsurance penalty when the agreed value option is in effect. Therefore, insurers underwrite agreed value carefully, requiring proof of value before providing agreed value coverage. At the very least, the insured ordinarily must submit a signed statement of values. Insurance Services Office, Inc. (ISO) Form CP 16 15, Statement of Values, can be used for this purpose.

The BPP Coinsurance condition does not apply to property insured under the agreed value option. However, it is replaced by a provision that, while not called coinsurance, is the practical equivalent of 100 percent coinsurance based on the agreed value. The agreed value option provides that if the limit of insurance equals or exceeds the agreed value stated in the declarations, losses will be paid in full up to the limit of insurance. If the limit of insurance is less than the agreed value, the amount of loss payment is calculated by this equation:

$$\text{Loss payment} = \left(\frac{\text{Limit of insurance}}{\text{Agreed value}} \times \text{Loss} \right) - \text{Deductible}$$

Coverage under this option extends until the agreed value expiration date shown on the declarations or the expiration date of the policy, whichever occurs first. If the coverage option is not renewed, the Coinsurance condition is reinstated.

Inflation Guard

Inflation Guard optional coverage is coverage for the effects of inflation that automatically increases the limit of insurance by the percentage of annual increase shown in the declarations. This percentage is applied on a pro rata basis, from the date the limit of insurance became effective to the date of the loss, before the loss payment is computed. The percentage of annual increase is shown separately for buildings and personal property.

Replacement Cost

The **Replacement Cost optional coverage** replaces the phrase "actual cash value" with "replacement cost" in the BPP Valuation condition. As a result, the insurer is obligated to pay the cost to replace the damaged or destroyed property with new property of like kind and quality without any deduction for depreciation or obsolescence.

Inflation Guard
optional coverage

Coverage for the effects of inflation that automatically increases the limit of insurance by the percentage of annual increase shown in the declarations.

Replacement Cost
optional coverage

Coverage for losses to most types of property on a replacement cost basis (with no deduction for depreciation or obsolescence) instead of on an actual cash value basis.

The insurer is not obligated to pay replacement cost until the property has been repaired or replaced, and then only if such repair or replacement is completed in a reasonable time. If repair or replacement is not completed in a reasonable time, the loss payment is based on the actual cash value (ACV) at the time of loss.

The insured may make a claim on the basis of ACV, with the difference between ACV and replacement cost to be paid upon completion of repair or reconstruction. The insurer must be notified within 180 days after the occurrence of loss that a claim will be made for replacement cost.

If the replacement cost option is activated, the Coinsurance condition continues to apply, but with one important difference. The amount of insurance required by the Coinsurance condition is calculated by multiplying replacement cost by the coinsurance percentage if the claim is made on a replacement cost basis. If the insured makes a claim on an ACV basis, coinsurance is also calculated on an ACV basis.

If the replacement cost option is selected, tenants' improvements and betterments are also valued at replacement cost if the tenant actually repairs or replaces them, at its own cost, as soon as reasonably possible after the loss.

The replacement cost option does not apply to property of others; contents of a residence; manuscripts; or works of art, antiques, or rare articles. It also does not apply to "stock" unless the declarations indicate that the replacement cost option includes stock. The BPP defines stock to mean merchandise, raw materials, goods in process, and finished goods.

Extension of Replacement Cost to Personal Property of Others

Insureds frequently lease photocopiers, computers, phone systems, and other equipment. These leases or agreements may make the insured responsible for the replacement cost of these items in the event they are damaged. To cover this loss exposure, insureds who have selected the replacement cost option may also elect to have the personal property of others valued at replacement cost. In such cases, the amount of the loss is calculated according to the written agreement between the insured and the owner of the property, but it cannot exceed the replacement cost of the property or the applicable limit of insurance.

COMMERCIAL PROPERTY CONDITIONS

Even if an insurance policy would otherwise cover an insured's loss, an insurer may deny coverage if the policy's conditions have not been met.

The Building and Personal Property Coverage Form and the other coverage forms that can be included in a commercial property coverage part each contain several conditions specific to those forms. In addition, the Commercial Property Conditions Form contains nine conditions that apply to any of the Commercial Property Coverage Forms to which they are attached. These nine conditions are titled as shown:

- Concealment, Misrepresentation, or Fraud
- Control of Property
- Insurance Under Two or More Coverages
- Legal Action Against Us
- Liberalization
- Transfer of Rights of Recovery Against Others to Us
- No Benefit to Bailee
- Other Insurance
- Policy Period, Coverage Territory

Concealment, Misrepresentation, or Fraud

The commercial property coverage part is void if the insured commits any fraudulent act related to the coverage or conceals or misrepresents any material fact pertaining to the coverage part, the covered property, or the insured's interest in the covered property. Concealment and misrepresentation are related but distinct acts:

- A misrepresentation is an active, deliberate misstatement of fact. For example, assume that John Doe, who has previously been convicted of arson, applies for fire insurance. If the application asks whether the applicant has ever been convicted of arson, and Doe responds that he has not, his answer is a misrepresentation.

- Concealment does not involve a misstatement of fact, but instead is an intentional failure to disclose a material fact. In the John Doe example, if the application does not ask about past convictions for arson, and Doe does not offer information about his conviction, some courts might consider Doe's action to be concealment.

Misrepresentation or concealment does not always void coverage: Only material misrepresentation or concealment voids coverage. A fact is material if knowledge of it would cause the insurer to charge a higher premium or decline to write the coverage. For example, an insured might state that his or her building is painted red when in fact it is painted yellow. This misstatement would have no bearing on the insurance and is therefore not material.

Control of Property

The Control of Property condition consists of two parts. The first part states that coverage under the policy will not be affected by acts or omissions of persons other than the insured if those persons are not acting under the direction or control of the insured. The second part of the condition states that violation of a policy condition at one location will not affect coverage at any other location.

To illustrate how this clause might apply, assume that a liquor store's policy is endorsed, requiring the store's burglar alarm system to be maintained in working order at all insured locations. Assume also that the insured leases these locations from other parties. The first part of the clause would protect the insured if the alarm system was disconnected by a building owner, provided that the owner was not under the insured's control.

The second part of the Control of Property condition would be important in this example if the liquor store's policy provides coverage at more than one location. In the absence of this part of the condition, the insured's failure to maintain the alarm system at one location might suspend coverage at all locations, even if the alarm systems are properly maintained at the other locations. Under the second part of the condition, only coverage at the location with the deficient alarm system would be affected.

Insurance Under Two or More Coverages

This policy condition is necessary because some property might be covered under two or more coverage parts that can be included in a single commercial package policy (such as commercial property and commercial inland marine). The Insurance Under Two or More Coverages condition prevents double recovery by the insured in such instances. The total payment under all applicable coverage parts is limited to the actual amount of the loss. Duplication, or "stacking," of the limits is avoided.

Legal Action Against Us

This condition spells out two requirements the insured must meet before legal action can be brought against the insurer ("Us") to enforce the policy. First, the insured must have complied with all conditions of the policy, including those in the coverage part and the Common Policy Conditions, as well as the applicable Loss Conditions. Second, the action must be brought within two years after the date on which the direct physical loss occurred.

Liberalization

If the insurer adopts any revision that would broaden coverage under the commercial property coverage part and for which there is no additional premium charge, the broader coverage is extended automatically to policies already in effect. This automatic coverage applies only if the broadening amendment is adopted during the policy term or within forty-five days before the effective date of the policy. Liberalization applies only to amendments that broaden coverage, not to those that restrict coverage.

Transfer of Rights of Recovery Against Others to Us

Subrogation is a term commonly used by insurance practitioners but not used in Insurance Services Office, Inc. (ISO) commercial property forms. If the insured takes any action that eliminates the insurer's right of recovery (other than one specifically authorized by this condition), the insurer may not be required to pay the loss. This condition specifically permits the insured to waive the right of recovery against any other party, provided the waiver is made in writing and before the loss occurs. A waiver of recovery may be given by the insured after loss only to another party insured under the same policy, a parent or subsidiary company, or a tenant of the insured property. Any other waiver given by the insured after loss has occurred may impair the insured's right to collect from the insurer for the loss.

Subrogation

The process by which an insurer can, after it has paid a loss under the policy, recover the amount paid from any party (other than the insured) who caused the loss or is otherwise legally liable for the loss.

 Reality Check

Subrogation

The importance of subrogation to insurers and their insureds can be illustrated by this hypothetical case. The insured's building and its contents, valued at $600,000, were destroyed by a fire that was covered under the insured's commercial property insurance. While investigating the claim, the insurer's claims representative discovered that the fire was caused by faulty electrical wiring that had been installed in the building only a few months before the loss. After paying its insured's loss in full, minus the policy's $1,000 deductible, the insurer exercised its subrogation rights against the contractor that did the faulty work and was legally liable for the resulting damage. The contractor's liability insurer paid the entire $600,000 loss to the commercial property insurer. Out of this subrogation recovery, the commercial property insurer reimbursed its insured for the $1,000 deductible and recovered the entire amount that the insurer had paid its insured for the loss.

[DA07822]

No Benefit to Bailee

A bailee is a person or business organization that has temporary custody of the property of another. Examples are dry cleaners, television repair shops, laundries, and fur-storage firms. Bailees may become legally liable to bailors (the owners of the property) for damage to the property they hold. Bailees sometimes try to limit their liability with contractual provisions stating that the bailee is not liable for damage if the damage is recoverable under insurance carried by the bailor. The No Benefit to Bailee condition is intended to defeat such provisions in the bailment contract and to reinforce the insurer's right of subrogation against the bailee.

Other Insurance

An insured may have more than one policy covering a given loss. In keeping with the principle of indemnity, the Other Insurance condition limits the total recovery from all applicable insurance to an amount not in excess of the actual loss sustained.

If the other insurance is provided by an additional policy subject to the same plan, terms, and conditions, then each policy pays in relation to all applicable policies. If the other insurance is not subject to all of the conditions of the commercial property coverage part, then the policy subject to the commercial property coverage part is considered excess coverage and pays only the covered loss amount that exceeds what is due from the other policy.

Policy Period, Coverage Territory

This condition states that coverage begins on the effective date and ends on the expiration date shown in the declarations. The declarations state that the beginning and ending time is 12:01 a.m., determined by standard time at the insured's mailing address as shown in the declarations, even though some or all of the insured property may be located in a different time zone. The insured property is covered only while it is located within the United States (including its territories and possessions), Puerto Rico, or Canada.

COMMON POLICY CONDITIONS

The Insurance Services Office, Inc. (ISO) *Commercial Lines Manual* (CLM) requires that a common policy conditions form be attached to every Commercial Package Policy (CPP) or monoline policy. The Common Policy Conditions (IL 00 17) form contains six conditions, which apply to all coverage parts in the policy unless a particular coverage part states otherwise. This approach avoids the need to repeat these common conditions in each coverage part. These are the six conditions contained in the form:

- Cancellation
- Changes
- Examination of Books and Records
- Inspections and Surveys
- Premiums
- Transfer of Rights and Duties Under This Policy

Cancellation

The insured may cancel the policy at any time by mailing or delivering written notice of cancellation to the insurer. If two or more insureds are listed in the declarations, only the one listed first (called the first named insured) can request cancellation.

The insurer can cancel the policy by mailing or delivering written notice of cancellation to the first named insured. To provide time for the insured to obtain other insurance, the insurer is required to give advance notice of cancellation. The notice must be mailed or delivered to the insured at least ten days before the date of cancellation if the cancellation is for nonpayment of premium. The notice must be mailed at least thirty days before the date of cancellation for any other reason. If the cancellation results in a return premium, the insurer will send the refund to the first named insured.

In almost every state, the Cancellation condition is superseded by state law and an endorsement is added to the policy. The endorsement modifies the cancellation provisions to conform with the applicable law.

The state laws commonly address permissible reasons for cancellation and a longer advance notification period if the cancellation occurs for a reason other than nonpayment of premium.

Changes

The Changes condition states that the policy constitutes the entire contract between the insurer and the named insured, and that the policy can be changed only by a written endorsement issued by the insurer.

In practice, changes are often first made by verbal communication and confirmed afterwards in writing. In most states, such verbal changes are binding because an authorized agent of the insurer is viewed as having the power to waive the written endorsement requirement. Such changes may be made, with the insurer's consent, upon the request of the first named insured.

Only the first named insured has the authority to request policy changes, and the insurer is authorized to make changes upon the request of the first named insured without specific permission of any other insured.

Examination of Books and Records

The insurer reserves the right to examine and audit the insured's books and records related to the policy at any time during the policy period and for up to three years after the policy's termination. This provision is included because many commercial insurance policies are issued with estimated premiums. The final premium is determined after the policy expires, based on reported values of the insured property, the amount of the insured's sales or payroll, or some other variable premium base. The insured is required to report the final figures to the insurer, and the insurer may accept the insured's reports without verification.

However, if the insurer prefers to verify the reports by making an on-site inspection of the insured's books and records, the condition permits the insurer to do that. An insurer may also choose to exercise its rights under this condition in the process of investigating a claimed loss.

Inspections and Surveys

The insurer has the right, but not the obligation, to inspect the insured's premises and operations at any reasonable time during the policy period.

The inspections may be made by the insurer's own personnel or by another organization acting on the insurer's behalf. Such inspections are important in determining the insurability of the insured's property and operations, in setting proper insurance rates, and in making risk control recommendations.

The insurer may inform the insured of the results of such inspections and may recommend changes. However, it does not have a duty to do either. The condition makes it clear that the insurer does not make safety inspections, does not guarantee that conditions are safe or healthful, and does not guarantee that the insured is in compliance with safety or health regulations.

These disclaimer clauses have been included in the policy to protect the insurer against suits made by persons who allege that their injuries would not have occurred but for the insurer's failure to detect a hazardous condition or a violation of laws or regulations, and that the insurer is therefore responsible for the resulting damages, fines, or penalties assessed against the insured.

Premiums

The first named insured is responsible for paying the policy premium. If the insurer owes a return premium, it will make payment only to the first named insured.

Transfer of Rights and Duties Under This Policy

The insured cannot transfer any rights or duties under the policy to any other person or organization without the insurer's written consent. For example, if the insured sells a building covered by the policy, the insurance cannot be transferred to the new owner of the property without the insurer's written consent.

Such a transfer of insurance is generally referred to as assignment of the policy. The condition also provides specifically for the automatic transfer of coverage if an individual named insured dies. (An individual named insured is a person whose name is listed on the "Named Insured" line in the policy declarations.) In that case, the insured's rights and duties under the policy are automatically transferred to the insured's legal representatives or, if the insured's legal representatives have not yet been appointed, to any person having proper temporary custody of the insured property.

COMMERCIAL PROPERTY ENDORSEMENTS ship

The Building and Personal Property Coverage Form, also referred to as the BPP, can be modified by a variety of endorsements.

The BPP's endorsements are useful for these tasks:

- Providing coverage enhancements that some insureds may want but that others either do not believe they need or cannot afford
- Eliminating coverage for certain exposures, enabling underwriters to accept applications that they would otherwise decline
- Changing policy provisions to match the specific characteristics of certain industries or insureds
- Amending the policy to comply with state insurance regulations

The Insurance Services Office, Inc. (ISO) portfolio of commercial property forms contains more than 100 multistate forms and endorsements and an even greater number of state-specific endorsements. In addition, many insurers use independently developed endorsements or draft manuscript endorsements to accommodate special requirements. This selection of endorsements illustrates their diversity:

- Ordinance or Law Coverage Endorsement
- Spoilage Coverage Endorsement
- Flood Coverage Endorsement
- Earthquake and Volcanic Eruption Coverage Endorsement
- Peak Season Limit of Insurance Endorsement
- Value Reporting Form

Ordinance or Law Coverage

The Ordinance or Law Coverage endorsement provides three coverages for losses resulting from the enforcement of building ordinances or laws:

- Coverage A covers the value of the undamaged portion of a building that must be demolished. For example, an entire structure may have to be totally demolished if it is a frame building in an area where only fire-resistive construction is currently permitted. Demolishing the undamaged

Skip

parts of the building changes what would have been a partial loss to a total loss.

- Coverage B covers the cost to demolish the undamaged portion of a building and remove its debris when demolition is required by the building code.

- Coverage C covers the increased cost to repair or rebuild the property resulting from the enforcement of a building, zoning, or land use law. Building codes may require that reconstruction of damaged property meet higher standards, such as heavier electrical service, elevators to upper floors, and fire-resistive stairwells. Coverage C pays the added expense for these improvements.

Coverages B and C can be provided under one blanket limit. The unendorsed commercial property coverage forms exclude these losses except for the additional coverage for increased cost of construction, which adds a small amount of coverage for the types of loss insured by Coverage C of the endorsement.

Spoilage Coverage

The Spoilage Coverage endorsement covers damage to perishable stock resulting from power outages; on-premises breakdown; or contamination of the insured's refrigerating, cooling, or humidity control equipment. The power outage must be caused by conditions beyond the insured's control. The coverage is not subject to coinsurance and cannot be provided under a blanket limit.

Flood Coverage

In the United States, losses from flooding accompany hurricanes, heavy rains, and melting snow. Collapsing dams can also cause floods. Any of these events can cause catastrophic losses. Because of the movable nature of the property they insure, auto physical damage insurance and many inland marine forms include flood as an insured peril. However, insurers are reluctant to write flood insurance on property at fixed locations, such as buildings and their contents. Therefore, all three of the causes of loss forms exclude flood.

Flood insurance for buildings and their contents is available, though, in two ways.

The National Flood Insurance Program (NFIP) is a federal government resource that provides insurance for properties located in eligible communities. The NFIP is administered by the Federal Insurance Administration, part of the Federal Emergency Management Agency (FEMA). For commercial properties, the maximum NFIP limit is $500,000 per building and $500,000 for the contents of a building. Although the demand for flood insurance is greatest from insureds in the most hazardous flood zones, NFIP provides coverage in all areas of eligible communities. National flood insurance is sold through private insurers and agents and is backed by the U.S. government.

Ship

The other source for flood insurance on buildings and contents is private insurers without federal participation. Most private insurers are unwilling to provide flood coverage for commercial properties located in zones that have more than a once-in-100-years flooding probability risk (shown in NFIP flood maps as Zone A). For properties located outside the high-hazard flood zones, private insurers often write flood coverage by endorsement to the insured's commercial property policy, subject to a substantial deductible (often $25,000 or more). The ISO commercial property program includes a Flood Coverage endorsement for use with the ISO commercial property coverage forms. In some cases, insurers will provide only excess flood coverage that applies in addition to the maximum limit available from NFIP.

Earthquake and Volcanic Eruption Coverage

Earthquake and volcanic eruption, like flooding, present potentially catastrophic loss exposures. Consequently, earthquake insurance is expensive and limited in availability in areas with a high probability of severe earthquake damage, principally in parts of California and locations near the New Madrid Fault, which extends into portions of Arkansas, Illinois, Indiana, Kentucky, Mississippi, Missouri, and Tennessee.

In other areas, earthquake insurance is generally available but is often overlooked. Overlooking the earthquake exposure can be a costly mistake. In the past 100 years, earthquakes have occurred in thirty-nine of the fifty states.[1] One of the most severe earthquakes in U.S. history was centered in Charleston, South Carolina.

Insurers can use either of two ISO endorsements to add earthquake and volcanic eruption as covered perils under a commercial property coverage part. Independently filed earthquake endorsements are also available from some insurers. The two ISO endorsements are these:

- Earthquake and Volcanic Eruption Endorsement
- Earthquake and Volcanic Eruption Endorsement (Sub-Limit Form)

Both endorsements extend commercial property coverage to include earthquake and volcanic eruption. The first endorsement includes coverage for the full policy limit and contains a coinsurance condition. The second endorsement includes earthquake and volcanic eruption coverage subject to a sublimit that is lower than the regular policy limit, and it does not contain a coinsurance condition.

Peak Season Limit of Insurance Endorsement

Many organizations experience wide fluctuations (increases and decreases) in personal property values, especially the value of goods held for sale. The BPP does not provide a totally satisfactory method to cover fluctuating values. If the insured organization carries high enough limits to cover the maximum value, it is overinsured for much of the year and pays too much in premiums. If it carries less than the maximum value, it is underinsured during its peak inventory period. Continually amending the amount of insurance to correspond to changes in value would be an administrative burden on the insured and the insurer.

The Peak Season Limit of Insurance endorsement covers the fluctuating values of business personal property by providing differing amounts of insurance for certain time frames during the policy period. For example, a toy store may have a policy providing $100,000 of coverage on personal property with a peak season endorsement increasing coverage to $200,000 from October 1 to December 31, when the store expects to have higher inventory values.

Using this endorsement would have exactly the same effect as endorsing the policy on October 1 to increase the coverage and endorsing it again on December 31 to reduce the coverage. The peak season endorsement eliminates the need for these extra transactions and the possibility that they may be overlooked.

The peak season endorsement is usually attached when the policy is issued (although it may be added midterm), and a pro rata premium is charged for the period during which the limit is increased.

Value Reporting Form

Unlike the peak season endorsement, which actually modifies the limit of insurance, the Value Reporting Form covers the fluctuating values of business personal property by providing insurance for the insured's maximum expected values and requiring the insured to periodically report property values to the insurer. The insurer calculates the final policy premium based on the reported values instead of the limit of insurance. In this way, the insured has an adequate limit to cover maximum personal property values but pays a premium based on the reported property values.

Under the Value Reporting Form, the insured is required to report the value of the insured business personal property to the insurer periodically during the policy period. The frequency of reporting is indicated by a symbol entered in the declarations. For example, MR, the most common choice, calls for reporting values on hand on the last day of the month, with the report due within thirty days after the end of the month. Daily, weekly, quarterly, and annual periods can also be selected as a basis for reports by entering other codes in the declarations.

As long as the insured reports values accurately and on time, the insurer will pay the full amount of any loss that occurs (but not more than the policy limit), even if the values on hand at the time of the loss are greater than those last reported to the insurer.

To encourage accurate and timely reports, the Value Reporting Form specifies penalties for failure to comply with its reporting requirements. Separate rules

Reality Check

Value Reporting Form

A wholesaler insures its business personal property under a Value Reporting Form subject to a limit of $1 million for its single warehouse location. Its last monthly report of values was made on time and accurately showed the full value of business personal property—$800,000—as of the date of the report. Three weeks later, a fire destroyed the warehouse and its contents. Even though the value of covered personal property had increased to $900,000 since the last report, the loss is covered in full (minus the deductible).

[DA07816]

apply when no report is made (loss payment is reduced to 75 percent of the otherwise collectible loss), one or more reports are past due after the initial report (loss payment is limited to the last reported values), and reports are inaccurate (the loss is reduced by the proportion that the value reported bears to the correct value).

The insured pays an advance premium at the inception of the policy. The advance premium is based on 75 percent of the limit of insurance. The final premium is determined after the policy anniversary, based on the reported values. The premium is based on the values reported, even if the values reported exceed the policy limit. However, the insurer is not obligated to pay more than the policy limit in the event of loss, even if the reported values are higher. Thus, care should be taken to set the limit high enough to cover any possible increase in value.

Although the Value Reporting Form can more effectively match coverage to exposures than the Peak Season Limit of Insurance endorsement, many smaller firms do not have accounting systems of sufficient sophistication to generate the required reports accurately and on time. Furthermore, many insurers would decline to issue a Value Reporting Form for a smaller insured because the premium may not be large enough to warrant the added expense of processing the reports and calculating the final premium.

FACTORS AFFECTING COMMERCIAL PROPERTY PREMIUMS

The factors that affect commercial property premiums are information that the producer often needs to transmit to the underwriter. Understanding these factors is also fundamental to reducing the cost of insurance, since many of the factors are within the insured's control.

Commercial property rating procedures are numerous and complex. Therefore, this discussion focuses on the rating factors that principally affect the premiums for commercial property coverage on buildings and business personal property, not on the actual mechanics of rating. Some of the factors affecting commercial property premiums are certain aspects of coverage provided by the commercial property coverage part. Other factors—such as type of building construction and type of business occupying the building—exist independently of the coverage being provided.

Rating Fundamentals

Rating is the process of applying a rate to a particular exposure and performing any other necessary calculations to determine an appropriate policy premium. As a simplified example, if the applicable rate for commercial property coverage on a building is $0.50 per $100 of insurance and the amount of insurance is $100,000, the premium for the coverage can be calculated in this manner:

$$\frac{\$0.50}{\$100} \times \$100,000 = \$500$$

Another way to reach the same result is to establish the number of exposure units by dividing the amount of insurance by the unit amount, and then multiplying the number of units by the rate:

$$\frac{\$100,000}{\$100} \times \$0.50 = \$500$$

In reality, rating is usually more complicated; additional calculations are often needed. For example, the rate or the premium must often be multiplied by additional factors to account for territorial differences, to reduce the premium when the insured has selected a higher deductible, to increase the premium when a coverage option has been added, and so forth.

In the past, every commercial building was inspected individually, and building and contents rates reflecting the exposure to loss of a particular business were published by rating bureaus. This approach to developing rates is known as specific rating, which bases a building's property insurance rate on inspecting and evaluating that particular building.

As the methods used to collect loss statistics became more sophisticated, insurers were better able to generalize about the probabilities of loss within large groups of similar risks and to formulate rates that reflected the average probability of loss for businesses within these groups. Class rating is a rating approach that uses rates reflecting the average probability of loss for businesses within large groups of similar risks. Class rating allows a building and its contents to be rated without inspecting the building and developing a specific rate.

Large businesses, as well as certain other businesses with operations involving unusual or increased exposures to loss, are still specifically rated. However, class rating is used to rate the majority of commercial insureds.

Aspects of Coverage Affecting Premiums

Certain aspects of the coverage provided affect premiums. For example, higher limits result in higher premiums, and Special Form coverage involves a higher rate than Broad Form coverage, which in turn is higher than Basic Form coverage. Likewise, the applicable coinsurance percentage, the amount of the deductible, and any optional coverages that apply to the commercial property coverage part all affect the amount of the premium.

Limit of Insurance

The limit of insurance applicable to the coverage is an important component of the final premium because it represents the exposure against which the applicable rate is multiplied to calculate the premium. In addition, many insurers use a rating system for commercial property that varies the rate depending on the amount of insurance selected. This approach, called limit of insurance (LOI) rating, is based on the observation that most commercial property losses are partial, as opposed to total, and property losses do not increase proportionately with the value of the insured property. LOI rating recognizes this observation by using rates that decrease as the insured value increases. Thus, even though the owner of a high-value property still pays a higher premium than the owner of a low-value property of the same type, the high-value owner is charged a lower property rate (cost of insurance per each $100 of coverage).

Covered Causes of Loss

The rate for the Causes of Loss—Basic Form consists of a Group I rate (for fire, lightning, explosion, vandalism, and sprinkler leakage) and a Group II rate (for all other causes of loss covered under the Basic Form). If the policy provides Broad Form coverage, an additional rate is added to the Basic Form rates (Group I and Group II) for the cost of covering the additional perils of the Broad Form. The same approach is used with the Special Form except that the additional rate is higher than the Broad Form additional rate. The premium is determined by multiplying the applicable rate times the amount of insurance.

Coinsurance Percentage

The rates ordinarily used for insuring buildings and personal property are calculated with the assumption that they will be used with an 80 percent coinsurance clause in the policy. These rates are therefore called the "80 percent coinsurance rates." When a policy requires a higher coinsurance percentage, the 80 percent coinsurance rate is reduced, both to reflect the reduced likelihood that a loss will reach the insured amount and also to encourage the purchase of higher limits. Thus, with 90 or 100 percent coinsurance, the insured must buy a greater amount of insurance to comply with the coinsurance requirement, but the rate is reduced. When the coinsurance requirement is less than 80 percent, the rate is increased.

Deductible Amount

Commercial property rates are developed with the assumption that the policy will be subject to a $500 deductible. Many policyholders are willing and able to retain a larger deductible that may make the risk more desirable to underwriters (small claims are disproportionately expensive for insurers to handle). Rates are reduced in return for the insured's acceptance of a higher deductible, because raising the deductible reduces the insurer's loss payments. If the deductible is reduced to $250, rates are increased.

Optional Coverages

Adding optional coverages to the Building and Personal Property Coverage Form, also referred to as the BPP, or another coverage form ordinarily increases the policy premium. In some cases, the optional coverage increases the premium only because the limit of insurance must be increased to cover the additional property values being insured. For example, replacement cost insurance does not involve a higher rate, but the amount of insurance needed to meet the coinsurance requirement on a replacement cost basis may be considerably higher than the amount needed on an actual cash value basis. In other cases, the charge for a coverage option is a separate rate applied to the amount of insurance. For example, a grocery store that wishes to buy optional spoilage coverage will pay an additional premium calculated by applying a rate for that coverage to the amount of insurance.

Other Factors Affecting Premiums

Apart from the terms of coverage, factors that affect commercial property premiums are the building's construction, occupancy, protection, external exposure, and location. The first four factors are often referred to by the acronym COPE. To a large extent, the COPE factors relate to fire, which is often the most significant cause of loss in a commercial property policy.

Construction

Some types of buildings resist fire more effectively than others, thereby reducing the fire risk for both the buildings and their contents. Although buildings can be classified in many ways, the system used to classify buildings for purposes of rating commercial property insurance is based on their ability to resist fire. The six construction classes used for purposes of rating commercial property insurance are these:

- Frame
- Joisted masonry
- Noncombustible
- Masonry noncombustible
- Modified fire resistive
- Fire resistive

Frame construction, which uses wood or other combustible material in the exterior walls of a building (even if covered by brick veneer or stucco), is the most susceptible to fire damage. Fire-resistive construction uses materials with a fire-resistance rating of at least two hours and is the least susceptible to fire damage.

Occupancy

Occupancy refers to the type of activity conducted inside the building. Some occupancies are riskier than others. To cite an extreme example, a building used for manufacturing fireworks will face a greater explosion and fire risk than if it were used for storing bottled water. Accordingly, commercial property rates are higher for buildings with more hazardous occupancies.

Protection

Fire protection can be either internal (such as a sprinkler system) or external (the local fire department). For rating purposes, external protection is graded on a scale of one (the best protection) to ten (the worst), indicating the availability of fire-fighting personnel and equipment. For internal protection, buildings classified as "sprinklered" receive rate reductions. In contrast, buildings that have certain fire hazards (such as unsafe heating or cooking devices or inadequate electrical wiring) are charged higher premiums.

External Exposure

External exposure is another factor that can affect a commercial property premium. In addition to hazards arising from a building's construction, occupancy, and protection, other properties adjacent to the building can increase the probability of loss to the insured building and its contents. For example, a fire or explosion in the previously described fireworks plant could damage an adjacent building and its contents. Insurers include a charge for external exposure only when a specific rate is calculated for a particular location. Even if external exposure is not a factor in calculating the rate, underwriters consider external exposure when deciding whether to accept a particular submission.

External exposure
A property outside the area owned or controlled by the insured that increases the probability of loss to the insured's building and its contents.

Location

The risk of loss caused by windstorm, theft, earthquake, and other perils varies depending on the location of the insured property. For example, buildings along the coastline of the southeastern United States are more exposed to hurricane damage than buildings in other areas; tornadoes and hailstorms occur more frequently in parts of the midwestern U.S. Thus, different rates apply to different areas, or the rates are modified by territorial multipliers that account for the differences.

DETERMINING WHETHER THE BPP COVERS A LOSS

Knowing how to apply the commercial property coverage provided by the Insurance Services Office, Inc. (ISO) Building and Personal Property Coverage Form, also referred to as the BPP, to the facts of a case is an important skill. This case study will help you make the transition from knowing policy language to applying policy language to losses to determine whether coverage applies. As you progress through the case study, you can check your understanding of the coverage provided by answering the Knowledge to Action questions.

Case Facts

Jim owns a building in a beach town on the New Jersey coast. During the tourist season, the building had been occupied by a surfing-supply retailer to whom Jim rented the premises. At the end of the tourist season, on September 15, 20X1, the retailer vacated the building and relocated to Florida, leaving it empty. Jim was unable to find a new tenant, so the building remained vacant.

A tropical storm struck just north of the New Jersey beach town on October 25, 20X1. The storm's precipitation did not reach Jim's area, but strong wind associated with the storm ripped shingles from the building's roof and shattered several windows with flying debris. A storm surge from the ocean caused salt water to enter Jim's building, causing extensive damage to its interior. See the exhibit "Damage Estimates."

Jim has a commercial package policy (CPP) that includes a BPP and a Causes of Loss—Broad Form covering the building. The CPP's Common Policy Declarations form indicates that the policy's coverage period is one year. The policy does not contain any endorsements.

Given the facts presented in the case, will the claim for damage related to the storm be covered? If so, what amount will the insurer pay for the claim? When answering the questions in this case-based activity, consider only the information provided as part of this case.

Damage Estimates

Item	Description	Replacement Cost	Actual Cash Value
Wind damage to building	Destroyed roof shingles and broken windows	$20,000	$12,000
Water damage to building	Damage to walls, floors, and fixtures	$95,000	$76,000
Water damage to maintenance equipment	Total loss to a lawnmower, an electric hedge trimmer, and a vacuum cleaner stored on the first floor	$750	$375
Total		$115,750	$88,375

[DA07841]

Necessary Reference Materials

To determine whether the BPP provides coverage for the losses associated with the storm, you need to consult the relevant portions of the declarations page and any policy provisions that apply to the loss.

Overview of Steps

When examining policy forms to determine whether coverage applies to a loss, you can apply the four steps of the DICE method. Next, you can determine the amount payable for the loss under the applicable policy or policies. Doing this involves applying the limit(s) of insurance and any deductibles that apply. It also involves determining whether more than one policy provides coverage for the same loss.

Determination of Coverage

Determining whether the BPP applies to this loss involves analyzing the relevant portions of the policy and determining whether any information found at each step in the DICE process precludes coverage at the time of the loss. You should also examine other categories of policy provisions, such as the insured's duties, general provisions, endorsements (if applicable), and terms defined in the policy in relation to the declarations, insuring agreement, conditions, and exclusions.

DICE Analysis Step 1: Declarations

The first DICE step is to review the declarations page. In this case, the review will determine whether Jim and the building were covered by the BPP when the storm struck. See the exhibit "Excerpt of Declarations Page."

Excerpt of Declarations Page

POLICY NO. SP 0001   **EFFECTIVE DATE** 07 / 01 / 20X1   ☐ **"X" If Supplemental Declarations Is Attached**

NAMED INSURED

Jim Smith

DESCRIPTION OF PREMISES

Prem. No.	Bldg. No.	Location, Construction And Occupancy
001	001	100 Beach View Blvd., Jersey Shore Town, NJ 08000 Joisted Masonry Retail Store

COVERAGES PROVIDED   **Insurance At The Described Premises Applies Only For Coverages For Which A Limit Of Insurance Is Shown**

Prem. No.	Bldg. No.	Coverage	Limit Of Insurance	Covered Causes Of Loss	Coinsurance*	Rates
001	001	Building	$1,000,000	Broad	80%	

*If Extra Expense Coverage, Limits On Loss Payment

OPTIONAL COVERAGES   Applicable Only When Entries Are Made In The Schedule Below

Prem. No.	Bldg. No.	Agreed Value			Replacement Cost (X)		
		Expiration Date	Cov.	Amount	Building	Pers. Prop.	Including "Stock"
001	001				X		

Inflation Guard (%)		*Monthly Limit Of Indemnity (Fraction)	Maximum Period Of Indemnity (X)	*Extended Period Of Indemnity (Days)
Bldg.	Pers. Prop.			

*Applies to Business Income Only

MORTGAGEHOLDERS

Prem. No.	Bldg. No.	Mortgageholder Name And Mailing Address

DEDUCTIBLE

$500. Exceptions:

Knowledge to Action

Action Task: Review the relevant portion of the declarations in Jim's policy.

According to your analysis of the excerpt of the declarations page, is coverage applicable for Jim and his building during the coverage period?

Feedback: The declarations page confirms Jim as the insured for the premises damaged. The loss occurred during the policy period.

DICE Analysis Step 2: Insuring Agreement

The second DICE step is to review the insuring agreement to determine whether it is applicable to the described loss. Specifically, it must be determined whether each item of damaged property qualifies as Covered Property under the Building description. For the purposes of this case, assume that none of the property damaged is Property Not Covered. Also assume that none of the additional coverages or coverage extensions apply.

An analysis of whether the insuring agreement is applicable to a loss requires not only determining whether the damaged property qualifies as Covered Property, but also whether the damage was caused by a Covered Cause of Loss and whether any exclusions apply to coverage. These two items will be considered in Step 4. The relevant excerpt of the BPP insuring agreement indicates the types of Building property that qualify as covered property:

> 1. Covered Property
>
> Covered Property, as used in this Coverage Part, means the type of property described in this section, A.1., and limited in A.2., Property Not Covered, if a Limit Of Insurance is shown in the Declarations for that type of property.
>
> a. Building, meaning the building or structure described in the Declarations, including:
>
> (1) Completed additions;
>
> (2) Fixtures, including outdoor fixtures;
>
> (3) Permanently installed:
>
> (a) Machinery and
>
> (b) Equipment;
>
> (4) Personal property owned by you that is used to maintain or service the building or structure or its premises, including:
>
> (a) Fire extinguishing equipment;
>
> (b) Outdoor furniture;
>
> (c) Floor coverings; and
>
> (d) Appliances used for refrigerating, ventilating, cooking, dishwashing or laundering;

Knowledge to Action

Action Task: Review the relevant portions of the BPP insuring agreement.

According to your analysis of the excerpt of the insuring agreement, does the definition of Covered Property in Jim's BPP include the damaged walls, floors, and fixtures; the destroyed roof shingles; and the broken windows?

Feedback: Yes, the definition of Covered Property in Jim's BPP includes all of these items because the walls, floors, roof shingles, and windows are parts of the building described in the declarations, and the Building description specifically includes fixtures.

According to your analysis of the excerpt of the insuring agreement, does the definition of Covered Property in Jim's BPP include the water-damaged maintenance equipment?

Feedback: Yes, the definition of Covered Property in Jim's BPP includes the water-damaged maintenance equipment because the Building definition includes "personal property owned by you that is used to maintain or service the building or structure or its premises."

DICE Analysis Step 3: Conditions

The third DICE step is to review the policy conditions to determine whether they affect coverage at the time of the loss. Jim protected the covered property from further loss by covering the damaged roof with a tarp, sent the insurer the required proof of loss, and fulfilled the other duties required of him after a loss. However, it is necessary to consider that Jim's building was vacant between September 15, 20X1, and October 25, 20X1, possibly making the Vacancy condition applicable to this loss. The Coinsurance condition also needs to be considered. If Jim does not have an amount of insurance that meets the Coinsurance requirement, a Coinsurance penalty will apply.

Knowledge to Action

Action Task: According to your analysis of the Vacancy condition, does it apply in this case? If so, how will it affect coverage?

Feedback: Part a. (Description Of Terms) of the Vacancy condition defines a building owned by the insured as being vacant "unless at least 31% of its total square footage is: (i) Rented to a lessee or sub-lessee and used by the lessee or sub-lessee to conduct its customary operations; and/or (ii) Used by the building owner to conduct customary operations." Because none of the building was being used by a lessee or sub-lessee or by Jim to conduct customary operations at the time of the loss, the building meets the definition of being vacant.

It is therefore necessary to consider Part b. (Vacancy Provisions) of the condition, which states that if "the building where loss or damage occurs has been vacant for more than 60 consecutive days before that loss or damage occurs," the insurer will not pay anything for loss caused by certain listed causes of loss and will reduce by 15 percent the amount that would otherwise be payable for loss caused by any other covered cause of loss.

Because Jim's building had been vacant for less than sixty days at the time of loss, neither the full exclusion of coverage nor the 15 percent reduction of loss payment applies. However, if another loss were to occur more than sixty days after the building became vacant, either of those consequences could apply, depending on the cause of the loss. To protect against that possibility in a future loss, Jim's insurance agent can ask the insurer to add (for an additional premium) a Vacancy Permit endorsement that suspends the Vacancy condition during a specified period while Jim's building is vacant.

Action Task: According to your analysis of the Coinsurance condition in relation to the facts in Jim's loss, does the amount of insurance carried by Jim satisfy the Coinsurance condition?

Feedback: The Coinsurance condition states that the insurer "will not pay the full amount of any loss if the value of Covered Property at the time of loss times the Coinsurance percentage shown for it in the declarations is greater than the Limit of Insurance for the property." The insurer determines that the value of Covered Property at the time of loss was $1,200,000. The declarations in Jim's policy show the Coinsurance percentage as 80 percent and the limit of insurance for the building as $1,000,000. Eighty percent of the value of the Covered Property ($1,200,000) at the time of loss is $960,000, which is less than the $1,000,000 limit of insurance. Therefore, the limit satisfies the Coinsurance condition and no coinsurance penalty applies.

DICE Analysis Step 4: Exclusions

The fourth DICE step is to determine whether the causes of loss are covered and, if so, if any exclusions affect coverage. In this case, it must be determined whether the windstorm that damaged the shingles and the windows and the water from the storm surge that damaged the building's interior are Covered Causes of Loss. The Causes of Loss—Broad Form indicates that windstorm is a Covered Cause of Loss. However, the Water exclusion may preclude coverage for losses related to the storm surge:

g. Water

(1) Flood, surface water, waves (including tidal wave and tsunami), tides, tidal water, overflow of any body of water, or spray from any of these, all whether or not driven by wind (including storm surge);

(2) Mudslide or mudflow;

(3) Water that backs up or overflows or is otherwise discharged from a sewer, drain, sump, sump pump or related equipment;

(4) Water under the ground surface pressing on, or flowing or seeping through:

(a) Foundations, walls, floors or paved surfaces;

(b) Basements, whether paved or not; or

(c) Doors, windows or other openings; or

(5) Waterborne material carried or otherwise moved by any of the water referred to in Paragraph (1), (3) or (4), or material carried or otherwise moved by mudslide or mudflow.

This exclusion applies regardless of whether any of the above, in Paragraphs (1) through (5), is caused by an act of nature or is otherwise caused. An example of a situation to which this exclusion applies is the situation where a dam, levee, seawall or other boundary or containment system fails in whole or in part, for any reason, to contain the water.

But if any of the above, in Paragraphs (1) through (5), results in fire, explosion or sprinkler leakage, we will pay for the loss or damage caused by that fire, explosion or sprinkler leakage (if sprinkler leakage is a Covered Cause of Loss).

Knowledge to Action

Action Task: Refer to the Causes of Loss—Broad Form Water exclusion.

According to your analysis of the Water exclusion, is the water damage to the building from the storm surge covered?

Feedback: Because the Water exclusion specifies that flood and waves, "whether or not driven by wind," are not Covered Causes of Loss, the Water exclusion eliminates coverage for the water damage caused by the storm surge, even though it resulted from the windstorm. (If Jim had purchased a flood endorsement to the BPP or other applicable flood coverage, this damage would have been covered elsewhere.)

Because Jim's building did not require demolition of undamaged portions of the structure or entail increased construction costs, the Ordinance or Law exclusion is not applicable in this case.

Determination of Amount Payable

Now that you have completed the DICE analysis, you can determine the amount payable. Doing this involves applying the limit(s) of insurance available to pay for the loss and any applicable deductibles and conditions. In this case, the DICE analysis has revealed that the wind damage to the building will be covered under the policy but that the water damage to the building and the maintenance equipment will not be covered.

In this case, the first step in calculating the amount payable is to determine whether the policy's coverage applies on a replacement cost or an actual cash value basis. A review of the BPP's Valuation condition reveals that none of the alternative valuation methods described in that condition (such as selling price valuation for "stock") apply to Jim's loss.

Knowledge to Action

Action Task: Review the relevant portion of the commercial property declarations in Jim's policy to determine the valuation method applicable to Jim's building.

According to your analysis of the declarations page, does Jim's coverage apply on a replacement cost or an actual cash value basis?

Feedback: Jim's coverage applies on a replacement cost basis, as indicated by the check mark below Replacement Cost in the Optional Coverages section of the declarations page.

The next step in the calculation is to determine how the BPP's limit of insurance and deductible affect the amount payable for the covered losses.

Knowledge to Action

Action Task: Review the relevant portion of the declarations page in Jim's policy to determine the policy limit and deductible that will be used to calculate the amount payable.

According to your analysis of the declarations page, what are the relevant policy limits and deductible that will be used to calculate coverage?

Feedback: The declarations page shows a $1,000,000 limit of insurance for the covered Building and a $500 deductible.

Action Task: Review the Damage Estimate exhibit to determine the amount claimed for each of the three categories of damaged items.

Given the information you have developed thus far, what is the amount payable for each of the three categories of damaged items?

Feedback: The amount payable for the wind damage to the building, which is a Covered Cause of Loss to Covered Property, is $20,000, the full amount claimed. Jim will not recover for the water damage to the first floor and to the maintenance equipment, both of which are excluded despite being Covered Property because they were not caused by a Covered Cause of Loss. Therefore, before accounting for any applicable deductible, the total amount payable is $20,000.

Action Task: Review the policy's deductible as shown on the commercial property declarations page. Accounting for the deductible, what is the total amount payable?

Feedback: The $500 deductible is subtracted from the amount payable, thus making the new amount payable $19,500.

The exhibit illustrates how the amount payable is determined. See the exhibit "Determination of Amount Payable."

Determination of Amount Payable

Item	Description	Claimed	Coverage Limits/ Issues	Amount Payable
Wind damage to building	Destroyed roof shingles and broken windows	$20,000	Within coverage limit	$20,000
Water damage to building	Repairs to first floor	$95,000	Excluded	$0
Water damage to maintenance equipment	A lawnmower, an electric hedge trimmer, and a vacuum cleaner stored on the first floor sustained damage	$750	Excluded	$0
Subtotal				$20,000
Effect of Policy Deductible			Loss recovery reduced by $500	($500)
Total Amount Payable				$19,500

[DA07843]

SUMMARY

The Loss Conditions and Additional Conditions sections of the BPP state the duties of the insured and the insurer after a loss has occurred, establish procedures for adjusting claims, explain methods for establishing the value of damaged property, outline requirements for coinsurance, and explain the interests of a mortgageholder (mortgagee).

The BPP contains four optional coverages: Agreed Value, Inflation Guard, Replacement Cost, and Extension of Replacement Cost to Personal Property of Others. Optional Coverages only apply when an appropriate notation is made on the declarations page.

The Commercial Property Conditions Form contains these conditions:

- Concealment, Misrepresentation, or Fraud
- Control of Property

- Insurance Under Two or More Coverages
- Legal Action Against Us
- Liberalization
- Transfer of Rights of Recovery Against Others to Us
- No Benefit to Bailee
- Other Insurance
- Policy Period, Coverage Territory

The Common Policy Conditions form is attached to every CPP or monoline policy written subject to ISO Commercial Lines Manual rules. The form contains these conditions: Cancellation; Changes; Examination of Your Books and Records; Inspections and Surveys; Premiums; and Transfer of Your Rights and Duties Under This Policy.

Hundreds of endorsements can be used to modify commercial property coverage. Examples of the exposures that can be covered by endorsement include building ordinance or law, spoilage, flood, and earthquake. The BPP can be supplemented in either of two ways to address the problem of fluctuating personal property values: the Peak Season Limit of Insurance endorsement and the Value Reporting Form.

Commercial property premiums are affected by the limit of insurance, the causes of loss covered, the applicable coinsurance percentage, deductible amounts, the inclusion of optional coverages, and the building's construction, occupancy, protection, external exposure, and location.

Just because damaged property qualifies as Covered Property does not mean that the loss is covered. The peril(s) causing the loss must also qualify as a Covered Cause of Loss. In this case, the property damaged directly by windstorm was covered, but the property damaged by flooding, even though it resulted from storm surge, was excluded.

ASSIGNMENT NOTE

1. Insurance Information Institute, "Few Homes Have Insurance Coverage for Earthquake or Tsunami, Although the U.S. Is At Risk for Both," March 23, 2011, www.iii.org/press_releases/few-homes-have-insurance-coverage-for-earthquake-or-tsunami-although-the-us-is-at-risk-for-both.htm (accessed July 11, 2011).

Business Income Insurance

Educational Objectives

After learning the content of this assignment, you should be able to:

▷ Describe the following aspects of the business income loss exposure:

- Measurement of business income loss

- Effect of business interruption on expenses

- Property and perils involved in business income losses

▷ Summarize the provisions of the Business Income and Extra Expense insuring agreements in the ISO business income coverage (BIC) forms.

▷ Explain how each of the additional coverages and the coverage extension supplement the business income coverage (BIC) forms.

▷ Summarize the Limits of Insurance, Loss Conditions, and Additional Condition (Coinsurance) of the business income coverage (BIC) forms.

▷ Explain how the optional coverages each modify the business income coverage (BIC) forms.

▷ Given a case, determine whether, and for what amount, a described loss would be covered either by the Business Income (and Extra Expense) Coverage Form or the Business Income (Without Extra Expense) Coverage Form.

Business Income Insurance

BUSINESS INCOME LOSS EXPOSURES

Commercial property coverage forms are tailored to insure buildings and personal property against damage by covered perils. However, the loss in value of the property and the expense of restoring it are not the only losses that a business may sustain.

Almost all of a commercial firm's property is acquired because of the income that it will generate or facilitate. This income can be lost when property is damaged or destroyed.

To evaluate the coverage needs an organization faces and determine how business income policy provisions are applied, an insurance practitioner should first understand how business income losses are measured, how a business interruption affects expenses, and the property and perils that business income losses can involve.

Measurement of Business Income Losses

Simply described, **business income insurance** covers the reduction in an organization's income when operations are interrupted by damage to property caused by a covered peril. The exact insurance recovery, of course, is determined by the terms and conditions of the policy. Because the severity of a business income loss is directly related to the length of time required to restore the property, business income coverage is considered a "time element" coverage. It is also called a "business interruption" coverage, because the loss of business income results from the interruption of the insured's business.

Business income losses are measured in terms of **net income**, which is the difference between revenues (such as money received for goods or services) and expenses (such as money paid for merchandise, rent, and insurance). It can be expressed by the formula:

Revenues – Expenses = Net income

Profit is net income that results when revenues exceed expenses. **Net loss** is the net income that results when expenses exceed revenues. For accounting purposes, the amount of a net loss appears in parentheses or is preceded by a minus sign (–).

Business income insurance covers the reduction in a firm's net income caused by accidental property damage. This reduction can be calculated by

> **Business income insurance**
> Insurance that covers the reduction in an organization's income when operations are interrupted by damage to property caused by a covered peril.
>
> **Net income**
> The difference between revenues (such as money received for goods or services) and expenses (such as money paid for merchandise, rent, and insurance).
>
> **Profit**
> Net income that results when revenues exceed expenses.
>
> **Net loss**
> Net income that results when expenses exceed revenues.

subtracting the amount of net income that a firm actually earned in a period of interruption from the amount of net income that the firm could reasonably have been expected to earn during the same period.

The following simplified example illustrates these concepts. Locksey Hardware Store suffered a partial fire loss and was closed for three months until the building could be repaired and the personal property replaced. During the three-month interruption, Locksey's revenue was reduced to nil, some ordinary expenses (payroll, electricity, and so on) were temporarily reduced or eliminated, and Locksey incurred some additional expenses (such as overtime labor and express freight on merchandise) to reopen the store as soon as possible. See the exhibit "Locksey's Revenue, Expenses, and Profit."

Locksey's Revenue, Expenses, and Profit

	Expected	Actual
Revenue	$300,000	$ 0
Expenses	240,000	120,000
Net profit (or loss)	$ 60,000	($120,000)

[DA02477]

The "Expected" column shows the revenue, expenses, and profit that Locksey could reasonably have expected during the three-month period, had no business interruption occurred. The "Actual" column shows its actual revenue, expenses, and net loss (indicated by parentheses) during the three-month period of interruption.

Locksey's business income loss is the $180,000 difference between the $60,000 profit it expected and the $120,000 net loss it actually experienced during the period of interruption. Locksey's loss can also be calculated by adding the $60,000 net income it would have earned to the $120,000 expenses that it actually incurred during the period.

For the sake of simplicity, this example assumes that Locksey's revenue returned to its normal level as soon as it reopened, which is seldom the case. In reality, Locksey's business income loss could have continued for several months after the store reopened.

Continuing expenses
Expenses that continue to be incurred during a business interruption.

Noncontinuing expenses
Expenses that will not continue during a business interruption.

Effect of Business Interruption on Expenses

During a business interruption, some of the organization's expenses (called **continuing expenses**) will continue, and other expenses (called **noncontinuing expenses**) will not continue. A business can also incur extra expenses during a business interruption. All changes in expenses must be considered when measuring a business income loss.

Continuing Expenses

If business is interrupted for only a short time, payroll of key employees, debt repayments, taxes, insurance, and many other expenses will continue during the interruption. If a longer interruption of business occurs, many expenses can be reduced or eliminated. Workers can be laid off, taxes are reduced (because of reduced income), and insurance premiums are smaller. It is often difficult to predict which expenses will continue and which will not.

Any reduction in expenses during a business interruption lessens the severity of the resulting business income loss. Nevertheless, continuing expenses can be, and ordinarily are, a significant part of business income losses. If, for example, an organization generates no revenue during a business interruption, its business income loss will be its lost profit for the period of interruption, plus the continuing expenses for that period, plus any extra expenses. In many cases, a company's continuing expenses exceed the profit that the company would have earned during the period.

Extra Expenses

Extra expenses are expenses, in addition to ordinary expenses, that an organization incurs to mitigate the effects of a business interruption. These are examples of extra expenses:

Extra expenses
Expenses, in addition to ordinary expenses, that an organization incurs to mitigate the effects of a business interruption.

- In order to reopen an assembly line that had been shut down because of an explosion, a factory owner pays the additional costs of overtime labor and overnight air shipment of repair parts.
- After sustaining fire damage to its warehouse, a wholesale distributor rents a similar warehouse and continues its operations within two weeks instead of shutting down entirely for several months.
- To continue classes while an elementary school building is rebuilt following hurricane damage, a school district rents mobile classrooms and situates them on the school's playground.

Extra expense measures often pay for themselves. For example, the extra cost of overtime labor and air freight of needed parts may have been considerably less than the income that would have been lost had such measures not been taken. Such measures actually reduce the business income loss, and most organizations will readily undertake measures that reduce loss.

Some organizations will incur extra expenses even when such expenditures exceed any reduction in the business income loss. For example, after a property loss occurs, a hospital might incur substantial extra expenses to maintain essential services for its patients even though such expenses increase its business income loss. The decision to incur such extra expenses depends on the organization's objectives. For some organizations, maintaining continuous service to customers may be more important than reducing the business income loss.

Property and Perils Involved in Business Income Losses

Business income losses typically result from physical damage to the affected organization's own buildings or personal property. However, a tenant's operations can be interrupted by damage to the building in which the tenant is located even though the part of the building the tenant occupies has not been damaged. For example, an explosion that debilitates heating, air conditioning, and ventilating equipment makes offices in sealed high-rise buildings uninhabitable in very hot or very cold weather, even though the offices themselves are not damaged.

In some cases, a physical loss at one location can cause a business interruption elsewhere. For example, a business may have to close because of damage to off-premises property that provides utilities such as electricity, water, or communications. Alternatively, one business may depend on another business as a major customer or as a key supplier. A business may be dependent simply because it is near a key facility or "magnet" property that attracts customers to the site (such as a major department store in a shopping mall). Damage to these kinds of properties could cause a business income loss at a location where no physical damage occurred.

The causes of loss for business income losses associated with property exposures are typically the same as those for physical damage losses. Thus, a fire or a windstorm that damages property may also cause a business income loss. A business income loss can also result when there has been no physical damage to buildings or personal property. For example, the closing of a road or a labor strike can cause a business income loss. However, such risks are generally not insurable. Any number of other events that are not covered by business income insurance can reduce an organization's net income. Prudent organizations use risk management techniques to avoid or lessen business income loss exposures that cannot be transferred by insurance. In order for business income insurance to apply, this must occur: an interruption of operations caused by property damage from a covered peril to property at locations or situations described in the policy resulting in a loss of business income and/or extra expense.

If any of these conditions are not met, there is no coverage under business income coverage.

BIC INSURING AGREEMENTS

A producer, underwriter, or risk management professional must understand what each business income coverage form covers in order to recommend the correct form to an insured who has business income that may be lost if a covered peril occurs.

Insurance for most business income exposures can be provided under either of the two Insurance Services Office (ISO) coverage forms for providing business income coverage:

- The Business Income (and Extra Expense) Coverage Form covers both business income and extra expense losses (even if the extra expenses do not reduce the business income loss).
- The Business Income (Without Extra Expense) Coverage Form covers business income loss but covers extra expenses only to the extent that they reduce the business income loss.

The Business Income insuring agreement is found in both of these forms and the Extra Expense insuring agreement is found only in the Business Income (and Extra Expense) Coverage Form. Either BIC form can be included in a commercial property coverage part, with or without another commercial property coverage form such as the Building and Personal Property Coverage Form. The causes of loss included in business income coverage can be designated by either the same causes of loss form that applies to other coverage forms or by a different causes of loss form that applies only to business income coverage.

Because the two ISO business income forms are similar in all respects except extra expense coverage, this section applies equally to both forms unless otherwise specified. The abbreviation "BIC" is used to refer to both forms. The phrases "BIC and extra expense" and "BIC without extra expense" are used to distinguish between the two forms.

Business Income Insuring Agreement

The BIC allows an insured to choose any one of these three options for business income coverage:

- Business income including rental value
- Business income other than rental value
- Rental value only

The option chosen by the insured should always be clearly indicated on the declarations page.

The first option covers both loss of rental value and loss of other business income. An insured that owns and operates out of a multi-tenant office building that it rents in part to other tenants might choose this. If the building became physically damaged and unable to be occupied, the insurer would pay for both the insured's loss of rental income from tenants and the insured's loss of business income from its own business.

The second option covers business income other than rental value. A business that has no rental income to lose might choose this.

The third option is less expensive, but it covers rental value only. This option might be purchased by a landlord whose only income is derived from renting property to others.

The insurer agrees to pay the actual loss of business income sustained by the named insured because of the necessary "suspension" of the named insured's "operations" during the "period of restoration." (The BIC definition of these terms is discussed in subsequent paragraphs.) The suspension must result from direct physical loss or damage to real or personal property caused by a covered cause of loss and occurring at the "premises" described in the declarations.

If the insured is a tenant, the definition of premises is broadened to include "any area within the building or on the site…if that area services, or is used to gain access to, the described premises." Thus, if fire damages the elevator motors in the basement of a building, a tenant on the thirtieth floor would be covered for any resulting business income loss even if no damage occurs above the first floor.

The BIC defines business income as the sum of these two items:

- Net profit or loss that would have been earned or incurred if the suspension had not occurred
- Normal operating expenses, including payroll, that continue during the suspension

The amount of profit or loss that would have been earned or incurred if the suspension had not occurred must be estimated based on past and prospective performance of the business.

The continuing expenses can be determined during the suspension. These expenses may include salaries of key employees, property taxes, and interest expenses.

The terms "operations," "period of restoration," and "suspension" are defined in the BIC's Definitions section. The "operations" of the insured are (1) the business activities of the insured that occur at the premises described in the declarations or (2) in the case of rental value coverage, the "tenantability" (suitability for occupancy) of the described premises.

The "period of restoration" is the period during which business income loss is covered under the BIC forms. For business income coverage, it begins seventy-two hours after the physical loss occurs and ends when the property is (or should have been) restored to use with reasonable speed. With regard to extra expense coverage, it begins immediately after the physical loss occurs. In both cases, the period of restoration ends on the date when the property should be restored with reasonable speed and similar quality or when the business is resumed at a new, permanent location. Thus, for business income coverage, there is no coverage for the first three days following the physical loss. The seventy-two hour deductible can be reduced to twenty-four hours or eliminated entirely by endorsement for an additional premium.

The period of restoration does not include any additional time that might be required to repair or reconstruct the building in order to comply with any building code or law unless the policy has been specifically endorsed to cover such additional time. The period of restoration also does not include any increased period required by ordinance or law to respond to or assess the effects of pollutants.

"Suspension" means the slowdown or cessation of business activities or, in the case of rental value coverage, that a part of the premises is rendered untenant-able (unfit for occupancy).

Whichever cause of loss form applies to the BIC determines what qualifies as a covered cause of loss for purposes of business income coverage. All of the provisions in the causes of loss form apply to business income claims, includ-ing a set of exclusions that apply only to business income and/or extra expense losses.

In summary, these are the key requirements for a business income claim to be covered in the BIC:

- Actual loss of business income you sustain resulting from the necessary suspension of your operations during the period of restoration caused by direct physical loss of or damage to property at the described premises
- Loss or damage caused by a covered cause of loss

Apply Your Knowledge

Department Store (DS) is insured under a commercial package policy that includes the Business Income (and Extra Expense) Coverage Form. For each of the loss scenarios described, determine whether the circumstances of the loss satisfy the conditions imposed by the Business Income insuring agreement in DS's Business Income (and Extra Expense) Coverage Form.

DS sustained an actual loss of business income at the described store premises as a result of decreased shopper traffic for several months while nearby streets were blocked off as part of a subway construction project.

Feedback: No. The circumstances of the loss do not meet the conditions of the Business Income insuring agreement because there was no direct physical loss to property at the described premises by a Covered Cause of Loss.

DS sustained an actual loss of business income while the second floor of the described store was necessarily shut down for repairs after a fire (a Covered Cause of Loss) caused physical loss to that floor. Although sales continued on the ground and first floors of the store, DS's net income was reduced by approximately 30 percent until the second floor was restored to use.

Feedback: Yes. The circumstances of the loss meet all the conditions of the Business Income insuring agreement:

- DS sustained an actual loss of business income.
- The loss of business income was due to the necessary suspension of DS's operations. (Partial interruption qualifies as "suspension.")
- DS incurred loss of business income during the period of restoration (before the property was restored).
- The suspension of DS's operations was caused by direct physical loss or damage to property at the described premises.
- The loss or damage was caused by a Covered Cause of Loss.

Extra Expense Insuring Agreement

The BIC and extra expense coverage form contains a second insuring agreement—Extra Expense. The Extra Expense insuring agreement provides coverage for expenses that the named insured incurs to avoid or minimize the suspension of operations. Examples of such extra expenses include the costs to move to a temporary location, increased rent at the temporary location, rental of substitute equipment (furniture, fixtures, or machinery), and the cost of substitute services such as for data processing.

The BIC and extra expense coverage form covers such expenses in full, subject to the policy limit. With the exception of extra expense to repair or replace property, these expenses are not limited to the amount by which they reduce the extra expense loss; coverage applies even if the business income loss is not reduced at all.

Even with the BIC and extra expense coverage form, extra expenses to repair or replace property are treated differently. Such expenses are covered only to the extent that they actually reduce the business income loss. For example, a business owner may pay a contractor at an overtime rate to work around the clock to repair damaged property so that the business can reopen promptly. The additional cost paid to do so would be payable as extra expense, but only to the extent that it actually reduced the business income loss. Thus, if reopening earlier reduced the business income loss by $20,000, the insurer would pay the overtime charges up to that amount (and subject to the limit of insurance).

BIC ADDITIONAL COVERAGES AND COVERAGE EXTENSION

The business income coverage (BIC) forms include additional coverages and a coverage extension that supplement the basic insuring agreement(s) in ways that are often vital to insureds recovering from business income losses.

Each version of the BIC form contains four additional coverages and one coverage extension to insure several sources of business income loss that would not otherwise be covered. The Business Income (Without Extra Expense) Coverage Form contains one more additional coverage, Expenses to Reduce Loss. The additional coverages and extension are shown in the exhibit. See the exhibit "BIC Insuring Agreements, Additional Coverages, and Coverage Extension."

BIC Insuring Agreements, Additional Coverages, and Coverage Extension

	Business Income (and Extra Expense) Coverage Form	Business Income (Without Extra Expense) Coverage Form
Insuring Agreement(s)	• Business Income • Extra Expense	• Business Income
Additional Coverages	• Civil Authority • Alterations and New Buildings • Extended Business Income • Interruption of Computer Operations	• Expenses to Reduce Loss • Civil Authority • Alterations and New Buildings • Extended Business Income • Interruption of Computer Operations
Coverage Extension	• Newly Acquired Locations	• Newly Acquired Locations

[DA02479]

Expenses to Reduce Loss

Instead of containing an Extra Expense insuring agreement, the BIC without extra expense form contains an additional coverage titled Expenses to Reduce Loss. This addition covers necessary expenses incurred by the named insured to reduce business income loss, other than the cost of extinguishing a fire.

Thus, the insured can incur the same types of expenses that are covered under the BIC and extra expense form, but they are covered only to the extent that they reduce business income loss.

A danger of the BIC without extra expense form is that the insured may incur extra expenses other than the reduction in business income loss. A large, uninsured extra expense loss can therefore result.

The BIC and extra expense form greatly reduces this possibility. Because the rate for the BIC and extra expense form is not much greater than the rate for the BIC without extra expense form, many businesses opt for the broader coverage form.

Civil Authority

In almost all cases, coverage under the BIC is related to damage to property at the insured's premises. However, Civil Authority additional coverage insures loss of business income that results when damage is to property other than the insured's and when access to the insured's premises is prohibited by civil authority. The insured's premises must be within one mile of the damaged property and access to the insured's premises must be denied by the civil authority because of a dangerous physical condition or to enable the civil authority unimpeded access to the damaged property. For example, fire damage to another building may make it unsafe for customers to go to the insured's premises.

If damage to the other premises resulted from a cause of loss covered by the insured's policy, the resulting income loss at the insured's premises would be covered for the period of suspension, beginning seventy-two hours after the time of the action by civil authority, up to a maximum of four consecutive weeks after the time of the action. The maximum period of coverage can be increased to 60, 90, or 180 days by endorsement. If the seventy-two hour period in the definition of "period of restoration" is reduced or eliminated in the BIC, the endorsement makes the same change in the Civil Authority additional coverage.

Apply Your Knowledge

Jennifer's shoe store has coverage under the BIC. A tenant situated a few doors away from Jennifer's store in the same shopping center had a fire that weakened the roof supports for part of the building. The civil authorities prohibited access to Jennifer's store because they were concerned that the building's roof could collapse. It took three and a half weeks (twenty-four days) before the civil authorities allowed Jennifer's customers to visit her store again. Does Jennifer have a covered business income claim? Explain.

Feedback: Yes, the Civil Authority additional coverage insures losses that occur somewhere other than at the insured's premises. Jennifer's premises is within one mile of the damaged property. Access was denied by the civil authority because of a dangerous physical condition—the threat of the roof collapsing—and the time period of the prohibited access was less than the coverage's allotted four consecutive weeks and access was denied beyond the seventy-two hour waiting period.

Alterations and New Buildings

In most cases, business income losses result from the interruption of operations that are already underway. However, the BIC form also provides coverage for loss of income resulting from a delay in starting operations if the delay results from damage at the described premises by a covered cause of loss to one of these:

- New buildings or structures, either completed or under construction
- Alterations or additions to existing buildings
- Machinery, equipment, supplies, or building materials located on or within 100 feet of the described premises (provided they are used in the construction, alterations, or additions or are incidental to the occupancy of new buildings)

The period of restoration for losses to new or altered buildings begins on the date that operations would have begun had the damage not occurred. The BIC and extra expense form specifically states that this additional coverage includes necessary extra expenses.

Extended Business Income

Business income coverage ceases when the period of restoration ends—that is, on the date when the property at the described premises should be repaired, rebuilt, or replaced with reasonable speed and similar quality. However, all of the insured business's former customers may not return immediately upon restoration, especially if the interruption has been long.

The Extended Business Income (EBI) additional coverage addresses this possibility by extending the regular business income coverage to include business income losses that continue after the period of restoration ends. The coverage begins when the damaged property has been restored and ends when the insured's business returns to normal, subject to a maximum of sixty days. For example, if a restaurant is closed because of fire damage, its regular customers will patronize other restaurants. Time will be needed for the insured's income to return to normal levels even after the physical repairs are completed.

Interruption of Computer Operations

A coverage restriction found in each of the BIC forms, titled Additional Limitation—Interruption of Computer Operations, states that no coverage applies when a suspension of operations is caused by destruction or corruption of, or any other loss or damage to, electronic data. An exception to this restriction is provided under the additional coverage Interruption of Computer Operations.

The additional coverage provides $2,500 of coverage for loss of business income or extra expense when business operations are suspended because of an interruption of computer operations resulting from the destruction or corruption of electronic data caused by a covered cause of loss. The $2,500 is an aggregate limit for all losses sustained in any one policy year that applies in addition to the regular limit of insurance. If the insurer is willing to provide a higher limit, it is shown in the declarations.

The $2,500 limit is not a meaningful amount of coverage for most insureds covered by commercial package policies, because losses can easily exceed that amount. Inland marine and cyber risk coverages are available to provide greater coverage.

The Interruption of Computer Operations additional coverage does not apply when loss to electronic data involves only electronic data that are integrated in and operate or control a building's elevator, lighting, heating, ventilation, air conditioning, or security system. This type of loss is specifically excepted from the Additional Limitation—Interruption of Computer Operations and is therefore covered by the business income insuring agreement without any of the restrictions of the additional coverage, such as the $2,500 aggregate limit and the limitation to specified causes of loss.

Newly Acquired Locations

The BIC forms' only coverage extension expands coverage to property at premises acquired during the policy period if a coinsurance of 50 percent or more is shown in the declarations. Titled Newly Acquired Locations, this optional coverage for insureds does not include property at fairs or exhibitions.

The coverage at any newly acquired location is limited to $100,000. This is an additional amount of insurance above the limit stated in the declarations and is not subject to the Coinsurance condition. An additional premium is charged for the automatic coverage from the date of acquisition of the new property.

The Newly Acquired Locations coverage terminates on the earliest of (1) the expiration date of the policy, (2) the date on which the insured reports the acquisition to the insurer, or (3) thirty days after the date of acquisition. This extension is intended to provide temporary protection until the insured obtains permanent coverage.

BIC LIMIT OF INSURANCE AND CONDITIONS

The sometimes overlooked Limits of Insurance, Loss Conditions, and Additional Condition (Coinsurance) sections of the business income coverage (BIC) forms can be crucial in determining how much will be paid for a business income loss.

The Limits of Insurance, Loss Conditions, and Additional Condition (Coinsurance) sections of the Insurance Services Office (ISO) BIC forms contain policy provisions that guide both the insured and insurer when deter-mining the amount payable for a business income loss. The Loss Conditions, in particular, also address these issues:

- Appraisal
- Duties in the Event of Loss
- Loss Determination
- Loss Payment

Limits of Insurance

The limit of insurance stated in the declarations is the maximum amount the insurer will pay for loss in any one occurrence.

Any amounts payable under these coverages of the BIC do not increase the limit of insurance:

- Extra Expense (in the Business Income [and Extra Expense] Coverage Form only)
- Expenses to Reduce Loss (in the Business Income [Without Extra Expense] Coverage Form only)
- Civil Authority
- Alterations and New Buildings
- Extended Business Income

The Interruption of Computer Operations additional coverage and the Newly Acquired Locations coverage extension are payable subject to their own limits. Any amounts the insurer pays for these two coverages do not reduce the limit of insurance shown in the declarations. Limits of insurance for business income can be written on either a specific or blanket basis. If they are written on a specific basis, a specific limit is set for each building insured. If they are written on a blanket basis, the limit applies to all buildings at one location or to all buildings at multiple locations. Writing coverage on a blanket basis can help a business with interdependent locations, with which a loss at one building could affect income at another building. For example, if a warehouse is damaged, it may be unable to supply goods to be sold at another building.

Loss Conditions

The Loss Conditions provide a forum to resolve disputes over amounts to be paid, require an insured to mitigate a loss, identify factors to apply when determining the amount of business income loss, and require prompt payment once an amount is agreed upon.

Appraisal

The Appraisal condition allows either the insured or the insurer to demand an appraisal of a loss if the insured and the insurer disagree on the amount of loss, but not in disputes as to coverage. The condition also describes the appraisal procedure to be followed in such cases.

Duties in the Event of Loss

The duties of the insured after loss—such as giving the insurer prompt notice of loss, protecting covered property from further loss, and cooperating with the insurer—are similar to the duties specified in the ISO Building and Personal Property Coverage Form, also known as the BPP. The BIC imposes one additional duty on any insured that intends to continue its business: to resume operations, in whole or in part, as quickly as possible.

Loss Determination

The amount of a business income loss can never be known precisely, but business income loss is determined on the basis of these items:

- Net income of the business before the loss occurred
- Probable net income of the business if no loss had occurred
- Operating expenses that must continue during the period of restoration to permit the insured to resume operations with the quality of service that existed prior to loss
- Other relevant sources of information

Not all expenses terminate when a business's operations are suspended. Continuous expenses include payroll and, depending on the insured's circumstances, utilities, rental payments, taxes, interest payable on loans, and similar items. Other relevant sources of information may include the insured's financial and accounting records, bills, invoices, notes, deeds, liens, and contracts.

The BIC states that the amount of loss will not be based on the net income that might have been earned as a result of an increase in business resulting from favorable business conditions caused by the effect of the covered cause of loss. This change was motivated by questions that arose following Hurricane Andrew in 1992. Insurers believed that the proper measure of damages for a hotel, for example, would be the room rentals that the hotel would normally have earned had the hurricane not occurred. The policy wording change makes it clear that the increase in business resulting from a catastrophe will not be included when estimating the likely net income.

Loss Payment

The insurer agrees to pay for a covered loss within thirty days after the date on which the amount of loss is agreed to (or an appraisal award is made).

The insured must have complied with all policy conditions, including filing a sworn statement of loss.

If the insured does not resume operations as quickly as possible, the insurer pays the loss based on the length of time it would have taken the insured to do so. If the insured does not resume operations at all (many businesses do not reopen after a serious fire or other damage), the period of restoration is based on the time it would have taken to resume operations as quickly as possible.

Additional Condition: Coinsurance

The BIC forms contain an additional condition establishing a coinsurance provision. The BIC coinsurance percentage may be 50, 60, 70, 80, 90, 100, or 125 percent. The policy may also be written with no coinsurance provision. The BIC loss payment calculation is:

$$\text{Loss payment} = \left(\frac{\text{Amount of insurance carried}}{\text{Amount of insurance required}}\right) \times \text{Loss amount}$$

The numerator of the fraction in this calculation is the amount of insurance carried. The denominator is the amount of insurance required; it is determined by multiplying the coinsurance percentage by the sum of the insured's net income (whether profit or loss) plus all operating expenses (less certain expenses specified in the form) that would have been incurred in the absence of a loss for the twelve-month period beginning at the inception or latest anniversary date of the policy.

Although the procedure is similar to that used with the BPP, the coinsurance basis used for business income insurance is significantly different. For other property coverages, the coinsurance basis is the same as the property covered. That is, if a building is the covered property, the coinsurance basis is either the replacement cost or the actual cash value of the building (depending on which valuation basis the policy provides). This is not the case with business income insurance. The item covered in business income insurance is net income plus continuing operating expenses; the coinsurance basis is the projected net income and all operating expenses except for certain deductible items.

Another difference between the item covered and the coinsurance basis is the period of time used in computing values. For coverage purposes, the time covered is the period of restoration plus thirty days of extended business income. For coinsurance purposes, coverage includes the estimated net income and expenses for one year, starting with the policy inception or anniversary. This makes calculating the amount of insurance needed to satisfy coinsurance more complicated for business income than for other property coverages.

To assist insureds in making the necessary calculations, ISO publishes a Business Income Report/Work Sheet. Completing this form requires a significant level of financial sophistication. Therefore, some small businesses prefer options that eliminate the coinsurance requirement.

The variety of coinsurance percentages from which the insured may choose reflects the fact that the maximum foreseeable loss for a given insured seldom equals the projected net income and operating expenses for twelve months. To be properly protected, insureds should carry, at minimum, an amount of insurance equal to their **probable maximum loss (PML)**.

Probable maximum loss (PML)

The largest loss that an insured is likely to sustain.

For some insureds, PML may constitute only a small fraction of the coinsurance basis. For example, a retail store operating in an area that contains numerous empty stores may be able to relocate and be fully operational within three months if its present location is totally destroyed. In contrast, a manufacturer that depends on sophisticated, special-order machinery might be shut down for eighteen months or more while waiting for replacement equipment if it sustains extensive damage to key equipment.

The retail store might need an amount of insurance equal to less than half its coinsurance basis and could thus choose 50 percent coinsurance; the manufacturer might need an amount of insurance much greater than its coinsurance basis. It could select 125 percent coinsurance, which would reduce the rate, because rates are lower when higher coinsurance percentages are selected.

☑ Reality Check

Effect of Coinsurance Penalty

This hypothetical example shows how an insured's failure to comply with the BIC Coinsurance condition can result in an insufficient loss recovery, even when the amount of loss is less than the limit of insurance.

Karen operates a retail store. Her store is insured under a Commercial Package Policy that includes the BIC. She selected a coinsurance percentage of 80 percent and an amount of $200,000 for coverage of her business income losses. The sum of her store's net income plus all operating expenses that would be incurred in the absence of a loss for the twelve-month period beginning at the inception or latest anniversary date of the policy is $400,000. This amount, the coinsurance basis, is twice the amount of the insurance coverage she bought. So Karen was substantially underinsured when she had a fire at her store. She lost $100,000 in business income as a result of the fire.

Applying the coinsurance formula to determine how much the insurer will pay her, the $400,000 coinsurance basis is multiplied by 80 percent. The result is $320,000, which is the minimum amount of coverage she should have bought to avoid a coinsurance penalty. The $200,000 amount of insurance she did buy is divided by the $320,000 amount she should have bought. The result is 0.625, which is multiplied by the $100,000 business income loss. That result is $62,500, which is the amount Karen's insurer will pay for her $100,000 loss, despite the $200,000 of coverage she purchased.

The difference between $100,000 and $62,500 is $37,500. That amount is the coinsurance penalty assessed against the loss as a result of purchasing an inadequate amount of coverage. Options are available to Karen and other insureds to omit or suspend the Coinsurance condition, thereby avoiding coinsurance penalties.

[DA07853]

BIC OPTIONAL COVERAGES Skip

Optional coverages that can be activated in either version of the business income coverage (BIC) forms allow the insured to obtain significant coverage enhancements.

The BIC forms each include four optional coverages that modify the basic coverage:

- Maximum Period of Indemnity
- Monthly Limit of Indemnity
- Business Income Agreed Value
- Extended Period of Indemnity

The first three optional coverages eliminate or suspend the Coinsurance condition, and the fourth optional coverage covers loss of business income that continues after the Extended Business Income additional coverage ends.

Maximum Period of Indemnity

The Maximum Period of Indemnity optional coverage negates the Coinsurance condition while limiting loss payment to the lesser of (1) the amount of loss sustained during the 120 days following the start of restoration or (2) the policy limit. The Maximum Period of Indemnity is not an additional coverage: It is a restriction of the period of restoration provided by the BIC, which, from the insured's point of view, has the advantage of avoiding any coinsurance penalty.

The period of restoration begins seventy-two hours after the time of direct physical loss. Therefore, an effective three-day deductible applies to these optional coverages in the same way that it applies to the standard BIC. (The seventy-two-hour period can be reduced to twenty-four hours or eliminated by endorsement.)

The coinsurance condition does not apply at any location to which the maximum period of indemnity is applicable. Therefore, this optional coverage should be used only when the insured is certain that any suspension of operations will last no more than four months.

Monthly Limit of Indemnity

Activated by inserting a fraction in the appropriate space in the declarations, the Monthly Limit of Indemnity optional coverage negates the Coinsurance condition while limiting the amount recoverable during any month of business interruption to the noted fraction of the insurance amount. This optional coverage applies only to business income coverage. Therefore, in the Business Income (and Extra Expense) Coverage Form, this optional coverage does not limit recovery for extra expense.

The Coinsurance condition does not apply to any location at which the monthly limit of indemnity is applicable. But this optional coverage is sometimes chosen because the insured does not want to disclose financial information to prove compliance with the Coinsurance condition or because the Coinsurance condition requires more insurance than the insured deems necessary.

Business Income Agreed Value

The Business Income Agreed Value optional coverage suspends the Coinsurance condition as long as the insured carries an amount of business income insurance that is equal to the value agreed on by the policyholder and the insurer. An insurer that is willing to provide this coverage—which, like the Maximum Period of Indemnity coverage, helps the insured avoid a potential coinsurance penalty—must take two steps to activate it.

 Reality Check

Example of Applying the Monthly Limit of Indemnity Optional Coverage

This hypothetical example shows how the Monthly Limit of Indemnity optional coverage would limit payment of a business income loss.

If the fraction shown in the declarations is 1/4 and the policy limit is $100,000, the maximum amount the insured could recover for any business income loss during any period of thirty consecutive days is $25,000. The claim payment would be the lesser of the actual loss sustained or $25,000 for the applicable thirty-day period. So if the business is suspended for three months following the start of the restoration period, and the actual loss of income is $30,000 for each of those months, the claim payment is only $25,000 per month, or a total of $75,000.

[DA07851]

First, the insurer must secure from the insured a completed business income report/worksheet showing this information:

- The insured's actual data for the most recent twelve-month accounting period before the date of the worksheet
- Estimated data for the twelve months immediately following inception of the coverage

Second, the insurer must enter the agreed value into the declarations. The agreed value must be at least equal to the product obtained by multiplying the coinsurance percentage shown in the declarations by the estimated net income and operating expenses shown on the worksheet for the twelve months following the inception of the optional coverage.

The agreed value is effective for a period of twelve months or until the policy expires, whichever comes first. The insured must submit a new worksheet to the insurer every twelve months for the agreed value coverage to remain in effect.

The Coinsurance condition is suspended while this optional coverage is in place. However, during this period, the insured must carry an amount of insurance at least equal to the agreed value if losses are to be paid in full. The Coinsurance condition is automatically reinstated if the agreed value coverage lapses. This could happen, for example, if the insured renews a policy but does not submit a new worksheet.

Extended Period of Indemnity

The Extended Period of Indemnity optional coverage extends the duration of the Extended Business Income (EBI) additional coverage to include business income losses that continue for more than sixty days after the property

Reality Check

Example of Applying the Business Income Agreed Value Optional Coverage

This hypothetical example illustrates the operation of the Business Income Agreed Value optional coverage.

ABC Corporation has a BIC with an agreed value of $200,000. If ABC carries insurance of $200,000 or more, its covered losses will be paid in full, without any possibility of a coinsurance penalty, up to the amount of insurance. However, if ABC carries only $150,000 of insurance, the Coinsurance condition will be reinstated and, consequently, only three-fourths of its covered losses will be paid (calculated as $150,000/$200,000 = 0.75).

[DA07852]

is restored. The period of indemnity can be extended up to 730 days, or two years. The actual number of days selected depends on the insured's estimate of the amount of time it would take for revenues to return to normal after the property is restored.

Many insureds, such as restaurants and clothing stores, depend on strong customer relationships and repeat business and would be unlikely to return to normal income levels within sixty days of reopening after a severe loss. For such insureds, this optional coverage can be highly attractive.

DETERMINING WHETHER THE BIC FORM COVERS A LOSS

Knowing how to apply business income coverage to the facts of a case is an important skill. This case study will help you make the transition from knowing policy language to applying policy language to losses to determine whether coverage applies. As you progress through this case study, you can check your understanding of the coverage provided by answering the Knowledge to Action questions.

Case Facts

Given the facts presented by the case, will the business income loss be covered? If so, what amount will the insurer pay for the claim? When answering the questions in this case-based activity, consider only the information provided as part of this case.

Fancy Wear Boutique (FWB), a retail clothing store in Chicago, is insured under a commercial package policy that includes the Business Income (and Extra Expense) Coverage Form, the Causes of Loss—Special Form, the

Commercial Property Conditions, and the Common Policy Conditions (as well as other forms that are not relevant to this case).

The Commercial Property Coverage Part Declarations Page describes the insured premises at the address of the store building owned by FWB and shows a $1 million Business Income limit of insurance for the location, subject to option (2), Business Income Other Than "Rental Value." The declarations also show that FWB had purchased the Business Income Agreed Value optional coverage and that the value agreed to by the insurer and FWB was $1 million. None of the other optional coverages of the Business Income (and Extra Expense) Coverage Form are in effect. Moreover, no endorsements apply to FWB's Business Income (and Extra Expense) Coverage Form or Causes of Loss—Special Form. The one-year policy period shown in the declarations began on January 1, 20X1.

On April 1, 20X1, FWB suffered a total direct physical loss to its store building and contents when a tornado touched down on FWB's premises but did not cause widespread damage in the immediate area. Replacement of the building and its contents was accomplished with reasonable speed and required one year. As a result of FWB's direct physical loss, both the revenues and normal operating expenses that FWB expected to experience were reduced as shown in the table. The resulting loss of business income that FWB sustained while operations were suspended at the described premises was $680,000. The business income loss for the first seventy-two hours following the physical loss totaled $4,000. See the exhibit "FWB's Expected and Actual Revenues, Expenses, Net Income."

FWB's Expected and Actual Revenues, Expenses, Net Income

	Expected	Actual
Revenues	$2,000,000	$1,000,000
Expenses	750,000	430,000
Net Income	$1,250,000	$570,000

Business income loss = $1,250,000 – $570,000
                     = $680,000

[DA07918]

To keep its business operating during the period of restoration, FWB rented and moved into a nearby building one month after the tornado occurred and continued operating the boutique at this location for the duration of the restoration period. During this period, FWB incurred additional costs totaling $34,000 ($20,000 for rent, $3,000 for moving expenses, $5,000 for leased equipment, and $6,000 for additional advertising expenses). FWB would not have incurred any of these expenses had the tornado damage not occurred.

After the period of restoration ended and FWB resumed operations at the insured premises, the boutique continued to sustain loss of business income for sixty days, in these amounts:

- First period of sixty days after reopening: $15,000
- Second period of sixty days after reopening: $10,000

All loss of business income that occurred after FWB reopened its store resulted from changes in customers' shopping behavior during FWB's year-long suspension of normal operations while temporarily relocated. The additional loss of business income did not result from unfavorable business conditions caused by the impact of the tornado in FWB's area. Moreover, there was nothing more that FWB could reasonably have done to restore its normal business income level any sooner than it did.

FWB and the insurer agreed on all loss determinations, and FWB fulfilled all its post-loss duties under the policy.

Necessary Reference Materials

To determine whether FWB's policy provides coverage for business income loss incurred as a result of the tornado, you need copies of the policy forms, and the declarations pages themselves. There are no endorsements that affect Business Income coverage, but if there were, they would need to be reviewed to see how they affect the Business Income (and Extra Expense) Coverage Form.

You will need to have copies of the following forms available for your reference while working on this coverage case:

- Business Income (and Extra Expense) Coverage Form (CP 00 30 10 12)
- Causes of Loss—Special Form (CP 10 30 10 12)
- Commercial Property Conditions (CP 00 90 07 88)

Determination of Coverage

When examining the policy forms to determine whether coverage applies to the losses, you can apply the four steps of the DICE method. This involves analyzing the policy declarations, insuring agreement, conditions, and exclusions and determining whether any information found at each step precludes coverage at the time of the loss. You should also examine other categories of policy provisions such as the insured's duties, general provisions, endorsements (if applicable), and terms defined in the policy in relation to the declarations, insuring agreements, conditions, and exclusions.

DICE Analysis Step 1: Declarations

The first DICE step is to review the declarations pages to determine whether it covers the person or the property at the time of the loss. Action Task: Review the declarations in FWB's policy. See the exhibit "Excerpt From FWB's Declarations Page."

A basic requirement, expressed in the Policy and Coverage Territory provision in the Commercial Property Conditions, is that the loss or damage must commence during the policy period shown in the declarations and must commence within the coverage territory in order for coverage to apply. The facts of FWB's claim satisfy this requirement because the business income loss commenced on April 1, 20X1, which is within the policy period stated in the declarations; and the loss commenced at the described premises, which is within the coverage territory. Even though the business income and extra expense loss continued for several months after the policy period ended, FWB's claim for the entire business income and extra expense claim would be covered under the policy in effect at the time the loss commenced. This result is supported by this sentence in the policy definition of period of restoration: "The expiration date of this policy will not cut short the 'period of restoration.'"

DICE Analysis Step 2: Insuring Agreement

The second DICE step is to review the insuring agreement to determine whether it is applicable to the described loss. The Business Income (and Extra Expense) Coverage form has two insuring agreements—one for the business income and a second for extra expense. You should determine what part of the loss is covered under the Business Income insuring agreement and what part is covered under the Extra Expense insuring agreement.

To be covered under the Business Income insuring agreement, a loss must be an actual loss of business income as defined and must meet several requirements imposed by the Business Income insuring agreement.

During its suspension of operations at the described premises, FWB sustained a $680,000 loss of business income, as defined in the Business Income insuring agreement. Because the claim is for business income other than rental income, the loss falls within option (2), Business Income Other Than "Rental Value," shown in the declarations. (A claim for loss of rental income, for example, would not be covered under FWB's business income coverage.)

3.26   Survey of Commercial Insurance

Excerpt From FWB's Declarations Page

COMMERCIAL PROPERTY
CP DS 00 10 00

COMMERCIAL PROPERTY COVERAGE PART DECLARATIONS PAGE

POLICY NO. 00123456   **EFFECTIVE DATE** 01 / 01 / 20X1   ☐ **"X" If Supplemental Declarations Is Attached**

NAMED INSURED   Fancy Wear Boutique

DESCRIPTION OF PREMISES

Prem. No.	Bldg. No.	Location, Construction And Occupancy
001	001	1234 Main St., Chicago, IL Joisted Masonry Clothing or Wearing Apparel Store

COVERAGES PROVIDED   Insurance At The Described Premises Applies Only For Coverages For Which A Limit Of Insurance Is Shown

Prem. No.	Bldg. No.	Coverage	Limit Of Insurance	Covered Causes Of Loss	Coinsurance*	Rates
001	001	Building	600,000	Special	80%	See Sched.
		Your Business Personal Property	700,000	Special		
		Personal Property of Others	50,000	Special		
		Business income/Extra Expense	1,000,000	Special		
		Option (2) Business Income Other Than Rental Value				
		Business Income Agreed Value optional coverage	1,000,000			

CP DS 00 10 00   Copyright, Insurance Services Office, Inc., 1999   Page 1 of 1   ☐

[DA07919]

Furthermore, the circumstances of the claim meet the other applicable requirements imposed by the insuring agreement:

- The actual loss of FWB's business income was due to the necessary suspension of FWB's operations.

- The suspension was caused by direct physical loss of or damage to property (in this case, building and contents) at the premises described in the declarations and for which a Business Income limit of insurance is shown.

- The loss or damage was caused by a Covered Cause of Loss (in this case, tornado, a type of windstorm that is not excluded by the Causes of Loss—Special Form and is therefore covered).

The Business Income insuring agreement states that the insurer will pay actual loss of Business Income only during the "period of restoration." According to the policy definition of this term, the period of restoration, for purposes of Business Income coverage (as opposed to Extra Expense coverage), begins "seventy-two hours after the time of direct physical loss or damage." Because FWB sustained $4,000 of business income loss during those first seventy-two hours (three days), that sum will be deducted from the covered amount of business income loss.

For expenses to be covered under the Extra Expense insuring agreement, the circumstances of the claim must meet the requirements imposed by that agreement. The requirements of the insuring agreement are satisfied by these case facts:

- FWB incurred $34,000 in additional costs during the period of restoration to continue its operations at a substitute store.

- FWB would not have incurred these costs if there had been no direct physical loss or damage or if the loss or damage had not been caused by or resulted from a Covered Cause of Loss (in this case, tornado).

Knowledge to Action

Do any additional coverages or coverage extensions apply?

Feedback: Yes, but the only additional coverage or coverage extension of the Business Income (and Extra Expense) Coverage Form that applies to FWB's claim is the Extended Business Income (EBI) additional coverage. EBI applies to the claim because FWB continued to sustain loss of Business Income after its property was replaced and operations resumed. Moreover, as explained in the case facts, the additional loss of business income did not result from "unfavorable business conditions caused by the impact of the Covered Cause of Loss in the area where the described premises are located."

Although EBI applies to FWB's claim, it is limited to the sixty consecutive days immediately following the date the property was replaced and operations resumed. FWB could have lengthened this sixty-day period by purchasing the

Extended Period of Indemnity optional coverage, but chose not to obtain that optional coverage.

DICE Analysis Step 3: Conditions

The third DICE step is to review the policy conditions to determine whether they preclude coverage at the time of the loss.

Numerous policy conditions are associated with FWB's business income and extra expense coverage. In addition to the conditions contained in the Business Income (and Extra Expense) Coverage Form, the Commercial Property Conditions and Common Policy Conditions also apply. In investigating the loss, the insurer must ascertain that the insured and the insurer have performed their respective duties imposed by these conditions and that the circumstances of the loss satisfy any other applicable conditions.

As stated in the case facts, the insurer determined that FWB performed all the duties required by the Duties in the Event of Loss condition. Because the insurer and FWB agreed on the determination of the amount of Business Income loss and the amount of Extra Expense incurred, the Appraisal condition was not applicable.

Also, because FWB has a $1 million limit, which satisfies the requirement in the Business Income Agreed Value optional coverage that FWB has purchased, the Coinsurance condition is suspended and therefore there is no possibility of a coinsurance penalty that would reduce the recovery amount. No other conditions had any negative effect on coverage.

Due to FWB complying with all the terms of the coverage part, once the insurer and FWB agree on the amount of loss, the insurer must pay the claim within thirty days after receiving FWB's sworn proof of loss.

Knowledge to Action

Of the following conditions required of the insured, FWB, which are found only as a condition of business income coverage?

a. Timely reporting of claim to the insurer

b. Cooperating with the insurer in investigation of claim

c. Providing a sworn proof of loss statement to the insurer

d. Resuming operations, in whole or in part, as quickly as possible

Feedback: d. Resuming operations is a condition that is unique to business income coverage.

DICE Analysis Step 4: Exclusions

The fourth DICE step is to review the policy exclusions to determine whether they exclude or limit coverage of the loss. The case facts presented provide no indication that any exclusion applies.

Determination of Amounts Payable

Now that you have completed the DICE analysis, you can determine the amounts payable. This involves analyzing the limit(s) of insurance available to pay for the loss and any deductibles that apply. It also involves determining whether more than one policy provides coverage for the same loss. FWB has no other policy that would cover this business income loss and therefore the Other Insurance provisions do not need to be considered.

The full amount of business income loss sustained before FWB's property was restored ($680,000) is covered, minus the amount sustained during the first three days after the physical loss occurred ($4,000), which results in the covered amount of $676,000 of business income loss.

All of FWB's $34,000 in additional costs are covered as extra expense. The period of restoration for Extra Expense coverage begins immediately after the direct physical loss occurs; there is no deductible for loss sustained during the first seventy-two hours, as in the case of business income coverage.

Only the $15,000 of business income loss sustained during the first sixty days following resumption of operations is insured under the EBI coverage extension. The additional $10,000 of business income loss sustained after the initial sixty-day period is not covered. FWB could have covered the additional income loss by purchasing the Extended Period of Indemnity optional coverage. See the exhibit "Amounts Payable to FWB."

Amounts Payable to FWB

Type of Loss	Amount of Loss Covered
Business Income	$676,000
Extra Expense	34,000
EBI	15,000
Total	$725,000

[DA07920]

The limit of insurance for FWB's Business Income (and Extra Expense) Coverage Form is $1 million, which is the maximum amount payable for loss in any one occurrence. Because the covered amount of FWB's losses is

$725,000, the limit of insurance does not reduce the amount payable. As discussed in connection with Step 3, the Business Income Agreed Value optional coverage is in effect, suspending the Coinsurance condition and therefore eliminating any possibility of a coinsurance penalty that would reduce the amount payable.

SUMMARY

A business income loss can sometimes be more devastating for an insured than the associated property loss. A business income loss is measured as the reduction in the insured's net income—the difference between expected net income had no loss occurred and actual net income after the loss. The causes of loss are often the same as for direct property losses.

Using either the Business Income (and Extra Expense) Coverage Form or the Business Income (Without Extra Expense) Coverage Form, most business income exposures can be insured. The Business Income insuring agreement is found in both of these forms, while the Extra Expense insuring agreement is found only in the Business Income (and Extra Expense) Coverage Form.

The basic coverage provided by the BIC form is supplemented by these additional coverages and one coverage extension:

- Expenses to Reduce Loss (BIC without extra expense only)
- Civil Authority
- Alterations and New Buildings
- Extended Business Income
- Interruption of Computer Operations
- Newly Acquired Locations

The amount payable by an insurer for a business income loss is determined in part by the BIC's Limits of Insurance, Loss Conditions, and Additional Condition (Coinsurance) sections. In particular, purchasing a limit of insurance that satisfies the BIC Coinsurance condition can help ensure an adequate recovery for business income losses.

The BIC includes four optional coverages that can be used to prevent application of a coinsurance penalty or to prolong business income coverage beyond the period of restoration.

The four optional coverages include:

- Maximum Period of Indemnity
- Monthly Limit of Indemnity
- Business Income Agreed Value
- Extended Period of Indemnity

You should now be able to apply policy language to business income losses to determine whether the losses are covered and the amount for which they are covered.

4

Commercial Crime and Equipment Breakdown Insurance

Educational Objectives

After learning the content of this assignment, you should be able to:

▷ Describe the basic characteristics of the ISO commercial crime program and financial institution bonds.

▷ Summarize the seven insuring agreements of the Commercial Crime Coverage Form in terms of these elements:

- Covered causes of loss

- Covered property

- Where coverage applies

▷ Apply the Commercial Crime Coverage Form's Limit of Insurance and Deductible provisions to a claim.

▷ Identify losses that the Commercial Crime Coverage Form excludes.

▷ Explain how the Commercial Crime Coverage Form's conditions address each of these issues:

- Interests insured

- Where coverage applies

- When coverage applies

- Claim-related duties and procedures

- Conditions applicable to Employee Theft only

▷ Given a case, determine whether, and for how much, a described loss would be covered by the Commercial Crime Coverage Form.

▷ Describe equipment breakdown insurance in terms of these elements:

- Why equipment breakdown insurance is needed

- Insuring agreements included in equipment breakdown coverage forms

- Conditions that distinguish equipment breakdown insurance from other types of insurance

Commercial Crime and Equipment Breakdown Insurance

OVERVIEW OF COMMERCIAL CRIME INSURANCE

Organizations use various techniques to manage their loss exposures resulting from criminal acts such as robbery, burglary, and other forms of theft. Among these techniques are avoidance (for example, paying employees by check or direct deposit instead of in cash), risk control (for example, installing burglar alarms), and insurance.

Many types of insurance provide coverage against some property losses that result from criminal acts. Because crime loss exposures can vary significantly among policyholders and require special underwriting skills, insurers prefer to insure certain types of crime-related property loss under separate commercial crime insurance forms. These forms allow organizations to cover crime losses that are not insured under other insurance policies.

Briefly described, commercial crime insurance covers money, securities, and other property against a variety of criminal acts, such as employee theft, robbery, forgery, extortion, and computer fraud. Many insurers use Insurance Services Office, Inc. (ISO) commercial crime forms. Financial institution bonds are used to meet the crime insurance needs of banks, insurance companies, and other types of financial institutions.

ISO Commercial Crime Program

The ISO commercial crime program includes crime coverage forms that can be added to a commercial package policy, as well as crime policy forms that can be written as monoline crime policies. The principal difference between the coverage forms and the policy forms is that the policy forms include the conditions contained in the ISO Common Policy Conditions form, thus eliminating the need to attach them to a monoline crime policy. Each coverage form and policy form comes in two versions: a discovery form and a loss sustained form. See the exhibit "Crime Forms: Discovery Form Versus Loss Sustained Form."

The ISO commercial crime coverage forms and policy forms are designed for insuring any type of nongovernment commercial or not-for-profit entity other than a financial institution. A separate set of ISO government crime coverage forms and policy forms is used to insure government entities, such as states, counties, and public utilities. See the exhibit "ISO Crime Forms and Policies."

Crime Forms: Discovery Form Versus Loss Sustained Form

Discovery Form	Loss Sustained Form
Form that covers losses discovered during the policy period even though they may have occurred before the policy period.	Form that covers losses actually sustained during the policy period and discovered no later than one year after policy expiration.

[DA07817]

Financial Institution Bonds

Few industries have crime loss exposures equal to those faced by banks and other financial institutions. A financial institution bond is an insurance policy that covers the crime loss exposures of financial institutions. Financial institution bonds were developed by the Surety & Fidelity Association of America (SFAA) and are called "bonds" because one of the key coverages that they provide is employee dishonesty insurance, which was traditionally called a "fidelity bond."

Although banks are the most common type of financial institution, other entities—such as savings and loan associations, credit unions, stockbrokers, finance companies, and insurance companies—are also eligible to be insured under financial institution bonds. Entities eligible for financial institution bonds are not eligible for the ISO commercial crime program.

The most widely used financial institution bond is Standard Form No. 24, used to insure banks and savings and loan associations. For many years, this form was called the "bankers blanket bond," a term still often used informally to refer to this coverage. The forms used for other types of financial institutions are similar to Form 24. ISO also publishes financial institution forms similar to the SFAA forms, and many of the insurers that specialize in financial institution coverage have developed their own forms.

ISO Crime Forms and Policies

Form	Form #	Type of Form	Description
Commercial Crime Coverage Form	CR 00 20	Discovery*	Designed for attachment to another policy to provide crime coverage (eight insuring agreements) for organizations other than financial institutions** and government entities.
Commercial Crime Coverage Form	CR 00 21	Loss sustained***	Designed for attachment to another policy to provide crime coverage (eight insuring agreements) for organizations other than financial institutions and government entities.
Commercial Crime Policy	CR 00 22	Discovery	Designed as a stand-alone policy to provide crime coverage (eight insuring agreements) for organizations other than financial institutions and government entities.
Commercial Crime Policy	CR 00 23	Loss sustained	Designed as a stand-alone policy to provide crime coverage (eight insuring agreements) for organizations other than financial institutions and government entities.
Government Crime Coverage Form	CR 00 24	Discovery	Designed for attachment to another policy to provide crime coverage (nine insuring agreements) for government entities.
Government Crime Coverage Form	CR 00 25	Loss sustained	Designed for attachment to another policy to provide crime coverage (nine insuring agreements) for government entities.
Government Crime Policy	CR 00 26	Discovery	Designed as a stand-alone policy to provide crime coverage (nine insuring agreements) for government entities.
Government Crime Policy	CR 00 27	Loss sustained	Designed as a stand-alone policy to provide crime coverage (nine insuring agreements) for government entities.
Employee Theft and Forgery Policy	CR 00 28	Discovery	Designed to provide only employee theft and forgery or alteration coverage in a monoline policy.
Employee Theft and Forgery Policy	CR 00 29	Loss Sustained	Designed to provide only employee theft and forgery or alteration coverage in a monoline policy.

* Loss is discovered during the policy period and sustained during the policy period, before it, or both.

**Financial institutions include banks, savings and loan associations, credit unions, insurers, and similar institutions. These organizations obtain their crime insurance under financial institution bonds (a specialized policy).

***Loss is sustained during the policy period and discovered no longer than one year after the policy period.

[DA05994]

COMMERCIAL CRIME INSURING AGREEMENTS

The Insurance Services Office, Inc. (ISO) Commercial Crime Coverage Form offers optional insuring agreements that enable organizations to customize crime coverage to meet their business needs.

The ISO Commercial Crime Coverage Form includes these insuring agreements, numbered in the form as shown:

1. Employee Theft
2. Forgery or Alteration
3. Inside the Premises—Theft of Money and Securities
4. Inside the Premises—Robbery or Safe Burglary of Other Property
5. Outside the Premises
6. Computer and Funds Transfer Fraud
7. Money Orders and Counterfeit Money

Insureds may select one or more of these insuring agreements and can add other crime coverages by endorsement.

Employee Theft

Insuring Agreement 1 covers an employer against theft of its property by its own employees. The scope of the coverage is determined by policy definitions of various terms. See the exhibit "Summary of Employee Theft Coverage."

Summary of Employee Theft Coverage

Cause of Loss	"Theft" committed by any "employee."
Property Covered	"Money," "securities," and "other property."
Where Coverage Applies	Covered territory is the United States (including its territories and possessions), Puerto Rico, and Canada. Coverage also applies to loss caused by an employee who is temporarily outside the covered territory for not more than ninety consecutive days.

[DA02511]

The policy defines "theft" as the unlawful taking of "money," "securities," or "other property" to the deprivation of the insured. No police report or criminal conviction is required for coverage to apply.

The Employee Theft insuring agreement also states that the term "theft" includes forgery—thereby clarifying that forgery committed by an employee is covered under this insuring agreement, not under the Forgery or Alteration insuring agreement.

The policy definition of "employee" is a natural person (not a corporation) who is currently employed by the insured or who was employed by the insured within the past thirty days; who is compensated by the insured by salary, wages, or commissions; and who is subject to the control and direction of the insured. The definition includes further details that are not discussed here.

The policy defines these types of covered property:

- "Money" means currency, coins, and bank notes in current use with a face value, and travelers' checks, register checks, and money orders held for sale to the public. Under insuring agreements 1, 2, and 6, money also includes deposits in the named insured's account at any financial institution as defined in the form.

- "Securities" means negotiable and nonnegotiable instruments or contracts representing money or other property, such as stocks, bonds, tokens, tickets, stamps, and evidences of debt issued in connection with credit cards other than cards issued by the insured.

- "Other property" means all other tangible property that has intrinsic value. Computer programs, electronic data, and other specified property are excluded. "Tangible" means "possible to touch." Copyrights, patents, intellectual property, and other intangible items are not covered property under the crime coverage form.

The Employee Theft insuring agreement extends the coverage territory to include loss caused by any employee while temporarily outside the regular policy territory (the United States, including its territories and possessions, Puerto Rico, and Canada) for up to ninety consecutive days.

Forgery or Alteration

Insuring Agreement 2 covers loss sustained for these reasons:

> "forgery" or alteration of checks, drafts, promissory notes, or similar written promises, orders or directions to pay a sum certain in "money" that are:
>
> (1) Made or drawn by or drawn upon you; or
>
> (2) Made or drawn by one acting as your agent;
>
> or that are purported to have been so made or drawn.[1]

The coverage pays losses of the insured or its representatives resulting from forgery or alteration of checks and similar instruments; it does not pay losses resulting from the insured's knowing acceptance of instruments that have been forged or altered by others. See the exhibit "Summary of Forgery or Alteration Coverage."

Forgery or alteration coverage does not apply to loss resulting from dishonest acts of the insured or of its partners, members, directors, trustees, representatives, or employees. Forgery committed against the insured by the insured's employees is covered under the Employee Theft insuring agreement, not under the Forgery or Alteration insuring agreement.

Summary of Forgery or Alteration Coverage

Causes of Loss	"Forgery" and alteration
Property Covered	Checks, drafts, promissory notes, or similar instruments made or drawn by the insured or the insured's agent
Where Coverage Applies	Worldwide

[DA07838]

Inside the Premises—Theft of Money and Securities

Insuring Agreement 3 covers money and securities inside the "premises" or "financial institution premises" against theft, disappearance, or destruction.

Under this insuring agreement, "premises" means the interior of any commercial building the named insured occupies. The form defines financial institution premises as the interior of that portion of any building occupied by a financial institution.

For purposes of Insuring Agreement 3, the form defines "financial institution" as "(1) A bank, savings bank, savings and loan association, trust company, credit union or similar depository institution; or (2) An insurance company."[2]

The insuring agreement extends coverage to apply to loss or damage to the premises if the insured is the owner or is liable for the damage, and to containers that hold covered property if damage is caused by safe burglary or attempted safe burglary.

The policy definition of theft includes any type of "unlawful taking" of covered property "to the deprivation of the insured." Hence, an insured loss (subject to exclusions) can be caused by burglary, robbery, observed or unobserved theft, or any other unlawful taking of money or securities.

However, for this coverage to apply, the thief must be present inside the premises or the banking premises; thus, theft committed through a remote computer is not covered.

Disappearance or destruction includes losses regardless of whether they are caused by unlawful acts. For example, coverage is provided for money and securities destroyed by fire, and disappearance of property is covered regardless of whether theft appears to be the cause. See the exhibit "Summary of Inside the Premises—Theft of Money and Securities Coverage."

Summary of Inside the Premises—Theft of Money and Securities Coverage

	Basic Coverage	Extension for Damage to Premises	Extension for Containers
Covered Causes of Loss	"Theft," disappearance, destruction	Actual or attempted "theft" of "money" or "securities"	Actual or attempted "theft" or unlawful entry
Covered Property	"Money," "securities"	The "premises" or their exterior	Locked safe, vault, cash register, cash box, or cash drawer
Where Coverage Applies	Inside the "premises" or "financial institution premises" (The thief must be present inside the premises.)	At the "premises"	Inside the "premises"

[DA02514]

Inside the Premises—Robbery or Safe Burglary of Other Property

Insuring Agreement 4 covers "other property" from actual or attempted "robbery" of a "custodian" and actual or attempted "safe burglary."

According to the policy definition, the unlawful taking of property is considered "robbery" if the person taking the property has caused or threatened to cause bodily harm to the person having care or custody of the property or if the custodian witnesses an obviously unlawful act (for example, seeing someone run out of the store with property for which he or she has not paid). See the exhibit "Summary of Inside the Premises—Robbery or Safe Burglary of Other Property Coverage."

For robbery coverage to apply, the property must be inside the premises when taken from the named insured, the named insured's partners, or any employee who is a custodian as defined in the policy. A custodian may be a salesperson or cashier working inside the insured's store but cannot be a watchperson (hired exclusively to have care and custody of property inside the premises with no other duties) or janitor (a doorkeeper or person who cleans or maintains the premises).

The other covered peril, "safe burglary," is the unlawful taking of a safe or vault from inside the premises or of property from within a locked safe or vault by a person unlawfully entering the safe or vault as evidenced by marks

Summary of Inside the Premises—Robbery or Safe Burglary of Other Property Coverage

	Basic Coverage	Extension for Damage to Premises	Extension for Containers
Covered Causes of Loss	Actual or attempted "robbery" of a "custodian" or "safe burglary"	Actual or attempted "robbery" or "safe burglary" of "other property"	Actual or attempted "robbery" or "safe burglary"
Covered Property	"Other property"	The "premises" or their exterior	Locked safe or vault
Where Coverage Applies	Inside the "premises"	At the "premises"	Inside the "premises"

[DA02521]

of forcible entry. Coverage is only provided if a burglar leaves marks of forcible entry into the safe or vault.

In an actual or attempted robbery or safe burglary, coverage extends for resulting damage to the premises and for loss of or damage to a locked safe or vault located inside the premises.

Outside the Premises

Insuring Agreement 5 covers money, securities, and other property while outside the premises and in the care and custody of either a "messenger" or an armored vehicle company. The policy defines "messenger" as the named insured, a relative of the named insured, any partner or member of the named insured, "or any 'employee' while having care and custody of property outside the 'premises.'"[3] For example, an employee who takes cash and checks to the bank for deposit in the insured's account is a messenger.

The perils insured against vary by the type of property involved in the loss. Money and securities are covered against theft, disappearance, or destruction. Other property is covered against actual or attempted robbery. See the exhibit "Summary of Outside the Premises Coverage."

Computer and Funds Transfer Fraud

Insuring Agreement 6 covers two types of loss that were, before the introduction of the 2012 editions of the ISO commercial crime forms, covered by separate Computer Fraud and Funds Transfer Fraud insuring agreements.

The first part of the Computer and Funds Transfer Fraud insuring agreement covers loss resulting directly from fraudulent entry of electronic data or com-

Summary of Outside the Premises Coverage

	Coverage for "Money" and "Securities"	Coverage for "Other Property"
Covered Causes of Loss	"Theft," disappearance, destruction	Actual or attempted "robbery"
Where Coverage Applies	Outside the "premises" while in care or custody of a "messenger" or an armored car company and inside the United States (including its territories and possessions), Puerto Rico, and Canada	Outside the "premises" while in care or custody of a "messenger" or an armored car company and inside the U.S. (including its territories and possessions), Puerto Rico, and Canada

[DA02522]

puter program into, or change of electronic data or computer program within, a computer system owned, leased, or operated by the named insured. The fraudulent entry or change must cause either of these results:

- Money, securities, or other property to be transferred, paid, or delivered
- The named insured's account at a financial institution to be debited or deleted

The second part of the insuring agreement covers loss resulting directly from a fraudulent instruction directing a financial institution to debit the named insured's transfer account and transfer, pay, or deliver money or securities from that account. See the exhibit "Summary of Computer and Funds Transfer Fraud Coverage."

Money Orders and Counterfeit Money

Insuring Agreement 7 covers loss from money orders that are not paid when presented and "counterfeit money" that the insured has accepted in good faith in exchange for merchandise, money, or services. See the exhibit "Summary of Money Orders and Counterfeit Money Coverage."

Summary of Computer and Funds Transfer Fraud Coverage

	Coverage for Computer Fraud	Coverage for Funds Transfer Fraud
Covered Cause of Loss	Use of a computer to fraudulently cause a transfer of covered property or cause the named insured's account at a financial institution to be debited or deleted.	Fraudulent instruction directing a financial institution to debit the named insured's transfer account and transfer covered property from that account.
Covered Property	"Money," "securities," and "other property."	"Money" or "securities."
Where Coverage Applies	Coverage applies to loss resulting directly from an occurrence taking place anywhere in the world.	

[DA11294]

Summary of Money Orders and Counterfeit Money Coverage

Covered Cause of Loss	Good-faith acceptance of: (1) Money orders that are not paid upon presentation or (2) "Counterfeit money"
Covered Property	Money orders issued by any post office, express company, or financial institution; and "counterfeit money" acquired during the regular course of business
Where Coverage Applies	United States (including its territories and possessions), Puerto Rico, and Canada

[DA02525]

COMMERCIAL CRIME LIMITS AND DEDUCTIBLE

Applying an insurance policy's limit of insurance and deductible to a claim covered under the policy is crucial to determining the amount payable. The Insurance Services Office, Inc. (ISO) Commercial Crime Coverage Form contains provisions that specify the manner in which the policy's limits and deductible(s) should be applied.

The Commercial Crime Coverage Form's Limit of Insurance provision states that the most the insurer will pay for all loss resulting directly from an "occurrence" (as defined in the policy) is the applicable limit shown in the declarations. Therefore, whether an act meets the policy's definition of occurrence and the limit that applies to the claim that stems from that act are components of the determination of the amount payable. The Deductible provision, which indicates how the deductible shown in the policy's declarations affects the insurer's payment, must also be applied to the claim.

Limit of Insurance

Under the Commercial Crime Coverage Form, a separate limit of insurance can be shown in the declarations for each insuring agreement that the insured selects. If a loss is covered under more than one insuring agreement, the insurer will pay no more than the highest limit of the insuring agreements that apply.

Definition of Occurrence

The definition of "occurrence" is key in determining how much the insurer is obligated to pay for a covered crime loss. Slightly different definitions of occurrence apply to employee theft coverage, forgery or alteration coverage, and all other coverages. Each of these definitions states that "occurrence" includes an individual act, the combined total of all separate acts (whether or not related), or a series of acts (whether or not related).

As defined for employee theft, the definition of occurrence requires that the act or acts must be committed by an employee (as defined in the form) acting alone or in collusion with others. Thus, if the employee theft limit is $100,000, the most the insurer would be required to pay for one instance of embezzlement—regardless of how many employees might have been involved in the crime—is $100,000. In addition, because of the definition of occurrence, the applicable limit is the most the insurer will pay for an individual act or a series of acts involving the same employee.

The definition of occurrence that applies to forgery or alteration requires that the act or acts must be committed by a person acting alone or in collusion with others and must involve one or more instruments. Therefore, if one person or a ring of perpetrators forged multiple documents, the resulting loss would be considered as having been caused by a single occurrence, and the insurer would pay no more for the combined loss than the forgery or alteration limit.

The definition of occurrence that applies to all coverages other than employee dishonesty and forgery or alteration includes not only acts but also events. The word "event" is included because some of the perils covered by these other coverages are events rather than acts committed by persons. For example, money and securities can be covered for theft, disappearance, or destruction. Although theft is an act committed by persons, disappearance and destruction can be caused by events such as windstorm or earthquake.

Each definition of occurrence comes in two different versions: one for the loss sustained forms and another for the discovery forms. The difference is found at the end of each definition:

- The loss sustained forms state that the act must be committed (or the event must occur) "during the Policy Period shown in the Declarations, except as provided" in the conditions pertaining to loss sustained under prior insurance
- The discovery forms state that the act must be committed (or the event must occur) "during the Policy Period shown in the Declarations, before such Policy Period or both."[4]

Special Limits of Insurance

In addition to the limits of insurance shown in the policy declarations for each insuring agreement, three of the insuring agreements are subject to special limits that apply only to specified types of covered property.

Inside the Premises—Robbery or Safe Burglary of Other Property is subject to a special limit of $5,000 per occurrence for these types of property:

(1) Precious metals, precious or semiprecious stones, pearls, furs, or completed or partially completed articles made of or containing such materials that constitute the principal value of such articles; or

(2) Manuscripts, drawings, or records of any kind or the cost of reconstructing them or reproducing any information contained in them.[5]

Outside the Premises coverage is subject to a special limit of $5,000 per occurrence for the types of property listed in items (1) and (2). Computer and Funds Transfer Fraud coverage is subject to a special limit of $5,000 per occurrence for loss of or damage to the types of property listed in item (2).

Deductible

No loss in any one occurrence is payable by the insurer unless the amount of loss exceeds the deductible shown in the declarations. If the amount of loss exceeds the deductible, the insurer will pay the amount of the loss in excess of the deductible, up to the limit of insurance.

To illustrate application of the deductible with a hypothetical case, assume that Tri-State Supply Company has employee theft coverage with a $100,000 limit and a $1,000 deductible. If one employee stole $5,000 of covered property, the insurer would pay the amount of loss in excess of the $1,000 deductible, or $4,000. If the amount of loss exceeded the limit of insurance by the deductible amount or more, the insured would be able to recover the full amount of insurance. For example, on a loss of $101,000 or more, the insurer would pay the full $100,000 limit in excess of the $1,000 deductible. In other words, the deductible is taken off the amount of the loss, not off the limit.

Apply Your Knowledge

An independent audit of the accounting records of a business insured under a Commercial Crime Coverage Form reveals that several employees in the organization's accounting department colluded over five years (and five policy periods) to embezzle $200,000 annually. The policy's limit of insurance is $500,000, with a per-occurrence deductible of $1,000. The insured submits a claim to its insurer for $1,000,000, the total that was stolen. Will the Commercial Crime Coverage Form apply to this claim and, if so, what amount will the insurer pay for this loss?

Feedback: Yes, the Commercial Crime Coverage Form will apply to this claim. The definition of "occurrence" applicable to employee theft coverage requires that the act or acts be committed by an employee, whether acting alone or in collusion with others, and that the act must be committed "during the Policy Period shown in the Declarations, before such Policy Period, or both." The facts of the claim meet this condition, as the theft occurred over a number of years prior to the discovery during the audit. Additionally, the definition of occurrence states the limit of insurance is the most the insurer will be liable for as a result of an individual act or a series of acts involving the same employee. In this circumstance, the most the insurer will pay for the act of employee theft, regardless of how many employees were involved and— equally importantly—regardless of the number of acts of employee theft, is $500,000. Finally, the amount of loss the insurer is obligated to pay under the Commercial Crime Coverage Form is the amount in excess of the deductible. The amount of the loss, $1,000,000, exceeds the limit of $500,000, so the insurer will pay the full limit in excess of the $1,000 deductible. The deductible is subtracted from the amount of the loss, not the limit of insurance.

COMMERCIAL CRIME EXCLUSIONS

As with most insurance coverage forms, the Commercial Crime Coverage Form excludes losses that are best covered under other insurance, are not insurable, or are not anticipated in the policy premium.

In the Insurance Services Office, Inc. (ISO) Commercial Crime Coverage Form, the basic crime insuring agreements are subject to several exclusions. The exclusions are divided into different groups, depending on whether they apply to all or only some insuring agreements.

Exclusions are presented in the coverage form and described in this section based on these groupings:

- General exclusions
- Exclusions applicable only to employee theft

- Exclusions applicable to inside the premises and outside the premises
- Exclusions applicable only to computer and funds transfer fraud

General Exclusions

Eleven general exclusions are applicable to any of the crime insuring agreements:

- Acts Committed by You, Your Partners or Your Members—The exclusion eliminates coverage for loss resulting from theft or any other dishonest act committed by the named insured, the named insured's partners, or (if the named insured is a limited liability company) the named insured's members, whether acting alone or in collusion with other persons.

- Acts Committed by Your Employees Learned of by You Prior to the Policy Period—The exclusion eliminates coverage for loss resulting from theft or any other dishonest act committed by an employee if the named insured, the named insured's partners, or the named insured's members, or any managers, officers, directors, or trustees, not in collusion with the employee, knew that the employee had committed theft or a dishonest act before the policy's effective date. This exclusion prevents the insurer from having to cover employee theft committed by employees who are known, prior to the policy period, to have committed any type of dishonest act.

- Acts Committed by Your Employees, Managers, Directors, Trustees or Representatives—The commercial crime form excludes theft or other dishonest acts committed by the named insured's employees, managers, directors, trustees, or authorized representatives. The exclusion applies regardless of whether such persons acted alone or in collusion with others and while such persons performed services for the named insured or otherwise. The exclusion states that it does not apply to loss covered under the Employee Theft insuring agreement.

- Confidential or Personal Information—The form excludes losses resulting from the use of another person's or organization's confidential or personal information, including, but not limited to, patents, trade secrets, processing methods, customer lists, credit card information, or health information.

- Data Security Breach—The form excludes fees, costs, fines, penalties, and other expenses the insured incurs related to the access to or disclosure of another person's or organization's confidential or personal information, which includes, but is not limited to, patents, trade secrets, processing methods, customer lists, financial information, credit card information, health information, or any other type of nonpublic information.

- Governmental Action—Like virtually any policy covering property loss, the commercial crime form excludes loss resulting from seizure or destruction of property by order of government authority.

- Indirect Loss—The form lists three examples of indirect loss that are not covered: (1) business income losses; (2) payment of damages for which the insured is legally liable (other than compensatory damages arising directly from a loss covered by the policy); and (3) expenses incurred in establishing either the existence or the amount of loss under the policy. The exclusion is not limited to just those three types of indirect loss; any indirect loss is excluded.

- Legal Fees, Costs and Expenses—The form excludes fees, costs, and expenses related to any legal action except when covered under the Forgery and Alteration insuring agreement.

- Nuclear Hazard—The exclusion eliminates coverage for loss or damage caused by any nuclear reaction, radiation, or radioactive contamination.

- Pollution—This exclusion eliminates coverage for any loss or damage that in any way results from pollution, which the exclusion defines as "the discharge, dispersal, seepage, migration, release or escape of any solid, liquid, gaseous, or thermal irritant or contaminant." Pollution includes residuals of pollutants, such as smoke, vapor, fumes, and so forth, along with materials to be recycled, reconditioned, or reclaimed.

- War and Military Action—This exclusion eliminates coverage for loss or damage resulting from war or civil war, whether declared or undeclared; warlike actions by a military force; or acts of rebellion or revolution, including governmental action to defend against such acts.

Exclusions Applicable Only to Employee Theft

This group of exclusions applies only to the Employee Theft insuring agreement:

- Inventory Shortages—The insurer will not pay for any loss that depends on inventory or profit-and-loss calculations to prove either the existence or the amount of the loss. An inventory shortage is the difference between a physical inventory and the inventory shown in the insured's books and records. An inventory shortage may occur for reasons other than employee theft. For example, there may have been bookkeeping or arithmetic errors, obsolete inventory may have been discarded, or samples may have been sent to customers but not deleted from the inventory records. Therefore, insurers will not accept an inventory calculation as proof that the insured has sustained an employee theft loss. However, if an insured establishes without inventory computations that it has sustained a loss, the form allows the insured to offer inventory records and actual physical count of inventory in support of the amount of loss claimed.

- Trading—An employer may sustain a large financial loss resulting from an employee's unauthorized trading in stocks, bonds, futures, commodities, or other similar items. Because employee theft coverage rates do not contemplate such losses, the form excludes loss resulting from trading, whether the trading occurs in the named insured's name or in a "genuine or fictitious account."

- Warehouse Receipts—The Warehouse Receipts exclusion eliminates coverage for "loss resulting from fraudulent or dishonest signing, issuing, canceling or failing to cancel, a warehouse receipt or any papers connected with it." Such a loss may occur, for example, when an employee releases merchandise without canceling the receipt or issues a receipt without having received the merchandise. The customer could then make a claim for missing goods based on the erroneous receipts. Such claims would not be covered because of this exclusion.

Exclusions Applicable Only to Inside the Premises and Outside the Premises

These eight exclusions apply specifically to the Inside the Premises—Theft of Money and Securities; Inside the Premises—Robbery or Safe Burglary of Other Property; and Outside the Premises insuring agreements:

- Accounting or Arithmetical Errors or Omissions—The form excludes losses resulting from accounting or arithmetical errors or omissions. Although many losses of this type are within the policy deductible, some losses could be sizable. The exposure falls within the general category of business risks that should be addressed by loss control measures, with any losses retained by the business.

- Exchanges or Purchases—Loss resulting from giving or surrendering property in an exchange or purchase is excluded. Thus, a fraudulent transaction that involves the loss of money, securities, or other property is not covered. For example, the loss sustained when a purchaser pays with a forged cashier's check is excluded from coverage.

- Fire—The three insuring agreements do not cover loss or damage resulting from fire, regardless of its cause. However, the exclusion does not apply to fire damage to a safe or vault. The exclusion also does not apply (under Inside the Premises—Theft of Money and Securities) to money or securities damaged or destroyed by fire. Nearly all organizations have commercial property insurance to cover the fire losses that the crime form excludes; money, however, is not covered under commercial property coverage forms.

- Money Operated Devices—Loss of property from money-operated devices (such as vending machines, amusement devices, or change machines) is not covered unless a continuous recording instrument inside the machine keeps track of the amount of money deposited. In the absence of a recording device, establishing the amount of the loss would be difficult or impossible.

- Motor Vehicles or Equipment and Accessories—The form excludes loss of or damage to motor vehicles, trailers, or semi-trailers, or for equipment and accessories attached to them. Theft of automobiles and related equipment can be insured under automobile physical damage coverage, and theft of mobile equipment can be insured under inland marine forms.

- Transfer or Surrender of Property—Loss of or damage to property after it has been transferred or surrendered to a person or place outside the premises or financial institution premises is excluded under several specified circumstances. For example, loss of property that the insured has voluntarily sent to an imposter on the basis of unauthorized instructions is excluded.

- Vandalism—Coverage extensions stated in the two inside the premises insuring agreements cover damage to the premises and their exterior and loss of or damage to various types of receptacles containing covered property if directly caused by a covered peril. The Vandalism exclusion eliminates coverage for damage to those types of property by vandalism or malicious mischief. Commercial property forms normally include coverage for damage to such property by vandalism or malicious mischief, including building damage caused by the breaking in or exiting of burglars.

- Voluntary Parting With Title to or Possession of Property—The voluntary parting exclusion eliminates coverage when the insured or an agent of the insured is tricked into voluntarily surrendering property to a thief. For example, a business owner tells the firm's cashier that a bank messenger is to pick up money at a given time each day. If a wrongdoer impersonates the messenger and succeeds in getting the cashier to part with the money voluntarily, the loss would not be covered by Inside the Premises—Theft of Money and Securities.

Exclusions Applicable Only to Computer and Funds Transfer Fraud

These five exclusions apply only to the Computer and Funds Transfer Fraud insuring agreement:

- Authorized Access—Loss resulting from fraudulent entry of or a fraudulent change to electronic data or a computer program in any computer system that is owned, leased, or operated by the insured that is executed by a person or organization with authorized access to the insured's computer system is excluded. The exclusion does not apply if the fraudulent entry or change is made by an employee acting on a fraudulent instruction from a computer software contractor who has a written agreement with the insured. It also does not apply to losses that may be covered under the Employee Theft Insuring Agreement.

- Credit Card Transactions—Loss resulting from the use or purported use of credit, debit, charge, access, convenience, identification, stored-value, or other cards or the information contained on such cards is excluded.

- Exchanges or Purchases—Loss resulting from the giving or surrendering of property in any exchange or purchase is excluded. For example, this exclusion may apply to an Internet-based transaction in which an insured knowingly exchanges a product for compensation whose value is less than the value the insured intended to receive in exchange for that product.

- Fraudulent Instructions—Loss resulting from an employee or financial institution acting upon a fraudulent instruction to transfer, pay, or deliver money, securities, or other property or from an employee or financial institution acting upon a fraudulent instruction to debit or delete the insured's account is excluded. However, the exclusion does not apply if the loss results directly from a fraudulent instruction that directs a financial institution to debit the insured's transfer account and pay, transfer, or deliver money or securities from that account. It also does not apply if the fraudulent entry or change is made by an employee acting on a fraudulent instruction from a computer software contractor who has a written agreement with the insured.

- Inventory Shortages—A separate Inventory Shortages exclusion applies to computer fraud coverage. Unlike the general exclusion, this exclusion does not include the wording permitting the insured to use inventory records in support of the amount of loss claimed.

Apply Your Knowledge

Identify any exclusions of the Commercial Crime Coverage Form that would apply to these losses. In each case, the insured has purchased all of the insuring agreements under this coverage form:

Tom, an employee of the insured, commits an act that meets all of the requirements under the Employee Theft insuring agreement. The insurer's claims investigation reveals that Tom had been arrested for shoplifting before the policy period began. However, Tom's employer had no knowledge of Tom's prior dishonesty until it was revealed by the investigation. Would the Acts of Employees Learned of by You Prior to the Policy Period exclusion eliminate coverage for this loss?

Feedback: No. The exclusion applies only if the insured learns of the prior dishonest act before the beginning of the policy period. In this case, Tom's employer did not know about Tom's prior dishonest act before the policy period, so the exclusion does not apply.

Vandals set the insured's building on fire. In addition to damaging the building and its contents, the fire destroys $5,000 of money that was in the insured's building. The loss of money meets all the requirements under the Inside the Premises—Theft of Money and Securities insuring agreement, which covers money and securities against theft, disappearance, or destruction. Would the Fire exclusion eliminate coverage for this loss?

Feedback: No. The Fire exclusion does not apply to loss of or damage to money or securities.

A thief breaks into and steals money from vending machines located in a convenience store. The vending machines do not contain recording instruments to track the money that was deposited. The loss of money meets all the requirements under the Inside the Premises—Theft of Money and Securities insuring agreement. Would the Money Operated Devices exclusion eliminate coverage for this loss?

Feedback: Yes. The Money Operated Devices exclusion eliminates coverage from such devices that do not have a continuous recording instrument inside them to keep track of the amount of money deposited.

COMMERCIAL CRIME CONDITIONS

The Insurance Services Office, Inc. (ISO) Commercial Crime Coverage Form includes numerous policy conditions that affect the application or extent of coverage provided.

As with all insurance policies, conditions are included in the ISO Commercial Crime Coverage Form that extend or eliminate coverage under various circumstances. Some conditions apply only to certain insuring agreements. Other conditions apply to all of the insuring agreements. The latter group, although listed alphabetically in the form, are presented here in logical order followed by two conditions that apply only to the Employee Theft insuring agreement.

Interests Insured

Several conditions help to clarify issues concerning the interests insured under a crime policy.

The Ownership of Property; Interests Covered condition states that the insurance applies only to property owned, leased, or held by the named insured, or for which the insured is legally liable, provided that the insured was liable for the property before the loss occurred. However, the insurance is for the insured's benefit only; any claim must be made by the insured. If the insured does not want to present a claim, the owner of the property cannot make a direct claim on the insurance. Coverage for theft by the insured's employee of client's property may be added by endorsement.

The Joint Insured condition appoints the first named insured as agent for all other insureds with regard to all transactions under the policy. It also provides that an employee of any insured is considered to be an employee of every insured and that knowledge possessed by any insured or any partner, officer, or limited liability company (LLC) member of any insured is considered to be known to all insureds.

If, during the policy period, the insured adds additional premises or employees other than by consolidation, merger, or acquisition, the Additional Premises or Employees condition states that policy coverage will be extended automatically.

No notice is required, and no additional premium is charged for the remainder of the policy period. On renewal, the insured must give the insurer full information, and the renewal premium will reflect the revised exposure.

If the insured acquires additional employees or premises by consolidation, merger, or acquisition, the Consolidation—Merger or Acquisition condition states that coverage will be extended automatically for ninety days to the new employees or premises. If the insured wishes to extend coverage beyond ninety days, the insured must notify the insurer of the consolidation, merger, or acquisition promptly and pay the appropriate additional premium.

Where Coverage Applies

Many of the crime insuring agreements limit coverage to occurrences inside the premises described in the policy. When coverage is not restricted to the premises, the Territory condition defines the geographical scope of coverage. This condition limits coverage for all insuring agreements to acts committed or events occurring within the United States (including its territories and possessions), Puerto Rico, and Canada. The territorial provision for employee theft coverage is extended to include coverage for loss caused by employees temporarily outside the coverage territory for not more than ninety days. The territorial provisions for forgery or alteration coverage and computer and funds transfer fraud coverage are extended to cover loss resulting from occurrences taking place anywhere in the world.

When Coverage Applies

Three conditions are principally concerned with determining when a loss must occur in order to be covered under the loss sustained version of the Commercial Crime Coverage Form:

- Extended Period to Discover Loss
- Loss Sustained During Prior Insurance Issued by Us or Any Affiliate
- Loss Sustained During Prior Insurance Not Issued by Us or Any Affiliate

Extended Period to Discover Loss

Under the loss sustained form, the insurer will pay for loss that the named insured sustains through acts committed or events occurring during the policy period. Moreover, coverage applies only to acts discovered during the policy period or within one year after the policy is canceled. However, the discovery period terminates immediately as of the effective date of any other insurance that the insured obtains (from any insurer) that replaces coverage in whole or in part. See the exhibit "Discovery Form."

Discovery Form

All of the ISO crime forms are available in loss sustained and discovery versions. The discovery form covers losses regardless of when they occurred if they are first discovered during the policy period or during the sixty-day discovery period that applies to most claims under the discovery form.

To limit the broad coverage for prior occurrences that discovery forms provide, the insurer may attach a retroactive date endorsement. This endorsement states that coverage is limited to losses the insured sustains through acts committed or events occurring after the retroactive date shown in the policy schedule. For coverage to apply, the loss must still be discovered during the policy period or the extended loss discovery period.

[DA07834]

Loss Sustained During Prior Insurance Issued by Us or Any Affiliate

Some losses occurring before the current policy period of a loss sustained crime policy may be covered by the policy currently in effect. Under the Loss Sustained During Prior Insurance Issued by Us or Any Affiliate condition, the insurer agrees to pay a loss that meets these criteria:

- The loss is discovered during the policy period shown in the declarations.
- The loss occurred while prior insurance, issued by the same insurer or an affiliated insurer, was in effect.
- The current insurance became effective when the prior insurance was canceled.
- The loss would have been covered by the present insurance if the insurance had been in force at the time of loss.

If these requirements are met, the current policy applies, but the most the insurer will pay is the amount recoverable under the prior insurance, if it had remained in effect.

The same condition also contains provisions for settling covered losses that occurred over more than one policy period. Such losses typically are associated with employee theft, in which an employee may have embezzled funds for years before the employer discovers the loss.

Coverage must be continuous; that is, the renewal policy must have commenced when the prior policy expired, but no limit of insurance accumulates from year to year. A policy in force for ten years with a $50,000 limit will pay a maximum of $50,000 for any one covered loss, not ten times $50,000. This is important to consider when selecting the amount of insurance for employee theft coverage. A dishonest employee often steals smaller amounts on numerous occasions over many years that can accumulate in significant losses.

This condition is found in the loss sustained form only; it is not needed in the discovery form because the discovery form covers loss, regardless of when it occurred, that is discovered during the current policy period.

Loss Sustained During Prior Insurance Not Issued by Us or Any Affiliate

If the prior insurance was not provided by the current insurer or an affiliate, the Loss Sustained During Prior Insurance Not Issued by Us or Any Affiliate condition applies. Under this condition, which is found in the loss sustained form but not in the discovery form, the insurer agrees to pay a loss that meets all of these criteria:

- The loss is discovered during the policy period shown in the declarations.
- The loss occurred while prior insurance, issued by another unaffiliated insurer, was in effect.
- The current insurance became effective when the prior insurance was canceled or terminated.
- The loss would have been covered by the present insurance if the insurance had been in force at the time of loss.

If these requirements are met, the insurer will pay the *lesser* of the amount recoverable under the present insurance or the prior insurance (if it had remained in effect).

The essential difference between these two provisions concerns the available limits. If the loss is covered by both the current insurance and prior insurance issued by the same or an affiliated company, the highest limit in force under any of the policies covering the loss will be available to the insured. If the loss occurred under prior insurance issued by another insurer, recovery is limited to, at most, the applicable limit in the policy in effect at the time of the loss.

Claim-Related Duties and Procedures

Several conditions establish the duties and procedures to follow after a loss involving covered property.

☑ **Reality Check**

Loss Sustained During Prior Insurance Not Issued by Us

This hypothetical example illustrates why an insurer would be willing to cover a loss that occurred during the prior policy period of another insurer.

Joanie, the proprietor of an electronics store, was alarmed when her commercial crime insurer raised the premium on her loss sustained crime policy by 20 percent. She consulted Mark, her insurance agent, because she wanted to change insurers. However, she was concerned that she would not be covered for any crime loss that occurred when that policy was in effect but was not discovered until after the policy was canceled.

Mark explained that another insurer offers loss sustained coverage using ISO's Commercial Crime Coverage Form. He told Joanie that the form has a condition that would cover a loss sustained during prior insurance not issued by the new insurer if the loss met specified criteria.

After Mark explained the criteria and quoted Joanie a lower premium on the new crime policy, Joanie was surprised that the new insurer would be willing to cover such a loss. Mark explained that without the offer of such coverage, it would be nearly impossible to persuade an insured to switch to a new insurer. In effect, providing this coverage for a prior period is one of an insurer's costs of acquiring new policyholders.

[DA07835]

The insured's duties stated in the Duties in the Event of Loss condition in a crime policy are essentially the same as such duties under other property policies. After discovering a loss or a situation that may result in a loss, the insured has these duties:

- Notify the insurer as soon as possible and, except for employee theft and forgery and alteration losses, notify the police if the insured believes that the loss involves a violation of law
- Submit a detailed, sworn proof of loss within 120 days
- Cooperate with the insurer in its investigation of the loss
- Produce all pertinent records for the insurer to examine
- Submit to examination under oath if requested by the insurer
- Secure all rights of recovery that the insured has against others responsible for the loss and do nothing to impair those rights.

The Records condition in a crime policy requires the insured to keep sufficient records to enable the insurer to verify the amount of loss.

Under the Valuation—Settlement condition of a crime policy, the value of a covered loss is determined differently for each of the three categories of covered property:

- Money is valued at its face value. If foreign money is lost, the insured has the option of receiving payment for the loss at the face value of the money or at its equivalent U.S. value on the date of the loss.

- Securities are valued as of the close of business on the day the loss is discovered. In many cases, duplicate securities can be issued if the insured posts a bond. The insurer will pay the cost of the bond as part of the loss. The insurer has the option of paying the market value of lost securities or replacing them in kind. If securities are replaced, the insured must assign to the insurer all rights, title, and interest in the lost securities.

- If property other than money and securities is lost or damaged, the insurer has the option of paying the replacement cost of the property, repairing the property, or replacing it. If the property is not promptly repaired or replaced as soon after the loss or damage as possible, the insurer will pay the loss on an actual cash value basis.

The Recoveries condition of a crime policy specifies how any subrogation or salvage recoveries will be divided between the insurer and the insured. First the insured is reimbursed for its covered loss that exceeded the limit of insurance.

The remaining amount of the recovery is paid to the insurer until it has recovered all that it paid. Any remaining value is paid to the insured to reimburse it for the deductible amount and for any loss not covered by the insurance.

As with most insurance policies, the crime general provisions include a subrogation provision. Under the Transfer of Your Rights Against Others to Us condition, for any loss the insurer pays to the insured, the insured must transfer its rights of recovery against others to the insurer. Moreover, the insured must do nothing after loss to impair those rights. (The insured is permitted to waive its rights of action against other parties if the waiver is made before loss occurs.)

The Other Insurance condition is split into two parts: primary and excess.

If the insurance is written as primary, a loss will be shared on a pro rata by limits basis with other insurance subject to the same terms and conditions. If the other insurance is not subject to the same terms and conditions, the insurance will apply as excess coverage over any other insurance available to the insured to cover a loss. Often, the other policy will have a similar clause. When two or more policies cover a loss and all policies purport to be excess over other insurance, courts usually require the insurers to contribute on a pro rata basis if the insurers are unable to agree on a mutually acceptable method.

If the insurance is written on an excess basis, the insurer will only pay the amount of loss that exceeds the limit and deductible of the other insurance.

Conditions Applicable to Employee Theft Only

The Termination as to Any Employee condition and the Employee Benefit Plans condition apply only to the Employee Theft insuring agreement.

The first part of the Termination as to Any Employee condition automatically terminates employee theft coverage with respect to any employee who has committed a dishonest act as soon as the act is known to the insured or any partner, officer, or director not in collusion with the employee. Coverage on the employee is terminated regardless of whether the act was committed against the insured or others (before or after the employee was hired by the insured) and regardless of whether the employer learns of it before or after policy inception.

If the insured first learns of an employee's dishonest act after the employee has committed an employee theft, the loss will be covered (assuming no other exclusions apply), but coverage with respect to that employee for any further claims will be terminated.

If, in another situation, a claim investigation of an employee theft loss reveals that the insured knew about a prior dishonest act by the same employee, the current claim will not be covered, because coverage for that employee was automatically terminated when the insured learned of the prior dishonest act.

The second part of the Termination as to Any Employee condition gives the insurer the right to cancel coverage with respect to any employee by providing thirty days' advance notice to the insured.

The Employee Benefit Plans condition explains how employee theft coverage applies when the policy includes one or more employee benefit plans as insureds for the Employee Theft insuring agreement. This condition eliminates the need to attach the Employee Retirement Income Security Act of 1974 (ERISA) compliance endorsement to the policy to satisfy the ERISA fidelity bonding requirement. Employee theft coverage was traditionally called a fidelity bond, and the term "fidelity" is still used to refer to employee theft coverage.

Apply Your Knowledge

On August 5, Millright Foods canceled its crime insurance policy, which it had purchased from Insurer A. Millright then purchased a new crime policy from Insurer A's affiliate, Insurer B, which took effect on the cancellation date of Insurer A's policy. Insurer B's policy uses the ISO Commercial Crime Coverage Form. Four months after Insurer B's policy became effective and during its policy period, Millright discovered that one of its former managers, who left Millright's employment on July 15 of that year, had been embezzling funds over the previous three months. Insurer A denied coverage for the loss because the loss was not discovered until after Insurer A's policy was canceled.

How would the Loss Sustained During Prior Insurance Issued by Us or Any Affiliate condition in Insurer B's policy affect coverage for this loss?

Feedback: This condition specifies that the loss will be covered under Insurer B's policy if these requirements are met: the loss is discovered during the policy period shown in the declarations, the loss occurred while the affiliate's insurance was in effect, the current insurance became effective when the prior insurance was canceled, and the loss would have been covered by the present insurance if the insurance had been in force at the time of loss.

DETERMINING WHETHER THE COMMERCIAL CRIME COVERAGE FORM COVERS A LOSS

Knowing how to apply commercial crime coverage to the facts of a case is an important skill. This case study will help you make the transition from knowing policy language to applying policy language to losses to determine whether coverage applies. As you progress through this case study, you can check your understanding of the coverage provided by answering the Knowledge to Action questions.

Case Facts

Office Myria, Inc. (OM) is an office supply store. Each day, the shift manager on duty at the end of the day prepares the deposit from all of the daily receipts and takes the deposit to the night depository of a nearby bank. Each night, $2,000 in cash is stored in a safe for use in the cash drawers the next day.

Brad, the principal owner and president of OM, purchased a commercial package policy that includes the Insurance Services Office (ISO) Commercial Crime Coverage Form (Loss Sustained Form). The Crime and Fidelity Coverage Part Declarations page shows the coverages, limits, and deductibles that Brad selected. See the exhibit "Excerpt From Office Myria's Crime Coverage Declarations Page."

In 20X1, OM sustained several losses. On July 3, 20X1, a thief entered OM through an unlocked window while the store was closed and broke into the safe, causing $1,200 damage to the safe. The thief found only $2,000 in cash in the safe, so he also stole $1,500 worth of electronic devices from the selling floor on his way out. OM repaired the safe and replaced the stolen property promptly after the loss.

Two employees, Daryl (OM's bookkeeper) and Jared (a shipping clerk), in collusion, stole money and merchandise from OM during 20X1. The thefts occurred as shown in the exhibit, "Office Myria Employee Thefts From 20X1."

Excerpt From Office Myria's Crime Coverage Declarations Page

Insuring Agreements	Limit Of Insurance Per Occurrence	Deductible Amount Per Occurrence
1. Employee Theft	$100,000	$1,000
2. Forgery Or Alteration	$100,000	$1,000
3. Inside The Premises – Theft Of Money And Securities	$25,000	$1,000
4. Inside The Premises – Robbery Or Safe Burglary Of Other Property	$25,000	$1,000
5. Outside The Premises	$25,000	$1,000
6. Computer And Funds Transfer Fraud	$100,000	$1,000
7. Money Orders And Counterfeit Money	Not Covered	

If "Not Covered" is inserted above opposite any specified Insuring Agreement, such Insuring Agreement and any other reference thereto in this policy are deleted.

When Daryl and Jared were hired, neither Brad nor anyone else at OM was aware of any criminal history of either of these men.

Because Brad had a high degree of trust in Daryl and did not check the store's accounting records frequently, he did not discover any of the thefts until late December, 20X1, after all the thefts had been committed. During a police investigation, Daryl and Jared blamed one another for the thefts, but later they both confessed to all the thefts. Brad immediately fired both Daryl and Jared. See the exhibit "Office Myria Employee Thefts From 20X1."

Office Myria Employee Thefts From 20X1

Date of Theft	Item(s) Stolen	Value of Stolen Item(s)
April 30, 20X1	Money	$10,000
September 12, 20X1	Merchandise	$15,000
August 20, 20X1	Merchandise	$30,000
November 24, 20X1	Merchandise	$20,000
December 18, 20X1	Money	$35,000
TOTAL		$110,000

[DA07924]

Given the facts presented in the case and assuming that no endorsements to OM's policy affect the coverage in these losses, determine whether the commercial crime form will cover the losses, and if so, what amount the insurer will pay for each loss. When answering the questions in this case-based activity, assume that the insured reported each loss to its crime insurer promptly after discovering it, cooperated with the insurer, and maintained records of all property covered under the policy. Otherwise, consider only the information provided as part of this case.

Necessary Reference Materials

To determine whether OM's crime form provides coverage for any losses of money, securities, or other property incurred as a result of criminal acts such as robbery, burglary, and other forms of theft, you need a copy of the crime form and the declarations page.

Overview of Steps

When examining the declarations page and crime form to determine whether coverage applies to each loss, you can apply the four steps of the DICE method. Doing this involves analyzing the policy declarations, insuring agreement, conditions, and exclusions and determining whether any information found at each step precludes coverage at the time of each loss. You should also examine other policy provisions such as the limit of insurance, deductible, endorsements (not applicable in this case), and terms defined in the policy.

Next, you determine the amounts payable for each loss under the applicable policy. Doing this involves analyzing the limit(s) of insurance and any deductibles that apply. Assume OM has no other policy that provides coverage for the same losses.

Determination of Coverage

To determine coverage, you must apply the four DICE steps to the case facts for each of OM's losses.

DICE Analysis Step 1: Declarations

The first DICE step is to review the declarations page to ascertain basic facts about the coverage.

Action Task: Review OM's Common Policy Declarations included with its commercial package policy. See the exhibit "Excerpt From Office Myria's Common Policy Declarations Page."

Excerpt From Office Myria's Common Policy Declarations Page

POLICY NUMBER:

IL DS 00 09 08

COMMON POLICY DECLARATIONS

COMPANY NAME AREA	PRODUCER NAME AREA

NAMED INSURED: **Office Myria, Inc.**

MAILING ADDRESS: **1225 East Nevada Avenue**

Anytown, US 12345

POLICY PERIOD: FROM   **03/12/20X1**   TO   **03/12/20X2**   AT 12:01 A.M. STANDARD TIME AT YOUR MAILING ADDRESS SHOWN ABOVE

BUSINESS DESCRIPTION	Office supply store with loading dock

Includes copyrighted material of Insurance Services Office, Inc. with its permission. Copyright, ISO Properties, Inc., 2007. [DA07925]

Knowledge to Action

To complete Step 1, answer these questions about the Common Policy Declarations:

- Is OM listed as an insured under the policy?
- Were the losses sustained during the policy period?

Feedback: The declarations page shows OM as the named insured. A review of the insuring agreements is needed to confirm whether coverages apply to each of the losses. The case facts indicate that each of the losses was sustained (and discovered) during the policy period.

DICE Analysis Step 2: Insuring Agreement

The second DICE step is to review the insuring agreements to determine whether those for which coverage is provided apply to the described losses.

Action Task: Refer to the insuring agreements in the excerpt from the crime coverage declarations page, and then examine the applicable insuring agreements from the Commercial Crime Coverage Form.

The $2,000 theft of money from the safe and $1,200 damage to the safe are covered under the Inside the Premises—Theft of Money and Securities insuring agreement.

We will pay for:

a. Loss of "money" and "securities" inside the "premises" or "financial institution premises":

(1) Resulting directly from "theft" committed by a person present inside such "premises" or "financial institution premises"; or

(2) Resulting directly from disappearance or destruction.

b. Loss from damage to the "premises" or its exterior resulting directly from an actual or attempted "theft" of "money" and "securities", if you are the owner of the "premises" or are liable for damage to it.

c. Loss of or damage to a locked safe, vault, cash register, cash box or cash drawer located inside the "premises" resulting directly from an actual or attempted "theft" of, or unlawful entry into, those containers.[6]

The $1,500 theft of electronic devices is not covered under the Inside the Premises—Theft of Money and Securities insuring agreement, because the stolen property does not qualify as money or securities. This theft is also not covered under the Inside the Premises—Robbery and Safe Burglary of Other Property, because the cause of the loss does not meet the policy definition of "robbery" or "safe burglary."

20. "Robbery" means the unlawful taking of property from the care and custody of a person by one who has:

a. Caused or threatened to cause that person bodily harm; or

b. Committed an obviously unlawful act witnessed by that person.[7]

In this case, the cause of loss was not robbery, because the thief did not harm or threaten a person having custody of the property, nor was there any custodian present to witness the thief's obviously unlawful act. Moreover, the cause of loss was not safe burglary because the devices were stolen from the selling floor, not from a locked safe or vault, as is required by the policy definition of safe burglary.

The Employee Theft insuring agreement applies to the employee theft losses committed by Daryl and Jared. Daryl and Jared both meet the policy definition of employee, they committed theft as defined, and their acts of theft resulted in the loss of money and other property as defined.

We will pay for loss of or damage to "money", "securities" and "other property" resulting directly from "theft" committed by an "employee", whether identified or not, acting alone or in collusion with other persons.[8]

DICE Analysis Step 3: Conditions

The third DICE step is to review the policy conditions to determine whether they preclude coverage at the time of the loss.

Action Task: Refer to the applicable Commercial Crime Coverage Form policy conditions.

OM has complied with the standard policy conditions contained in the Commercial Crime Coverage Form, such as Cooperation, Duties in the Event of Loss, and Records. The only other condition that would apply is the Valuation—Settlement condition. This condition, which explains how money and property are valued, will be helpful to you when you determine the amounts payable for the insured's claims.

If OM had not immediately fired Daryl and Jared, then the Termination As to Any Employee condition (provision E.2.a.) that applies to the Employee Theft insuring agreement would have automatically terminated OM's employee theft coverage with regard to any further acts committed by Daryl or Jared.

DICE Analysis Step 4: Exclusions

The fourth DICE step is to review the policy exclusions to determine whether they exclude or limit coverage of the loss.

Action Task: Refer to the exclusions in the Commercial Crime Coverage Form, (section D).

Based on these loss scenarios, no exclusions apply. However, under different circumstances, two exclusions might have been applicable to the employee theft loss.

If Brad had been aware of any past criminal acts of either Daryl or Jared prior to the policy period, the Acts of Employees Learned of by You Prior to the Policy Period exclusion (D.1.b.) would apply.

If the only evidence of the employee theft loss was the inventory shortage that Brad noticed in January, then the Inventory Shortages exclusion that applies to the Employee Theft insuring agreement (A.1) would apply. However, in this case, Daryl and Jared confessed their crime to the police.

> Insuring Agreement A.1. does not cover:
>
> a. Inventory Shortages
>
> Loss, or that part of any loss, the proof of which as to its existence or amount is dependent upon:
>
> (1) An inventory computation; or
>
> (2) A profit and loss computation.
>
> However, where you establish wholly apart from such computations that you have sustained a loss, then you may offer your inventory records and actual physical count of inventory in support of the amount of loss claimed.[9]

Knowledge to Action

Based on the Inventory Shortages exclusion in the commercial crime form, would OM's inventory records from January of 20X2 serve any useful purpose in OM's claim for merchandise losses from employee theft? Explain your answer.

Feedback: Yes, OM could use the inventory records from January 20X2 to support the amount of loss it claims from the employee theft because Brad was able to "establish wholly apart from such computations" that OM sustained a loss.

Determination of Amounts Payable

Now that you have completed the DICE analysis, you can determine the amounts payable. Doing this involves applying the limits of insurance available to pay each of the losses and any deductibles that apply. Typically, it also involves determining whether more than one policy provides coverage for the same loss; however, in this case no other policy applies. See the exhibit "Office Myria's Claims and Applicable Limits."

Office Myria's Claims and Applicable Limits

Claim	Applicable Insuring Agreement(s)	Coverage Limit(s)	Claim Amount(s)
July 3, 20X1 Theft:			
• Theft of money from safe ($2,000) • Damage to safe ($1,200) • Theft of small electronics (not covered)	Inside the Premises—Theft of Money and Securities	$25,000	$3,200
20X1 Employee Theft:			
• Theft of money ($45,000) • Theft of merchandise ($65,000)	Employee Theft	$100,000	$110,000

[DA07926]

The Limit of Insurance provision (B) in the Commercial Crime Coverage Form restricts the amount that the insurer will pay for losses.

The most we will pay for all loss resulting directly from an "occurrence" is the applicable Limit Of Insurance shown in the Declarations.

If any loss is covered under more than one Insuring Agreement or coverage, the most we will pay for such loss shall not exceed the largest Limit of Insurance available under any one of those Insuring Agreements or coverages.[10]

The Commercial Crime Coverage Form's definition of "occurrence" is crucial in applying the Limit of Insurance provision correctly. Part a. of the definition (F.17.a.) applies specifically to the Employee Theft insuring agreement.

"Occurrence" means:

a. Under Insuring Agreement A.1.:

(1) An individual act;

(2) The combined total of all separate acts whether or not related; or

(3) A series of acts whether or not related; committed by an "employee" acting alone or in collusion with other persons, during the Policy Period shown in the Declarations, except as provided under Condition E.1.k. or E.1.l.[11]

Consequently, all the separate acts of employee theft that Daryl and Jared committed (for both money and merchandise) qualify as only one occurrence when applying the limit of insurance applicable to employee theft loss. Therefore, the most the crime insurer will pay for OM's employee theft losses is $100,000.

The July 3, 20X1, theft of money from the safe and safe damage claim is within the policy limit for the applicable coverage and will be paid fully, minus the deductible.

The Deductible provision of the crime form explains how the deductible should be applied to a loss.

We will not pay for loss resulting directly from an "occurrence" unless the amount of loss exceeds the Deductible Amount shown in the Declarations. We will then pay the amount of loss in excess of the Deductible Amount, up to the Limit of Insurance.[12]

The July 3 money theft amounts to $3,200, which is less than the applicable limit of insurance. The insurer will pay OM the amount of loss in excess of the $1,000 deductible: $2,200.

The employee theft losses (one occurrence) amount to $110,000, which exceeds the $100,000 limit of insurance for employee theft. The insurer will pay the amount of the loss in excess of the deductible ($110,000 − $1,000 = $109,000), up to the limit of insurance. Therefore the insurer's loss payment is $100,000. (The deductible comes off the amount of the loss, not the limit.)

EQUIPMENT BREAKDOWN INSURANCE

Because commercial property policies exclude loss caused by mechanical or electrical breakdowns and steam boiler explosions, most businesses need equipment breakdown insurance, which covers those perils.

The Insurance Services Office (ISO) Equipment Breakdown Protection Coverage Form is a typical example of the various equipment breakdown policies offered by insurers. This form contains ten insuring agreements that cover property damage, expediting expenses, business income and/or extra expense, and other loss consequences of equipment breakdown. Some of the leading insurers in this line use independently developed forms but keep them similar to the ISO form in most ways. All equipment breakdown policies, whether standard or independent, contain conditions that distinguish them from other types of policies.

Need for Equipment Breakdown Insurance

Traditionally called boiler and machinery insurance, equipment breakdown insurance covers loss caused by the accidental breakdown of almost any type of equipment that operates under pressure or that controls, transmits, or uses mechanical or electrical power.

Common examples of such equipment include steam boilers (used for heating buildings and other purposes); electrical generating and transmitting equipment; pumps, compressors, turbines, and engines; air conditioning and refrigeration systems; production machinery used in manufacturing operations; and all types of electrically powered office equipment such as copiers, computers, and telephone systems. Nearly all businesses rely on one or more of these types of equipment.

The types of equipment covered by equipment breakdown insurance are covered under the Building and Personal Property Coverage Form, also referred to as the BPP, but only with regard to the perils insured against by the causes of loss forms used with the BPP. The commercial property causes of loss forms exclude electrical breakdown, mechanical breakdown, and steam boiler explosion, all of which can damage such equipment and the property around it.

Equipment breakdown insurance can fill this coverage gap, covering physical damage to both the covered equipment and other property of the insured that results from the accidental breakdown of covered equipment. Equipment breakdown insurance can also cover business income, extra expense, and other losses resulting from such physical damage.

A relatively small line of insurance, equipment breakdown insurance is important for businesses of all sizes. Few insurers have the expertise to underwrite and provide risk control services for equipment breakdown coverage, but many provide it in their commercial package policies through reinsurance arrangements with insurers that specialize in equipment breakdown coverage.

Because of the potentially catastrophic effects of equipment breakdown, loss prevention is a key goal for both the equipment breakdown insurer and the insured. Therefore, the inspection and risk control services provided by equipment breakdown insurers are important adjuncts to the insurance they provide. An insurer's inspection expenses for equipment breakdown coverage often equal or exceed its loss payments.

Insuring Agreements

The ISO Equipment Breakdown Protection Coverage Form contains ten insuring agreements. The coverages that apply in a particular policy are indicated on the policy's Declarations page by either a limit of insurance or the word "included." If neither is noted for a particular coverage, then that coverage does not apply. Several of the insuring agreements function more as coverage extensions than as basic coverages. See the exhibit "Insuring Agreements of the ISO Equipment Breakdown Form."

Insuring Agreements of the ISO Equipment Breakdown Form

- Property Damage
- Expediting Expenses
- Business Income and Extra Expense
- Spoilage Damage
- Utility Interruption
- Newly Acquired Premises
- Ordinance or Law
- Errors and Omissions
- Brands and Labels
- Contingent Business Income and Extra Expense

[DA07890]

The covered cause of loss in the Equipment Breakdown Protection Coverage Form is a "breakdown" to "covered equipment." The form defines breakdown as direct physical loss that causes damage to covered equipment and necessitates the equipment's repair or replacement as a result of any of these malfunctions:

- Failure of pressure or vacuum equipment
- Mechanical failure, including rupturing or bursting caused by centrifugal force
- Electrical failure, including arcing

Various exclusions apply to the definition of "breakdown," such as leakage, defects, or viruses in computer equipment and programs; damage to vacuum or gas tubes; and damage to foundations or structures supporting the equipment.

The policy definition of covered equipment is extremely broad and includes these equipment groupings:

- Equipment built to operate under internal pressure or vacuum
- Electrical or mechanical equipment used in the generation, transmission, or utilization of energy
- Communication and computer equipment

This definition is broad enough to encompass all of the previously discussed types of property, as well as some additional types that insurers are generally not willing to insure under equipment breakdown policies. Accordingly, the definition excludes various types of property that are outside the intended scope of coverage. The list of excluded property includes, but is not limited to, computer media; vehicles, aircraft, and watercraft (including any attached equipment); excavation or construction equipment; parts and tools subject to periodic replacement (such as brake pads); medical diagnostic equipment; and equipment manufactured by the named insured for sale.

 Reality Check

Coverage for an Explosion From a Steam Boiler

This hypothetical case shows how equipment breakdown coverage applies to the various losses that can result from an accident to covered equipment.

A steam boiler in Galbi Manufacturing's factory exploded, causing destruction of the boiler; bodily injury to some of Galbi's employees; and damage to Galbi's building, Galbi's business personal property, a customer's patterns in Galbi's possession, and a neighboring firm's building.

Because the explosion was an accident to covered equipment, Galbi's equipment breakdown insurance would cover the damage to Galbi's building and business personal property and to its customer's patterns in its possession (its care, custody, or control). Galbi's equipment breakdown insurance would not cover damage to the neighboring firm's building, because equipment breakdown coverage does not cover property of others unless it is personal property in the insured's care, custody, or control at a described location. The equipment breakdown coverage would not apply to bodily injury to Galbi's employees (or to anyone else). Galbi's responsibility for injury to its own employees would be covered under its workers compensation insurance.

[DA07891]

Property Damage

Under the Property Damage insuring agreement, the insurer agrees to pay for direct damage to "covered property." The policy definition of covered property differs from, and is much broader than, the policy definition of covered equipment. Covered property means property that the named insured owns or that is in the named insured's care, custody, or control and for which the named insured is legally liable. In either case, the property must be situated at a location described in the Declarations.

Thus, the Property Damage insuring agreement covers loss to a much broader classification of property than covered equipment. The purpose of equipment breakdown coverage is not merely to cover damage to the covered equipment but also to cover damage to other property that results from damage to the covered equipment.

For example, a steam boiler explosion may not only destroy the steam boiler but also damage the building in which the steam boiler is contained as well as the contents of the building. The commercial property causes of loss forms] - hey! would cover none of this damage because they all exclude damage resulting from steam boiler explosion.

The ISO equipment breakdown form does not include any coinsurance provision applicable to property damage coverage; a coinsurance provision applies only to the business income and extra expense coverage. Debris removal is covered as part of the property damage limit.

Expediting Expenses

The Expediting Expenses insuring agreement covers the reasonable extra cost to make temporary repairs in order to speed up (expedite) permanent repairs or replacement of covered property. An example of expediting expenses is overtime wages paid to speed up repairs.

Expediting expenses coverage can overlap with the extra expense coverage available through another insuring agreement of the form. However, expediting expenses coverage is not as broad as extra expense coverage. For example, the cost of renting substitute facilities to continue operations could be covered as extra expense but not as expediting expenses. When expenses fall within both coverages, the insured can collect under either one, but not both.

Business Income and Extra Expense

Equipment breakdown (and resulting damage to covered property in addition to the covered equipment) can interrupt operations and cause the insured to lose business income, incur extra expenses, or both. Accordingly, equipment breakdown policies normally offer business income and extra expense coverage. The ISO form allows the insured to select coverage for both business income and extra expense, or coverage for extra expense only.

The form also offers a Contingent Business Income and Extra Expense insuring agreement that covers the insured's loss of business income and extra expenses resulting from equipment breakdown occurring at a location, shown in the Declarations, that the insured does not own or operate. For example, an insured that manufactures computers might buy this coverage and show the location of the single company that supplies microprocessors to the insured.

Other Insuring Agreements

Several additional insuring agreements are included in the form. The insured can choose the ones that meet their particular business needs. These insuring agreements are available:

- Spoilage Damage—Covers loss caused by the spoilage of perishable goods as a result of a breakdown to covered equipment.

- Utility Interruption—Extends the business income and extra expense coverage to include loss sustained by the insured because of breakdown of equipment owned by a utility or other supplier that has contracted to provide the insured with any of these services: electricity, communications, air conditioning, heating, gas, sewer, water, or steam.

- Newly Acquired Premises—Extends all of the equipment breakdown coverages to property situated at newly acquired locations that the insured has purchased or leased after policy inception.

- Ordinance or Law—When equipment breakdown damages a building, this insuring agreement covers losses (such as increased construction costs) that result from the enforcement of ordinances or laws that regulate the repair or construction of buildings.

- Errors and Omissions—Covers loss or damage that would otherwise not be covered because of certain unintentional errors or omissions made in arranging the insurance, such as incorrectly describing an insured building's location.

- Brands and Labels—Covers the reasonable costs to label damaged merchandise as salvage or to remove the brands or labels from the merchandise before the insurer takes the property for disposition.

Conditions

Most of the general conditions contained in equipment breakdown policies are comparable to those contained in other property insurance policies. The noteworthy conditions that distinguish equipment breakdown policies from other policies include these: Suspension, Joint or Disputed Loss Agreement, and Jurisdictional Inspections.

Suspension

The Suspension condition allows the insurer to immediately suspend equipment breakdown insurance on an item of equipment that the insurer determines to be in a dangerous condition. The insurer can suspend coverage by delivering or mailing a written notice of coverage suspension to the named insured. Once coverage for an item of equipment has been suspended, coverage can be reinstated only by endorsing the policy.

The Suspension condition is reasonable considering the enormous loss potential some equipment breakdown exposures entail. The condition allows a boiler inspector or risk control representative of the insurer to act immediately when imminent danger of an accident exists. Most insureds want a loss-free operation and willingly cooperate when a dangerous situation is discovered. Therefore, the Suspension condition is seldom invoked. However, it serves as a last resort that the insurer can use when the insured cannot or will not cooperate in remedying a dangerous situation.

Joint or Disputed Loss Agreement

When separate insurers provide an organization's equipment breakdown insurance and its commercial property insurance, coverage disputes may occur when the cause of loss is uncertain. For example, disputes may occur when fire breaks out following the breakdown of covered equipment. The insurers may disagree on how much of the damage was caused by breakdown and how much by the fire.

When both policies contain the Joint or Disputed Loss Agreement condition or its equivalent, each insurer will (after receiving a written request from the insured) pay the entire amount of loss that each agrees is covered under its own policy plus one-half of the amount in dispute. In this way, the insured is fully paid without having to wait for the insurers to reach agreement on their respective liabilities.

Jurisdictional Inspections

Many states and municipalities require boilers and other pressure vessels to be inspected by a qualified inspector. The inspectors working for equipment breakdown insurers are usually licensed to perform these inspections, which are often referred to as "jurisdictional inspections." Some insurers' equipment breakdown policies state that the insurer will make jurisdictional inspections for their insureds. The ISO form does not contain such a statement, but most insurers arrange for the required inspections for their equipment breakdown insureds regardless of whether the form includes a jurisdictional inspection provision.

SUMMARY

The ISO commercial crime program includes crime coverage forms that can be added to a commercial package policy and crime policy forms that can be written as monoline crime policies. ISO offers two versions of crime forms, the discovery form and the loss sustained form. Financial institution bonds provide employee dishonesty insurance and other crime coverages designed for banks, insurance companies, and other types of financial institutions.

Insureds can select from among the seven insuring agreements of the ISO Commercial Crime Coverage Form to tailor coverage for their businesses. These insuring agreements cover money, securities, and other property against a variety of covered perils, such as employee theft, forgery or alteration, robbery, safe burglary, theft, disappearance, destruction, computer and funds transfer fraud, and good-faith acceptance of counterfeit money.

The ISO Commercial Crime Coverage Form contains provisions that specify the policy's limits and the manner in which a deductible should be applied.

In the commercial crime form, the exclusions are divided into different groups, depending on whether they apply to all or only some insuring agreements.

The ISO Commercial Crime Coverage Form includes numerous policy conditions that extend or eliminate coverage under various circumstances. While some conditions apply only to particular insuring agreements, such as two that apply to Employee Theft, other conditions apply to all insuring agreements.

You should now be able to apply policy language to commercial crime losses to determine whether the losses are covered and the amount for which they are covered.

Most businesses need equipment breakdown insurance because commercial property policies exclude loss caused by mechanical or electrical breakdown and steam boiler explosion. The ISO Equipment Breakdown Protection Coverage Form contains insuring agreements covering property damage, expediting expenses, business income and extra expense, and several other loss consequences. Equipment breakdown policies contain conditions related to suspension, joint or disputed loss agreement, and jurisdictional inspections, distinguishing them from other types of policies.

ASSIGNMENT NOTES

1. Includes copyrighted material of Insurance Services Office, Inc. Copyright, Insurance Services Office, Inc., 2012.
2. Includes copyrighted material of Insurance Services Office, Inc. Copyright, Insurance Services Office, Inc., 2012.
3. Includes copyrighted material of Insurance Services Office, Inc. Copyright, Insurance Services Office, Inc., 2012.
4. Includes copyrighted material of Insurance Services Office, Inc., with its permission. Copyright, Insurance Services Office, Inc., 2012.
5. Includes copyrighted material of Insurance Services Office, Inc., with its permission. Copyright, Insurance Services Office, Inc., 2012.
6. Copyright, Insurance Services Office, Inc., 2012.
7. Copyright, Insurance Services Office, Inc., 2012.
8. Copyright, Insurance Services Office, Inc., 2012.
9. Copyright, Insurance Services Office, Inc., 2012.
10. Copyright, Insurance Services Office, Inc., 2012.
11. Copyright, Insurance Services Office, Inc., 2012.
12. Copyright, Insurance Services Office, Inc., 2012.

Inland and Ocean Marine Insurance

Educational Objectives

After learning the content of this assignment, you should be able to:

▷ Describe inland marine insurance in terms of these elements:

- The role of the Nationwide Marine Definition

- The distinction between filed and nonfiled classes of inland marine business

- The role of judgment rating

▷ Summarize the key provisions of each of these traditionally nonfiled classes of inland marine insurance:

- Contractors equipment

- Builders risk

- Transit

- Motor truck cargo liability

- Difference in conditions

- Electronic data processing (EDP) equipment

- Bailees

- Instrumentalities of transportation and communication

▷ Describe what is covered by each of the filed classes of inland marine insurance.

▷ Describe ocean marine insurance in terms of the following elements:

- The types of loss exposures that can be covered

- The role of judgment rating

5

▷ Summarize the key provisions of these three main types of ocean marine insurance:

- Cargo insurance

- Hull insurance

- Protection and indemnity insurance

▷ Given a case describing an organization's loss exposures, recommend appropriate types of inland and ocean marine insurance.

Inland and Ocean Marine Insurance

5

OVERVIEW OF INLAND MARINE INSURANCE

A century ago, inland marine insurance developed as a way to cover emerging loss exposures linked to transportation. Today, inland marine insurance continues to be a source of flexible coverage solutions.

These concepts provide a foundation for understanding the types of inland marine insurance and why inland marine policy forms and rates are more flexible than those for most other types of insurance:

- Nationwide Marine Definition
- Distinction between filed and nonfiled classes of inland marine business
- Role of judgment rating

Nationwide Marine Definition

The term **inland marine insurance** was coined in the early 1900s, when United States insurers were restricted to writing one of three general kinds of insurance: fire insurance, casualty insurance, and **marine insurance**. Although fire insurers could insure buildings and their contents against fire and allied perils, they were not permitted to insure against most crime perils. In addition, they were generally not interested in providing fire and allied coverage on property in transit or on valuable property such as jewelry.

Marine insurers, however, were accustomed to covering ocean cargos of all types against many different causes of loss, including theft, while the property was either at sea or ashore. Consequently, they were willing to provide broad perils or "all-risks" coverage on the types of property that fire insurers avoided covering. The inventories of jewelry stores, property in the course of inland transit, and bridges were typical properties covered by marine insurers in the early 1900s. The insurance became known as inland marine insurance.

By the 1930s, inland marine insurance had grown to cover so many types of property that fire insurers believed that marine insurers were encroaching on their territory. To resolve the conflict, in 1933 the National Association of Insurance Commissioners (NAIC) adopted a **Nationwide Marine Definition**, a statement used mainly to determine whether a particular coverage is marine insurance (inland or ocean). The definition restricted the underwriting powers of marine insurers to specified types of property.

Inland marine insurance

Insurance that covers many different classes of property that typically involve an element of transportation.

Marine insurance

Insurance that, in the U.S., includes both ocean and inland marine coverage and, in the rest of the world, is limited to insurance for vessels and cargo.

Nationwide Marine Definition

Statement of the types of property that may be insured on inland marine and ocean marine insurance forms.

5.3

The enactment of legislation in the 1950s permitted a single insurer to offer fire, casualty, and marine coverages. Hence, the Nationwide Marine Definition was no longer needed for restrictive purposes. However, many states continue to use a similar, updated definition to determine whether a particular coverage is marine insurance (either inland or ocean) under their form and rate filing laws. Typically, commercial inland and ocean marine insurance is subject to less rate and form regulation than other lines of insurance. See the exhibit "Summary of Nationwide Marine Definition."

Summary of Nationwide Marine Definition

This summary lists many, but not all, types of coverage that can be classified as marine.

A. Imports

B. Exports

C. Domestic shipments

D. Bridges, tunnels, and other instrumentalities of transportation and communication, such as piers, wharves, docks, pipelines, power and telephone lines, radio and television towers and communication equipment, and outdoor cranes and loading equipment

E. Various types of property owned or used by individuals, such as jewelry, furs, musical instruments, silverware, coin collections, and stamp collections

F. Various types of property pertaining to a business, a profession, or an occupation, such as mobile equipment, builders risks, property in the custody of bailees, live animals, property at exhibitions, and electronic data processing equipment

[DA02503]

Filed and Nonfiled Classes of Business

A variety of inland marine policies cover many classes of business (such as contractors equipment, builders risk, motor truck cargo, and so forth). Insurance regulatory authorities have recognized this diversity by dividing inland marine classes of business into two categories: filed and nonfiled.

The filed classes are the classes of inland marine business for which the policy forms and/or rates must be filed with the state insurance department. Filed classes are characterized by a large number of potential insureds and reasonably homogeneous loss exposures. Examples of filed classes are policies that cover musical instruments and photographic equipment.

Insurance Services Office, Inc. (ISO) and the American Association of Insurance Services (AAIS) file forms and rates for these classes on behalf of their member companies. Many states, however, specify additional classes for which forms and rates must be filed.

Nonfiled classes are the classes of inland marine business for which neither policy forms nor rates must be filed with the state insurance department. The classes of inland marine insurance that are nonfiled vary by state. To avoid violating state laws that require the filing of insurance forms and/or rates, insurers must determine which classes of inland marine insurance can be written on a nonfiled basis in every state in which the insurer wishes to write those classes of business. The term "traditionally nonfiled classes" is sometimes used to denote those classes that are nonfiled in some states but not others.

Nonfiled classes are characterized by a relatively small number of potential insureds, diverse loss exposures, or both. The contractors equipment floater is an example of a class of inland marine insurance that has traditionally been nonfiled because of the diverse loss exposures that can be covered by this type of policy. (The term "floater" is often used to denote an inland marine policy that covers property moved between different locations, or, in other words, "floating" property.)

Many types of property may be covered, ranging from simple hand tools and small power equipment to very large cranes and earthmovers. The property may be used in a variety of locations and climates such as in a desert, in a rain forest, or on the Arctic tundra. It may be used for many purposes, such as to build roads, buildings, pipelines, or other structures, or to remove snow or mow grass in public areas. Policies must be drafted, rates calculated, and underwriting keyed to all of these variables. In states where these policies do not need to be filed with state regulators, insurers can customize appropriate policy provisions and rates for individual insureds.

Role of Judgment Rating

Rating methods for the filed commercial inland marine forms are based on procedures contained in the ISO *Commercial Lines Manual* (CLM). The CLM does not contain rating methods for the traditionally nonfiled classes of inland marine insurance. However, many nonfiled inland marine policies are so widely written that both their coverage provisions and rates have become standardized to an extent. Motor truck cargo liability insurance, for example, is a common form of inland marine coverage with rates based on many years of loss experience. Insurers active in insuring truck shipments have developed their own manuals and rate schedules for this coverage.

In other cases, the property being insured under a nonfiled policy may be so unusual or the coverage terms so specialized that there is not enough previous loss information to give the insurer a statistically accurate idea of what the coverage should cost. What is a fair price for transporting a priceless painting from one museum to another for a special exhibit? How much should be charged for coverage on a one-of-a-kind piece of machinery that could be damaged as it is custom-fitted and installed in a new factory? How could an insurer rate coverage on a drawbridge?

When faced with such questions, inland marine underwriters must rely on their best judgment to set rates. Judgment rating is a rating method used by underwriters to rate one-of-a-kind risks. As opposed to manual rating (the method used to determine the premium for filed lines of insurance), judgment rating requires a thorough knowledge of the class of business for which coverage is being written. An underwriter might have to draw on expertise in any of several specialized fields—fine arts, heavy equipment, construction, or communications—to determine an adequate rate for the unique risks that are eligible for inland marine coverage. Realistically, rates are also influenced by market conditions.

NONFILED CLASSES OF INLAND MARINE INSURANCE

The largest classes of inland marine business (as measured by premiums written) are the traditionally nonfiled classes. Historically, each insurer has developed its own forms for these coverages, though both the American Association of Insurance Services (AAIS) and Insurance Services Office, Inc. (ISO) offer advisory nonfiled forms for their affiliated insurers. Nonfiled forms can range from preprinted documents and endorsements used by most insureds to one-of-a-kind manuscript policies drafted for unusual risks.

Though there are many other classes of nonfiled inland marine insurance, these are significant examples:

- Contractors equipment
- Builders risk
- Transit
- Motor truck cargo liability
- Difference in conditions
- Electronic data processing equipment
- Bailees
- Instrumentalities of transportation and communication

Contractors Equipment

Contractors
equipment floater
A policy that covers mobile equipment or tools while located anywhere in the coverage territory.

Contractors equipment typically represents the largest class of commercial inland marine business. The equipment used by contractors may include cranes, earthmovers, tractors, stone crushers, bulldozers, mobile asphalt plants, portable offices, and scaffolding. All such equipment can be covered under a **contractors equipment floater**.

This policy normally contains a schedule that lists each piece of equipment and its corresponding limit of insurance. A policy may also provide blanket coverage on unscheduled hand tools and miscellaneous equipment.

It is difficult, if not impossible, to maintain a current insurance schedule of all items when several hundred pieces of equipment are used by an insured. A large contractor may therefore obtain blanket coverage applying to all equipment, whether owned, rented, or borrowed by the contractor. A policy providing such blanket coverage is subject to an annual accounting of value of the insured equipment.

Coverage may be provided for named perils only or on an open perils basis, an approach that covers causes of loss that are not specifically excluded. When coverage is on a named perils basis, the perils commonly included are fire, lightning, explosion, windstorm, hail, vandalism, theft, earthquake, flood, collision, overturn, and collapse of bridges and culverts.

Contractors equipment floaters frequently include rental reimbursement coverage, which pays the cost of renting substitute equipment when covered property has been put out of service by a covered cause of loss.

Builders Risk

Although an ISO Builders Risk Coverage Form can be issued as a component of a commercial property coverage part, buildings or other structures in the course of construction can also be insured under a nonfiled inland marine **builders risk policy**. The nonfiled approach is often preferred by both insureds and insurers because it allows more coverage and rating flexibility.

Inland marine builders risk policies typically cover the structure under construction, temporary structures at the building site, and building materials that have not yet become part of the building. Building materials are covered while on the insured location, in transit, or in storage at another location. Business income coverage may be provided as part of the policy.

Inland marine builders risk policies usually cover losses on an open perils basis, and many insurers provide coverage for losses usually excluded under standard commercial property forms, such as these:

- Flood
- Earthquake
- Theft of building materials that have not been installed

Many insurers that write inland marine builders risk policies offer an endorsement providing soft costs coverage. Soft costs coverage covers various incidental expenses that might result from a physical loss to a building project, such as additional interest, advertising expenses, or real estate taxes. Incidental expenses may also include additional costs and commissions incurred during lease renegotiation.

Builders risk policy
Policy that covers a building in the course of construction, including building materials and supplies while on or away from the building site.

Closely related to the builders risk policy is the installation floater, which covers a contractor's interest in building supplies or fixtures that the contractor has been hired to install. It does not cover the entire building, as in the case of a builders risk policy.

Transit

Transit insurance, also called transportation insurance, covers owners of property against damage to their property while in the course of transit by land, air, or water carriers. Shippers use this coverage because their property may be damaged in circumstances under which a carrier has no legal obligation to pay the shipper's loss.

Two basic types of transit insurance are available. The trip transit policy covers a particular shipment of goods specified in the policy. This kind of policy is purchased by occasional shippers. Designed for frequent shippers, the annual transit policy covers all shipments made or received by the insured throughout a one-year policy period.

Examples of property excluded in an annual transit policy include these:

- Contraband is not insurable as a matter of law and is therefore explicitly excluded by most insurance policies.

- Other types of property are commercially insurable but are especially attractive to thieves and therefore expensive to insure (for example, precious metals, furs, jewelry, and money and securities). Most annual transit policies exclude these items.

- Some insurers also exclude certain high-risk commodities such as electronics, tobacco products, alcoholic beverages, or fresh and frozen food.

If coverage for these items is wanted, and the insured is willing to pay an additional premium, the exclusions can be deleted or modified to provide coverage. Coverage may also be obtained under another policy, such as a jewelers or furriers block policy or a crime policy covering money and securities.

Most annual transit policies cover on an open perils basis. For example, flood and earthquake are not excluded.

Many annual transit policies cover only within the continental United States, Alaska, and Canada, including airborne shipments between those places. The continental U.S. does not include Hawaii, Puerto Rico, or any overseas possessions. Such wording precludes the insurer from having to cover air or water shipments to or from overseas locations. Overseas shipments by plane or ship (even between places within the coverage territory) are usually insured under ocean marine cargo policies.

Property covered under an annual transit policy is usually valued at the amount of invoice, including shipping charges, if the property is being transported between buyer and seller. If no invoice applies—such as when a company is shipping its own property between its own locations—the property may be valued at actual cash value.

Motor Truck Cargo Liability

A motor carrier (a trucking company) can be held liable for damage to the property it is transporting in certain circumstances. To cover this exposure, a motor carrier can purchase a **motor truck cargo liability policy**. This form of insurance applies only to cargo damage for which the motor carrier is legally liable. It is not direct property insurance for the benefit of the cargo owner.

In addition to limiting coverage to losses for which the insured is legally liable, some policies also limit coverage to losses caused by specified perils. Other forms cover any loss for which the insured is liable as long as the loss is not subject to any of the exclusions expressed in the form.

The description of covered property usually encompasses most property accepted by the insured for transportation. However, as in transit policies, certain types of valuable property likely to be targeted by thieves are commonly excluded, such as precious metals, jewelry, and fine arts. Some policies exclude liquor and cigarettes, two other commodities that attract hijackers. A motor carrier that transports such commodities can usually have the exclusions deleted in return for an additional premium.

The property is covered only while in or on a land vehicle operated by the insured (including connecting carriers) or while located at the insured's terminal. Terminal coverage, however, is usually limited to a certain time period, such as seventy-two hours. The insurer will usually extend the duration of terminal coverage for an additional premium.

> **Motor truck cargo liability policy**
>
> Policy that covers a trucker's liability for damage to cargo of others being transported by the trucker.

Difference in Conditions

A **difference in conditions (DIC) policy** can serve a variety of needs. Its basic purpose is to fill in gaps left by the insured's commercial property insurance. Originally, a DIC policy was intended to provide open perils coverage to insureds whose basic policy provided only named perils coverage. DIC policies are still used for that purpose, but with the widespread availability of the Causes of Loss—Special Form, which provides open perils coverage in commercial property policies, organizations now buy DIC policies for these reasons:

> **Difference in conditions (DIC) policy, or DIC insurance**
>
> Policy that covers on an "all-risks" basis to fill gaps in the insured's commercial property coverage, especially gaps in flood and earthquake coverage.

- To provide coverage for flood and earthquake exposures not covered by basic policies

- To provide excess limits over flood and earthquake coverages included in basic policies

- To cover loss exposures not covered in basic policies, such as property in transit or loss of business income resulting from theft or transit losses

- To cover property at overseas locations

DIC policies are a nonfiled class of inland marine insurance in most states. Thus, insurers have great flexibility in arranging the insurance to address the specific needs or exposures of their insureds.

Electronic Data Processing Equipment

An electronic data processing (EDP) equipment floater covers computer equipment, software, and electronic data owned by the insured, as well as similar property of others in the insured's care, custody, or control. "Electronic data processing equipment" basically means "computer equipment." Some insurers expand the term to include medical equipment, robotics, and even computerized gaming equipment such as slot machines. Although such equipment is covered as business personal property in commercial property forms, an inland marine EDP equipment floater can provide added benefits. Many EDP equipment floaters cover perils that are not usually covered in commercial property policies, such as mechanical or electrical breakdown. They may also insure covered property while it is in transit or at unlisted locations. Moreover, because EDP equipment is a nonfiled class of inland marine in many states, an EDP equipment floater can be tailored to meet the insured's individual needs.

The policy definition of "equipment" usually includes, but is not limited to, mainframe computers, servers, server racks or server "farms," display terminals, monitors, printers, imaging devices (optical scanners), disk drives and other storage devices, network components, and laptops and other portable devices. The term "data" includes both computer programs—which direct the processing of data—and data files—which store processed data, such as customer mailing lists. "Media," such as disks and tapes, are the materials used to store data.

An EDP policy usually includes coverage for extra expenses incurred as the result of covered loss. Business income coverage can often be added when the insured requests it. Coverage is usually on an open perils basis but without all the exclusions found in the Causes of Loss—Special Form. In addition, breakdown coverage can usually be added to an EDP policy. Subject to a separate deductible, breakdown coverage insures loss to equipment resulting from such perils as mechanical failure, electrical disturbance, and changes in temperature resulting from breakdown of air conditioning equipment.

Equipment and data are usually subject to separate valuation methods. Equipment may be valued at its actual cash value, replacement cost, or upgraded value. Upgraded value is the cost to replace the property with the latest, comparable, state-of-the-art equipment available. For data and media, property can be valued at the actual cost of reproduction or for an agreed dollar amount.

Bailees

Insurers use two basic approaches to insuring bailees for the property in their custody.

The first approach covers loss to customers' goods only if the insured bailee is legally liable for the loss. A common example of this type of coverage is a warehouse operator's legal liability policy, which covers warehouse operators against liability for damage to the property of others being stored in operators' warehouses.

The second approach covers damage to customers' goods, regardless of whether the insured bailee is legally liable for the loss. An inland marine policy that takes this approach is called a bailees' customers policy; this policy covers damage to customers' goods while in the possession of the insured, regardless of whether the insured is legally liable for the damage. Because this type of policy allows the bailee to pay customers' losses even when the bailee is not legally obligated to do so, it can preserve customer goodwill under circumstances in which a legal liability policy would not cover the loss. Bailees' customer policies are written for dry cleaners, laundries, furriers, tailors, upholsterers, and appliance repair shops, among others.

Instrumentalities of Transportation and Communication

Property essential to transportation or communication can be insured under an inland marine policy. The major types of properties in this class are bridges, tunnels, pipelines, and radio and television broadcasting equipment.

FILED CLASSES OF INLAND MARINE INSURANCE

Though an insurer may file its own inland marine rates, rules, and forms, Insurance Services Office, Inc. (ISO) and the American Association of Insurance Services (AAIS) file inland marine coverage forms, endorsements, manual rules, and loss costs for several classes of commercial inland marine business.Insurers affiliated with ISO or AAIS can use these forms and endorsements to compose a commercial inland marine coverage part. The coverage part can be included in a commercial package policy or issued as a monoline policy that provides inland marine insurance only.

The ISO commercial inland marine coverage forms are briefly described in this section. These forms provide coverage on an open perils basis, meaning that they cover direct physical loss by any cause other than those that are specifically excluded. Valuation is typically on an actual cash value basis. However, ISO *Commercial Lines Manual* (CLM) rules permit the valuation clause to be modified to provide for any other basis of valuation to which the insurer and the insured might agree.

Commercial Articles

The Commercial Articles Coverage Form covers photographic equipment and musical instruments used commercially by photographers, motion picture producers, professional musicians, and others. It is not intended for dealers of these types of property. Coverage can be provided on a scheduled or blanket basis.

Camera and Musical Instrument Dealers

The Camera and Musical Instrument Dealers Coverage Form covers the stock in trade (inventory) of camera dealers or musical instrument dealers and similar property of others in the insured's care, custody, or control. Coverage can be provided by endorsement for other types of equipment while it is on the insured's premises.

Equipment Dealers

The Equipment Dealers Coverage Form covers the stock in trade of dealers that sell agricultural or construction equipment. The form also covers similar property of others in the insured's care, custody, or control. Coverage under a reporting form is available.

Physicians and Surgeons Equipment

The Physicians and Surgeons Equipment Coverage Form covers the professional equipment, materials, supplies, and books of physicians, surgeons, and dentists. It also covers the insured's office equipment and (if the insured is a tenant) improvements and betterments that the insured has made to a leased building.

These coverages can be added by endorsement:

- Office equipment while off premises for no more than thirty consecutive days
- Extra expenses following a covered loss
- Money and stamps on premises
- Personal effects of the insured or others while on premises
- Valuable records

Signs

The Signs Coverage Form covers neon, fluorescent, automatic, or mechanical signs. The covered signs must be scheduled with a limit of insurance shown for each item. This form (or a comparable commercial property endorsement) is used by many businesses because commercial property coverage forms severely limit coverage for signs.

Theatrical Property

The Theatrical Property Coverage Form covers stage scenery, costumes, and other personal property used in theatrical productions. It covers similar property of others in the insured's care as well as property owned by the insured. The insured must have used or must intend to use the property in a production stated in the declarations.

Film

The Film Coverage Form covers exposed motion picture film and magnetic tapes or videotapes, including related soundtracks or sound records. The amount of insurance reflects—and the form covers—the cost of reshooting the film if it is lost or damaged.

Floor Plan

The Floor Plan Coverage Form covers merchandise that is being held for sale and financed through a floor plan. The Floor Plan Coverage Form may be used to insure the dealer's interest in the merchandise, the lender's interest in it, or both. Coverage is written on a reporting form basis. The Nationwide Marine Definition includes policies covering floor plan merchandise, but only for merchandise other than automobiles. Therefore, floor plan insurance on automobiles is not handled as inland marine.

Jewelers Block

The Jewelers Block Coverage Form covers the merchandise of retail jewelers, including similar property of others in the insured's care, custody, or control. It was designed to meet the needs of small retail jewelers. Depending on the nature of the insured's operations, this can be either a filed or nonfiled coverage. The filed coverage form covers damage to the insured's stock of jewelry, precious and semiprecious stones, watches, precious metals, and similar merchandise, along with other stock used in the insured's business.

Mail

The Mail Coverage Form is written for banks, trust companies, insurance companies, investment brokers, and other financial institutions that frequently ship securities and other valuable items through a government postal service. The form covers the insured against loss of securities (such as bonds, stock certificates, and certificates of deposit) and other negotiable instruments (such as bills of lading and warehouse receipts) while in transit by first-class mail, certified mail, express mail, or registered mail. Valuable items such as bullion, currency, and jewelry are covered property only if sent by registered mail.

 Reality Check

Financing Merchandise Under a Floor Plan

Retailers (dealers) who offer certain types of high-priced merchandise often open a line of credit with a lender (a finance company or manufacturer) to obtain product inventory. This arrangement, called a floor plan, enables the dealer to display a number of models, colors, or options for products on its sales floor or lot, which encourages sales. Floor plan financing is often used for autos, recreational vehicles, manufactured homes, agricultural and construction equipment, and major home appliances.

Under a floor plan, the lender holds title to each item of merchandise (the collateral) until the dealer sells it. As property is sold, the dealer uses the proceeds to pay the lender for the merchandise, restoring that amount to the dealer's credit line, and the lender transfers the title to the buyer. When sales of floor plan merchandise are slower than expected, the lender can demand payment of interest and depreciation from the dealer for the collateral.

[DA07867]

Accounts Receivable

Many businesses would be unable to collect their accounts receivable (monies owed to them) if the records of those accounts were destroyed. This exposure can be significant, but it is easily overlooked.

The Accounts Receivable Coverage Form covers losses (including uncollectible accounts) resulting from destruction of the insured's records of accounts receivable. The insurer pays the amount of accounts receivable the insured is unable to collect because of the destruction of records. The form also covers the cost to reconstruct accounts receivable records, interest on loans made necessary by an inability to collect accounts receivable, and increased collection costs resulting from loss of records. Coverage may be written on either a reporting or nonreporting form.

Because many businesses keep backup (duplicate) copies of all their computer records, including records of accounts receivable, at a secure off-premises location, they do not buy accounts receivable insurance. However, insurers frequently include a certain amount of accounts receivable coverage in their package policies. An insured may use the inland marine form to obtain a higher coverage limit than the insurer is willing to include in a package policy.

Valuable Papers and Records

The Valuable Papers and Records Coverage Form covers printed or otherwise recorded items such as an architect's blueprints and plans, as well as the cost of necessary research to reconstruct the records. Irreplaceable records, such as original manuscripts or rare books, are scheduled with an agreed value shown for each item.

OVERVIEW OF OCEAN MARINE INSURANCE

Parties involved in the transportation of property in vessels are exposed to common and unique hazards. Various types of ocean marine insurance are available to cover those exposures.

The transportation of property in vessels (watercraft) over oceans or other bodies of water creates several types of loss exposures that can be covered by ocean marine insurance. The three most common types of ocean marine insurance policies are cargo, hull, and protection and indemnity. Ocean marine insurers typically develop their own rates for these types of insurance based on their underwriters' judgment.

Ocean Marine Loss Exposures

Ocean marine loss exposures exist for these parties:

- Cargo owners (shippers)
- Vessel owners
- Carriers

Cargo owners, often called shippers, include manufacturers, importers, and exporters. Owners of cargo face the possibility that their cargo could be damaged or destroyed while in transit, either on board the vessel or on land between the vessel and the cargo's point of origin or destination. This loss exposure can be covered by ocean marine **cargo insurance**.

Vessel owners face the possibility that their vessels could be damaged or destroyed by largely the same perils that can damage or destroy the cargo they carry. These perils include the action of wind and waves, striking of rocks or other vessels, shifting of cargo, fire, war, and breakage of machinery. This loss exposure can be covered by **hull insurance**.

A carrier that is prevented by an accident from delivering the cargo aboard its ship may face an additional exposure, called loss of freight. Freight is the compensation the carrier receives for transporting cargo. If the cargo cannot

Cargo insurance

Insurance that covers loss of or damage to property shipped primarily by water or, if in foreign trade, by air.

Hull insurance

Insurance that covers physical damage to vessels, including their machinery and fuel but not their cargo.

be delivered as promised, the carrier may lose the freight that the shipper would otherwise have paid. More frequently, however, the shipper guarantees that freight charges will be paid regardless of whether the cargo is delivered, provided that the failure to deliver the cargo results from causes beyond the carrier's control. When freight is guaranteed, the shipper, and not the carrier, is primarily exposed to loss of freight.

A vessel owner's freight exposure can be covered under a freight insurance policy, but such policies are not frequently requested. A shipper's freight loss exposure can be covered under an ocean marine cargo policy by including freight in the valuation clause.

Finally, a vessel owner faces exposure to legal liability for damage to cargo and other property and bodily injury to crew members, passengers, and other persons. If, for example, an oil tanker operator's negligence results in a collision with another vessel, the operator could become liable to the cargo owner for loss of oil, to the owner of the other vessel for damage to that vessel and its cargo, to persons on either vessel injured in the accident, and for the costs of cleaning up a resulting oil spill.

Protection and indemnity (P&I) insurance

Insurance that covers shipowners against various liability claims due to operating the insured vessel.

These vessel-related liability exposures can be covered by **protection and indemnity (P&I) insurance**. Many hull policies also include a collision liability clause, which covers the vessel owner's liability for damage to another vessel and its cargo resulting from collision with the insured vessel.

The Role of Judgment Rating in Ocean Marine Insurance

No advisory organization computes ocean marine loss costs. Moreover, ocean marine insurance is generally not subject to rate-filing laws in the various states. Thus, each insurer writing ocean marine insurance develops its own ocean marine rates, guided by the judgment of its underwriters. A marine underwriter's judgment in rating may be influenced by many factors.

A cargo insurance underwriter usually considers past loss experience, the product being shipped, the type of packing, the trade route over which the product is to be shipped, the time of year, the volume of shipments, port conditions, the ocean and inland carriers, and, significantly, the shipper's reputation and quality of management.

Hull and P&I insurance underwriters consider past loss experience; the size, type, and age of the insured vessel; the area of navigation; the trade in which the vessel is employed; the nation in which the vessel is registered (the loss experience of ships registered under one flag may differ dramatically from ships under another flag); and the vessel owner's reputation and quality of management.

✓ Reality Check

Oil Tanker Collision Loss Exposures

Details of a January 24, 2010, collision between an oil tanker and a barge in Port Arthur, Texas, demonstrate some of the exposures that cargo shippers and owners and operators of vessels face.

According to the U.S. Coast Guard, a vessel towing two barges struck and ruptured the side of the oil tanker *Eagle Otome*. It was estimated that 450,000 gallons of crude oil were spilled into the Sabine Neches Waterway, which was then closed to all marine traffic.[1]

The damage to the tanker represents a property loss exposure of the tanker's owner and a liability loss exposure of the barge operator, who could be held legally liable for the damage to the tanker.

The loss of oil is a property loss exposure of the shipper who owns the oil and pollution liability exposure for the barge owner and possibly the tanker owner, if the tanker owner is held to be partially at fault in the collision.

One or both of the vessel owners or operators could also incur liability because of the waterway's closure to other vessel traffic while the spill is being cleaned up. According to news reports, one officer reported that 150 barges and 15 tankers typically use the waterway daily—so the closure could create a significant economic loss.

Any bodily injuries would have created an additional liability for the responsible vessel owner. Fortunately, no injuries were reported in this case.

Finally, the tanker owner may have suffered loss of freight for the portion of oil that was lost, unless the shipper had guaranteed that the freight charges would be paid.

[DA07901]

OCEAN MARINE INSURANCE POLICIES

While ocean marine insurance may sound exotic, any company whose business involves importing or exporting has ocean cargo loss exposures. Similarly, any enterprise that uses watercraft in its operations has vessel property and liability loss exposures. Ocean marine insurance is used to insure these loss exposures.

Ocean marine insurance is written using a variety of forms. Because ocean marine policies can vary widely, this discussion focuses on the general characteristics of these three most common types of ocean marine policies:

- Cargo
- Hull
- Protection and indemnity

Cargo Insurance

There are two basic types of ocean marine cargo policies. A voyage policy is a policy that covers cargo for a single trip specified in the policy. In contrast, an open cargo policy is a policy that covers all goods shipped or received by the insured during the policy's term and is comparable to an inland marine annual trip transit policy, but without a set policy expiration date. The insured periodically pays premiums to the insurer based on reports from the insured of covered shipments.

The open cargo policy is well suited to the needs of an insured who frequently ships or receives goods overseas. Open cargo policies are often extended to cover air shipments as well as ocean shipments. An open cargo policy does not have an end date; the policy remains in force until either the insured or the insurer cancels it.

Warehouse to Warehouse Clause

Many importers and exporters are not located in a seaport. Consequently, their overseas shipments may be exposed to loss while in transit to the port facility by truck or railcar or by barge on an inland waterway, while aboard the cargo vessel, and while being transported again by land or inland waterway to the final destination.

To accommodate shippers' needs for continuous coverage during the entire course of transit, including inland transportation, ocean cargo policies contain a warehouse to warehouse clause. This clause covers the insured cargo during the ordinary course of transit (including land transit) from the time the cargo leaves the point of shipment until it is delivered to its final destination. If the cargo is discharged at the final port and not delivered to an inland destination, coverage ceases after a stipulated number of days.

The warehouse to warehouse clause is often supplemented by the marine extension clauses, which expand the coverage to include unavoidable deviations from the ordinary course of transit or delays caused by natural disasters, orders of civil authorities, or strikes of port workers. For example, a vessel may become damaged and have to dock for repairs at an unintended port. If the cargo owner arranges for transshipment of the cargo by another carrier to the final destination, the policy will cover the remainder of the trip. The insured must pay the additional premium required by the insurer.

Covered Causes of Loss

In the past, ocean cargo policies insured against specified causes of loss. Today, most ocean cargo policies use the "all-risks" approach. When cargo insurance is written on an "all-risks" basis, the insurer covers any unexpected or fortuitous loss not specifically excluded. Typically, an "all-risks" open cargo policy excludes loss caused by delay, inherent vice, war, strikes, riots, or civil commotion. Coverage for loss caused by strikes, riots, or civil commotion is reinstated in virtually every open cargo policy by endorsement. Loss caused by war can usually be insured under a separate cargo war risk policy.

Virtually every ocean cargo policy contains a sue and labor clause, which is a clause that covers the cost of reasonable measures that the insured is required to take to protect property from damage at the time of loss. In return, the insurer agrees to pay expenses the insured incurs in carrying out this duty.

General average situations arise when some of the vessel's cargo is jettisoned (thrown overboard) or otherwise sacrificed in order to save the entire venture. Under maritime law, all parties to the venture, including the vessel owner and all cargo owners, are required to share the losses of the owner(s) whose property was sacrificed. Similarly, if the vessel owner incurs certain expenses (such as the cost of being towed to a port of refuge) to ensure the safety of a voyage following a collision or other casualty, the vessel owner and all owners of cargo aboard the vessel will be required to share the expenses.

Ocean cargo policies specifically cover the insured's liability for general average and salvage charges. "Salvage" refers to situations in which owners of cargo aboard a vessel that falls in distress become liable to pay awards to other parties, such as salvage contractors, that put themselves at risk to rescue the vessel.

General average

Partial loss that must, according to maritime law, be shared by all parties to a voyage (cargo owners and vessel owner).

Valuation of Property

If a policy covers only one particular voyage, the property can be insured for a specific agreed value. It would be impractical, however, for an open cargo policy to list an individual valuation for every shipment made under the policy, especially if the insured makes many shipments each year. Consequently, the usual practice is to value a shipment of cargo by a formula, which typically includes the amount of invoice, all freight charges included in the invoice, and a stated percentage to cover additional expenses. The stated percentage varies depending on the circumstances, but 10 percent is often used. Thus, a typical valuation of an ocean shipment is calculated as shown:

Amount of invoice + Freight + 10%

Open cargo policies are ordinarily subject to a maximum limit of insurance for cargo shipped on any one vessel. Open cargo loss payments are usually subject to a dollar deductible.

Hull Insurance

A hull is the body of a vessel. Hull insurance covers physical damage to vessels, including their machinery and fuel but not their cargo. Hull insurance also covers provisions and stores for the operation of the vessel. Hull policies ordinarily exclude any cargo on board the vessel, as well as personal effects of passengers and crew.

Hull insurance policies usually cover on a specified perils basis but can also apply on an "all-risks" basis. These are the typically covered causes of loss:

• Perils of the seas—Perils of the seas are accidental causes of loss that are peculiar to the sea and other bodies of water. Examples include abnormally high winds and rough seas, strandings, groundings, and collisions with other vessels or objects.

• Fire, lightning, and earthquake—The inclusion of earthquake provides coverage for the possibility that a vessel might be damaged by earthquake while docked.

• Barratry—Barratry is serious misconduct by the vessel's master or crew that is contrary to the owner's interest, such as a fraudulent or criminal act that causes damage to the vessel.

• All other like perils—"All other like perils" refers to perils similar to the perils specifically listed in the policy. The phrase does not provide "all-risks" coverage.

In addition to these basic perils, many hull policies include an additional perils clause covering losses caused by several other perils, such as electrical breakdown, bursting of boilers, breakage of shafts, latent defects, and negligence of the crew.

Hull policies exclude loss caused by war, piracy, strikes, riots, and virtually any situation in which the vessel is taken by another party. Coverage for many of the excluded perils can be added to the policy by endorsement.

A vessel is normally insured for a value agreed upon by the insurer and the insured. If the vessel sustains a total loss caused by a covered cause of loss, the insurer pays the agreed value stated in the policy. In the event of a partial loss, the insurer pays the cost of repairs.

Most hull policies contain a collision liability clause (also known as a running down clause), which covers the insured's liability for collision damage to other vessels and their cargoes. Collision liability coverage is a separate amount of insurance ordinarily equal to the amount of insurance on the hull. The costs of defending a suit alleging covered damages are also covered, and such costs do not reduce the amount of insurance available for paying damages.

The collision liability clause does not cover liability for bodily injury, nor does it cover property damage resulting from some cause other than collision. Usually, it does not apply to liability for collision damage to any property besides other vessels and their cargoes.

Protection and Indemnity Insurance

Protection and indemnity (P&I) insurance covers vessel owners against various liability claims resulting from the operation of the insured vessel.

P&I insurance is usually provided in a separate policy. These are some of the important sources of liability claims that may be covered by P&I insurance:

- Damage to bridges, piers, wharves, and other structures along waterways
- Injury to passengers, crew, and other persons on the insured vessel
- Injury to persons on other vessels
- Damage to cargo of others aboard the insured vessel

P&I policies cover several miscellaneous exposures as well, such as expenses incurred to remove the wreck of an insured vessel, the costs of entering an unscheduled port to obtain medical assistance for a passenger or crew member, and fines resulting from the violation of laws.

Some P&I policies do not cover the insured's liability for discharging pollutants. Separate pollution liability insurance for vessel owners is available from underwriting syndicates or industry pools.

 Reality Check

Application of Ocean Marine Coverages

This hypothetical loss and claim scenario shows how the hull and P&I policies of two vessels typically apply to a collision at sea between the two vessels.

The owners of cargo vessel A and cargo vessel B both have hull insurance and P&I insurance. Vessel A negligently runs into vessel B. Both vessels and their cargoes are damaged. In addition, crew members of vessels A and B are injured. Vessel A is held legally liable for damage to vessel B, to vessel B's cargo, to vessel A's cargo (owned by others), and for injury to crew members on each vessel. Coverage will apply as follows:

- Vessel A's hull policy will cover the damage to vessel A.
- Vessel A's hull policy (under the collision liability clause) will cover vessel A's liability for damage to vessel B and vessel B's cargo.
- Vessel A's P&I policy will cover vessel A's liability for damage to vessel A's cargo and injury to the crew members of both vessels A and B.

[DA07922]

RECOMMENDING INLAND AND OCEAN MARINE COVERAGES

Knowing how to select inland marine and ocean marine coverages based on the facts of a case is an important skill. This case study should help you transition from simply knowing inland marine and ocean marine insurance concepts to being able to apply those concepts and recommend inland and ocean marine insurance coverages for a commercial customer's loss exposures. As you progress through the case study, you can check your understanding by answering the Knowledge to Action questions.

Case Facts

RBC, Inc., a commercial construction contractor, owns an office building, a large garage for storing RBC's building materials and other equipment, a fleet of trucks, and more than 100 units of mobile construction equipment.

RBC purchases all its building materials from suppliers located in the United States. These materials are delivered by motor carriers to either RBC's construction sites or RBC's garage. RBC, as opposed to its suppliers, is usually the party that bears the risk of loss of the materials during transit.

When RBC constructs a building under contract with the building's owner, RBC's ownership of building supplies continues until all supplies are installed in the building under construction, at which point they become the building owner's property and are insured under the building owner's builders risk or commercial property policy. When RBC constructs a building on speculation (not under contract with an owner), RBC owns the construction materials and the building until the building is sold.

For each building project, RBC's architects and engineers develop blueprints and building plans with specifications that are stored in its office building and at work sites. All of these records are backed up daily on RBC's computer system, and duplicates are stored at a secure, remote location.

RBC employs a mechanic to service its mobile construction equipment in RBC's garage. However, because maintaining RBC's equipment does not keep the mechanic busy full time, the mechanic also earns revenue for RBC by repairing other contractors' equipment. Depending on the circumstances of each loss, RBC could be held legally liable for damage to other contractors' equipment while it is in RBC's care, custody, or control.

RBC has an in-house accounting department that handles accounts receivable from RBC's customers. Its accounts receivable are often valued in the millions of dollars, exceeding the limit of coverage that RBC's commercial property insurance provides for this exposure. RBC's records of accounts receivable are backed up daily on the company's computer system, and duplicates are stored at a secure, remote location.

RBC has recently entered into a contract to convert a commercial wharf into a shopping mall. To complete this work, RBC will need to lease several barges and other workboats under agreements that require RBC to provide insurance for both of these exposures:

- Accidental damage to the leased barges and workboats
- Liability for bodily injury or property damage to others arising out of RBC's operation of the leased barges and workboats

Based on the facts presented in this case, what are RBC's loss exposures that can be covered by inland and ocean marine insurance? What types of inland and ocean marine insurance should RBC purchase to cover these loss exposures?

When answering the questions in this case-based activity, consider only the information supported by the facts of the case.

Overview of Steps

Assuming that RBC wishes to insure its inland and ocean marine loss exposures, these steps can be used to recommend appropriate types of inland and ocean marine insurance for RBC:

- Identify RBC's loss exposures that can be covered by inland or ocean marine insurance.
- Consider the available types of inland and ocean marine insurance, matching each identified loss exposure with the specific type, or types, of inland or ocean marine insurance that would cover each exposure.
- Recommend the most appropriate types of inland or ocean marine insurance for each of RBC's inland marine and ocean marine loss exposures.

Identify RBC's Loss Exposures That Can Be Covered by Inland or Ocean Marine Insurance

RBC has these property loss exposures that can be covered by inland marine insurance:

- Mobile construction equipment
- Property in transit by motor carriers
- A computer system and electronic data
- Blueprints and building plans with specifications
- Records of accounts receivable
- Building materials delivered to RBC but not yet installed in buildings
- Buildings under construction (owned by RBC)

RBC's only property loss exposures that can be covered by ocean marine insurance are the leased barges and workboats that RBC has agreed to insure against accidental damage.

RBC's only liability loss exposure that can be covered by inland marine insurance is its liability for damage to other contractors' equipment in RBC's care, custody, or control.

RBC's only liability loss exposure that can be covered by ocean marine insurance is its liability for bodily injury or property damage resulting from its use of leased barges and workboats.

Knowledge to Action

Explain why RBC's office building, garage, and trucks are not included on the list of RBC's loss exposures that can be covered by inland or ocean marine insurance.

Feedback: Buildings and automobiles are not eligible for inland or ocean marine insurance, as determined by the Nationwide Marine Definition. The only exceptions are builders risk policies (which RBC can purchase on buildings under construction) and difference in conditions (DIC) policies.

How might RBC benefit from an inland marine DIC policy?

Feedback: RBC could use a DIC policy to cover causes of loss, such as flood or earthquake, in addition to the basic perils insurable under commercial property policies. RBC could also use a DIC policy to cover loss of income resulting from theft or transit losses, to cover property at overseas locations, or to fill other gaps left by RBC's commercial property insurance.

Consider the Available Types of Inland and Ocean Marine Insurance

In this step, each of the identified loss exposures is matched with the corresponding type(s) of inland or ocean marine insurance. The exhibit shows the types of inland and ocean marine insurance that could be used to cover RBC's loss exposures. See the exhibit "Applicable Inland Marine and Ocean Marine Insurance Options."

Recommend the Most Appropriate Types of Inland and Ocean Marine Insurance

For most of RBC's inland and ocean marine loss exposures, as shown in the exhibit, one coverage applies for each loss exposure. In such cases, these specified coverages serve as valid recommendations for RBC to consider. But for some of RBC's exposures, two or more alternative coverages might be available. In these cases, you must consider which coverages should be recommended.

For example, consider RBC's loss exposure for building materials after they have been delivered to RBC and before RBC installs them in buildings under construction. Builders risk policies and installation floaters both can cover this loss exposure. If RBC buys a builders risk policy on a structure that RBC is building on speculation, that policy can be arranged to cover the building materials before they become part of the building. Additionally, to cover building materials before they become part of a building that RBC does not own, RBC can buy an installation floater.

Applicable Inland Marine and Ocean Marine Insurance Options

Loss Exposures	Insurance Options
Inland Marine Property:	
• Mobile construction equipment	• Contractors equipment floater
• Property in transit by motor carriers	• Builders risk policy
	• Installation floater
	• Trip transit policy
	• Annual transit policy
• RBC's computer system and electronic data	• Electronic data processing (EDP) equipment floater
• Blueprints and building plans with specifications	• Valuable Papers and Records Coverage Form
• Records of accounts receivable	• Accounts Receivable Coverage Form
• Building materials delivered to RBC but not yet installed in buildings	• Builders risk policy
	• Installation floater
• Buildings under construction (owned by RBC)	• Builders risk policy
Ocean Marine Property:	
• Leased barges and workboats	• Hull policy
Inland Marine Liability:	
• Liability for other contractors' equipment in RBC's care, custody, or control	• Bailees' customers policy
Ocean Marine Liability:	
• Liability for bodily injury or property damage resulting from the use of leased barges and workboats	• Protection and indemnity policy

[DA07909]

Knowledge to Action

As shown in the exhibit, RBC's building materials in transit from suppliers can be covered by these four types of inland marine policies:

- Builders risk policy
- Installation floater
- Trip transit policy
- Annual transit policy

Assuming that RBC will purchase an installation floater and a builders risk policy as just discussed, which of the four alternative policies would you recommend for covering RBC's building materials in transit from suppliers?

Feedback: Builders risk policies and installation floaters, because they are traditionally nonfiled classes of inland marine insurance, are often written to include coverage for building materials while in transit or storage before being installed in the building under construction. If RBC can obtain this coverage under its builders risk policies and installation floater, then it does not need to purchase separate transit insurance, and the first two policies can be recommended.

If RBC needed to purchase separate transit insurance policies on multiple shipments during the year that are not covered by RBC's builders risk policy or installation floater, would you recommend a trip transit policy or an annual transit policy? Explain your answer.

Feedback: An annual transit policy would be the better choice because RBC receives multiple shipments during the year. With trip transit, a separate policy would need to be issued for each shipment. An annual transit policy automatically covers all shipments made during the policy period.

Retention

A risk financing technique by which losses are retained by generating funds within the organization to pay for the losses.

Once your coverage recommendations are made to RBC, RBC's management might decide to use **retention** instead of insurance for some of its loss exposures. For example, because RBC has implemented appropriate risk control techniques (daily backup and storage of duplicates at a remote location) for its valuable papers and records and for its records of accounts receivable, RBC may choose not to insure either or both of these types of property.

SUMMARY

Inland marine insurance provides a variety of flexible coverage solutions. Many states continue to use an updated NAIC Nationwide Marine Definition to differentiate marine insurance from other types of insurance for form and rate regulation. Inland marine business can be filed or nonfiled with state insurance departments, and underwriters use judgment rating for less common types of nonfiled, inland marine insurance.

ISO and AAIS file various forms on behalf of their members. However, the largest classes of inland marine insurance are, in many states, nonfiled and include contractors equipment, builders risk, transit, motor truck cargo liability, difference in conditions, and electronic data processing equipment.

Filed classes of inland marine insurance include coverage forms for commercial articles, camera and musical instrument dealers, equipment dealers, physicians and surgeons equipment, signs, theatrical property, film, floor plan merchandise, jewelers block, mail, accounts receivable, and valuable papers and records.

The transportation of property in vessels creates several types of loss exposures that can be covered by ocean marine insurance. Insurers typically develop rates for ocean marine insurance based on their underwriters' judgment, which may be influenced by a number of factors.

Ocean marine loss exposures can be insured by three basic types of marine insurance: cargo insurance, hull insurance, and P&I insurance. The open cargo policy covers all goods shipped or received by the insured during the term of the policy. Hull insurance covers the vessel, its machinery, fuel, and supplies. P&I insurance covers vessel owners against various liability claims resulting from the operation of the insured vessel.

You should now be able to apply inland and ocean marine insurance concepts to loss exposures and recommend inland and ocean marine insurance coverages for a commercial business.

ASSIGNMENT NOTE

1. Angel Gonzalez and Naureen Malik, "Collision Causes Crude Oil Spill in Texas," The Wall Street Journal, Digital Network, January 24, 2010, www.online.wsj.com/article/SB10001424052748704562504575021540843701582.html (accessed July 21, 2011).

Commercial General Liability Insurance, Part I

Educational Objectives

After learning the content of this assignment, you should be able to:

▷ Describe commercial general liability insurance in terms of these elements:

- The types of losses that can be covered by general liability insurance

- The components of a commercial general liability coverage part

▷ Determine whether a described claim meets the conditions imposed by the Coverage A insuring agreement of the Commercial General Liability Coverage Form (occurrence version).

▷ Determine whether any of the exclusions applicable to Coverage A of the Commercial General Liability Coverage Form eliminate coverage for a described claim.

▷ Determine whether a described claim meets the conditions imposed by the Coverage B insuring agreement of the Commercial General Liability Coverage Form and whether any of the Coverage B exclusions eliminate coverage for the claim.

▷ Determine whether a described claim meets the conditions imposed by the Coverage C insuring agreement of the Commercial General Liability Coverage Form and whether any of the Coverage C exclusions eliminate coverage for the claim.

▷ Summarize the supplementary payments of the Commercial General Liability Coverage Form.

Commercial General Liability Insurance, Part I

OVERVIEW OF COMMERCIAL GENERAL LIABILITY INSURANCE

All businesses, including not-for-profit and governmental organizations, face the possibility of incurring liability losses arising out of their premises, operations, products, and other sources. Purchasing general liability insurance is one method that businesses and other organizations can use to finance these potential liability losses.

The most widely used general liability form, the Insurance Services Office, Inc. (ISO) Commercial General Liability (CGL) Coverage Form, covers these two broad categories of liability loss:

- Bodily injury and property damage liability
- Personal and advertising injury liability

The CGL form also includes medical payments coverage, which pays for the medical expenses of persons injured on the insured's premises or because of the insured's activities, regardless of whether the insured is legally liable.

A variety of other general liability coverage forms and endorsements are available for covering situations or loss exposures not adequately covered under the CGL form. The particular general liability coverage forms and endorsements that an insured selects are combined into a general liability coverage part that can be included in a commercial package policy (CPP) or issued as a monoline policy.

Bodily Injury and Property Damage Liability

The primary type of liability loss covered by general liability forms is covered under the Coverage A—Bodily Injury and Property Damage Liability insuring agreement of the CGL form. Although this insuring agreement is subject to many exclusions, it covers the insured's liability for bodily injury and property damage arising out of a wide range of sources.

Traditionally, these sources of bodily injury and property damage liability have been categorized, for premium-development purposes, as the premises and operations hazard and the products and completed operations hazard. Ordinarily, a separate insurance rate applies to each of these two hazards. Each of these descriptors is also used to refer to loss exposures (such as "premises and operations liability exposure") or to coverage (such as "products and completed operations liability coverage").

Premises and Operations

The premises and operations liability exposure is the possibility that an organization will be held liable because of bodily injury or property damage caused by an accident that either occurs on the organization's premises or arises out of the organization's ongoing (as opposed to completed) operations on or off those premises. These are two examples of accidents that could result in premises and operations liability claims:

- A customer inside a food store is injured when he slips and falls on a wet floor that has just been mopped by a store employee who failed to put up a warning sign.
- A passerby at a contractor's job site is injured when an employee of the contractor accidentally drops a tool while working on a ladder above the sidewalk.

An organization's liability for accidents associated with the premises and operations liability hazard is usually based on negligence: that is, that the organization (or a person for whose actions the organization is legally responsible) failed to exercise the appropriate degree of care owed to a person under the circumstances, and the person suffered injury as the direct result of the organization's failure to exercise due care.

The premium for a CGL policy is typically calculated by applying a premises and operations rate and a products and completed operations rate to the appropriate exposure base for each. The coverage that corresponds with the premises and operations rate includes the contractual liability coverage provided by the CGL form. Therefore, contractual liability for bodily injury or property damage is often considered to be part of the premises and operations liability exposure.

Although premises and operations liability includes bodily injury or property damage arising out of the use of mobile equipment (such as a bulldozer or crane) as defined in the CGL form, bodily injury or property damage arising out of the use of aircraft, autos (as defined in the CGL form), or watercraft is excluded in almost all instances. Liability for injury or illness of the organization's employees is also excluded.

Products and Completed Operations

The products and completed operations liability exposure is the possibility that an organization will be held liable because of bodily injury or property damage caused by an accident arising out of products manufactured, sold, or distributed by the organization and occurring after the products are no longer on the organization's premises or in the organization's physical possession or by an accident arising out of the organization's completed work, including defective parts or materials furnished with the work. These are two examples of accidents that could result in products and completed operations claims:

- A consumer dies because of impurities in a medicine sold by a pharmaceutical firm.
- The tenants of an apartment building are injured by smoke inhalation, and their personal property is destroyed by a fire that resulted from faulty electrical work completed by a contractor several hours earlier.

An organization's liability for products or completed operations can, depending on the circumstances of the claim and the jurisdiction in which the claim is made, be based on a variety of recovery theories, including (but not limited to) negligence, strict liability in tort, misrepresentation, fraud, and breach of warranty.

Personal and Advertising Injury Liability

Another coverage included in the CGL form is Coverage B—Personal and Advertising Injury Liability, which covers the insured's liability for "personal and advertising injury." The form defines this phrase to mean any kind of injury (such as loss of reputation, humiliation, economic loss, or even consequential bodily injury) arising out of any of several listed offenses. Examples of the listed offenses are false arrest, wrongful eviction, libel, slander, and infringing upon another's copyright in the insured's advertisement.

Liability for personal and advertising injury was once so rare that most businesses did not insure against it. It is now such a common exposure that it is an integral part of the CGL form, but it can be omitted if the insured does not want to buy it.

Medical Payments

The CGL form also includes Coverage C—Medical Payments, which pays medical expenses of others in certain circumstances. Coverage C—Medical Payments does not require the insured to be legally liable and, therefore, is not technically liability insurance.

To be covered, the medical expenses (as defined in the form) must result from bodily injury because of an accident occurring on the insured's premises or arising out of the insured's operations (other than completed operations) anywhere in the coverage territory.

Medical payments coverage has a much lower limit of insurance than either Coverage A or Coverage B. Its role is to pay small bodily injury claims without having to establish liability, perhaps reducing the likelihood that an accident victim will sue the insured.

Other General Liability Exposures

Several other ISO general liability coverage forms are available for covering either special situations or specific loss exposures that are not adequately covered by the CGL form. See the exhibit "Liability Coverage Forms That Provide Coverage That Is Not Adequately Addressed Under the CGL Policy."

Liability Coverage Forms That Provide Coverage That Is Not Adequately Addressed Under the CGL Policy

Coverage Form	Basic Purpose
Owners and Contractors Protective Liability Coverage Form	Is bought by an independent contractor but issued in the name of the property owner for whom the contractor is performing operations. Covers the property owner against liability arising out of (1) operations being performed by a contractor or (2) the named insured's negligent supervision of the contractor's operations.
Railroad Protective Liability Coverage Form	Protects the named railroad owner against bodily injury and property damage liability claims resulting from the operations of a contractor performing operations on, over, under, or adjacent to railroad property. The coverage is usually bought by the contractor at the railroad's request.
Liquor Liability Coverage Form	Available for insuring bars, restaurants, stores, and any other businesses that sell or serve alcoholic beverages. Covers "liquor liability" arising out of the sale or serving of alcoholic beverages, a loss exposure that the CGL form excludes if the insured is in the business of selling alcoholic beverages.
Electronic Data Liability Coverage Form	Covers the insured's liability for loss of electronic data caused by an electronic data incident as defined in the form, an exposure that the CGL form excludes.
Product Withdrawal Coverage Form	Covers the costs of withdrawing or recalling products from the market.
Various pollution liability coverage forms	Available for insuring bodily injury, property damage, or cleanup costs resulting from pollution incidents not covered under the CGL form.

[DA07819]

Components of a General Liability Coverage Part

A general liability coverage part consists of these components:

- One or more general liability declarations forms
- One or more general liability coverage forms
- Any applicable endorsements

Under ISO procedures, a general liability coverage part can be included in a CPP or issued in a monoline policy that provides general liability coverage only.

General Liability Declarations

ISO has developed separate declarations forms for use with each of its general liability coverage forms. Typically, each of these declarations forms contains spaces for showing these common items of information:

- The insurer's and producer's names.
- The named insured's name and mailing address.
- The policy inception and expiration dates.
- A condition stating, "In return for the payment of the premium, and subject to all the terms of this policy, we agree with you to provide the insurance as stated in the policy."
- The limits of insurance.
- Description of the named insured's business.
- Rating and premium auditing information.
- A list of endorsements attached to the policy.

Some of the declarations forms also contain spaces for showing additional information relevant to the associated coverage form.

General Liability Coverage Forms

Each of the various ISO general liability coverage forms typically contains these major sections:

- Coverages—This section contains one or more insuring agreements and applicable exclusions, as well as supplementary payments in some forms.
- Who Is an Insured—This section describes the individuals and organizations that qualify as insureds.
- Limits of Insurance—This section explains how the limits of insurance apply to covered claims.
- Conditions—This section contains various conditions that the insurer and insured must abide by.
- Definitions—This section defines certain words and phrases used in the coverage form.

Some of the coverage forms have two versions, which differ only with respect to whether they have an occurrence coverage trigger or a claims-made coverage trigger. Some coverage forms come in only a claims-made version. The claims-made forms typically contain an additional section, titled Extended Reporting Periods, which describes the coverage that the policy provides for claims first made after the end of the policy period for accidents that occurred before the end of the policy period.

Endorsements

Many endorsements are available to tailor the general liability coverage forms to meet the specialized needs of particular insureds, to make the policy comply with particular state laws, or to eliminate exposures that insurers are not willing to insure.

CGL COVERAGE A—INSURING AGREEMENT

Coverage A—Bodily Injury and Property Damage Liability of the Insurance Services Office, Inc. (ISO) Commercial General Liability (CGL) Coverage Form insures against claims arising out of premises, operations, products, completed operations, and contractual liability exposures. Coverage A provisions include a broad insuring agreement.

The CGL policy's Coverage A insuring agreement contains the insurer's promise to pay damages on behalf of the insured and to defend the insured against claims or suits seeking damages covered under the policy. A claim that meets all of the conditions in the insuring agreement is still subject to the Coverage A exclusions.

Insurer's Duty to Pay Damages

In the occurrence version of the CGL, the insuring agreement imposes seven conditions on the insurer's duty to pay damages, all of which must be fulfilled for a claim to be covered. See the exhibit "Conditions Imposed on the Insurer's Duty to Pay Damages Under CGL Coverage A."

Legally Obligated (Legally Liable) to Pay Damages

Whether the insured is legally obligated (legally liable) to pay damages can be determined either through a court proceeding or by the insurer's claims investigation. Often, the insurer's investigation reveals that the insured is legally liable. If the insurer also believes that the policy covers the claim, it will

---

Conditions Imposed on the Insurer's Duty to Pay Damages Under CGL Coverage A

- The insured must be legally obligated (legally liable) to pay damages.
- The damages must result from bodily injury or property damage as defined in the policy.
- The policy must apply to the bodily injury or property damage.
- The bodily injury or property damage must be caused by an occurrence.
- The occurrence must take place in the coverage territory.
- The bodily injury or property damage must occur during the policy period. (The claims-made form contains a different provision in this regard.)
- The bodily injury or property damage must not be known to the named insured or certain other persons before the policy period.

[DA07840]

usually attempt to negotiate an out-of-court settlement with the third-party claimant. The basic types of damages that a court might award include these:

- Special damages, for such out-of-pocket costs as medical expenses and loss of earnings
- General damages, for such intangibles as pain and suffering
- Punitive damages, awarded to punish or make an example of the wrongdoer

Although the insurer promises to pay all damages for which the insured is liable, a few states do not recognize the concept of punitive damages, and others do not permit insurers to pay punitive damages on behalf of an insured. Even in states that do allow insurers to pay punitive damages, insurers are not likely to pay them in an out-of-court settlement.

Bodily Injury and Property Damage

The CGL coverage form broadly defines bodily injury as "bodily injury, sickness or disease sustained by a person, including death resulting from any of these at any time." The insuring agreement contains a statement that damages resulting from bodily injury include damages for care, loss of services, or death resulting at any time from the bodily injury. Damages for pain and suffering are part of bodily injury. The policy definition of property damage includes both of these elements:

- Physical injury to tangible property, including resulting loss of use of that property. An example of physical injury is the destruction of a customer's building by fire caused by the insured contractor's negligence. Resulting loss of use would include the loss of income sustained by the customer until the building could be rebuilt.

- Loss of use of tangible property that is not physically injured. An example of this kind of loss is a retail store's loss of business income resulting from the interruption of utility services when a contractor severed utility lines.

The definition of property damage also states that electronic data are not tangible property. The policy defines electronic data broadly to include "information, facts, or programs stored as or on, created or used on, or transmitted to or from computer software or any type of electronic medium or device."

Injury or Damage to Which the Insurance Applies

The insurer is not obligated to pay damages if any of the Coverage A exclusions apply to the claim or if the claim is not covered for any other reason.

Caused by an Occurrence

To be insured, the bodily injury or property damage must be caused by an occurrence. The policy definition of occurrence is an "accident, including continuous or repeated exposure to substantially the same general harmful conditions."

Accident is not defined in the policy. However, the intent is to provide coverage either for an event that happens suddenly and results in immediate bodily injury or property damage or for any adverse condition that continues over a long period and eventually results in bodily injury or property damage. In either case, the bodily injury or property damage must have been caused by an occurrence.

Unintended results of intentional acts generally qualify as accidents. For example, in using a propane torch to thaw a customer's frozen water pipe (an intentional act), a plumber may accidentally set the building on fire. The fire, because it is an unintended result, qualifies as an accident. In contrast, if a plumber intentionally set a customer's house on fire, it would not be considered an accident and therefore would not meet the definition of occurrence in the plumber's CGL policy.

Coverage Territory

Coverage A applies only to occurrences that take place in the coverage territory defined in the policy. The coverage territory that applies to most claims is the United States (including its territories and possessions), Puerto Rico, and Canada. International waters and international airspace are included in the coverage territory if the injury or damage occurs in the course of travel or transportation between places included in the basic coverage territory.

The coverage territory is extended to include the entire world with respect to these:

- Goods or products made or sold by the named insured in the basic coverage territory
- Activities of a person whose home is in the basic coverage territory but who is away for a short time while pursuing the named insured's business

These extensions apply only if the insured's liability for damages is determined either in a suit filed in the basic coverage territory (the U.S., its territories or possessions, Puerto Rico, or Canada) or in a settlement to which the insurer agrees.

Injury or Damage Occurring During the Policy Period

The occurrence version of the CGL policy requires that the bodily injury or property damage occur during the policy period. This requirement is known as the occurrence coverage trigger. Therefore, the policy that applies to a particular claim is the one that is in effect when the bodily injury or property damage occurs. This is true even if the claim is not made until many years after the policy period ends.

Injury or Damage Not Known Before the Policy Period

The occurrence version of the CGL coverage form eliminates coverage for bodily injury or property damage that was known by designated insureds or by designated employees of the insured to have occurred in whole or in part before the policy's inception date. Designated insureds are those described in the Who Is an Insured section of the CGL coverage form. Designated employees are persons, such as the named insured's risk manager, who are authorized by the named insured to give or receive notice of an occurrence or a claim.

This provision was developed in response to a court case in which the court adopted a continuous injury trigger. The continuous injury trigger holds that injury or damage is deemed to occur continuously over time as long as an injury continues, thus triggering coverage under all occurrence-based policies that were in effect throughout the course of the injury. The provision is referred to as either the continuous or progressive injury provision or the Montrose provision (after the name of the plaintiff in the court case).

The claims-made version of the CGL requires that the claim for bodily injury or property damage first be made during the policy period. However, several additional conditions apply.

Insurer's Duty to Defend

The Coverage A insuring agreement also stipulates that the insurer has the right and duty to defend the insured against any suit that seeks damages for bodily injury or property damage to which the insurance applies. The policy defines suit to include arbitration or other alternative dispute resolution proceedings as well as formal lawsuits.

Courts frequently describe the insurer's duty to defend as broader than its duty to pay damages. The insurer must defend its insured whenever a claimant alleges a wrongful act or omission of the insured that could conceivably fall within the policy's coverage. The insurer's duty to defend the insured against a suit exists even if the allegations are later proven groundless, false, or fraudulent. Many cases entail a plaintiff alleging multiple acts or omissions, some of which may clearly fall outside the scope of coverage. However, as long as at least one of the alleged acts or omissions may conceivably be covered, the insurer is usually obligated to defend the insured against the entire complaint.

Apply Your Knowledge

When a construction company's crane accidentally drops a steel beam on a parked car, it becomes legally obligated to pay damages because of property damage that results. The accident occurs during the policy period at a work site in Mexico. Does this claim meet all the conditions imposed by the Coverage A insuring agreement in the company's CGL policy?

Feedback: No. The claim does not meet the condition requiring that the occurrence take place in the coverage territory, which does not include Mexico.

Retail Store in Denver, Colorado, becomes legally obligated to pay damages because of the false detention of a customer whom the store's security guards wrongly believed to be a shoplifter. The incident takes place during the policy period. The shopper alleges that she suffered humiliation and inconvenience as a result of her detention. Does this claim meet all conditions imposed by the Coverage A insuring agreement in Retail Store's CGL policy?

Feedback: No. Even though the insured was legally liable to pay damages for an incident that occurred during the policy period and in the coverage territory, the claim does not meet the requirement that the damages must result from bodily injury or property damage to which the policy applies.

Manufacturer, Inc. becomes legally obligated to pay damages to a German citizen who sustains bodily injury in Germany because of a product the manufacturer built in the United States. The injury resulted from an accident, and the accident and injury occurred during the current policy period. Neither Manufacturer, Inc., nor any of its employees had knowledge of the claimed injury before the current policy period began. The injured person wins a suit in a U.S. court. Does this claim meet all the conditions imposed by the Coverage A insuring agreement in Manufacturer, Inc.'s CGL policy?

Feedback: Yes. The circumstances of the claim meet all of the conditions contained in the Coverage A insuring agreement. Although the accident occurred in Germany, the fact that the product was built in the U.S. and that the injured person brought suit in the U.S. brings this claim within the CGL's coverage territory.

CGL COVERAGE A—EXCLUSIONS

Even if a claim meets the conditions of the Commercial General Liability (CGL) Coverage Form's Coverage A—Bodily Injury and Property Damage Liability insuring agreement, the claim is not covered if one or more of the Coverage A exclusions applies to it.

Coverage A of the CGL coverage form contains seventeen exclusions, labeled a. through q. Some of the exclusions eliminate coverage for exposures that are customarily insured under other policies, such as automobile liability, workers compensation, or pollution liability. Other exclusions address exposures that are uninsurable or, at best, difficult to insure, such as intentional injury, damage to the insured's products, or war.

Expected or Intended Injury

Exclusion a. eliminates coverage for bodily injury or property damage that is expected or intended by the insured. Thus, coverage does not apply if the insured intentionally injured the claimant.

However, the exclusion does not apply to bodily injury resulting from the use of reasonable force to protect persons or property. For example, a storeowner can use reasonable force to restrain a customer from damaging merchandise. This act of protecting property would be covered despite the storeowner's intentional use of force.

Contractual Liability

Exclusion b. eliminates coverage for liability assumed by the insured under a contract. This exclusion applies only if the liability would not have existed in the absence of the contract. That is, if liability for a claim could have been imposed on the insured by tort law, the exclusion does not apply, even though the insured may have also assumed liability for the claim under a contract.

More significantly, the exclusion also does not apply to liability assumed under an "insured contract" if the bodily injury or property damage occurs after the contract or agreement is executed. The definition of "insured contract" includes many, but not all, types of contracts under which the insured might assume the liability of others. Therefore, determining whether the CGL form would cover a particular type of contract requires a careful review of the CGL form's definition of "insured contract."

Liquor Liability

Exclusion c. applies only to insureds in the business of manufacturing, distributing, selling, serving, or furnishing alcoholic beverages. It eliminates coverage if liability arises from causing or contributing to the intoxication of any person, from furnishing alcoholic beverages to a person under the legal drinking age, or from otherwise violating the laws governing the sale and distribution of such beverages.

The Liquor Liability exclusion applies only if the named insured is in the alcoholic beverage business. Therefore, the exclusion does not apply to an organization that is not in the alcoholic beverage business that becomes liable for injury resulting from serving alcoholic beverages at a company picnic or holiday office party.

The exception also clarifies that allowing patrons to furnish their own alcoholic beverages for consumption is not, by itself, considered the business of selling, serving, or furnishing alcoholic beverages. However, "bring your own" establishments, for whom this clarification is designed, are still well advised to purchase full liquor liability insurance because various actions by the establishment or its employees, beyond allowing patrons to bring their own bottles, could be the basis for a legal determination that they are in the business of selling, serving, or furnishing alcoholic beverages and therefore subject to the Liquor Liability exclusion.

Apply Your Knowledge

Art Gallery, whose business is limited to selling contemporary art, served complimentary alcoholic beverages at the opening night of an exhibition. One of the guests became intoxicated and caused an auto accident while driving home.

The other motorist injured in the accident made a claim against Art Gallery for his injuries, alleging that Art Gallery was negligent in serving alcoholic beverages to the guest who caused the accident. Would the Liquor Liability exclusion in Art Gallery's CGL policy apply to this claim?

Feedback: No. The Liquor Liability exclusion applies only if the named insured is "in the business of manufacturing, distributing, selling, serving or furnishing alcoholic beverages." Because Art Gallery's business is limited to selling contemporary art, the Liquor Liability exclusion does not apply to Art Gallery.

Workers Compensation and Employers Liability

Exclusions d. and e. prevent the CGL form from duplicating workers compensation and similar coverages for occupational injury or disease to employees.

Exclusion d. (Workers' Compensation and Similar Laws) eliminates coverage for obligations of the insured under any workers compensation, disability benefits, unemployment compensation, or similar law.

Exclusion e. (Employer's Liability) eliminates coverage for bodily injury to any employee of the insured if the injury arises out of and in the course of employment, thus eliminating CGL policy coverage for employee injuries that would otherwise be covered by the employer's liability coverage of the standard Workers Compensation and Employers Liability Insurance Policy.

Pollution

Exclusion f. eliminates coverage for pollution liability claims related to the insured's premises and operations. The exclusion is worded broadly to encompass the many ways pollutants can enter the environment. The exclusion applies to bodily injury, property damage, and cleanup costs resulting from pollution incidents.

The exclusion is subject to a few exceptions, which allow coverage for certain pollution liability exposures. Here are two examples of these exceptions:

• Bodily injury or property damage caused by heat, smoke, or fumes from a hostile fire. (A hostile fire is a fire that becomes uncontrollable or breaks out from where it was intended to be.)

• Bodily injury or property damage resulting from the escape of fuels, lubricants, or other operating fluids needed to perform the normal functions of mobile equipment. The fuels, lubricants, or operating fluids must escape from a vehicle part designed to hold them, and the escape must be accidental.

If an organization has pollution loss exposures that are not covered by the CGL form, various types of environmental insurance are available. Some insurers are willing to cover pollution loss exposures under separate environmental insurance policies because that gives them the opportunity to evaluate the covered loss exposures, charge an adequate policy premium, and provide appropriate risk control services to the insured.

Aircraft, Auto, or Watercraft

Exclusion g. eliminates coverage for bodily injury and property damage arising from the ownership, maintenance, or use (including loading or unloading) of any aircraft, auto, or watercraft. Although the CGL coverage form does not define aircraft or watercraft, it does define auto. Thus, the actual scope of the auto exclusion depends on the policy definition of auto:

2. "Auto" means:

a. A land motor vehicle, trailer or semitrailer designed for travel on public roads, including any attached machinery or equipment; or

b. Any other land vehicle that is subject to a compulsory or financial responsibility law or other motor vehicle insurance law where it is licensed or principally garaged.

However, "auto" does not include "mobile equipment".

Some coverage for claims involving aircraft, autos, and watercraft is provided through five exceptions to exclusion g. The exclusion does not apply to any of these:

- Watercraft while ashore on the insured's premises
- A watercraft that the named insured does not own and that is less than twenty-six feet long and not being used to carry persons or property for a fee
- Parking an auto on or next to the insured's premises if the auto is not owned by, rented to, or loaned to any insured
- Liability assumed under an insured contract for the ownership, maintenance, or use of aircraft or watercraft (but not autos)
- The operation of certain types of equipment attached to autos

The third exception primarily benefits organizations that provide valet parking service. If, for example, a restaurant employee negligently strikes another car while parking a patron's car in the restaurant's parking lot and injures the other car's driver, the restaurant's CGL policy would cover the damage to the other car and the injury to its driver.

Damage to the customer's auto would not be covered by the CGL policy, however, because of exclusion j., which (in part) applies to personal property in the insured's care, custody, or control.

Apply Your Knowledge

A restaurant uses its own employees to provide valet parking to customers. When an employee was parking a customer's auto on its premises, the employee accidentally ran the auto into a pedestrian, who sued the restaurant for her bodily injury resulting from the accident.

Because the restaurant did not have a commercial auto policy, it asked its CGL insurer to cover the claim. Would the Aircraft, Auto or Watercraft exclusion in the restaurant's CGL policy eliminate coverage for the claim against it?

Feedback: No. Although the exclusion applies to bodily injury or property damage arising out of the ownership, maintenance, or use of an auto operated by an insured (in this case, the employee), the exclusion specifically does not eliminate coverage for parking an auto on the named insured's premises, provided the auto is not owned by or rented or loaned to an insured.

Mobile Equipment

Mobile equipment is any of various types of vehicles designed for use principally off public roads, such as bulldozers and cranes. The policy definition of mobile equipment includes a variety of motorized land vehicles and any machinery or equipment attached to them.

The only CGL policy exclusion that specifically applies to mobile equipment is exclusion h., which applies in narrow circumstances. Thus, the CGL form generally covers liability arising out of the ownership, maintenance, or use of mobile equipment.

Exclusion h., the Mobile Equipment exclusion, eliminates coverage for these:

- The transportation of mobile equipment by an auto that is owned, operated, rented, or borrowed by an insured
- The use of mobile equipment in a prearranged racing, speed, or demolition contest or in a stunting activity

The CGL policy's definition of "mobile equipment" is long and complicated. The types of vehicles included in the definition of mobile equipment are summarized in the exhibit. Although most claims involving autos are excluded from CGL policy coverage, claims arising from the operation of mobile equipment are covered as long as they are not excluded by exclusion h.

A recent revision of the CGL form modified the definition of mobile equipment to exclude any land vehicle—even one that otherwise meets the mobile equipment definition—if the vehicle is subject to a compulsory or financial responsibility law or other motor vehicle insurance law where it is licensed or principally garaged. Such vehicles are considered autos. See the exhibit "Types of Vehicles Included in the CGL Form's Definition of Mobile Equipment."

War

Exclusion i., the War exclusion, eliminates coverage for bodily injury or property damage arising, directly or indirectly, out of war in its various forms and other warlike actions. For example, assume that several people are injured because of an act of war that another nation committed against the United States.

The victims later make a liability claim against the owner of the building in which they were injured. The claim alleges that the owner failed to provide suitable means of exit from the building. The War exclusion would preclude coverage for this claim under the building owner's CGL policy.

Types of Vehicles Included in the CGL Form's Definition of Mobile Equipment

Mobile equipment includes these types of land vehicles, including attached equipment:

- Vehicles used primarily off public roads, including bulldozers, farm machinery, and forklifts
- Vehicles used solely on or next to premises owned or rented by the named insured
- Vehicles that travel on crawler treads
- Vehicles maintained primarily to provide mobility to various kinds of construction vehicles and equipment
- Vehicles that do not meet the descriptions in the first four items that are not self-propelled and are maintained primarily to provide mobility to permanently attached equipment such as air compressors, pumps, generators, and devices used to raise or lower workers
- Vehicles that do not meet the descriptions in the first four items that are maintained primarily for purposes other than transportation of persons or cargo

---

[DA07927]

Damage to Property

Exclusion j. eliminates coverage for damage to any of these:

- Property owned, rented, or occupied by the named insured
- Premises the named insured has sold, given away, or abandoned if the damage arises out of any part of such premises
- Property loaned to the named insured
- Personal property in the care, custody, or control of an insured
- That particular part of any real property on which work is being done by the named insured or any contractor or subcontractor working for the named insured if the damage arises from the work
- That particular part of any property that must be restored, repaired, or replaced because the named insured's work was incorrectly performed on it

It is possible to purchase other policies to cover many of the excluded items. The insured's property, excluded by the first listed item, can be insured by commercial property insurance. Property of others in the insured's possession, excluded by the first, third, and fourth items, can be covered by commercial property or inland marine forms.

The second item does not apply to premises that the named insured worked on if they were never occupied, rented, or held for rental by the insured. This exception provides coverage for a builder who constructs a building for sale (without occupying it, renting it, or holding it for rental) and later becomes liable for damage to the building after it has been sold.

The fifth and sixth items often cause confusion. The fifth item excludes only "that particular part" of real property on which the named insured is working. The exclusion does not, therefore, apply to personal property under any circumstances, and it applies only to "that particular part" of real property on which the insured is working.

For example, if the insured is an electrician who is installing electrical components in a building under construction and, while working on an electrical control panel, negligently causes a fire that burns down the entire building, the fifth item will only exclude damage to "that particular part" on which the insured was working.

"That particular part" would presumably be limited to the control panel. Damage to the rest of the building would be covered.

The sixth item applies to "that particular part" of either real property or personal property that must be repaired or replaced because the insured's work on it was done incorrectly. That is, the insurer will not pay the cost of redoing the insured's faulty work. The insurer will, however, pay for damage to property other than "that particular part" that must be redone.

The CGL policy states that the sixth item does not apply to property damage involving completed work projects. Therefore, for the sixth item to apply to a property damage claim, the property damage would need to occur before work on the project was completed or put to its intended use.

An exception to exclusion j. provides limited coverage for property damage (other than damage by fire) to premises, including contents of such premises, rented to the named insured for seven or fewer consecutive days. This coverage is subject to the Damage to Premises Rented to You limit shown in the policy declarations. Fire damage to premises rented to or occupied by the named insured is covered separately by an additional provision discussed subsequently.

Insured's Products and Work

Four CGL policy exclusions (k. through n.) relate directly to the insured's products and work. These exclusions prevent the insurer from having to pay for failures of the insured's products or work—other than bodily injury or damage to property that is not the insured's own product or work. The CGL form contains detailed definitions of "your product" and "your work."

Damage to Your Product

Exclusion k. eliminates coverage for any damage to the insured's product that results from a defect in any part of the product. For example, if defective cabinets manufactured by the insured collapse, the damage to the cabinets would not be covered. However, the insured's CGL policy would cover claims for breakage of the contents of the cabinets, assuming that no other exclusions or conditions eliminated coverage.

Damage to Your Work

Exclusion l. is similar to exclusion k., but it applies to claims for property damage to the insured's work rather than to the insured's products. The exclusion applies only to completed work—not to work that is still being performed when the property damage occurs. (Damage to property being worked on is addressed by exclusion j.)

Exclusion l. does not apply to claims if either the damaged work or the work from which the damage arose was performed for the insured by a subcontractor. For example, assume that defective plumbing caused extensive water damage to a house built by a construction company for the property owner.

If the construction company performed all of the work, including the plumbing, the construction company's CGL policy would exclude any claim based on damage from the faulty plumbing. If, instead, a subcontractor installed the plumbing, then the Damage to Your Work exclusion in the construction company's policy would not apply to claims against it for water damage to the house caused by the plumbing subcontractor's work.

Damage to Impaired Property or Property Not Physically Injured

Exclusion m. eliminates coverage for claims for property damage to "impaired property" or property that has not been physically injured if the damage arises from a defect in the insured's product or work or failure of the insured or anyone acting on behalf of the insured to complete a contract or agreement in accordance with its terms. The form defines impaired property as tangible property, other than the insured's product or work, that cannot be used or is less useful because it includes the insured's defective product or defective work or because the insured has failed to fulfill a contract or agreement.

For example, assume that a manufacturing company manufactures electric motors that are incorporated in drills produced by other companies. If the motors are defective and must be replaced in order for the drills to function properly, the drills would be deemed impaired property. Accordingly, the manufacturing company's CGL policy would not cover claims against it for the loss in value of the drills or for the cost of replacing the motors.

Recall of Products, Work, or Impaired Property

Manufacturers sometimes must recall products that pose a risk of serious injury to users or others. Exclusion n. eliminates coverage for any loss, cost, or expense resulting from loss of use, withdrawal, recall, inspection, repair, replacement, adjustment, removal, or disposal of the insured's product, the insured's work, or impaired property.

Apply Your Knowledge

A steam boiler in an apartment building exploded because of a defect in the boiler. The explosion destroyed the boiler and damaged the apartment building.

The building owner made a claim against the boiler manufacturer for property damage to the boiler and the building. Would the Damage to Your Product exclusion in the manufacturer's CGL policy eliminate coverage for this claim?

Feedback: The Damage to Your Product exclusion in the manufacturer's CGL policy would eliminate coverage only for the damage to the boiler because the exclusion applies only to property damage to "your product," not property damage to other property, such as the apartment building.

Personal and Advertising Injury

To avoid duplication of coverage, the Personal and Advertising Injury exclusion (exclusion o.) eliminates coverage—under Coverage A only—for bodily injury arising out of "personal and advertising injury." Bodily injury resulting from a personal and advertising injury offense (such as bodily injury caused by a security guard's false arrest and detention of a store customer) is covered under Coverage B—Personal and Advertising Injury Liability—of the CGL coverage form.

Electronic Data

The definition of property damage in the CGL is limited to tangible property, and the definition states that electronic data are not considered tangible property.

The Electronic Data exclusion reinforces the property damage definition that electronic data are not considered tangible property. Limited coverage for liability for the electronic data loss exposure can be added by the Electronic Data Liability endorsement (CG 04 37).

Broader coverage can be provided by the Electronic Data Liability Coverage Form (CG 00 65). The exclusion does not apply to liability for damages because of bodily injury.

Recording and Distribution of Material or Information in Violation of Law

The CGL excludes bodily injury or property damage resulting from violation of the Telephone Consumer Protection Act (TCPA); the CAN-SPAM Act of 2003; the Fair Credit Reporting Act; the Fair and Accurate Credit Transactions Act (FACTA); or any other statute, ordinance, or regulation that "addresses, prohibits, or limits the printing, dissemination, disposal, collecting, recording, sending, transmitting, communicating or distribution of material or information."

The TCPA and the CAN-SPAM Act are federal laws that restrict the use of telephones, fax machines, and computers for transmitting unsolicited advertisements or email messages. The exclusion also applies to similar state or local laws. For example, if a company sends an unsolicited electronic communication containing a code that causes damage to the computers of the recipients, coverage for the damage to the computers is excluded.

Fire Legal Liability Coverage

The Coverage A exclusions section concludes with this statement, which provides what is commonly called fire legal liability coverage:

> Exclusions c. through n. do not apply to damage by fire to premises while rented to you or temporarily occupied by you with permission of the owner. A separate limit of insurance applies to this coverage as described in Section III—Limits of Insurance.

For example, assume that the insured occupies, under lease, part of a multitenant building. Assume also that the insured's negligence causes a fire in the insured's own part of the building.

In this case, the insured's liability to the building owner for fire damage would be covered by the fire legal liability coverage in the insured's CGL policy because the exclusion of damage to property rented or occupied by the insured would not apply. This coverage is subject to the Damage to Premises Rented to You limit shown in the policy declarations.

CGL COVERAGE B—PERSONAL AND ADVERTISING INJURY LIABILITY

The Coverage B—Personal and Advertising Injury Liability of the Commercial General Liability (CGL) Coverage Form addresses a variety of loss exposures related to communication and interaction with the public that businesses encounter.

Coverage B of the CGL form insures against claims based on torts such as libel, slander, and wrongful eviction. The provisions relating exclusively to

Coverage B, as with those relating to Coverage A, consist of an insuring agreement and several exclusions.

Coverage B Insuring Agreement

The CGL coverage form's Coverage B insuring agreement parallels the Coverage A insuring agreement: the insurer agrees both to pay those sums that the insured becomes legally obligated to pay as damages and to defend the insured against any suit seeking such damages. However, instead of responding to claims for bodily injury and property damage, Coverage B responds to claims for personal and advertising injury to which the insurance applies. The CGL policy defines personal and advertising injury to include several specific offenses. See the exhibit "CGL Policy Definition of Personal and Advertising Injury."

CGL Policy Definition of Personal and Advertising Injury

"Personal and advertising injury" means injury, including consequential "bodily injury", arising out of one or more of the following offenses:

- False arrest, detention or imprisonment;

- Malicious prosecution;

- The wrongful eviction from, wrongful entry into, or invasion of the right of private occupancy of a room, dwelling or premises that a person occupies, committed by or on behalf of its owner, landlord or lessor;

- Oral or written publication, in any manner, of material that slanders or libels a person or organization or disparages a person's or organization's goods, products or services;

- Oral or written publication, in any manner, of material that violates a person's right of privacy;

- The use of another's advertising idea in your "advertisement"; or

- Infringing upon another's copyright, trade dress* or slogan in your "advertisement".

*The term "trade dress" refers to the overall appearance and image of a product.

The CGL form defines "personal and advertising injury" as injury, including bodily injury, arising out of any of the listed offenses. The CGL form does not define "injury," but, in its usual and ordinary sense, injury has a broad meaning and can include not only bodily injury but also any other type of injury, such as mental anguish, mental injury, fright, shock, humiliation, and loss of reputation.

Courts can award damages for any injury that results from the offenses included in the CGL definition of personal and advertising injury.

To be covered, a personal and advertising injury offense must be committed within the CGL coverage territory. The coverage territory includes worldwide coverage for personal and advertising injury offenses that take place through the Internet or similar electronic means of communication.

This does not mean that the CGL form covers all Internet-related liability for personal and advertising injury liability. In fact, some of the Coverage B exclusions directly exclude certain Internet-related loss exposures.

Under the occurrence CGL coverage form, the coverage trigger for Coverage B is a covered offense committed during the policy period. That is, the policy in effect when the insured committed the offense is the policy that covers any damages resulting from that offense (even if the claim is not made until after the policy has expired).

Apply Your Knowledge

An electrical contracting company is sued by an electrician who applied for a job with the company but was not hired. The electrician alleges that the company engaged in illegal discrimination in not hiring him and is seeking $1 million in damages.

The alleged discrimination occurred in the United States during the current policy period. Assuming that the company is legally liable to pay damages for the alleged wrong and that no Coverage B exclusion applies to the competitor's claim, does this claim meet the conditions for being covered under the Coverage B insuring agreement?

Feedback: No. The only offense alleged against the company is discrimination, and discrimination is not listed in the policy definition of personal and advertising injury. Consequently, the claim does not meet the condition requiring damages to result from personal and advertising injury.

Coverage B Exclusions

As with the Coverage A insuring agreement, the Coverage B insuring agreement is subject to several exclusions that further define the scope of insurance provided by Coverage B. Some of the fifteen Coverage B exclusions—those applying to contractual liability, pollution, and war—are comparable to Coverage A exclusions. The remaining Coverage B exclusions are unique because they relate to the different types of claims covered as personal and advertising injury liability.

Knowing Violation of Rights of Another

This form provides no insurance under Coverage B for injury caused by or at the direction of an insured who had knowledge that the act would violate the rights of another person and inflict personal and advertising injury. The exclusion would apply, for example, if the insured knowingly used a competitor's advertising ideas in his or her own advertisements.

Material Published With Knowledge of Falsity

Injury arising out of oral or written publication of material, if done by or at the direction of the insured with knowledge of its falsity, is excluded under Coverage B. For example, the form excludes coverage if the insured knowingly makes false statements about a competitor.

Material Published Prior to Policy Period

This form excludes under Coverage B any injury arising out of releasing of material whose first publication took place before the beginning of the policy period. For example, an insured's CGL policy with an inception date of January 1, 20X2, would not cover any injury resulting from an advertisement used by the insured from late 20X1 through early 20X2.

Criminal Acts

The Criminal Acts exclusion under Coverage B eliminates coverage for injury arising out of a criminal act committed by or at the direction of the insured.

For example, a suit was filed against the insured after the insured paid an individual to spray-paint defamatory graffiti on a competitor's building. Because spray-painting a building without permission is a criminal act (vandalism), the insured's CGL policy did not cover the suit against the insured for personal or advertising injury resulting from the criminal act.

Contractual Liability

The Contractual Liability exclusion under Coverage B applies to injury for which the insured has assumed liability in a contract or agreement.

This exclusion is subject to only one exception: liability that the insured would have in the absence of the contract or agreement. Unlike the Coverage A Contractual Liability exclusion, this exclusion does not contain an exception for liability assumed under an insured contract.

For example, assume that the insured, a department store owner named Jim, enters into a contract with a provider of security services. In this contract, Jim assumes liability for all personal injury occurring on his store's premises.

After an employee of the security firm detains a customer suspected of shoplifting, the customer sues the security firm for false imprisonment, and the security firm demands that Jim provide a defense. Because of the Contractual Liability exclusion, the insurer denies coverage for this claim.

Breach of Contract

Coverage B excludes injury arising out of a breach of contract. For example, after the insured failed to deliver goods to a buyer in accordance with a sales contract, the buyer alleged injury resulting from the insured's breach of contract. Coverage for this type of claim, even though the claim may have resulted from a fraudulent advertisement declaring that the insured had an abundant supply of the goods, would be eliminated because of the Breach of Contract exclusion.

Quality or Performance of Goods—Failure to Conform to Statements

This exclusion eliminates coverage for injury arising out of the failure of goods, products, or services to conform to any statement of quality or performance made in the named insured's advertisement. There is no insurance under Coverage B, for example, when a buyer of the insured's "wrinkle cream" sues the insured, alleging that the cream did not "eliminate wrinkles," as promised in the insured's advertising.

Wrong Description of Prices

Coverage B does not insure against injury arising out of wrong descriptions of the price of goods, products, or services in the named insured's advertisements.

For example, an insured who is an auto dealer advertises a new car for $3,399 instead of its actual price of $33,999. When the insured refuses to sell the car for the advertised amount, several potential buyers sue for the $30,600 difference between the actual price and the advertised price. No coverage is provided for the claim.

Infringement of Copyright, Patent, Trademark, or Trade Secret

This exclusion eliminates coverage for any injury arising out of the infringement of copyright, patent, trademark, trade secret, or other intellectual property rights. The exclusion does not apply to infringement, in the named insured's advertisement, of copyright, trade dress, or slogan.

Insureds in Media and Internet-Type Businesses

The form provides no insurance under Coverage B for injury committed by an insured whose business is in advertising, broadcasting, publishing, or telecasting; designing or determining the content of websites for others; or providing Internet searches, access, content, or service.

However, this exclusion does not apply to paragraphs a., b., and c. of the CGL policy's definition of personal and advertising injury. Furthermore, the exclusion states that placing frames, borders, links, or advertising material for the named insured or others anywhere on the Internet is not considered the business of advertising, broadcasting, publishing, or telecasting.

Because of this exclusion, organizations that engage in the businesses listed need to obtain special policies covering personal or advertising injury. For example, a publishing company insured under a CGL policy would not be covered under that policy against a suit alleging libelous statements that appear in a book it published.

Electronic Chatrooms or Bulletin Boards

Coverage B excludes injury arising out of an electronic chatroom or bulletin board that the insured hosts, owns, or controls. For instance, the insured, a public-interest group, posted a newspaper editorial on its electronic bulletin board.

The editorial falsely accused a public official of criminal behavior. Because of this exclusion, Coverage B would not protect the insured against a libel suit made by the public official.

Unauthorized Use of Another's Name or Product

This exclusion eliminates coverage for injury arising out of the unauthorized use of another organization's name or product in the named insured's email address, domain name, or metatag, or out of any other similar tactics to mislead the potential customers of another organization. For example, if an organization selects a domain name that is deceptively similar to a principal competitor's name, Coverage B will not apply if the competitor sues for unauthorized use of its name.

Pollution

The Coverage B Pollution exclusion applies to any injury arising out of the actual, alleged, or threatened discharge of pollutants at any time. Unlike the Pollution exclusion under Coverage A, the Coverage B exclusion has no exceptions.

For example, if caustic liquid chemicals and fumes escape because of an accident in a manufacturer's plant, Coverage B will provide no coverage for resulting claims, even if they allege personal or advertising injury.

Pollution-Related

The Pollution-Related exclusion eliminates coverage for any loss, cost, or expense arising out of any request, demand, or order to test for, monitor, or clean up pollutants or out of any claim or suit by or on behalf of a governmental authority for damages because of testing for, monitoring of, or cleaning up pollutants.

War

The War exclusion eliminates coverage for personal and advertising injury arising directly or indirectly out of war in its various forms or warlike actions.

Recording and Distribution of Material or Information in Violation of Law

This exclusion eliminates coverage for bodily injury, property damage, or personal or advertising injury arising directly or indirectly out of any action or omission that violates or is alleged to violate the Telephone Consumer Protection Act, the CAN-SPAM Act of 2003, the Fair Credit Reporting Act and any amendment to that law (including the Fair and Accurate Credit Transaction Act [FACTA]), or any other legislation "that addresses, prohibits or limits the printing, dissemination, disposal, collecting, recording, sending, transmitting, communicating or distribution of material or information."

Apply Your Knowledge

Identify any of the Coverage B exclusions in the CGL that apply to each of these claims:

The insured, a manufacturer, is sued by a competitor who alleges that the insured published an advertisement that infringes upon the competitor's copyright. The competitor does not allege that the insured knowingly infringed.

Because "infringing upon another's copyright" is included in the policy definition of "personal and advertising injury," the insured asks his insurer to pay the claim under Coverage B of its CGL policy.

Feedback: Absent an allegation or evidence that the insured knowingly committed the copyright infringement, none of the Coverage B exclusions apply to this claim.

The insured—the owner of a chain of discount stores—erroneously advertises in newspapers that a certain television model is on sale for $99.99 instead of its actual sale price of $999.99. Because of this error, the store honors the advertised price and sells out its entire stock of the sale model at a net loss of $250,000.

Because the owner views the loss as resulting from "personal and advertising injury," she asks her insurer to pay the claim under Coverage B of the store's CGL policy.

Feedback: The Wrong Description of Prices exclusion applies to this claim.

CGL COVERAGE C—MEDICAL PAYMENTS

Coverage C—Medical Payments of the Commercial General Liability (CGL) Coverage Form pays, on a no-fault basis, the medical expenses of persons who are injured on the insured's premises or as a result of the insured's operations away from the premises.

The medical payments coverage provided by the CGL coverage form's Coverage C is not considered liability insurance, because coverage is provided regardless of whether the insured is legally liable. However, it does provide a modest amount of insurance for settling minor injury cases without requiring determination of liability. Therefore, the coverage provides a means of making prompt settlements, satisfying potential liability claimants, and avoiding possibly larger liability claims.

Coverage C Insuring Agreement

Under the Coverage C insuring agreement, the insurer agrees to pay medical expenses (including, by definition, funeral expenses) for bodily injury caused by an accident. The coverage applies to accidents that occur on premises owned or rented by the insured, including the ways (roads, streets, paths, or passages) adjacent to such premises. The coverage also applies to accidents that occur away from the insured's premises and adjacent ways, but only if the accident results from the named insured's operations.

The accident must also occur in the CGL policy's coverage territory and during the policy period. The medical expenses must be incurred and reported to the insurer within one year after the date of the accident. An injured person who wishes to receive medical payments coverage must agree to be examined by a physician designated by the insurer.

Apply Your Knowledge

A customer at a home improvement store was injured when merchandise accidentally fell from a high storage rack and struck the customer's left foot. The customer was taken by paramedics to a hospital for emergency treatment and was released in satisfactory condition that day. Total medical expenses (for ambulance, medical services, and x-rays) were $2,100. Two weeks later, the customer made a claim under Coverage C of the store's CGL policy. Assuming that the injury occurred in the coverage territory and during the policy period, and that no exclusions or other provisions eliminated coverage for the claim, would the circumstances of the customer's claim meet all of the conditions of the Coverage C insuring agreement? Explain why or why not.

Feedback: Yes. The medical expenses are of the qualifying types, and they resulted from bodily injury caused by an accident on premises owned or rented by the named insured. The expenses were also incurred and reported to the insurer within one year after the accident. As long as the customer submits to medical examination as may be reasonably required by the insurer, the customer's claim will meet all of the conditions of the Coverage C insuring agreement.

Coverage C Exclusions

The CGL policy's medical payments coverage does not apply to bodily injury to these categories of persons:

- Any insured (other than a volunteer worker of the named insured)
- Anyone hired to do work for an insured or for a tenant of an insured
- A person injured on that part of the named insured's premises that the person normally occupies
- A person entitled to workers compensation benefits for the injury
- A person injured while taking part in any physical exercises, games, sports, or athletic contests

Medical payments coverage also does not apply to bodily injury included within the products-completed operations hazard or bodily injury excluded under Coverage A.

Apply Your Knowledge

Roberta, an employee of a warehouse facility, sprained her ankle when she stepped off a forklift on the facility's premises. A visit to the emergency department of a nearby hospital resulted in medical expenses of $850. With her employer's assistance, Roberta made a claim for payment of these expenses under Coverage C—Medical Payments of the facility's CGL form. Identify any Coverage C exclusions in the facility's CGL policy that would apply to Roberta's claim.

Feedback: The exclusion that precludes coverage for any insured would apply to Roberta's claim because Roberta is an employee of the named insured, and employees of the named insured are insureds under the CGL policy. Assuming that Roberta is subject to a workers compensation law, coverage would also be precluded because she is entitled to workers compensation benefits for her injury.

David, a self-employed janitor who is not covered by or subject to a workers compensation or similar law, suffered a deep gash in his hand when he attempted to move a paper cutter while working on the premises of a printing company. Because it was unlikely that the printing company could be held liable for David's injury, David made a claim with the company's CGL insurer under Coverage C—Medical Payments. Identify any Coverage C exclusions in the printing company's CGL policy that would apply to David's claim.

Feedback: The exclusion precluding coverage for anyone hired to do work would apply to David's claim because he had been hired to do work for the named insured.

CGL SUPPLEMENTARY PAYMENTS   skip

The Commercial General Liability (CGL) Coverage Form contains a section, Supplementary Payments—Coverages A and B, that supplements the Coverages A and B insuring agreements.

The CGL policy's supplementary payments section describes specific items that the insurer will pay in addition to damages payable under Coverage A or Coverage B. The supplementary payments are payable in addition to the limits of insurance that apply to the CGL policy's coverage. However, the insurer's obligation to pay these supplementary payments ends as soon as the applicable limit of insurance has been exhausted in paying damages for judgments or settlements.

The supplementary payments consist of these items:

- All expenses incurred by the insurer, such as fees for attorneys, witness fees, the cost of police reports, and similar items. (The payments do not, however, include attorneys' fees or attorneys' expenses taxed against the insured.)

- Up to $250 for the cost of bail bonds required because of accidents or traffic-law violations involving any covered vehicle (typically mobile equipment).

- The cost of bonds to release any property of the insured's held by a plaintiff to ensure payment of any judgment that may be rendered against the insured. The insurer is not required to provide either of the bonds previously described; its only obligation is to pay the premium.

- Reasonable expenses incurred by the insured at the insurer's request, including loss of earnings (up to $250 a day) if the insured must miss work to testify, attend court, or otherwise assist in the defense.

- Court costs or other costs (other than actual damages) assessed against the insured in a suit.

- Interest on judgments awarded against the insured. In some cases, courts will award either **prejudgment interest** or **postjudgment interest**, or both, to a plaintiff.

The supplementary payments section also contains a provision relating to the costs of defending a person or an organization (an indemnitee) that the insured has agreed to hold harmless or indemnify under an insured contract.

Prejudgment interest
Interest that may accrue on damages before a judgment has been rendered.

Postjudgment interest
Interest that may accrue on damages after a judgment has been entered in a court and before the money is paid.

The Contractual Liability exclusion states that any defense costs paid to an indemnitee under an insured contract are payable within the policy limits. In contrast, the supplementary payments section states that the insurer will pay an indemnitee's defense costs in addition to the policy limits if an indemnitee and an insured are both named as parties in the same suit. This applies only if the insured has assumed the obligation to defend the indemnitee under an insured contract and no conflict appears to exist between the interests of the insured and the interests of the indemnitee. Moreover, the indemnitee must cooperate with the insurer in the defense and perform essentially the same duties as any other insured would have to perform. The insurer's duty to defend ends when the insurer has paid the applicable limit of insurance for damages.

Apply Your Knowledge

Carol sued a wholesaler for damages resulting from bodily injury she sustained while visiting the wholesaler's premises. The wholesaler was insured under a CGL policy. The wholesaler's insurer defended against the suit in accordance with the Coverage A insuring agreement in the CGL policy. The court awarded Carol a judgment for $490,000, and the insurer paid the full amount of the judgment because the each occurrence limit of insurance in the wholesaler's CGL policy was $500,000. In addition, the court awarded prejudgment interest of $5,000 against the wholesaler, and the insurer's cost of defending the wholesaler totaled $15,000. How much of these two additional items will the insurer pay in accordance with the supplementary payments provisions in the CGL policy?

Feedback: The wholesaler's insurer will pay the prejudgment interest and defense costs in full, for a total of $20,000. Both of these items are covered as supplementary payments, and they are payable in addition to the limit of insurance.

SUMMARY

The major categories of liability losses covered by general liability insurance are bodily injury and property damage liability and personal and advertising injury liability. Bodily injury and property damage liability can be further categorized as premises and operations and as products and completed operations. General liability policies can also cover medical payments or special loss exposures excluded by the CGL form. A general liability coverage part consists of one or more declarations forms, one or more corresponding coverage forms, and any applicable endorsements. It can be included in a CPP or issued in a monoline policy.

The occurrence version of the Coverage A insuring agreement of the CGL coverage form consists of two distinct insurer promises:

- The promise to pay damages on behalf of the insured
- The promise to defend the insured against claims or suits seeking damages covered under the policy

Coverage A is subject to several exclusions that further define the coverage granted by the Coverage A insuring agreement. Several of the exclusions contain exceptions that allow coverage to apply to certain aspects of exposures that would otherwise be excluded.

Coverage B of the CGL form consists of an insuring agreement and several exclusions. Its coverage insures against claims based on "personal and advertising injury" offenses such as libel, slander, and wrongful eviction.

Coverage C of the CGL policy provides coverage, other than liability insurance, for medical treatment of injuries resulting from minor accidents on the insured's premises or as a result of the insured's operations. Its coverage is subject to several exclusions.

The CGL coverage form's Supplementary Payments—Coverages A and B section describes the specific items that the insurer will pay in addition to damages.

Direct Your Learning ▶▶

7

Commercial General Liability Insurance, Part II

Educational Objectives

After learning the content of this assignment, you should be able to:

▷ Determine whether a described person or organization is an insured under the Commercial General Liability Coverage Form.

▷ Explain how the following limits of insurance in the Commercial General Liability (CGL) Coverage Form are applied:

- Each occurrence limit
- Personal and advertising injury limit
- Damage to premises rented to you limit
- Medical expense limit
- General aggregate limit
- Products-completed operations aggregate limit

▷ Apply the Commercial General Liability Conditions to claims or other interactions between the insurer and the insured.

▷ Explain how the premium for CGL coverage is determined.

▷ Given a case, determine whether, and for what amount, the Commercial General Liability Coverage Form (occurrence version) covers a described claim.

▶▶

Commercial General Liability Insurance, Part II

7

CGL WHO IS AN INSURED PROVISIONS

Because determining whether a party qualifies as an insured is essential to advising a customer or settling a claim, the Commercial General Liability (CGL) Coverage Form's Who Is an Insured section is important because it specifies the parties to whom coverage applies and to whom coverage does not apply.

Section II of the CGL coverage form describes who is an insured. Depending on circumstances, persons or organizations in these three categories qualify as insureds under the CGL policy:

- Named insured and related parties
- Named insured's employees and volunteer workers
- Other persons and organizations

Named Insured and Related Parties

The named insured may be an individual, a partnership, a joint venture, a corporation, a limited liability company (LLC), or a trust, among others.

If the named insured is an individual, his or her spouse is also an insured. However, coverage applies only to claims arising from the conduct of a business owned solely by the named insured. The named insured and spouse are not covered for their nonbusiness activities. Coverage is not provided for any business owned by the unnamed spouse unless that business is named as an insured in the policy.

If the named insured is a partnership or joint venture, the named partnership or joint venture and all partners or members and their spouses also are insureds, but only for liability claims arising out of the conduct of the business of the partnership or joint venture. If the named insured is an LLC, the named company is an insured, as are these persons:

- The controlling members of the company, but only with respect to the conduct of the named insured's business
- The managers of the company, but only with respect to their duties as managers of the named insured

If the named insured is an organization other than a partnership, joint venture, or LLC (for example, a corporation, a school district, a municipality, or an association), then all executive officers, directors, and stockholders are insureds, but only with respect to their liability as officers, directors, or stockholders.

If the named insured is a trust (a legal entity created for the benefit of designated beneficiaries), the named trust is an insured. The named insured's trustees are also insureds, but only with respect to their duties as trustees.

Named Insured's Employees and Volunteer Workers

The named insured's employees and volunteer workers are also insureds for liability claims arising from their duties as such. However, an employee or volunteer worker (other than an executive officer or LLC manager) is not an insured when these situations occur:

- Bodily injury or personal and advertising injury to the named insured, to the named insured's partners or members (if the named insured is a partnership or joint venture), or to a coemployee or other volunteer worker while in the course of his or her duties as such
- Bodily injury or personal and advertising injury arising out of the employee's or volunteer worker's providing or failing to provide professional healthcare services (for example, a nurse employed by the named insured who provides improper medical treatment to a guest visiting the named insured's place of business)
- Property damage to property owned, occupied, used, rented to, or in the care, custody, or control of the named insured, the named insured's employees, volunteer workers, or partners or members

---

Apply Your Knowledge

Hazel, an employee of a business insured under a CGL policy, received third-degree burns at work when Hal, a co-worker, accidentally spilled coffee on Hazel's arm. Hazel sued Hal for damages resulting from her injury. Would Hal be an insured for Hazel's claim under the employer's CGL policy? Explain why or why not.

Feedback: Hal is not an insured for this claim. Even though he is an employee of the named insured, the provision in Who Is an Insured that gives insured status to employees of the named insured also states that no employee is an insured for bodily injury to a co-employee while in the course of his or her employment.

Byron is a volunteer worker for a food bank. While operating a forklift (mobile equipment) outside the food bank's warehouse, Byron accidentally ran into and damaged the car of a donor who had just brought canned goods to the warehouse. The donor (who was not a volunteer worker or an employee of the food bank) sued Byron for the damage to her car. Would Byron be an insured under the food bank's CGL? Explain why or why not.

Feedback: Byron, as a volunteer worker of the named insured, is an insured under Who Is an Insured, and no exclusion contained in Who Is an Insured applies.

Other Persons and Organizations

In addition to the named insured and the named insured's employees, several other persons and organizations, including real estate managers, legal representatives, and newly acquired organizations, are insureds under certain circumstances.

Real Estate Managers

Any person (other than an employee or a volunteer worker) or organization acting as real estate manager for the named insured is an insured. Coverage applies only while the person or organization is serving as real estate manager for the named insured.

Legal Representatives

If the named insured dies, any person or organization having proper temporary custody of the named insured's property is an insured under the CGL until a legal representative is appointed. The coverage for a temporary custodian applies only to liability arising out of the maintenance or use of the property. The appointed legal representative is also an insured, but only with respect to his or her duties as legal representative.

Newly Acquired Organizations

Any subsidiary or affiliated organization of the named insured that is in existence at or before the inception of the CGL policy must be shown in the declarations as a named insured in order to be covered. If the named insured acquires or forms a new organization during the policy period, the new organization qualifies as a named insured and is covered for ninety days after its formation or until the end of the policy period, whichever comes first. This provision does not extend to partnerships, joint ventures, or LLCs that are not named in the policy.

Moreover, Coverage A does not apply to bodily injury or property damage occurring before the organization was acquired or formed, and Coverage B does not apply to personal and advertising injury arising out of any offense committed before the organization was acquired or formed.

Unlisted Partnership, Joint Venture, or LLC— Excluded

Coverage does not apply to the conduct of any current or past partnership, joint venture, or LLC that is not shown as a named insured in the policy declarations. Such entities are covered only if they are specifically declared and named in the policy. The insurer will usually charge an additional premium for covering the added loss exposure.

This provision can present problems for insureds who form temporary partnerships that are dissolved once their purpose is achieved. For example, contractors and construction firms often form joint ventures that are terminated when the construction project for which they were formed is complete. Although the joint venture is terminated, both parties are potentially liable for bodily injury or property damage arising out of the joint venture's construction operations, even after the CGL policy under which the joint venture was insured is no longer in effect. If the contractor's subsequent CGL policies do not specifically declare and name the original joint venture as an insured, the contractor will not be covered for any losses associated with the joint venture's operations.

Individuals who began their businesses as sole proprietors and subsequently incorporated can have problems similar to those encountered by unnamed partnerships or joint ventures. The CGL policy issued in the name of the corporation will not cover the former sole proprietor (who is a current executive officer or director) who is sued in his or her personal capacity as an individual for injury arising out of work completed when the business was a sole proprietorship.

Apply Your Knowledge

Properties, LLC, the owner of several apartment buildings, hired an independent contractor to serve as the LLC's real estate manager. A tenant in one of the apartment buildings sued the real estate manager for damage allegedly caused to some of the tenant's personal property through the real estate manager's negligence. Would the real estate manager be an insured under the LLC's CGL policy? Explain why or why not.

Feedback: The independent contractor, as the LLC's real estate manager, is an insured under Who Is an Insured.

CGL LIMITS OF INSURANCE

The most an insurer will pay for claims is indicated in the limits of insurance shown in the declarations of the Insurance Services Office, Inc. (ISO) Commercial General Liability (CGL) Coverage Form. These limits are applied according to the provisions contained in the Limits of Insurance section of the policy.

The CGL coverage form contains a general aggregate limit and a products-completed operations aggregate limit, along with a limit for each covered occurrence. These limits are the most the insurer will pay, regardless of the number of insureds, suits, claims made, or entities bringing suit.

The dollar amounts of the CGL coverage form's limits are shown in the policy declarations, while provisions under Section III—Limits of Insurance explain how the limits apply. See the exhibit "CGL Limits of Insurance."

Limits and Sublimits

The each occurrence limit is the most the insurer will pay for any one occurrence, regardless of the number of persons insured, the number of claims or lawsuits brought, or the number of persons or organizations making claims, and including all damages under Coverage A and all medical payments under Coverage C. Defense costs do not apply to the each occurrence limit. A commonly used each occurrence limit is $1 million.

Two sublimits subject to the Coverage A each occurrence limit are these:

- Damage to premises rented to you limit—The damage to premises rented to you limit is the most the insurer will pay under Coverage A for damage to any one premises while rented to the named insured or, in the case of fire damage, while rented to or temporarily occupied by the named insured. The basic amount for this limit is $100,000.
- Medical expense limit—The medical expense limit is the most the insurer will pay under Coverage C to any one person. The basic amount for this limit is $5,000.

The personal and advertising injury limit is the most the insurer will pay under Coverage B for damages arising out of personal and advertising injury to any one person or organization. It is usually the same as the policy's each occurrence limit, although a different amount can be used.

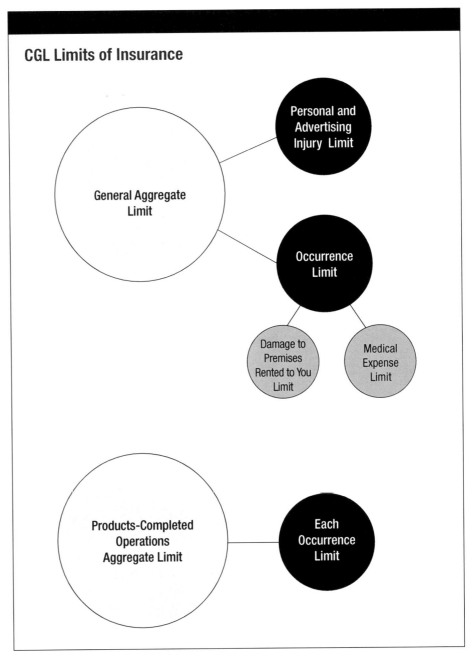

CGL Limits of Insurance

Personal and Advertising Injury Limit

General Aggregate Limit

Occurrence Limit

Damage to Premises Rented to You Limit

Medical Expense Limit

Products-Completed Operations Aggregate Limit

Each Occurrence Limit

[DA07740]

Aggregate limit

The maximum amount an insurer will pay for all covered losses during the covered policy period.

The CGL has two **aggregate limits**, which cap the total amount of damages that the insurer will pay for the entire policy period, although defense costs do not apply:

- General aggregate limit—This limit is the most the insurer will pay for the sum of damages under Coverage A (except those that arise out of the products-completed operations hazard) and Coverage B, and medical expenses under Coverage C.

- Products-completed operations aggregate limit—This limit is the most the insurer will pay under Coverage A for bodily injury or property damage included in the "products-completed operations hazard." The CGL defines this hazard to include bodily injury and property damage occurring away from premises owned or rented by the named insured and arising out of the named insured's product or work.

For example, the insured is an appliance store that sells used appliances that have been repaired by the owner. A customer shopping in the store is burned when she tries out a toaster oven that overheats because of improper repair. The damages paid for this injury would be subject to the general aggregate limit because the product had not left the insured's premises. Another customer purchases a stove and takes it home, where it causes a fire because of improper wiring during the repair. The damage would be subject to the products-completed operations aggregate limit.

Not all insureds have products-completed operations aggregate limits in their CGL policies. Many businesses have only incidental products-completed operations exposures, such as accounting firms, apartment complexes, office buildings, nursing homes, and a variety of other organizations. Any damages paid by an insurer for a products or completed operations liability claim for an insured that does not have a products-completed operations aggregate limit would apply to the policy's general aggregate limit.

Applying the Limits

It is important for insurance professionals to understand and be able to explain to customers that a CGL, unlike some other coverage forms, has annual caps on the amounts that will be paid in addition to caps for each accident.

Apply Your Knowledge

Becky owns a small toy-manufacturing company. She has a CGL with these limits:

- General aggregate limit: $2,000,000
- Products-completed operations aggregate limit: $2,000,000
- Each occurrence limit: $1,000,000
- Personal and advertising injury limit: $1,000,000
- Damage to premises rented to you limit: $100,000
- Medical expense limit: $5,000

All of the events and claims described occur within the same one-year policy period.

Becky leases premises in a factory complex, where the toys are manufactured. One night, an employee tosses a cigarette into a trash can on his way out. A fire starts in the building and spreads to another building in the complex. The damage to the premises Becky leases is $100,000. The damage to the other building, where the fire caused an explosion, is $600,000. Apply the damages to the appropriate limits.

Feedback: The $100,000 damage to the premises Becky leases is applied to the damage to premises rented to you limit, and that limit is now exhausted. The $600,000 damage and the $100,000 damage are applied to the each occurrence limit and are within that limit of $1,000,000. The sum of $700,000 applies to the general aggregate limit, leaving $1,300,000 available.

Becky develops a new toy oven. She leases a store in a mall, where she sells her toys. A fire starts in one of the toy stoves at the store. Three children sustain burns. Their bodily injury claims are $1,000,000. Apply the damages to the appropriate limits.

Feedback: The $1,000,000 damage applies to the each occurrence limit and is within the $1,000,000 limit. The damage also applies to the general aggregate limit. There is $1,300,000 remaining of the general aggregate limit of $2,000,000. After this loss is applied, $300,000 remains.

A second toy oven purchased by a customer catches fire and causes damage to the customer's home and injury to the child playing with the oven. The damages awarded are $600,000. Apply the damages to the appropriate limits.

Feedback: The $600,000 damage applies to the products-completed operations limit. The amount of the damages is within the each occurrence limit of $1,000,000. The products-completed operations aggregate limit is reduced by $600,000, and $1,400,000 remains.

The manager of Becky's store detained a customer, who was shopping with her child, for suspected shoplifting. The child was injured in the process. No evidence was found to support the allegation, and the customer sued the store. The damages awarded were $250,000 for the child's injury and $100,000 for the false detention. Apply the damages to the appropriate limits.

Feedback: The $350,000 applies to the personal and advertising injury limit. This is within the each occurrence limit for personal and advertising injury. However, the damages also apply to the general aggregate limit. Only $300,000 remains of the general aggregate limit. Therefore, $50,000 will be Becky's responsibility.

CGL CONDITIONS

Section IV—Commercial General Liability Conditions of the Commercial General Liability (CGL) Coverage Form establishes standards and procedures to which an insured and insurer must adhere during the claims process and other interactions.

CGL conditions are vitally important when a claim occurs, because the failure of an insured to act in accordance with the conditions can invalidate coverage for an otherwise-covered claim. Besides obligating the insured to perform certain duties in the event of a loss, the conditions also contain several provisions that govern insurer conduct and delineate how coverage is determined if more than one policy covers a claim. This discussion focuses on the conditions described in Section IV of the CGL coverage form, which work in tandem with the Common Policy Conditions that are attached to every commercial package policy or monoline CGL policy.

Bankruptcy

The Bankruptcy condition establishes that the bankruptcy or insolvency of an insured (or of the insured's estate) will not relieve the insurer of any of its policy obligations. The insurer remains obligated to defend the insured and pay judgments or settlements as though the insured had remained solvent.

Duties in the Event of Occurrence, Offense, Claim or Suit

If the insured does not perform the duties required by the Duties in the Event of Occurrence, Offense, Claim or Suit condition, the insurer may be relieved of its duty to defend and pay claims. Thus, the insured must understand and fulfill these duties.

Whenever the named insured becomes aware of an occurrence or an offense that may result in a claim, notice must be given to the insurer as soon as practicable. The notice may be either oral or written, and it should include, to the extent possible, this information:

• How, when, and where the occurrence or the offense took place
• The names and addresses of any injured persons and any witnesses
• The nature and location of any damage or injury resulting from the occurrence or offense

When a claim or suit is brought against any insured, the named insured must take these actions:

• Immediately record the details of the claim or suit and the date received
• Notify the insurer in writing as soon as practicable

Skip
7.12 - 7.27

The named insured (or any other insured involved in a claim or suit) is then required to perform these duties:

- Immediately forward to the insurer copies of any legal papers (such as a demand or a summons) received in connection with the claim or suit

- Authorize the insurer to obtain any legal records or other documents

- Cooperate with the insurer in the investigation or settlement of the claim or in the insurer's defense against the suit

- Assist the insurer (if requested) in any action against any third party that may be liable to the insured because of the injuries or damage for which claim is made

Finally, the condition states that no insured may make voluntary payment, assume any obligation, or incur any expense without the insurer's consent. Any voluntary payments made by an insured or expenses incurred by an insured without the insurer's consent must be paid by the insured. The only exception is that the insured may incur expenses for first aid at the time of the occurrence.

Legal Action Against Us

The Legal Action Against Us condition provides that no person or organization can bring the insurer into any suit seeking damages from an insured. Insurers believe that a suit that includes an insurer as a defendant may encourage a jury to award higher damages or to award damages in cases where damages would not be awarded otherwise. (Some states permit third-party claimants to sue insurers directly, regardless of this provision.)

The condition also states that no person or organization can bring suit to enforce the CGL policy coverage part unless that party has fully complied with all policy conditions. For example, the insured could not sue the insurer to force it to pay a third-party claim unless the insured had first forwarded all legal papers to the insurer, cooperated in the defense, and so forth.

Other Insurance

The CGL policy's Other Insurance condition explains the determination of the amount the insurer is obligated to pay on a claim if the insured has other insurance that also covers the claim. For the purposes of this condition, all applicable coverages are classified as either primary insurance or excess insurance. Primary insurance pays a covered claim from the first dollar, subject to any deductible that might apply. Excess insurance covers the part of the claim that exceeds the primary coverage's limit, up to its own, separate limit. For large risks, additional "layers" of excess insurance may apply above the first excess layer. For example, a small to mid-size account might have a primary CGL policy with a $1,000,000 each occurrence limit and an excess liability policy (often called an umbrella liability policy) with a limit of $5,000,000.

If a claimant obtains a judgment of $1,250,000 against the insured for bodily injury covered by the primary policy, the primary policy will pay the judgment up to its limit of $1,000,000, and the excess policy will pay the remaining $250,000.

Because more than one policy can cover a particular claim, the CGL contains detailed rules for determining which policy is primary, which policy is excess, and how losses will be shared when two or more policies are all excess or all primary.

When CGL Is Primary

The CGL policy's Other Insurance condition stipulates that the CGL policy's coverage is considered primary insurance unless there is other applicable insurance that meets any of the criteria that define excess insurance in paragraph b. of the condition. If the CGL policy is considered primary insurance, the insurer must meet all of its obligations under the policy—unless there is other insurance that is also primary, in which case the claim payment will be shared by the primary insurers as discussed subsequently.

When CGL Is Excess

Paragraph b. of the Other Insurance condition states that the CGL policy's coverage is excess insurance if the other insurance is any of these types:

- Fire, extended coverage, builders risk, installation risk, or similar coverage on the named insured's work
- Fire insurance on premises rented to the named insured or that the named insured temporarily occupies with the owner's permission
- Insurance that the named insured purchases to cover its liability as a tenant for damage to premises rented to the named insured or temporarily occupied by the named insured with the owner's permission
- Aircraft, auto, or watercraft coverage
- Any primary insurance available to the named insured covering liability for damages arising out of premises or operations, or out of products and completed operations, for which the named insured has been added as an additional insured

If the CGL policy's coverage is excess, the insurer has no obligation under Coverages A or B to provide defense for any claim or suit against which another insurer has a duty to defend. However, if no other insurer provides defense, the excess CGL insurer will do so.

Methods of Sharing

If two or more policies apply at the same level, either primary or excess, the policy provides for two methods of sharing: contribution by equal shares and contribution by limits. If all applicable policies permit contribution by equal shares, that method is used. Otherwise, contribution by limits is used.

Contribution by equal shares is one method of sharing loss when two or more policies apply. Each insurer pays an equal amount until the claim is fully paid or until one insurer exhausts its limit, in which case the other insurer pays the remainder of the claim (up to its limit).

Assume, for example, that a manufacturing company has two liability claims arising from separate occurrences and that these claims are covered under two of the company's primary liability policies. These are the applicable each occurrence limits of insurance for the two policies:

Insurer	Limit
A	$500,000
B	$1,000,000

For a claim of $300,000, each insurer would contribute $150,000. That amount would cover the claim in full and is within the limits of both policies. A claim of $1,200,000 would be distributed in two stages. First, each insurer would contribute $500,000, equal to Insurer A's limit. Since Insurer B has not exhausted its limit, it would contribute an additional $200,000 to cover the rest of the claim.

Contribution by limits is another method of sharing loss when two or more policies apply. Each insurer pays that proportion of the claim that the insurer's limit bears to the total of all applicable insurance. However, no insurer pays more than its applicable limit of insurance.

In the previous example, Insurer A's limit ($500,000) is one-third of the total applicable limits of both policies ($1,500,000). Consequently, Insurer A would pay one-third of each claim, but not more than its limit of $500,000. Insurer B's limit ($1,000,000) is two-thirds of the total applicable limits. Thus, Insurer B would pay two-thirds of any claim, but not more than its limit. Using the contribution by limits method, the two claims against the company would be distributed in this fashion:

Insurer	$300,000 Claim	$1,200,000 Claim
A	$100,000	$400,000
B	$200,000	$800,000

Note that Insurer A paid less when the claims were shared using contribution by limits. As a general rule, the contribution by equal shares method is more advantageous to the insurer with the higher limits, and the contribution by limits method is more advantageous to the insurer with the lower limits.

Premium Audit

CGL policies are often issued with estimated premiums. The final premium is determined after the policy has expired, based on the insured's payroll, sales, or some other premium base that cannot precisely be determined at the policy inception. The Premium Audit condition requires the named insured to keep adequate records to permit correct calculation of the premium and to make such records available to the insurer on request. The named insured must promptly pay for any additional premiums resulting from the audit. If the audit shows the earned premium to be less than the original estimate, the insurer is obligated to return the excess to the named insured, subject to any policy minimum premium.

Representations

The CGL policy's Representations condition states that the named insured, by accepting the policy, agrees to these:

- The statements in the declarations are accurate and complete.
- The statements in the declarations are based on representations made by the named insured to the insurer.
- The insurer has issued the policy in reliance on the named insured's representations.

This condition places a heavy burden on the named insureds to read the policy declarations and ensure that the representations are accurate.

Separation of Insureds

The Separation of Insureds condition states that the insurance provided by the policy applies separately to each person insured. This condition can benefit an insured under certain circumstances.

For example, the policy should not provide any coverage if one insured intentionally injures a third party (unless the injury is inflicted with reasonable force to protect a person or property from harm). However, this condition stipulates that the policy would still provide coverage for any other insured (such as an employer or partner) that may be liable for the injury. An employer or partner could be held vicariously liable because they are assumed to have some level of control over the person causing the injury, even though they did not personally cause the injury. Also, if one insured sues another insured, coverage is still provided for the insured who has been sued, subject to the other conditions and exclusions of the policy.

The condition is subject to two restrictions. First, the limits of insurance apply to all persons insured and are not increased because two or more persons are insured. Second, any rights or duties specifically assigned to the first named insured are not applicable to any other insured.

Transfer of Rights of Recovery Against Others to Us

Known as a subrogation provision in earlier policies, the Transfer of Rights of Recovery Against Others to Us condition stipulates that when the insured has rights to recover all or any part of a claim paid by the insurer from any third party, it must transfer those rights to the insurer. The insured must not impair these rights, and, upon the insurer's request, must assist the insurer in any reasonable manner to enforce them.

When We Do Not Renew

If the insurer opts not to renew the policy, the When We Do Not Renew condition requires it to give written notice of nonrenewal to the first named insured at least thirty days before the expiration date of the policy. If a state has a law or regulation that requires a notification period other than thirty days, the law or regulation will take precedence over this policy provision.

Apply Your Knowledge

A company is insured under two CGL policies, both of which are considered primary insurance. The each occurrence limit under Policy A is $500,000. Under Policy B, the each occurrence limit is $2,000,000. The company was held to be legally liable for $1,000,000 in damages arising from one occurrence. Under the contribution by equal shares method, how much would each insurer contribute to fulfill the claim?

Feedback: Under the contribution by equal shares method, each insurer pays an equal amount until the claim is fully paid or until one insurer exhausts its limit. Therefore, each insurer in this case would pay half of the $1,000,000 claim, or $500,000, an amount that does not exceed either insurer's limit.

Given the same set of circumstances as in the previous question, how much would each insurer contribute to fulfill the claim under the contributions by limits method?

Feedback: Under the contribution by limits method, each insurer pays the proportion of the claim that the insurer's limit bears to the total of all applicable insurance. In this case, the total of all applicable insurance is $2,500,000 (the sum of the two limits). Policy A's limit of $500,000 is 20 percent of the total limit of $2,500,000. Policy B's limit of $2,000,000 is 80 percent of the total limit of $2,500,000. Therefore, Insurer A will pay 20 percent of the claim—but not more than its limit of $500,000. Twenty percent of the $1,000,000 claim is $200,000. Insurer B will pay 80 percent of the claim, but not more than its limit of $2,000,000. Eighty percent of the $1,000,000 claim is $800,000.

RATING CGL COVERAGE

Most insurance professionals are not responsible for premium calculation. Nevertheless, understanding the basic procedure used to determine commercial general liability (CGL) premiums can be useful to those who work in commercial insurance.

The premium for a CGL coverage form is determined using a basic formula to calculate both a premises-operations premium and a products-completed operations premium, which are then combined. The premium could also be affected by other factors. For example, the premium is increased if the basic limits of insurance are increased, and the premium is reduced if a coverage is omitted from the coverage form.

CGL Rating Formula

The basic formula used to determine the premium for a CGL policy is this:

$$\text{Rate} \times \text{Exposure} = \text{Premium}$$

The rate, a reflection of the organization's susceptibility to liability losses, depends on the classification of the insured organization's operations. The exposure is a measure of the size of the business operations to be insured, not the type of losses to which the business is susceptible. For example, because of its production volume, a manufacturer that produces 1 million toys a year is more likely to be sued for products liability than one that produces 50,000 similar toys a year. Such differences are reflected in the exposure, which is expressed in terms of the **premium base**.

Premium base
The unit in which the exposure is measured, such as gross sales or payroll.

CGL Rates for Business Classifications

An insurer that writes CGL insurance develops a rate for each business classification that it is willing to insure. The classifications tied to these rates are listed in the classification table of the Insurance Services Office (ISO) *Commercial Lines Manual*. The classification table lists more than 1,000 types of operations, ranging from abrasive wheel manufacturing to zoos. Each is assigned an identification number called a **class code**. More than one class code may apply to an organization whose business operations involve two or more separately described classifications. These two CGL rates apply for most classifications:

Class code
A numeric code representing the description in the rating classification table that best fits a particular organization's operations.

- A premises-operations rate
- A products-completed operations rate

For organizations having little or no risk of incurring products-completed operations liability losses (such as photo finishing labs or florists), only a premises-operations rate is used. The small cost of providing products liability coverage for such insureds is included in their premises-operations rate.

Premium Base

The premium base used in rating CGL coverage for any given business is also indicated in the classification table. In general, similar organizations have the same premium bases:

- Mercantile businesses (retail stores, for example) are rated using a premium base of gross sales.

- Contracting businesses are rated on the basis of payroll.

- Building and premises risks (apartments, hotels, and offices) may be rated on the basis of area, gross sales, or the number of units in the building.

- Special events (concerts, sporting events, exhibitions, and so on) may be rated on the number of admissions.

Once the premium base to be used in the rating of a particular policy is known, information about the organization must be gathered carefully and completely in order to measure the exposure accurately. Specific rules govern what is and is not to be included in any of the exposures used to rate CGL insurance.

The actual premium for a CGL policy is often calculated at the end of the policy period after the exposure can be determined accurately. That premium is then reconciled with the estimated premium the insured paid at the beginning of the policy period.

Other Rating Considerations

Depending on the coverage choices the insured has made, other factors may contribute to CGL premium determination. An increased limits factor (a number, such as 1.35, by which the rate is multiplied) is used to generate higher premiums for policies written with coverage amounts greater than the basic limits. If the insured has chosen not to buy or the underwriter is unwilling to provide certain coverages included automatically in the CGL form—for instance, personal and advertising injury, medical payments, or fire legal liability—it receives premium credits. Any coverages added to the CGL form by endorsement will entail charges that increase the premium. Coverage can be written subject to a deductible, which reduces the premium.

Reality Check

CGL Rating Procedure

The CGL rating procedure can be illustrated by a hypothetical example in which a florist's CGL premium is determined. The insurer classifies the florist with class code 12841 from the ISO *Commercial Lines Manual*, indicating "Florists." The premium base for this class is gross sales, with products-completed operations included.

The exposure to measure this premium base is expressed in thousands of dollars. For example, if the florist's most recent annual gross sales totaled $1.6 million, its exposure for rating purposes is 1,600. Suppose the insurer has developed a rate of $1.20 for class code 12841. (Only one rate is used because the insured has one of the classifications that is charged only a premises-operations premium. Products-completed operations coverage is included in that rate.) The premium for the florist's CGL policy is calculated as $1.20 (rate) × 1,600 (exposure) = $1,920. This premium could be modified by the application of higher limits, coverage restrictions, or a deductible.

[DA07850]

DETERMINING WHETHER THE CGL COVERS A CLAIMS CASE

Knowing how to apply the Commercial General Liability (CGL) Coverage Form to the facts of a case is an important skill. This case study will help you make the transition from knowing policy language to applying policy language to losses to determine whether coverage applies. As you progress through this case study, you can check your understanding of the coverage provided by answering the Knowledge to Action questions.

Case Facts

Diana is the sole proprietor of a bakery, Diana's Bakery, that occupied the first floor of a two-story building owned by a real estate agency. The agency used the second floor for its office, while leasing the first floor to Diana. One afternoon in June 20X2, as Diana was caramelizing sugar on a crème brûlée with a small blowtorch, she unwittingly used the open flame too close to a stack of paper bags. The blowtorch ignited the paper bags, causing a fire that quickly grew out of control and destroyed the building and the business personal property of the bakery and the realtor. Diana and her employees, as well as the employees of the upstairs office, escaped uninjured, but a customer of the real estate agency was seriously injured when he tripped and fell down the stairs while evacuating the building.

The real estate agency made a claim against Diana for the loss of its building and business personal property. The injured customer made a claim against

Diana for his bodily injury. Diana submitted a claim to her CGL insurer to pay for the damage to her business personal property. The insurer determined that Diana was legally liable for all of the damages claimed by the real estate agency and its customer. Therefore, if the insurer also determines that the claims are covered under the CGL, it will settle the claims out of court, thus avoiding any legal fees or defense costs. See the exhibit "Damages."

Damages

Item	Damages
Property damage to Diana's business personal property	$60,000
Property damage to bakery premises (building only)	$150,000
Property damage to remainder of building	$200,000
Property damage to realtor's business personal property	$75,000
Bodily injury to the agency's customer	$500,000

[DA07929]

Diana's Bakery is covered under a CGL policy (occurrence version) with no deductible and no endorsements. Diana does not have any other commercial insurance covering her bakery operations or the building and her business personal property. Given the facts presented in the case, and assuming that no claims were made under Coverage C—Medical Payments, will Diana's CGL policy cover her against the claims made by the real estate agency and its injured customer? If so, what amount will the insurer pay for the claims? When answering the questions in this case-based activity, consider only the information provided as part of this case.

Necessary Reference Materials

To determine whether the CGL policy provides coverage for the losses incurred as a result of the fire, you need to consult the relevant portions of the declarations page and any policy provisions that apply to the loss.

Overview of Steps

When examining the policy forms to determine whether coverage applies to a loss, you can apply the four steps of the DICE method. Next, you can determine the amounts payable for the loss under the applicable policy. Doing this involves applying the limits of insurance and any other relevant provisions that apply. It also involves determining whether more than one policy provides coverage for the same loss. In this case, more than one policy does not apply.

Determination of Coverage

Determining whether the CGL policy applies to this loss involves analyzing the relevant portions of the policy and determining whether any information found at each step in the DICE process precludes coverage at the time of the loss. You should also examine other categories of policy provisions such as the insured's duties, general provisions, endorsements (if applicable), and terms defined in the policy in relation to the declarations, insuring agreement, conditions, and exclusions.

DICE Analysis Step 1: Declarations

The first DICE step is to review the declarations page. In this case, the review will determine whether Diana's Bakery was covered by the CGL policy at the time of the fire. See the exhibit "Excerpt of Declarations Page."

Excerpt of Declarations Page

POLICY NUMBER:

COMMERCIAL GENERAL LIABILITY
CG DS 01 10 01

COMMERCIAL GENERAL LIABILITY DECLARATIONS

COMPANY NAME AREA	PRODUCER NAME AREA

NAMED INSURED: Diana Smith, DBA Diana's Bakery
MAILING ADDRESS: 1 Main St.
Workingtown, PA 19000
POLICY PERIOD: FROM 10/1/20X1 TO 10/1/20X2 AT 12:01 A.M. TIME AT YOUR MAILING ADDRESS SHOWN ABOVE

IN RETURN FOR THE PAYMENT OF THE PREMIUM, AND SUBJECT TO ALL THE TERMS OF THIS POLICY, WE AGREE WITH YOU TO PROVIDE THE INSURANCE AS STATED IN THIS POLICY.

LIMITS OF INSURANCE		
EACH OCCURRENCE LIMIT	$ 1,000,000	
DAMAGE TO PREMISES RENTED TO YOU LIMIT	$ 100,000	Any one premises
MEDICAL EXPENSE LIMIT	$ 5,000	Any one person
PERSONAL & ADVERTISING INJURY LIMIT	$ 1,000,000	Any one person or organization
GENERAL AGGREGATE LIMIT	$ 2,000,000	
PRODUCTS/COMPLETED OPERATIONS AGGREGATE LIMIT	$ 2,000,000	

CG DS 01 10 01 © ISO Properties, Inc., 2000 Page 1 of 3

Knowledge to Action

Action Task: Review the relevant portion of the declarations in Diana's Bakery's policy.

According to your analysis of the excerpt of the declarations page, is coverage applicable for Diana's Bakery during the coverage period?

Feedback: The declarations page confirms that Diana, doing business as Diana's Bakery, is the named insured. The loss occurred during the policy period.

DICE Analysis Step 2: Insuring Agreement

The second DICE step is to review the CGL coverage form's three insuring agreements to determine whether any of them apply to the described claims. Because all the claims were for bodily injury or property damage, Coverage A—Bodily Injury and Property Damage Liability is the insuring agreement that needs to be considered. Coverage B applies only to personal and advertising injury, and (as stated previously) no claims were made under Coverage C—Medical Payments. In this case, you must determine whether each of the five consequences of the fire listed in the Damages exhibit meets the conditions imposed by the CGL policy's Coverage A insuring agreement:

1. Insuring Agreement

a. We will pay those sums that the insured becomes legally obligated to pay as damages because of "bodily injury" or "property damage" to which this insurance applies. We will have the right and duty to defend the insured against any "suit" seeking those damages. However, we will have no duty to defend the insured against any "suit" seeking damages for "bodily injury" or "property damage" to which this insurance does not apply. We may, at our discretion, investigate any "occurrence" and settle any claim or "suit" that may result. But:

(1) The amount we will pay for damages is limited as described in Section III—Limits Of Insurance; and

(2) Our right and duty to defend ends when we have used up the applicable limit of insurance in the payment of judgments or settlements under Coverages A or B or medical expenses under Coverage C.

No other obligation or liability to pay sums or perform acts or services is covered unless explicitly provided for under Supplementary Payments—Coverages A and B.

b. This insurance applies to "bodily injury" and "property damage" only if:

(1) The "bodily injury" or "property damage" is caused by an "occurrence" that takes place in the "coverage territory";

(2) The "bodily injury" or "property damage" occurs during the policy period; and

(3) Prior to the policy period, no insured listed under Paragraph 1. of Section II—Who Is An Insured and no "employee" authorized by you to give or receive notice of an "occurrence" or claim, knew that the "bodily injury" or "property damage" had occurred, in whole or

in part. If such a listed insured or authorized "employee" knew, prior to the policy period, that the "bodily injury" or "property damage" occurred, then any continuation, change or resumption of such "bodily injury" or "property damage" during or after the policy period will be deemed to have been known prior to the policy period.

c. "Bodily injury" or "property damage" which occurs during the policy period and was not, prior to the policy period, known to have occurred by any insured listed under Paragraph 1. of Section II—Who Is An Insured or any "employee" authorized by you to give or receive notice of an "occurrence" or claim, includes any continuation, change or resumption of that "bodily injury" or "property damage" after the end of the policy period.

d. "Bodily injury" or "property damage" will be deemed to have been known to have occurred at the earliest time when any insured listed under Paragraph 1. of Section II—Who Is An Insured or any "employee" authorized by you to give or receive notice of an "occurrence" or claim:

(1) Reports all, or any part, of the "bodily injury" or "property damage" to us or any other insurer;

(2) Receives a written or verbal demand or claim for damages because of the "bodily injury" or "property damage"; or

(3) Becomes aware by any other means that "bodily injury" or "property damage" has occurred or has begun to occur.

Knowledge to Action

Action Task: Review the relevant portions of the CGL Coverage A insuring agreement.

According to your analysis of the CGL Coverage A insuring agreement, do the losses described in the Damages exhibit satisfy the requirements of the Coverage A insuring agreement?

Feedback: All of the consequences satisfy most of the requirements of the Coverage A insuring agreement. All of the claims were for bodily injury or property damage that was caused by an occurrence (the fire) that took place in the coverage territory, and the bodily injury or property damage occurred during the policy period.

However, the damage to Diana's business personal property does not satisfy the requirement that the insured must be "legally obligated to pay damages," because Diana cannot be held legally liable to herself for damage to her own property. Therefore, this consequence is not covered.

The insurer considered Diana to be legally liable for all the other consequences of the fire. Therefore, the claims made against Diana for these consequences satisfy all of the requirements of the Coverage A insuring agreement except, perhaps, the requirement that there must be bodily injury or property damage "to which this insurance applies," because an exclusion or condition could eliminate coverage. The conditions and exclusions will be considered in steps 3 and 4.

DICE Analysis Step 3: Conditions

The third DICE step is to review the policy conditions to determine whether they preclude coverage at the time of the loss. None of the conditions in Section IV—Commercial General Liability Conditions would preclude coverage in this case. Diana performed all the duties in the event of occurrence or claim (such as reporting the occurrence promptly and cooperating with the insurer's investigation), and she did not make any misrepresentations that would have voided coverage.

DICE Analysis Step 4: Exclusions

The fourth DICE step is to determine whether any exclusions affect coverage. In this case, you must determine whether coverage for losses related to any of the consequences of the fire listed in the Damages exhibit would be precluded by any of the CGL Coverage A exclusions.

The first listed consequence involves the bakery's destroyed business personal property. The analysis of the insuring agreement indicated that one cannot be held legally liable to pay damages to oneself, thereby eliminating coverage for this consequence. The Damage to Property exclusion reinforces the insurer's denial of coverage for damage to the insured's own property:

j. Damage To Property

(1) Property you own, rent, or occupy, including any costs or expenses incurred by you, or any other person, organization or entity, for repair, replacement, enhancement, restoration or maintenance of such property for any reason, including prevention of injury to a person or damage to another's property;

Knowledge to Action

Action Task: Refer to the Damage to Property exclusion.

According to your analysis of the Damage to Property exclusion, would this exclusion also eliminate coverage for the property damage to the part of the building occupied by Diana's Bakery?

Feedback: The Damage to Property exclusion excludes property damage to property rented or occupied by the named insured. Therefore, this exclusion, read in isolation from other policy provisions, would seem to eliminate coverage for property damage to the part of the building occupied by Diana's Bakery. However, an exception, found at the end of the Coverage A exclusions, applies.

Because of this exception, the Damage to Property exclusion would not apply to the fire damage to the part of the building rented to Diana's Bakery:

Exclusions c. through n. do not apply to damage by fire to premises while rented to you or temporarily occupied by you with permission of the owner. A separate limit of insurance applies to this coverage as described in Section III—Limits of Insurance.

None of the CGL Coverage A exclusions apply to the real estate agency's claim for damage to the rest of its building and its business personal property.

Similarly, none of the exclusions apply to the bodily injury claim made by the real estate agency's customer.

Determination of Amounts Payable

Now that you have completed the DICE analysis, you can determine the amounts payable. Doing this involves applying the limits of insurance available to pay for the loss and any applicable deductibles and conditions. In this case, the DICE analysis has revealed that four of the five consequences of the bakery fire listed in the Damages exhibit are covered under the bakery's CGL policy. To calculate the amount payable for each of these items, you must first apply the applicable limits of insurance.

Knowledge to Action

Action Task: Review the relevant portion of the declarations page to determine the limits of insurance that will be used to calculate the amount payable.

According to your analysis of the declarations page, what are the relevant policy limits that will be used to calculate coverage?

Feedback: The limits shown on the declarations page will apply to the amount payable for the covered consequences in this way:

- Property damage to bakery premises—The $100,000 limit on damage to premises rented to the named insured applies to this consequence of the fire, as well as the $1,000,000 each occurrence limit.

- Property damage to remainder of building—The $1,000,000 each occurrence limit applies to this consequence of the fire.

- Realtor's business personal property—The $1,000,000 each occurrence limit applies to this consequence of the fire.

- Bodily injury to realtor's customer—The $1,000,000 each occurrence limit applies to this consequence of the fire.

Action Task: Review the Damages exhibit to determine the amount claimed for each of the consequences of the fire. (There are no "other insurance" issues that would need to be resolved by applying the Other Insurance condition.)

Given the information you have thus far, what is the amount payable for each of the consequences of the fire? See the exhibit "Determination of Amounts Payable."

Determination of Amounts Payable

Item	Damages	Amount Payable
Property damage to Diana's business personal property	$60,000	$0
Property damage to bakery premises (building only)	$150,000	$100,000
Property damage to remainder of building	$200,000	$200,000
Property damage to realtor's business personal property	$75,000	$75,000
Bodily injury to agency's customer	$500,000	$500,000
Sub-Total		$875,000
Total Amount Payable After Application of $1,000,000 Each Occurrence Limit		$875,000

[DA07931]

Both of the liability claims against Diana were covered by her CGL policy, but she was not indemnified for the full amount of the damage to her rented premises. She could have prevented this problem by having the $100,000 Damage to Premises Rented to You limit increased to an adequate amount. Her CGL policy also didn't cover the loss of her own business personal property, which she could have covered with commercial property insurance.

SUMMARY

In addition to the named insured, various other persons and organizations may also be insured under the CGL coverage form. These other insureds include (but are not limited to) spouses of individual named insureds, employees and volunteer workers of the named insured, the named insured's real estate manager or legal representative, and organizations newly acquired by the named insured.

In order to assist customers in their purchase of commercial liability insurance, it is important to understand the CGL limits and how they apply. Customers should carefully evaluate their CGL loss exposures when they make decisions regarding the limits of insurance that are available to their organizations.

The conditions included in the CGL coverage form relate to bankruptcy of the insured, the insured's duties in the event of loss, legal action against the insurer, other insurance, premium audits, representations, separation of insureds, subrogation, and the insurer's duties when it does not renew the policy.

A CGL policy's premium is a product of the insured's CGL rate, the insured's exposure (the premium base), and other considerations.

Determining whether, and for what amount, the occurrence version of the CGL coverage form covers a described claim requires analysis of the declarations page to confirm that coverage applies to the loss, the CGL coverage form's three insuring agreements to determine whether any of them apply to the described claims, the policy conditions to determine whether they preclude coverage at the time of the loss, and any exclusions to determine if they affect coverage. Any applicable deductibles and limits must be incorporated into the calculation of the amounts payable for the claim.

8

Commercial Auto Insurance

Educational Objectives

After learning the content of this assignment, you should be able to:

▷ Describe commercial auto insurance in terms of these elements:

- The loss exposures that can be covered
- The components of a commercial auto coverage part

▷ Select the symbols needed to provide a described organization with appropriate commercial auto coverage(s) under the Business Auto Coverage Form.

▷ Summarize the provisions contained in Section II—Covered Autos Liability Coverage of the Business Auto Coverage Form.

▷ Summarize the provisions contained in Section III—Physical Damage of the Business Auto Coverage Form.

▷ Describe the conditions contained in the Business Auto Coverage Form.

▷ Describe the following coverages that may be added by endorsement to the Business Auto Coverage Form:

- Medical payments
- Personal injury protection and added personal injury protection
- Uninsured and underinsured motorists

▷ Explain how the following are rated for commercial auto coverage:

- Private passenger vehicles
- Trucks, tractors, and trailers

▷ Given a case, determine whether, and for what amount, the Business Auto Coverage Form covers a described claim.

Commercial Auto Insurance

8

OVERVIEW OF COMMERCIAL AUTO INSURANCE

Before studying commercial auto coverage forms or endorsements, it is helpful to understand commercial auto loss exposures and the components of a commercial auto coverage part.

Commercial auto insurance can be used to cover liability loss exposures, property loss exposures, and personal loss exposures arising out of the ownership, maintenance, or use of autos. A common format for insuring these loss exposures is the commercial auto coverage part of Insurance Services Office, Inc. (ISO). A commercial auto coverage part consists of an appropriate declarations form, a coverage form, and any applicable endorsements. ISO commercial auto coverage forms include the Business Auto Coverage Form, the Auto Dealers Coverage Form, and the Motor Carrier Coverage Form.

Commercial Auto Loss Exposures

The ownership, maintenance, or use of autos creates liability loss exposures, property loss exposures, and personal loss exposures.

Liability Loss Exposures

Because liability arises from the use of owned, hired, or borrowed autos or from employees' operation of their own autos on behalf of a business, most organizations are exposed to auto liability. Liability can also arise when one organization assumes the auto liability of another organization by contract.

Under common law (the law that is made and applied by court decisions), the owner of an auto was not liable for losses resulting from the negligent operation of the vehicle by someone who is not acting on behalf of the owner. However, many states have enacted laws that hold the owner of an auto liable for injuries arising out of the use of the auto by those who borrow it. Commercial auto insurance covers liability of the insured arising out of the "ownership, maintenance, or use" of a covered auto, and so would cover the insured's liability in either instance, assuming the owned auto is a covered auto.

Perhaps the most common way a business can incur auto liability is through the negligent injury of persons or damage to property by an employee operating an auto owned by the business. As long as the employee operates the vehicle within the scope of his or her employment, the liability for resulting injuries and damage ordinarily falls on the employer as well as the employee. This rule of placing liability on the employer, known as the doctrine of *respondeat superior* ("let the master answer"), is based on the fact that the employee was acting on behalf of the employer at the time of loss. The employer's liability in this situation is also referred to as vicarious liability.

Employers nonownership liability

An employer's liability for its employees' operation of their autos in the employer's business.

If an employee uses his or her own auto in performing job duties, the employer is exposed to liability, called **employers nonownership liability** because the auto is being used to further the employer's business. A sales representative, for example, may use his or her own car to drive to customers' offices. These instances of liability are also covered by commercial auto insurance.

In several situations, an organization can become liable for injury or damage to others that results from the use of autos it does not own. An organization may hire autos from other organizations for terms ranging from a few hours to a number of years. Whatever the period of time, the hiring organization can be held legally liable for injury that results from the vehicle's operation. Similarly, a person or an organization that borrows an auto from another can be held liable for injury arising from its operation.

An organization that hires or borrows autos can also become liable for damage to the hired or borrowed auto itself, based upon user negligence or a contractual duty to return the auto in the same condition as when it was hired, normal wear and tear excepted. These exposures are typically insured by auto physical damage insurance on hired autos.

Subject to certain restrictions, commercial auto insurance also covers auto liability assumed by the insured under contracts, including auto rental agreements and leases. Although the lessee is normally liable for damage resulting from the use of the vehicle, even in the absence of the contract, a hold-harmless agreement also could obligate the lessee to reimburse the owner for amounts the owner is required to pay for injury to others arising out of the owner's faulty maintenance of the auto.

Any business that services, repairs, or otherwise attends to customers' autos can become liable for damage to cars temporarily left in its custody. Such businesses are said to face bailee loss exposures. A bailee is legally liable for damage to customers' property only if the damage occurs as a result of the bailee's negligence. However, in order to maintain good customer relations, many bailees choose to make "goodwill" payments for customers' losses even when not obligated to do so.

The Auto Dealers Coverage Form contains optional garagekeepers coverage for insuring loss to customers' autos while they are in the custody of the insured auto or trailer dealer. All other businesses that have a bailee exposure for customers' autos can insure this loss exposure under a garagekeepers endorsement to their commercial auto coverage forms.

Property Loss Exposures

Any organization that has a financial interest in one or more autos is exposed to loss if those vehicles are damaged or destroyed. The main consequences of damage to or destruction of an auto are these:

- Decrease in or loss of the auto's value
- Loss of use of the auto until it can be repaired or replaced

Auto physical damage insurance covers damage to or destruction of a covered auto. Ordinarily, the insurer pays the cost of repairing the vehicle or its actual cash value, whichever is less.

To a limited extent, the loss of use of an auto is insurable under a rental reimbursement endorsement to auto physical damage insurance. If a covered auto is destroyed, stolen, or disabled by a covered cause of loss, the insurer will reimburse the insured, up to a stated limit, for the cost to rent a substitute vehicle. This allows the insured to continue operations and avoid loss of income.

Automobiles are subject to many of the same causes of loss that can damage property at a fixed location, such as fire, hail, windstorm, and vandalism.

Because autos are mobile, they are highly susceptible to some additional perils, such as collision, overturn, and theft. However, their mobility also makes them less susceptible than fixed property to certain other perils. For example, a car can often be quickly driven away from rising floodwaters, an approaching forest fire, or other perils that could destroy stationary property.

Personal Loss Exposures

Personal loss exposure describes the possibility of financial loss resulting from injury, sickness, or death. Anyone who could suffer injury in an auto accident—either while occupying an auto or as a pedestrian—has a personal loss exposure. In many cases, an auto accident victim can sue or otherwise make a liability claim against the responsible party, in which case the responsible party may also incur a liability loss.

In other cases, an auto accident victim may not be able or willing to sue the responsible party (typically an at-fault driver or the at-fault driver's employer). For example, the injured person may also have caused the accident or may be a friend of the at-fault driver and unwilling to sue. In other cases, the injured party may be willing but unable to sue because the at-fault driver cannot be identified or may have no insurance or other assets with which to pay a judgment. In each of these instances, the injured person is exposed to loss for the costs of his or her injuries as well as a resulting loss of income if temporarily or permanently disabled.

Various commercial auto coverages cover personal loss exposures arising from auto accidents. These coverages include auto medical payments coverage, personal injury protection (PIP) coverage, and uninsured motorists coverage.

Some states require auto owners to maintain certain amounts of PIP coverage and/or uninsured motorists coverage to ensure that auto accident victims are compensated through insurance.

Components of a Commercial Auto Coverage Part

A commercial auto coverage part includes the declarations, a commercial auto coverage form, and any applicable endorsements. A commercial auto coverage part can be included in a commercial package policy (CPP) or issued as a monoline policy. See the exhibit "Components of a Commercial Auto Coverage Part."

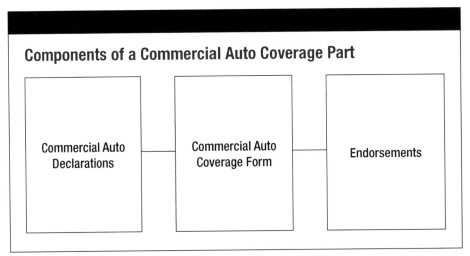

Components of a Commercial Auto Coverage Part

Commercial Auto Declarations — Commercial Auto Coverage Form — Endorsements

[DA07868]

Declarations

A separate declarations form is available for use with each of the commercial auto coverage forms:

- Business Auto Declarations
- Auto Dealers Declarations
- Motor Carrier Declarations

The commercial auto declarations forms are longer and more detailed than the declarations forms for most other lines of business. In addition to the usual information contained in any declarations form, the commercial auto declarations forms include various schedules for recording applicable coverages, covered autos, applicable limits, deductibles, premiums, and rating and classification information.

Coverage Forms

Insurers use the Business Auto Coverage Form to insure the auto loss exposures of any organizations that are not motor carriers (businesses that transport the property of others) or auto or trailer dealers. In addition to providing liability insurance, the Business Auto Coverage Form includes optional provisions for insuring physical damage to autos owned, leased, or hired by the named insured. Other auto coverages, such as no-fault, uninsured/underinsured motorists, and auto medical payments, can be added by endorsement.

Under ISO *Commercial Lines Manual* rules, auto dealers, trailer dealers, and other land motor vehicle dealers are the only organizations eligible for the Auto Dealers Coverage Form. Because the business of dealers involves both the sale and service of autos and trailers, their general liability and auto liability exposures are sometimes difficult to separate. Accordingly, the Auto Dealers Coverage Form provides the equivalent of commercial general liability insurance and business auto insurance in a single coverage form, an approach that prevents coverage gaps that could occur if an auto dealer had separate general liability and auto policies.

Other features of the Auto Dealers Coverage Form that are designed to meet the needs of eligible insureds include **garagekeepers coverage** and value reporting provisions for determining premiums for physical damage coverage on an auto dealer's fluctuating inventory values.

Garagekeepers coverage
Coverage for damage to customers' autos left in the named insured's care while the insured is attending, servicing, repairing, parking, or storing them.

ISO's commercial auto coverage forms also include the Motor Carrier Coverage Form, which can be used to insure any person or organization providing transportation by auto in furtherance of a commercial enterprise. This includes for-hire carriers of property or passengers, as well as commercial insureds that use autos to transport their own property or to transport passengers.

Endorsements

A variety of endorsements are available for modifying the terms and conditions of the commercial auto coverage forms. Endorsements are commonly used to add coverages, to designate additional insureds, to add or omit exclusions, and to bring standard coverage forms into conformity with state insurance regulations.

BACF COVERED AUTOS

The coverage symbols that the Business Auto Coverage Form (BACF) uses to designate covered autos allow for customizing commercial auto coverage to meet each insured's particular needs. Insurance professionals should understand the symbols and how they work in order to use them effectively.

The BACF consists of five sections:

- Section I—Covered Autos
- Section II—Covered Autos Liability Coverage
- Section III—Physical Damage Coverage
- Section IV—Business Auto Conditions
- Section V—Definitions

This discussion focuses on Section I—Covered Autos. The coverage symbols described in Section I define which autos qualify as covered autos. With the use of the appropriate symbol or symbols, coverage can be provided on autos owned by the named insured, autos hired or borrowed by the named insured, and other nonowned autos (such as employees' cars) used in the named insured's business.

How Coverage Symbols Work

The BACF allows great flexibility in designating covered autos for its various coverages. A coverage chosen by the named insured need not apply to all covered autos. For example, the insured might want to provide liability coverage for all autos and physical damage coverage only for specifically described autos.

The mechanism used to indicate the autos to which each coverage applies is a series of ten numerical coverage symbols, defined in Section I of the BACF. The appropriate symbol or symbols are entered beside each coverage in the Schedule of Coverages and Covered Autos in the business auto declarations. The exhibit shows how the symbols are shown to signal the coverages wanted by a particular insured. See the exhibit "Business Auto Coverage Form Coverage Symbols."

Defining the Term "Auto"

The BACF's definition of "auto" is crucial to understanding the coverage. This is the BACF definition of "auto":

> 1. A land motor vehicle, "trailer" or semitrailer designed for travel on public roads; or

> 2. Any other land vehicle that is subject to a compulsory or financial responsibility law or other motor vehicle insurance law where it is licensed or principally garaged.

> However, "auto" does not include "mobile equipment".[1]

The BACF's definition of "mobile equipment" is the same as that in the Commercial General Liability (CGL) Coverage Form. Consequently, mobile equipment (generally covered under the CGL coverage form) is excluded under the BACF unless it is subject to motor vehicle or financial responsibility laws, in which case it is an auto, not mobile equipment. See the exhibit "Types of Vehicles Included in the CGL Form's Definition of Mobile Equipment."

Business Auto Coverage Form Coverage Symbols

Coverages	Covered Autos
Liability	1
Personal Injury Protection	5
Added Personal Injury Protection	—
Auto Medical Payments	—
Uninsured Motorists	2
Underinsured Motorists	2
Physical Damage Comprehensive	7, 8
Physical Damage Specified Causes of Loss	—
Physical Damage Collision	7, 8
Physical Damage Towing and Labor	—

[DA07900]

Types of Vehicles Included in the CGL Form's Definition of Mobile Equipment

Mobile equipment includes these types of land vehicles, including attached equipment:

- Vehicles used primarily off public roads, including bulldozers, farm machinery, and forklifts

- Vehicles used solely on or next to premises owned or rented by the named insured

- Vehicles that travel on crawler treads

- Vehicles maintained primarily to provide mobility to various kinds of construction vehicles and equipment

- Vehicles that do not meet the descriptions in the first four items that are not self-propelled and are maintained primarily to provide mobility to permanently attached equipment such as air compressors, pumps, generators, and devices used to raise or lower workers

- Vehicles that do not meet the descriptions in the first four items that are maintained primarily for purposes other than transportation of persons or cargo

[DA07927]

BACF's Auto Coverage Symbols

The BACF's ten commercial auto coverage symbols are defined in Section I. The appropriate symbol or symbols appear beside each coverage in the schedule of coverages and covered autos in the declarations:

- Symbol 1—Any Auto—If symbol 1 is entered for a coverage, that coverage is provided for any auto, including autos owned by the named insured, autos the named insured hires or borrows from others, and other nonowned autos used in the insured's business. Symbol 1 provides the best protection for the insured. Ordinarily, this symbol is used for liability coverage only.

- Symbol 2—Owned Autos Only—If symbol 2 is entered for a coverage, that coverage applies to all autos owned by the named insured. Symbol 2 can be used for signaling any coverages under the BACF. However, when it is used to signal liability coverage, it also includes trailers (or semi-trailers) the named insured does not own while attached to power units owned by the named insured. "Trailer," as defined in the BACF, includes but is not limited to a semitrailer. Symbol 2 does not cover hired or borrowed autos or other autos the named insured does not own.

- Symbol 3—Owned Private Passenger Autos Only—Symbol 3 entered for a coverage indicates that coverage is provided only for private passenger autos owned by the named insured. Symbol 3 can be used for signaling any coverages under the BACF. This symbol does not include trucks or buses owned by the named insured or any kind of auto not owned by the named insured.

- Symbol 4—Owned Autos Other Than Private Passenger Autos Only—Symbol 4 entered for a coverage indicates that coverage is provided for all autos owned by the named insured except private passenger autos. Symbol 4 can be used for signaling any coverages under the BACF.

- Symbol 5—Owned Autos Subject to No-Fault—Symbol 5 is entered only on the personal injury protection (PIP) or added PIP line of the declarations. It provides PIP coverage only for those autos that are required by law to have it.

- Symbol 6—Owned Autos Subject to a Compulsory Uninsured Motorists Law—Symbol 6 is used only for uninsured motorists coverage. It indicates that coverage is provided only for autos that are required by law to have uninsured motorists coverage.

- Symbol 7—Specifically Described Autos—If symbol 7 is used, coverage applies only to those autos specifically described in the policy and for which a premium is shown in the policy. Symbol 7 can be used for signaling any coverages under the BACF. It also includes, for liability coverage only, any trailer not owned by the insured while it is attached to one of the covered power units.

- Symbol 8—Hired Autos Only—Symbol 8 provides coverage only for autos leased, hired, rented, or borrowed by the named insured. It does not cover autos leased, hired, rented, or borrowed from the named insured's employees or family members. Symbol 8 normally is only used for liability and physical damage coverage.

- Symbol 9—Nonowned Autos Only—Symbol 9, which is used only for signaling liability coverage, provides covered auto status for autos not owned, leased, hired, or borrowed by the named insured while such autos are used in connection with the named insured's business. This description includes autos owned by the named insured's employees or members of their households, but only while used in the named insured's business or personal affairs.

- Symbol 19—Mobile Equipment Subject to Compulsory or Financial Responsibility or Other Motor Vehicle Insurance Law Only—Symbol 19 can be used for signaling any coverages under the BACF.

Symbols 1 and 19 Explained

If symbol 1 (any auto) is used for liability coverage, then symbols 8 and 9 do not need to be shown in order to provide coverage for hired and nonowned autos; symbol 1 includes such coverage. If another symbol is shown for liability coverage—for example, symbol 2 or 7—symbols 8 and 9 must also be shown for liability coverage if the insured wants to have liability coverage for hired and nonowned autos.

Symbol 19 provides a way to cover land motor vehicles that would meet the definition of mobile equipment if they were not subject to a motor vehicle insurance law where they are licensed or principally garaged. Because such vehicles qualify as autos, they are covered under each of the covered auto symbols to the extent of the applicable symbol description. For example, if the insured has symbol 1 (any auto) for liability coverage, this symbol will include any vehicle that meets the definition of an auto, including an auto that would be considered mobile equipment if it were not subject to a motor vehicle insurance law.

The main situation in which symbol 19 is useful is when an insured has coverage through symbol 7 (specifically described autos). If the insured believes that a vehicle is mobile equipment automatically covered by the insured's CGL policy, the insured will not see any reason to ask the insurer to add this vehicle to the insured's BACF. If, after an accident, the vehicle is discovered to be subject to a motor vehicle insurance law, it will be considered an auto and therefore excluded by the CGL. Moreover, it will not be covered under symbol 7 in the BACF, because the vehicle is not described in the declarations. By showing symbol 19 for any desired coverages, the insured has coverage under the BACF in such situations.

Coverage for Newly Acquired Autos

If any of symbols 1 through 6, or 19, is shown for a coverage, that coverage applies to vehicles of the type indicated by the symbol if such vehicles are acquired during the policy term. Coverage for newly acquired vehicles of the type indicated by the symbol is automatic, without any requirement that the insurer be notified of the acquisition. (The insurer typically discovers any newly acquired autos when it audits the insured at the end of the policy period.) Likewise, a premium auditor will determine the actual nonowned and hired auto exposure. The insured must then pay an additional premium for the actual exposures covered during the policy period. However, many insurers do not audit policies that generate smaller premiums.

If symbol 7 is shown for a coverage, autos acquired during the policy term are covered from the time of acquisition only if both of these conditions are met:

- The insurer insures all autos owned by the named insured, or the newly acquired auto replaces a covered auto.
- The named insured asks the insurer to cover the newly acquired auto within thirty days of the acquisition.

Other Covered Items

If the BACF provides liability insurance, trailers with a load capacity of 2,000 pounds or less are covered automatically for liability insurance. Mobile equipment is automatically covered for liability while being carried or towed by an auto that has liability coverage. An auto used as a temporary substitute for a covered auto that is out of service because of its breakdown, repair, service, loss, or destruction is also covered for liability insurance only.

Apply Your Knowledge

A particular computer consulting firm does not own any autos. However, the firm's employees use their own autos to drive to and from customers' offices, and they also rent autos under the name of the named insured after flying to more-distant job sites. Accordingly, the firm wants liability coverage for hired and nonowned autos. The firm also wants collision and comprehensive physical damage coverage for hired autos because rental companies hold the renter responsible for physical damage to the rented car. The firm's auto insurance needs are currently met by using symbols 8 and 9 for liability coverage and symbol 8 for comprehensive and collision coverage.

The firm has bought a car for its president to use and wants to have liability, collision, and comprehensive coverage on the vehicle. Which symbols, if any, would need to be shown in the firm's BACF if the insurer is willing to provide symbol 1 for liability coverage?

Feedback: If symbol 1 were used, symbols 8 and 9 would no longer need to be shown for liability coverage, because symbol 1 covers "any auto." However, symbol 8 would still need to be shown for collision and comprehensive physical damage. An additional symbol would need to be added for collision and comprehensive on the owned car. Assuming the insurer was willing to use symbol 2 for physical damage coverage, coverage would be signaled by showing symbol 1 for liability and symbols 2 and 8 for comprehensive and collision.

If the insurer agrees only to use symbol 7 for the new car, how would coverage be signaled?

Feedback: If the insurer agrees only to use symbol 7 for the new car, coverage would be signaled by showing symbols 7, 8, and 9 for liability and symbols 7 and 8 for comprehensive and collision.

BACF COVERED AUTOS LIABILITY COVERAGE

Section II—Covered Autos Liability Coverage of the Business Auto Coverage Form (BACF) is an important coverage because liability can arise from an organization's owned, hired, or borrowed autos or from employees' autos operated on behalf of the organization.

The liability coverage provisions of the BACF include an insuring agreement, a definition of who is insured, coverage extensions, exclusions, and a limit of insurance provision.

Insuring Agreement

In the liability coverage agreement, the insurer expresses three distinct duties:

- A duty to pay damages
- A duty to pay "covered pollution cost or expense"
- A duty to defend the insured

Duty to Pay Damages

The insurer agrees to pay all sums an "insured" must legally pay as damages because of "bodily injury" (BI) or "property damage" (PD) to which the insurance applies, caused by an "accident" and resulting from the ownership, maintenance, or use of a covered auto. The terms in quotation marks are defined in Section V of the BACF:

"Insured" means any person or organization qualifying as an insured in the Who Is An Insured provision of the applicable coverage.

"Bodily injury" means bodily injury, sickness or disease sustained by a person including death resulting from any of these.

"Property damage" means damage to or loss of use of tangible property.

"Accident" includes continuous or repeated exposure to the same conditions resulting in "bodily injury" or "property damage".[2]

Whether a vehicle qualifies as a covered auto depends on what coverage symbols are indicated in the schedule of coverages and what covered autos are listed in the business auto declarations. The insurer's obligation to pay damages is also governed by exclusions, policy limits, and other conditions.

Duty to Pay "Covered Pollution Cost or Expense"

The BACF is subject to a broad pollution exclusion that eliminates almost all coverage for bodily injury or property damage resulting from the escape of pollutants being transported by a covered auto. However, the BACF covers certain pollution costs and expenses, such as those resulting from the escape of fuel or other fluids needed for the normal running of the covered auto.

In the event of an incident that produces pollution, damages for bodily injury and property damage are not the only consequences for which the insured can be held liable. The insured can incur various costs and expenses as the result of demands by governmental authorities or private citizens that the insured clean up or otherwise respond to the effects of pollutants.

To address this exposure, the insurer agrees to pay all sums that the insured must legally pay as "covered pollution cost or expense." For pollution cost or expense to be covered, it must be caused by an accident and must result from the ownership, maintenance, or use of a covered auto. In addition, the same accident that causes the pollution cost or expense must also result in bodily injury or property damage covered by the policy. All payments for covered pollution cost or expense reduce the applicable limit of insurance.

Duty to Defend

The insurer has the right and duty to defend an insured against any claim or suit alleging damages that would be covered under the policy. The claim or suit only needs to allege damages that would be covered. Hence, the insurer must defend against even false or fraudulent claims or suits as long as they allege covered damages.

The BACF defines "suit" to include not only a civil proceeding but also an arbitration proceeding or any other alternative dispute resolution proceeding to which the insured must submit or does submit with the insurer's consent. The duty to defend ends when the insurer has paid its applicable policy limit in full or partial settlement of the claim. The costs of defending the claim are payable in addition to the limit of insurance.

Who Is an Insured

The named insured is an insured for any covered auto. If, for example, symbol 1 is shown for liability coverage, the named insured is an insured for any auto. If only symbol 7 is shown for liability coverage, the named insured is an insured only for specifically described autos.

Anyone other than the named insured is an insured while using with the named insured's permission a covered auto owned, hired, or borrowed by the named insured. However, these restrictions apply:

- The owner or anyone else from whom the named insured hires or borrows a covered auto is not an insured, unless the covered auto is a trailer connected to a covered auto owned by the named insured. If, for example, ABC Company hires a car from A-1 Auto Rentals, A-1 will not be an insured under ABC's BACF liability coverage.

- An employee of the named insured is not an insured if the covered auto is owned by the employee or a member of the employee's household. For example, Sue is not an insured under her employer's BACF liability coverage while operating her car on an errand for her employer. (Sue's employer, however, is insured for this use of Sue's car if the policy includes either symbol 1 or symbol 9 for liability coverage.)

- A person using a covered auto while working in the business of selling, servicing, repairing, or parking autos is not an insured unless that business is the named insured's. For example, a mechanic of Bob's Brake Shop is not an insured under ABC's BACF liability coverage while test-driving ABC's car.

- Anyone other than the named insured's employees or partners, or a lessee or borrower of a covered auto or any of their employees, is not an insured while moving property to or from a covered auto. If, for example, employees of Jones Warehouse are unloading ABC Company's truck, the Jones employees are not covered under ABC's BACF liability coverage.

- If the named insured is a partnership, a partner of the named insured is not an insured for a covered auto owned by that partner or by someone residing in that partner's household.

- If the named insured is a limited liability company, a member of the named insured is not an insured for a covered auto owned by that member or by someone residing in that member's household.

Person Held Liable for the Conduct of the Insured

Any person or organization (other than those previously noted as excluded) held liable for the conduct of an "insured" is also an insured. For example, assume that an employee of XYZ Corporation operates an auto covered under ABC's BACF and causes an accident for which XYZ is held to be liable. This provision states that XYZ will be an insured under ABC's auto insurance. (XYZ's employee also will be an insured because of the earlier provision relating to "anyone else" other than the named insured.)

Coverage Extensions

The BACF liability provisions include coverage extensions for supplementary payments and for increased protection while a covered auto is out of the state in which it is licensed. BACF liability coverage provides six supplementary payments, which are payable in addition to the limit of insurance:

- All expenses incurred by the insurer
- Up to $2,000 for the cost of bail bonds required because of a covered accident

- The cost of bonds to release attachments in any suit against the insured that the insurer defends
- All reasonable expenses incurred by the insured at the insurer's request
- All court costs taxed against the insured in any suit against the insured defended by the insurer
- All interest on the full amount of any judgment that accrues after entry of the judgment in any suit against the insured that the insurer defends

If a covered auto is outside the state in which it is licensed, the limit of insurance is, if necessary, increased on that auto to the minimum required by the outside jurisdiction in which the auto is being operated. Also, if the outside jurisdiction requires a different type of coverage, the policy provides such coverage automatically.

For example, assume that a BACF has a $50,000 limit for liability insurance and that a covered auto is driven out of state through two other states. If the first outside state requires a minimum limit of $100,000, the limit is increased automatically to $100,000 while the auto is in that state. If the second outside state requires no-fault coverage, the insured's policy will automatically provide no-fault coverage while the auto is in that state.

Exclusions

The exclusions that appear in the BACF's liability coverage section impose several limitations on the liability insuring agreement.

Expected or Intended Injury and Contractual Liability Exclusions

Bodily injury or property damage expected or intended from the standpoint of the insured is excluded. Liability assumed by contract or agreement is excluded, but the exclusion does not apply to these items:

- Liability that the insured would have in the absence of the contract
- Damages assumed in an "insured contract," provided the injury or damage occurs after the contract is executed

Section V's definition of "insured contract" lists the types of contracts in which an assumption of liability is covered. In many ways, this definition resembles the definition of "insured contract" in the Commercial General Liability (CGL) Coverage Form. For example, both definitions include leases of premises. The BACF covers liability assumed under a lease of premises only if the liability being assumed arises out of the ownership, maintenance, or use of an auto; the CGL form covers liability assumed under a lease of premises if the liability being assumed does not arise out of the ownership, maintenance, or use of an auto. The same distinction applies to the other types of insured contracts.

Workers Compensation and Related Exclusions

The BACF excludes any liability under a workers compensation, disability benefits, or unemployment compensation law. The BACF effectively eliminates, subject to two exceptions, coverage for bodily injury to employees of the insured that should be covered under workers compensation and employees liability insurance. The two exceptions that allow coverage for employee injury are injury to domestic employees not entitled to workers compensation and liability assumed by the insured under an insured contract.

The Fellow Employee exclusion eliminates coverage for bodily injury to any fellow employee of any insured that arises in the course of the fellow employee's employment. If, for example, one of ABC's drivers negligently strikes another ABC employee with a truck while at work, ABC's BACF will not protect the driver against any legal action the injured employee may bring against the driver.

Care, Custody, or Control Exclusion

No coverage exists for property owned by the insured or in the care, custody, or control of the insured. Property owned by the insured can be insured under an appropriate form of property insurance. Property of others in the care, custody, or control of the insured is frequently insured under inland marine coverage. For example, motor truck cargo insurance covers property of others that is being transported by the insured.

Exclusions Related to Loading and Unloading

The Handling of Property exclusion helps to define the scope of coverage for accidents that occur during the loading or unloading of autos. The exclusion eliminates coverage for bodily injury or property damage resulting from the handling of property under these conditions:

- Before property is moved from the place where it is accepted by the insured for movement into a covered auto

- After it has been moved from a covered auto to the place where it is finally delivered by the insured

Consequently, the Handling of Property exclusion does not apply to—and thus coverage exists for—accidents that occur while property is being moved into a covered auto from the place where the insured has accepted the property or from a covered auto to the place where the property is finally delivered.

If, for example, two employees of an appliance store damage a hallway wall while moving a clothes washer from their delivery truck to a second-floor apartment, the store's BACF will cover the damage to the wall, because the property damage occurred before the washer was moved to the place of final delivery.

The CGL coverage form excludes "loading and unloading" and defines that term in the same manner as previously discussed, thus avoiding duplication of business auto coverage. The CGL form covers the liability loss exposures that exist in connection with property before loading begins or after unloading is completed.

The BACF excludes bodily injury or property damage resulting from movement of property by a mechanical device unless the device is attached to the covered auto or is a hand truck. For example, movement of property by a mechanical hoist attached to a flatbed truck is covered; movement of property by a conveyor belt not attached to the truck is excluded by the BACF (but covered by the CGL form).

Operations and Completed Operations Exclusions

The Operations exclusion eliminates coverage for the operation of several specified types of equipment attached to covered autos. In the absence of this exclusion, the BACF might otherwise be considered to cover the operation of such equipment because the equipment is attached to a covered auto. The CGL policy covers the operation of such equipment, regardless of whether it is attached to an auto.

For example, assume C&D Electric has a service truck on which a cherry picker (or "bucket" for raising and lowering workers) is mounted. If the driver of the truck causes an accident while driving to a work site, the resulting liability is covered under C&D's BACF. If, after the truck reaches its work site, a passerby is injured as a result of C&D's operation of the cherry picker, the resulting liability is excluded by C&D's BACF and covered by C&D's CGL insurance.

The Completed Operations exclusion clarifies that the BACF provides no coverage for completed operations performed with the insured's autos. For example, injury resulting from allegedly negligent snowplowing performed (and completed) by the insured would not be covered.

Pollution, War, and Racing Exclusions

With few exceptions, the Pollution exclusion eliminates coverage for bodily injury or property damage resulting from the discharge of any pollutants being transported or stored in, or moved to or from, a covered auto. By a specific exception, the exclusion does not apply to the escape of fuels, lubricants, fluids, exhaust gases, or other similar pollutants needed for the functioning of the covered auto. If, for example, gasoline leaks from the fuel tank of a covered auto after a collision, liability for the spill is covered.

Liability for damage caused by war, warlike actions, civil war, insurrection, rebellion, or revolution is excluded. The BACF excludes covered autos while they are used in organized races or demolition contests. Practice or preparation for such activities is also excluded.

☑ Reality Check

Is This Pollution Claim Covered?

While she was driving the delivery truck owned by her floral store, Isabella negligently collided with an oil tank truck owned by an oil company. As a result of the collision, the oil in the oil company's tank truck leaked on the ground and into a nearby stream. The cost to clean up the resulting pollution exceeded $200,000.

If Isabella were held legally liable for the cleanup costs, would the Pollution exclusion in her BACF eliminate coverage for the cleanup costs?

No, the Pollution exclusion applies to pollutants that are discharged from a covered auto or being transported by or on behalf of the insured. Because the oil that spilled was not being transported by Isabella or in a covered auto under Isabella's policy, the exclusion would not apply.

[DA07935]

Limit of Insurance

BACF liability coverage is subject to a combined single limit of insurance applicable to all bodily injury, property damage, and covered pollution cost or expense arising from a single accident. No annual aggregate limit applies. The single limit is the maximum amount the insurer will pay for all claims arising from a single accident, regardless of the number of vehicles, the number of drivers, or the number of claimants involved. Repeated exposure to essentially the same circumstances is considered to be a single accident.

BACF PHYSICAL DAMAGE COVERAGE

Section III—Physical Damage of the Business Auto Coverage Form (BACF) provides auto physical damage insurance. The primary purpose of the coverage is to insure loss of or damage to autos owned by the insured. However, coverage can also be arranged to cover autos hired or borrowed by the insured.

The BACF offers three basic physical damage coverages that may be purchased individually or in combination, as well as coverage extensions. Coverage is subject to a relatively small number of exclusions, a limit, and a deductible.

Available Coverages

Under the BACF, the insured may choose from three basic physical damage coverages:

- Collision Coverage
- Comprehensive Coverage
- Specified Causes of Loss Coverage

Any of these coverages can be purchased individually. Usually, however, the named insured selects either Collision Coverage and Comprehensive Coverage or Collision Coverage and Specified Causes of Loss Coverage. Because Comprehensive Coverage encompasses all of the specified causes of loss (and more), it is never purchased with Specified Causes of Loss Coverage on the same autos. In addition to these basic physical damage coverages, the BACF includes provisions for optional towing and labor coverage, an extension covering transportation expenses, and an extension covering loss of use of rental autos.

Collision Coverage

Collision Coverage insures direct and accidental loss or damage to a covered auto caused by collision with another object or by overturn. The BACF defines loss as "direct and accidental loss or damage." The BACF does not define collision or overturn. Collision is generally understood to mean a striking together with violent impact. Overturn is generally considered to include any incident in which a vehicle loses its equilibrium; the vehicle need not turn over completely.

Comprehensive Coverage

Comprehensive Coverage insures direct and accidental loss or damage to a covered auto by any peril except collision or overturn or a peril specifically excluded. This is essentially the same approach to defining covered perils as is used in the Causes of Loss—Special Form, which covers unnamed, unanticipated perils as long as they are not specifically excluded.

Glass breakage, damage resulting from hitting an animal, and damage caused by falling objects or missiles (generally, any object that is thrown or projected), although they might otherwise be considered losses caused by collision, are paid under comprehensive coverage. This provision usually benefits the insured, since most insureds carry lower deductibles on Comprehensive Coverage than on Collision Coverage.

If glass breakage is caused by collision, however, it can be covered by collision (and not under comprehensive) at the option of the insured. In that way, the insured can avoid the application of two deductibles when collision damage to the auto includes glass breakage.

Apply Your Knowledge

A company insures its commercial autos under a BACF with Collision Coverage that has a $2,500 deductible and Comprehensive Coverage that has a $1,000 deductible.

Assuming that no exclusions apply to any of these losses, indicate whether the damage to a covered auto in each of the described accidents would be insured under Collision Coverage or Comprehensive Coverage. If the company would have a choice of coverages to apply, select the choice that would result in application of the lowest possible deductible amount(s) to the loss.

a. One of the company's covered autos was damaged when it ran into a bridge abutment. (No glass damage occurred.)

b. One of the company's covered autos was damaged by a falling rock in a mountainous area.

c. One of the company's covered autos was damaged by colliding with a deer.

d. A company employee backed one of the company's covered autos into a utility pole, damaging the auto's body and shattering its rear window.

e. One of the company's covered autos was damaged when its driver ran a red light and struck an auto in the intersection. (No glass damage occurred.)

f. During a windstorm, one of the company's covered autos was crushed by a falling tree.

Feedback:

a. The loss would be insured under Collision Coverage.

b. The loss would be insured under Comprehensive Coverage.

c. The loss would be insured under Comprehensive Coverage.

d. The entire loss (both body damage and glass breakage) could, at the company's choice, be covered under Collision Coverage to avoid having to pay the collision deductible for auto body damage and the comprehensive deductible for the glass breakage.

e. The loss would be insured under Collision Coverage.

f. The loss would be covered under Comprehensive Coverage.

Specified Causes of Loss Coverage

A somewhat less expensive alternative to Comprehensive Coverage is Specified Causes of Loss Coverage, which is coverage for direct and accidental loss caused by fire, lightning, explosion, theft, windstorm, hail, earthquake, flood, mischief, vandalism, or loss resulting from the sinking, burning, collision, or derailment of a conveyance transporting the covered auto.

Towing Coverage

Towing Coverage pays for necessary towing and labor costs due to the disablement of a covered private passenger auto. The labor must be performed at the place of disablement. The limit for Towing Coverage is the most that the insurer will pay for each disablement.

Transportation Expenses

Transportation Expenses is a coverage extension for substitute transportation costs incurred when a private-passenger-type auto has been stolen. The insurer agrees to pay the cost of substitute transportation actually incurred by the named insured, subject to a daily limit of $20 and a total limit of $600. Payments begin forty-eight hours after the theft and end when the insured auto is returned to use or when the insurer pays for the auto. Such payments may extend beyond the expiration of the policy.

This coverage extension applies only if the auto is of the private passenger type and is stolen. Some insureds want broader coverage that can be provided through the Rental Reimbursement Coverage endorsement, which covers the cost of renting a substitute auto for a designated auto of any type that has suffered a loss due to any covered peril, subject to daily and aggregate limits.

Loss of Use Expenses

When the insured rents an auto, the rental agreement may obligate the insured to pay for physical damage to the auto that occurs during the rental period, as well as resulting loss of use of the auto, regardless of whether the insured is at fault. Although an organization can buy physical damage insurance on hired autos (through symbol 8), such coverage applies only to the physical loss and not to the resulting loss of use. Loss of Use Expenses is a coverage extension that pays for loss of use of a rental auto when an insured becomes contractually obligated to make such payments. The coverage extension for loss of use expenses provides up to $20 a day, to a maximum of $600, to cover that exposure. These limits can be increased by endorsement.

Apply Your Knowledge

A company is insured under a commercial package policy that includes a BACF.

Two of the company's autos—a delivery truck and a company car driven by the company's president—were stolen from the company's parking lot on the same day. Both were covered autos for comprehensive coverage. Until it could replace both autos, the company rented a temporary substitute delivery truck and a temporary substitute car for the president. The company rented the delivery truck for ten days at a cost of $100 per day. The company rented the car for six days at a cost of $40 per day. What amount, if any, of these rental expenses would be payable under the Transportation Expenses extension in the company's BACF for each rented vehicle?

Feedback: Under the BACF's Transportation Expenses coverage extension, nothing will be payable for the expense of renting the delivery truck because the delivery truck that was stolen was not a private passenger auto. The amount payable for the president's company car is $80, calculated as 4 days × $20 maximum per day. No coverage applies to the expenses incurred for the first two days.

The substitute delivery truck the company rented was damaged when the company's driver negligently caused the truck to collide with a tree. The rental agreement made the company legally responsible to pay for the damage to the truck, as well as its loss of use, at a rate of $100 per day for the fifteen days required to repair the truck. Because the company had selected symbol 8 (hired autos) for collision coverage, the company's insurer covered the physical damage to the truck, less the collision deductible. What additional amount, if any, would the company's insurer be obligated to pay for the loss of use expenses for which the company was held responsible?

Feedback: Under the BACF's Loss of Use coverage extension, the insurer would be obligated to pay $300, calculated as 15 days × $20 maximum per day.

Exclusions

Auto physical damage insurance is subject to relatively few exclusions. Like virtually any other type of property insurance, it excludes nuclear hazards and war or military action. Notably, however, auto physical damage insurance does not exclude earthquake, flood, or other water damage.

Business auto physical damage insurance excludes certain types of losses that are likely to occur as a normal consequence of prolonged use of the vehicle or the owner's neglect. Thus, wear and tear, freezing, mechanical or electrical failure, and road damage to tires are excluded unless they result from other loss insured by the BACF. For example, an auto with comprehensive coverage may be stolen. If the auto suffers a mechanical breakdown and tire damage resulting from abusive driving by the thief, the mechanical breakdown and tire damage would not be excluded, because the proximate cause of the loss was a covered peril (theft).

The BACF excludes many, but not all, types of electronic equipment in a covered auto. The insurer will not pay for loss to these items:

- Tapes, records, discs, or similar devices
- Radar detectors, laser detectors, and similar devices
- Any equipment, regardless of whether it is permanently installed, that reproduces, receives, or transmits audio, visual, or data signals
- Any accessories used with the previously described equipment

However, the exclusion does not apply to equipment that is designed to be powered only by the auto's electrical system and that at the time of loss meets any of these descriptions:

a. Permanently installed in or upon the covered "auto";

b. Removable from a housing unit which is permanently installed in or upon the covered "auto";

c. An integral part of the same unit housing any electronic equipment described in Paragraphs a. and b. above; or

d. Necessary for the normal operation of the covered "auto" or the monitoring of the covered "auto's" operating system.[3]

Coverage for the types of electronic equipment that are excluded can usually be added to the BACF by endorsement. Like business auto liability coverage, the physical damage section excludes coverage for autos while used in organized races or demolition contests, including practice or preparation for such activities. Finally, the physical damage section excludes "diminution in value," which the form defines as "the actual or perceived loss in market value" resulting from a covered auto being repaired.

Apply Your Knowledge

Wholesale Distributor, Inc. (WDI) insures its fleet of commercial autos under a BACF that includes collision and comprehensive physical damage coverage on all of WDI's owned autos. For each of the described losses, identify any of the BACF's physical damage exclusions that would apply.

One of WDI's trucks was severely damaged in a covered collision. After the truck was repaired, WDI asked the insurer to pay the cost of repairs and to compensate for the truck's decreased market value.

Feedback: The diminution in value exclusion would eliminate coverage for the decrease in the truck's market value.

One of WDI's covered autos was a total loss because of radioactive contamination that resulted from an incident at a nuclear power plant.

Feedback: The nuclear hazard exclusion would eliminate coverage for this loss.

One of WDI's autos experienced a tire blowout, which resulted in a collision in which the auto was damaged.

Feedback: The exclusion of loss "due and confined to" blowouts or other road damage to tires would eliminate coverage for the tire that experienced the blowout. However, the exclusion would not apply to the damage to the rest of the covered auto that resulted from the subsequent collision, which is a covered cause of loss.

Limit of Insurance

The most the insurer will pay for a physical damage loss is the lesser of these values:

*   The actual cash value of the property at the time of loss
*   The cost of repairing or replacing the property with other property of like kind or quality

Deductible

The insurer's payment for each covered auto is reduced by any applicable deductible shown in the declarations. Thus, if two of the insured's vehicles collide with each other, two deductibles will apply.

The deductible applicable to comprehensive coverage does not apply to loss by fire or lightning. This exception can be of considerable value to an owner of a fleet of autos that are garaged at the same location and therefore susceptible to total loss by fire. In the absence of this exemption, the insured would have to bear a portion of the loss equal to the amount of the deductible times the total number of cars destroyed.

BUSINESS AUTO COVERAGE FORM CONDITIONS

Section IV of the Business Auto Coverage Form, Business Auto Conditions, contains all conditions that apply to all coverages under the business auto form.

Some of the conditions in the Business Auto Coverage Form are similar to those found in the CGL form; others are specific to auto insurance. The conditions can be categorized as loss conditions or general conditions.

Loss Conditions

The first five conditions of Section IV of the Business Auto Coverage Form, Business Auto Conditions, are loss conditions:

*   Appraisal for Physical Damage Losses
*   Duties in the Event of an Accident, Claim, Suit or Loss
*   Legal Action Against the Insurer
*   Loss Payment—Physical Damage Coverages
*   Transfer of Rights Against Others

Appraisal for Physical Damage Losses

If the named insured and the insurer cannot agree on the amount of a covered loss, either may call for an appraisal. Each will then appoint an appraiser, and the appraisers will appoint a "competent and impartial" umpire.

The appraisers then determine actual cash value and the amount of loss payment. Any item on which the appraisers cannot agree is submitted to the umpire, and an award in writing, signed by any two of the three, binds both parties.

Each party pays its own appraiser, and both parties share the cost of the umpire. This procedure applies only to disagreements about the amount of loss, not to coverage disagreements.

Duties in the Event of an Accident, Claim, Suit or Loss

The insured's duties after loss are essentially the same as those imposed by the CGL policy. The named insured must give prompt notice of accident or loss to the insurer or its agent and assist the insurer in obtaining the names of injured persons or witnesses. Also, both the named insured and any other person who seeks liability coverage under the policy (for example, the driver of an insured vehicle) must take these actions:

- Cooperate with the insurer in its investigation and defense of the accident or loss
- Immediately send to the insurer copies of any notices or legal papers received in connection with the accident or loss
- Submit to physical examinations by physicians selected and paid by the insurer as often as the insurer may reasonably request
- Authorize the insurer to obtain medical reports and other medical information

Moreover, no insured can commit the insurer to make any payment either for damages or expenses.

If the claim is for loss or damage to a covered auto, the named insured must take these actions:

- Promptly notify the police if the insured auto or any of its equipment is stolen
- Do what is reasonably necessary to preserve the property from further loss
- Permit the insurer to inspect and appraise the damaged vehicle before it is repaired
- Agree to be examined under oath at the insurer's request and give a signed statement

Legal Action Against the Insurer

No legal action can be brought against the insurer under any coverage until the named insured and the insured bringing the action, if different, have complied with all provisions of the coverage form.

In addition, under the liability coverage, no action can be brought against the insurer until either a court has determined that the insured is liable for the loss or the insurer has agreed in writing that the insured is liable for the loss.

Loss Payment—Physical Damage Coverages

The insurer has three options with regard to damaged or stolen property:

- Pay to repair or replace the property
- Return the property at the expense of the insurer and repair any damage caused by theft
- Keep all of the property and pay an agreed or appraised value

Transfer of Rights Against Others

The insured may have a right to recover a loss from some other party, usually because the other party caused the loss.

If the insurer pays the loss, it is entitled, under this condition, to take over the insured's right of recovery from the other party. This right is referred to as subrogation. The insured must not do anything to impair the insurer's right of recovery and must do everything reasonably necessary to secure and preserve that right.

General Conditions

The last eight conditions of Section IV of the Business Auto Coverage Form, Business Auto Conditions, are general conditions:

- Bankruptcy
- Concealment, Misrepresentation, or Fraud
- Liberalization
- No Benefit to Bailee—Physical Damage Insurance Only
- Other Insurance
- Premium Audit
- Policy Period, Coverage Territory
- Two or More Coverage Forms or Policies Issued by the Insurer

Bankruptcy

Bankruptcy or insolvency of the insured does not relieve the insurer of any of its obligations under the policy.

If the insured is relieved through bankruptcy of any obligation to pay a liability claim, the insurer is still obligated to make payment just as it would have been had the insured remained solvent.

Concealment, Misrepresentation, or Fraud

In the case of fraud by the named insured relative to business auto coverage, the coverage is void.

It is also void if any insured intentionally conceals or misrepresents a material fact about the coverage form, any autos covered, the insured's interest in any covered auto, or a claim under the coverage form.

A material fact is one that would have changed the underwriting decision in some way.

Liberalization

If, during the policy term, the insurer revises the Business Auto Coverage Form to provide more coverage at no increase in premium, the insured's policy will provide that additional coverage, automatically, as of the date the revision becomes effective in the insured's state.

That is, the policy is liberalized (by providing more coverage at no extra cost) when the insurer's revised business auto form becomes effective, rather than on the policy renewal date.

No Benefit to Bailee—Physical Damage Insurance Only

Railroads and other transporters of property sometimes try to gain the benefit of the property owner's insurance by inserting a provision in their bill of lading stating that they are not liable for any loss for which the shipper is reimbursed by insurance. This provision in the bill of lading could invalidate the insurer's right of subrogation against the transporting company. Accordingly, the "no benefit to bailee" condition attempts to preserve the insurer's subrogation rights by stating that the insurer does not recognize any assignment of coverage or any other grant of coverage to any person or organization that holds, stores, or transports property for a fee.

Other Insurance

Business auto coverage may be either primary or excess, depending on the circumstances of the accident or loss.

For any covered vehicle owned by the named insured, the coverage is primary.

For any covered auto not owned by the named insured, the coverage is excess, and the insurance, if any, carried by the owner of the auto is primary.

For purposes of hired auto (symbol 8) physical damage coverage, any auto the named insured leases, hires, rents, or borrows is deemed to be a covered auto owned by the named insured. Such an auto is therefore covered on a primary basis. However, no coverage exists for an auto that is hired or borrowed with a driver.

Coverage for trailers follows the autos to which they are attached. Thus, coverage is excess for a trailer attached to an auto not owned by the named insured, and coverage is primary for a trailer attached to an auto owned by the named insured. The coverage is primary for a covered trailer owned by the named insured when it is not attached to any auto.

Regardless of these provisions, business auto liability coverage is primary for any liability assumed under an insured contract.

If two or more policies of the same level (either excess or primary) apply to the same loss, each policy contributes to the loss in the proportion that its limit bears to the total limits of all policies of its level. See the exhibit "Illustration of Other Insurance Provisions."

Illustration of Other Insurance Provisions

To illustrate the Other Insurance provision when two primary policies apply to the same claim, assume that Policy A has a $100,000 limit and Policy B has a $300,000 limit. If the covered amount of the claim was $40,000, Policy A, which has one-fourth of the total limits, would pay $10,000, and Policy B, which has three-fourths of the total limits, would pay $30,000.

[DA02611]

Premium Audit

The premium shown on the declarations, which the insured pays at policy inception, is an estimate. The actual premium is determined by a premium audit and based on actual exposures at the end of the policy period.

If the final premium is less than the estimate, the named insured gets a refund. If the final premium is greater than the estimate, the named insured must pay the difference.

Policy Period, Coverage Territory

Accidents and losses are covered if they occur during the policy period shown on the declarations and occur within the coverage territory. The coverage territory includes the United States, its territories and possessions, Puerto Rico, and Canada. Losses and accidents involving a covered auto while it is being transported between the covered territories are also covered.

A worldwide coverage territory applies to covered autos of the private passenger type that are leased, hired, rented, or borrowed without a driver for a period of thirty days or less. The insured's liability for damages must be determined in a suit in the U.S., its territories and possessions, Puerto Rico, or Canada, or in a settlement to which the insurer agrees.

Two or More Coverage Forms or Policies Issued by the Insurer

When an accident or a loss is covered by two or more policies issued by the same insurer or affiliated insurers, the maximum amount the insurer or affiliated insurers will be required to pay is the highest limit provided under any one policy.

However, this does not apply to any coverage specifically purchased as excess over business auto coverage, such as a commercial umbrella liability policy.

BUSINESS AUTO COVERAGES ADDED BY ENDORSEMENT

Apart from the Business Auto Coverage Form's (BACF's) liability and physical damage coverages, all of the coverages listed in the schedule of coverages and covered autos in the business auto declarations must be added by endorsement to the BACF if they are purchased.

These coverages are commonly included in commercial auto coverage parts or policies:

- Medical payments
- Personal injury protection and added personal injury protection
- Uninsured and underinsured motorists

The provisions for these coverages do not appear in the BACF. Therefore, if any of these coverages are to be included in a commercial auto coverage part, the provisions must be added to the BACF by attaching the appropriate endorsement(s).

Medical Payments

Auto medical payments coverage pays for medical expenses incurred by occupants of a covered auto, regardless of whether the auto's driver was at fault in the accident. Medical payments coverage, by paying a small bodily injury claim without any determination of liability, can sometimes prevent an injured passenger from making a costlier liability claim against the driver.

More specifically, the Auto Medical Payments Coverage endorsement covers the reasonable and necessary medical and funeral expenses incurred by a person injured by an accident while "occupying" (entering into, riding in, or alighting from) a covered auto. If the named insured is an individual, the endorsement covers the named insured and members of his or her family while occupying any auto or if struck by an auto while a pedestrian.

Payments for any one person may not exceed the limit stated in the declarations. Because no aggregate limit applies, the insurer may pay several times the limit if several persons are injured. Because medical payments coverage is designed for minor bodily injury claims, insureds typically choose medical payments limits that are much lower than limits for bodily injury liability coverage. For example, an insured with a $1,000,000 combined single limit for bodily injury and property damage liability might carry medical payments coverage with a $10,000 limit.

No coverage exists if the injury occurs in the course of employment and is covered under workers compensation. War, nuclear radiation, and radioactive contamination are also excluded.

Personal Injury Protection and Added Personal Injury Protection

In an attempt to reduce litigation arising from auto accidents, several states have enacted auto no-fault laws, which are state statutes that require motorists to purchase (or require insurers to make available) insurance that provides minimum first-party benefits to injured persons regardless of fault.

Some of these laws also limit the injured person's right to sue for noneconomic losses ("pain and suffering") unless the injuries meet a certain threshold. In some states, the threshold is expressed in terms of a dollar amount of damages resulting from the injury. For example, motorists cannot sue unless $5,000 in medical expenses has been incurred. In other states, the threshold is expressed as a definition of "serious injury." Unless a motorist sustains "serious injury" as defined, he or she cannot sue for noneconomic losses.

Personal injury protection (PIP) coverage pays benefits, regardless of fault, for medical expense, income loss, and other expenses resulting from bodily injury to occupants of a covered auto. If the insured is subject to an auto no-fault law, this coverage can be added to the policy by endorsement.

PIP coverage is a first-party coverage, like medical payments coverage. That is, both medical payments and PIP pay benefits to an insured (the first party). In contrast, under liability coverage, the insurer agrees to pay all sums the insured is legally obligated to pay to someone who has made a claim against the insured (the third party).

Because benefit levels and other features of no-fault laws vary from state to state, a separate PIP endorsement exists for each no-fault state. In some no-fault states, benefit levels can be increased above the minimum required levels by using an added personal injury protection endorsement. PIP benefits are paid regardless of fault. The exclusions applicable to PIP coverage vary with state law.

The benefits provided by a typical PIP endorsement are payable for expenses resulting from bodily injury to occupants of a covered auto because of an auto accident, and they consist of these items:

- Coverage for medical and rehabilitation expenses
- Income loss benefit
- Substitute services benefit
- Death benefits to survivors

The substitute services benefit pays the cost of purchased services that would have been performed by the injured person if the injury had not occurred. An example is the cost of a housekeeper to do the work that a person usually performed before his or her injury. See the exhibit "Medical Payments and PIP Coverages."

Medical Payments and PIP Coverages

Both PIP and medical payments coverage provide first-party medical benefits to insureds injured in auto accidents. (PIP provides other benefits as well.) Are they redundant (totally overlapping) coverages? In some ways, yes. Medical payments coverage was available in auto policies before the introduction of no-fault laws. Then, as now, it provided a path to compensation for medical costs in auto-related accidents, with the goal of preventing lawsuits. In states that have since introduced mandatory no-fault laws requiring PIP coverage, medical payments coverage is redundant in many cases and certainly less important than such coverage in states without no-fault laws. However, medical payments coverage is typically inexpensive in PIP states and can be a valuable coverage gap filler due to variations in state PIP laws and in PIP eligibility rules.

[DA07928]

Uninsured and Underinsured Motorists Insurance

Uninsured and underinsured motorists laws are state statutes that require auto insurers to offer uninsured and underinsured motorists coverage to all insured motorists who are their policyholders. These laws are in effect in most states. They establish that a vehicle owner can obtain insurance, under his or her auto policy, to pay for injuries caused by another motorist who is uninsured (or underinsured) and, as a result, unable to pay. Some states allow the policyholder to sign a release stating that the coverage is not wanted. Uninsured and underinsured motorists insurance can be added to the BACF by endorsement.

Uninsured Motorists (UM) Coverage

Uninsured motorists (UM) coverage covers any person injured by an uninsured motorist while riding in an auto insured under the policy. In addition, if the named insured is an individual proprietorship, the policy covers the named insured and members of his or her family while riding in any auto or if struck by an uninsured motorist while a pedestrian. "Uninsured motorist" is typically defined in the applicable UM endorsement to include these parties:

- A driver of a vehicle for which no liability insurance is provided at the time of the accident
- A driver of a vehicle for which liability insurance is provided, but with limits less than those required by state law
- A hit-and-run driver

A driver of a governmental vehicle or a vehicle owned by a person or an organization that has qualified as a self-insurer under state law is not an uninsured motorist for purposes of this coverage. UM coverage is a first-party type of insurance, which means that benefits are paid to the injured person by his or her own insurer. Benefits are paid only if the injuries were caused by an uninsured motorist under circumstances that make the uninsured motorist liable for the injuries.

If these conditions are met, the UM coverage provides a source of recovery that the uninsured motorist's liability insurance would have paid if he or she had been insured. In essence, the insured is buying the coverage that the uninsured driver should have purchased. In most states, UM coverage is applicable only to bodily injury. In some states, uninsured motorists coverage can be extended to cover property damage as well. The endorsement for adding UM coverage varies by state.

Underinsured Motorists (UIM) Coverage

An insured can also purchase underinsured motorists coverage (UIM). Although the details of coverage differ from state to state, the basic purpose of UIM coverage is to cover injuries caused by motorists who have liability insurance but for an amount less than the insured's limit for underinsured motorists coverage. In some states, UIM coverage is included in UM coverage and does not need to be purchased separately.

Like medical payments and PIP coverage, UM and UIM coverage can compensate the insured for medical costs from an auto accident. UM and UIM can be applied to all damages resulting from bodily injury in an auto accident, including funeral costs, lost income, and loss of services. Unlike either medical payments or PIP coverage, insureds may find compensation under UM or UIM for noneconomic losses that are not directly tied to a specific monetary amount. The most common instance of noneconomic loss is a settlement (offered by the insurer or determined in court) of an amount of money to compensate for "pain and suffering" related to injuries sustained in an auto accident.

RATING COMMERCIAL AUTO INSURANCE

Private passenger vehicles are rated from private passenger premium tables. The methodology for rating trucks, tractors, and trailers depends on whether the vehicle must be zone rated or not. A vehicle is zone rated if it is a "medium" or "large" truck operating more than 200 miles from its principal garaging location. The premiums for zone rated vehicles reflect the various zones in which they are operated.

Commercial autos can be rated using rules found in the automobile division of the ISO CLM. Under these rules, the rating procedure to be used for a particular insured depends on which of the five classification subsections apply to the insured's autos:

1. Private passenger vehicles
2. Trucks, tractors, and trailers
3. Public transportation vehicles
4. Garages
5. Special types of vehicles

Private Passenger Vehicles

Premiums for private passenger autos insured under a business auto form are obtained directly from private passenger premium tables. Liability premium tables list premiums by rating territory and policy limit. Physical damage tables list comprehensive and collision premiums by rating territory, the vehicle's "original cost new," and the deductible amount chosen. These premiums are not multiplied by rating factors.

Trucks, Tractors, and Trailers

A large part of the loss experience for any trucking operation depends directly on the area in which the insured's trucks are operated. The exposures faced by a local delivery truck are different from those encountered by a large tractor-semitrailer used for cross-country hauling. Except for light trucks, any vehicle in the truck, tractor, or trailer category that is regularly operated over a route that takes it more than 200 miles from its principal garaging location must be zone rated to account for the different hazards facing local and long-distance driving.

Primary Factor

The first step in rating a vehicle (whether zone rated or not) is to determine its primary factor. The primary factor depends on the vehicle's size class, its business use, and its radius class. The exhibit lists the characteristics that determine the primary factor. See the exhibit "Primary Rating Factors for Trucks, Tractors, and Trailers."

Primary Rating Factors for Trucks, Tractors, and Trailers

1. Size Class (determined by gross vehicle weight—GVW)
   - Light
   - Medium
   - Heavy
   - Extra-heavy
2. Business Use
   - Service
   - Retail
   - Commercial
3. Radius Class
   - Local (within 50 miles)
   - Intermediate (between 51 and 200 miles)
   - Long distance (beyond 200 miles)

[DA02606]

Size class—There are four size classes for trucks (light, medium, heavy, and extra-heavy), determined by the vehicle's gross vehicle weight (GVW). GVW is the vehicle's maximum loaded weight specified by the manufacturer. In addition, there are two size classes for truck-tractors (heavy and extra-heavy), determined by the vehicle's gross combination weight (GCW). GCW is the maximum loaded weight for a truck-tractor and its semitrailer or trailer together.

Business use—Business use for trucks, tractors, and trailers is categorized as service, retail, or commercial. Service use describes the use of vehicles to carry workers, equipment, supplies, and so forth to or from job sites at which the vehicle generally remains parked for most of the workday. Retail use principally involves pickup and delivery of property to or from individual households. Commercial use is the category into which vehicles are placed if they do not qualify for the service or retail use categories.

Radius class—Primary factors are also governed by the radius of the area within which the vehicle is operated—within 50 miles of the principal garaging location (local), between 51 and 200 miles (intermediate), and beyond 200 miles (long distance). **Zone rated vehicles** are trucks in the medium and larger size classes that are operated beyond a 200-mile radius of the principal garaging location and that are subject to zone rating, which considers the territories in which insured vehicles operate.

Zone rated vehicles

Trucks in the medium and larger size classes that are operated beyond a 200-mile radius of the principal garaging location and that are subject to zone rating, which considers the territories in which insured vehicles operate.

Premium Computation

After the primary factor has been determined, premium computation methods differ depending on whether the vehicle is zone rated.

Non-zone rated vehicles—A truck, tractor, or trailer is not zone rated if it is a light truck operating over any distance, or a medium or larger truck operating predominantly within 200 miles of its principal garaging location. When a commercial auto is not zone rated, the primary factor is added to a secondary factor associated with the nature of the insured's business operations. The sum of the primary factor and the secondary factor is called the combined factor.

Secondary factors correspond to a number of industry classifications. Depending on the degree of hazard that is characteristic of the particular industry, these factors either increase or decrease the primary factor.

The base premiums for liability and physical damage coverage are multiplied by the combined factor. Base liability premiums are determined on the basis of the policy limit and the territory in which the auto is principally garaged. Base physical damage premiums are determined on the basis of the vehicle's age and its cost new.

Zone rated vehicles—After the primary factor has been determined for a zone rated vehicle, its physical damage and liability premiums are calculated by applying the primary factor to base premiums. Secondary factors are not used for zone rated autos.

Base premiums for zone rated autos are affected by the various geographical zones in which the vehicles are operated, because liability and collision losses are much more likely in metropolitan areas than on the open road. Moreover, the probability of some comprehensive physical damage losses, such as theft or windstorm, varies from one region of the country to another. Base physical damage premiums also depend on the vehicle's cost new, the current age of the vehicle, the type of vehicle (with respect to collision coverage), and the chosen deductible.

DETERMINING WHETHER THE BACF COVERS A CLAIM

Knowing how to apply the auto liability and physical damage coverages provided by the Insurance Services Office, Inc. (ISO) Business Auto Coverage Form (BACF) to the facts of a case is an important skill. This case study will help you make the transition from knowing policy language to applying policy language to losses to determine whether coverage applies. As you progress through the case study, you can check your understanding of the coverage provided by answering the Knowledge to Action questions.

Case Facts

Office Equipment Company (OEC) is insured under a commercial package policy that includes the BACF. The only coverage endorsements attached to the BACF are for providing uninsured and underinsured motorists coverage, as required by the state in which OEC is located and in which its autos are registered. On February 6, 20X0, Hector, an OEC sales representative, was scheduled to make sales calls at customers' offices. In accordance with OEC policy, Hector used his own auto to make the sales calls. Hector's auto was insured under a Personal Auto Policy (PAP) with a $500,000 single limit of insurance for liability coverage.

While driving to the first customer's office, located in the same state as OEC, Hector did not see a traffic light turn red and improperly entered the intersection, colliding with a car that had the right of way. This other car was driven by Michael, who was seriously injured. Hector's airbag deployed, and he received only some bruises that did not require medical treatment. Michael subsequently made a claim against Hector and OEC for bodily injury to himself and property damage to his car.

After investigating the facts of Michael's claim, OEC's insurer concluded that Hector and OEC were legally liable for the $650,000 in damages sustained by Michael. Hector was primarily liable because his negligent driving resulted in the accident that injured Michael. OEC was also liable because Hector was operating his car in the course of employment for OEC at the time of the accident.

Before offering a settlement, however, the insurer needs to determine whether Michael's claim is covered under Section II—Covered Autos Liability Coverage of OEC's BACF and, if so, for what amount. OEC's BACF is not subject to any endorsements that would affect coverage for Michael's claim.

Necessary Reference Materials

To determine whether the BACF provides coverage for Michael's claim, for which Hector and OEC both sought coverage under OEC's BACF, you need to consult the relevant information drawn from OEC's BACF declarations page and any policy provisions that apply to the loss.

Overview of Steps

When examining the declarations page to determine whether coverage applies to each loss, you can apply the four steps of the DICE method. Doing this involves analyzing the policy declarations, insuring agreement, conditions, and exclusions and determining whether any information found at each step precludes coverage at the time of each loss. You should also examine other policy provisions such as the limit of insurance, deductible, endorsements (not applicable in this case), and terms defined in the policy.

Determination of Coverage

Determining whether the BACF applies to this claim involves analyzing the relevant portions of the policy and determining whether any information found at each step in the DICE method precludes coverage at the time of the loss. You should also examine other categories of policy provisions such as the insured's duties; general provisions; endorsements (if applicable); and terms defined in the policy in relation to the declarations, insuring agreement, conditions, and exclusions.

DICE Analysis Step 1: Declarations

The first DICE step is to review the declarations page. See the exhibit "Excerpt of Declarations Page."

Knowledge to Action

Action Task: Analyze the excerpt of OEC's BACF declarations page.

According to your analysis of OEC's BACF declarations page, what information shown is relevant to OEC's claim and how will this information be used to determine whether coverage is applicable in this case?

Feedback: The policy inception and expiration dates allow you to determine whether the bodily injury and property damage occurred during the policy period. The Named Insured line allows you to determine that OEC is an insured under the policy, and the covered auto symbol and limit of insurance entered verify that the policy includes liability coverage. The covered auto symbol will be key to determining whether the accident involved a covered auto, and the amount of the limit will be important in deciding what amount of the loss is covered.

DICE Analysis Step 2: Insuring Agreement

The second DICE step is to review the insuring agreement to determine whether it is applicable to the described loss.

For damages to be covered under the insuring agreement in Section II—Liability Coverage, a claim must meet several conditions stated in the insuring agreement:

A. Coverage

We will pay all sums an "insured" legally must pay as damages because of "bodily injury" or "property damage" to which this insurance applies, caused by an "accident" and resulting from the ownership, maintenance or use of a covered "auto".

We will also pay all sums an "insured" legally must pay as a "covered pollution cost or expense" to which this insurance applies, caused by an "accident" and resulting from the ownership, maintenance or use of covered "autos". However, we will only pay for the

Excerpt of Declarations Page

POLICY NUMBER:

COMMERCIAL AUTO
CA DS 03 03 10

BUSINESS AUTO DECLARATIONS

ITEM ONE

Company Name: Office Equipment Company	**Producer Name:**
Named Insured: Office Equipment Company	**Mailing Address:**

Policy Period	
From: January 1, 20X0	
To: January 1, 20X1	At 12:01 AM Standard Time at your mailing address shown above
Previous Policy Number:	

Form Of Business:

[X] Corporation   [ ] Limited Liability Company   [ ] Individual

[ ] Partnership   [ ] Other:

ITEM TWO
Schedule Of Coverages And Covered Autos

This policy provides only those coverages where a charge is shown in the premium column below. Each of these coverages will apply only to those "autos" shown as covered "autos". **"Autos" are shown as covered "autos" for a particular coverage by the entry of one or more of the symbols from the Covered Autos Section of the Business Auto Coverage Form next to the name of the coverage.**

Coverages	Covered Autos	Limit	Premium
Liability	1	$ 1,000,000	$

Copyright, ISO Properties, Inc. [DA07934]

"covered pollution cost or expense" if there is either "bodily injury" or "property damage" to which this insurance applies that is caused by the same "accident".

We have the right and duty to defend any "insured" against a "suit" asking for such damages or a "covered pollution cost or expense". However, we have no duty to defend any "insured" against a "suit" seeking damages for "bodily injury" or "property damage" or a "covered pollution cost or expense" to which this insurance does not apply. We may investigate and settle any claim or "suit" as we consider appropriate. Our duty to defend or settle ends when the Liability Coverage Limit of Insurance has been exhausted by payment of judgments or settlements.[4]

The first condition is that the insured must be legally liable to pay damages. The insurer's investigation found that Hector and OEC were legally liable to pay damages to Michael. However, the insurer must now determine whether both Hector and OEC qualify as insureds under OEC's BACF under the circumstances of this claim by reviewing the BACF's Who Is An Insured section:

1. Who Is An Insured

The following are "insureds":

a. You for any covered "auto".

b. Anyone else while using with your permission a covered "auto" you own, hire or borrow except:

(1) The owner or anyone else from whom you hire or borrow a covered "auto". This exception does not apply if the covered "auto" is a "trailer" connected to a covered "auto" you own.

(2) Your "employee" if the covered "auto" is owned by that "employee" or a member of his or her household.

(3) Someone using a covered "auto" while he or she is working in a business of selling, servicing, repairing, parking or storing "autos" unless that business is yours.

(4) Anyone other than your "employees", partners (if you are a partnership), members (if you are a limited liability company), or a lessee or borrower or any of their "employees", while moving property to or from a covered "auto".

(5) A partner (if you are a partnership), or a member (if you are a limited liability company) for a covered "auto" owned by him or her or a member of his or her household.

c. Anyone liable for the conduct of an "insured" described above but only to the extent of that liability.[5]

Knowledge to Action

Action Task: Analyze the BACF's Who Is An Insured section and the relevant excerpts of OEC's BACF declarations page.

According to your analysis of the BACF's Who Is An Insured section and the relevant excerpts of OEC's BACF declarations page, is OEC an insured for Michael's claim and was Hector's car a covered auto at the time of the accident?

Feedback: Paragraph a. of Who Is An Insured states that "you" (OEC) are an insured for any covered auto, and OEC has symbol 1 (any auto) for liability coverage. Therefore, OEC is an insured for this claim. Paragraph b. of Who Is An Insured states that "anyone else while using with your permission a covered 'auto' you own, hire or borrow" is an insured. Hector was driving his own car, which has already been established to be a covered auto under OEC's BACF. However, Hector's car is not "a covered 'auto' you [OEC] own, hire or borrow." Moreover, even if it were, paragraph b.(2) of Who Is An Insured excludes any employee of the named insured if the covered auto is owned by that employee. Therefore, Hector is not an insured under OEC's policy for Michael's claim. (If the Employees as Insureds endorsement were attached to the policy, Hector would be an insured for this claim under OEC's policy, but that endorsement is not attached to OEC's policy.)

Action Task: Analyze the Coverage section of the BACF insuring agreement.

According to your analysis of the BACF insuring agreement, does the claim meet the remainder of the conditions that the insuring agreement imposes on coverage?

Feedback: The second condition is that the damages claimed must result from bodily injury or property damage. The insurer's investigation of the claim found that Michael's damages were all for bodily injury or property damage. The third condition is that the insurance must apply to the bodily injury or property damage. Determination of whether the claim meets this requirement must wait until the exclusions and other policy conditions are analyzed. The fourth condition is that the bodily injury or property damage must be caused by an accident. The insurer's investigation found that to be the case. The fifth condition is that the bodily injury or property damage must result from the ownership, maintenance, or use of a covered auto. As already established in connection with the first condition, Hector's auto was a covered auto at the time of the accident.

DICE Analysis Step 3: Conditions

The third DICE step is to review the policy conditions to determine whether they affect coverage at the time of the loss.

In addition to meeting the conditions imposed by the liability coverage insuring agreement, the circumstances of the claim must meet all other applicable policy conditions contained in Section IV—Business Auto Conditions.

The Duties in the Event of Accident, Claim, Suit or Loss apply to any claim scenario. OEC satisfactorily performed all the duties described in that condition.

The Policy Period, Coverage Territory condition also must be considered for every claim. In Michael's claim, the accident occurred within both the policy period and the coverage territory.

The Other Insurance condition is also applicable to this claim:

> 5. Other Insurance
>
> a. For any covered "auto" you own, this Coverage Form provides primary insurance. For any covered "auto" you don't own, the insurance provided by this Coverage Form is excess over any other collectible insurance. However, while a covered "auto" which is a "trailer" is connected to another vehicle, the Liability Coverage this Coverage Form provides for the "trailer" is:
>
> (1) Excess while it is connected to a motor vehicle you do not own.
>
> (2) Primary while it is connected to a covered "auto" you own.[6]

Knowledge to Action

Action Task: Review the Case Facts section and the BACF's Other Insurance condition.

According to your analysis of the Case Facts section, how would the BACF's Other Insurance condition affect coverage for Michael's claim?

Feedback: Hector insures his car under a PAP with a $500,000 limit of insurance applicable to liability coverage. Paragraph a. of the Other Insurance condition states that for any covered auto that OEC does not own, the BACF is excess over any other collectible insurance.

The investigation conducted by OEC's insurer revealed that Hector's insurer had settled with Michael for its full $500,000 limit for liability coverage. Moreover, OEC qualified as an insured under Hector's policy. Thus, the $500,000 settlement was "other collectible insurance," and OEC's policy will pay (on behalf of OEC, not on behalf of Hector) Michael's damages in excess of the $500,000 settlement.

DICE Analysis Step 4: Exclusions

The fourth DICE step is to determine whether the exclusions in Section II—Liability Coverage apply to the claim. None of the BACF's exclusions apply in this case.

Coverage Extensions

The coverage extensions in Section II of the BACF include both supplementary payments and out-of-state coverage extensions. Each of these must be considered when determining the BACF's coverage of Michael's claim:

- If the insurer settles the claim out of court, most of the supplementary payments will not be needed. However, paragraph (1), which covers "All expenses we incur," clarifies that the insurer will pay all the costs it incurs to investigate and settle the claim. The insurer's payment for these expenses does not reduce the limit of insurance that is available for covering damages.

- Because the claim against OEC did not involve out-of-state insurance limits or requirements, the out-of-state coverage extensions do not apply.

Determination of Amounts Payable

Now that you have completed the DICE analysis, you can determine the amount payable. Doing this involves applying the limit(s) of insurance available to pay for the loss and any applicable deductibles and conditions.

Knowledge to Action

Action Task: Review the Case Facts section and your DICE analysis.

How much will OEC's BACF insurer pay on behalf of OEC for Michael's claim?

Feedback: OEC's insurer will pay the amount by which Michael's $650,000 in damages exceeds the $500,000 in damages paid by Hector's policy. Because the resulting $150,000 in damages is less than the $1 million limit of insurance for liability coverage in OEC's policy, the insurer will pay $150,000 to Michael. No deductible applies to liability coverage in the BACF. Therefore, OEC's BACF insurer will pay $150,000 (plus all costs the insurer incurs) for Michael's claim.

SUMMARY

Commercial auto insurance can be used to cover liability exposures, property exposures, and personal exposures arising out of the ownership, maintenance, or use of autos. A common format for insuring these exposures is the ISO commercial auto coverage part. The components of a commercial auto coverage part include a declarations form, a commercial auto coverage form, and any applicable endorsements. The coverage part can be included in a CPP or issued as a monoline commercial auto policy.

The BACF contains five sections. Section I contains ten descriptions of covered auto symbols. These symbols are entered in a schedule in the declarations to indicate which autos are covered for each coverage selected.

Section II—Covered Autos Liability Coverage of the BACF covers the insured against claims alleging bodily injury or property damage resulting from the insured's ownership, maintenance, or use of a covered auto. The provisions contained in Section II include an insuring agreement, a definition of who is insured, coverage extensions, exclusions, and a limit of insurance provision.

Section III of the BACF insures loss of or damage to autos owned by the insured and, if specified, autos hired or borrowed by the insured.

Section IV of the Business Auto Coverage Form, Business Auto Conditions, contains all conditions that apply to all coverages under the Business Auto Form. These can be categorized as loss conditions and general conditions.

Coverages for medical payments, personal injury protection, added personal injury protection, and uninsured and underinsured motorists are commonly included in the BACF by endorsement. Auto medical payments coverage pays a small bodily injury claim without any determination of liability, which can sometimes prevent an injured passenger from making a costlier liability claim against the driver. Personal injury protection coverage pays benefits, regardless of fault, for medical expense, income loss, and other expenses resulting from bodily injury to occupants of a covered auto. Uninsured and underinsured motorists coverage can be applied to all damages resulting from bodily injury in an auto accident, including funeral costs, lost income, and loss of services.

Private passenger vehicles are rated from private passenger premium tables. The methodology for rating trucks, tractors, and trailers depends on whether the vehicle must be zone rated or not. A vehicle is zone rated if it is a "medium" or "large" truck operating more than 200 miles from its principal garaging location. The premiums for zone rated vehicles reflect the various zones in which they are operated.

Determining whether the BACF covers a particular claim requires applying the policy's declarations, insuring agreement, conditions, exclusions, and coverage extensions to the details of the claim to determine whether the loss is covered and for what amount. The insuring agreement's Who Is An Insured section is crucial to this determination, as is the application of the Other Insurance condition, which can affect the amount payable.

ASSIGNMENT NOTES

1.   Copyright, Insurance Services Office, Inc., 2011.

2.   Includes copyrighted material of Insurance Services Office, Inc., with its permission. Copyright, Insurance Services Office, Inc., 2011.

3.   Includes copyrighted material of Insurance Services Office, Inc, with its permission. Copyright, ISO Properties, Inc., 2005.

4.   Includes copyrighted material of Insurance Services Office, Inc. Copyright, Insurance Services Office, Inc., 2011.

5.   Includes copyrighted material of Insurance Services Office, Inc. Copyright, Insurance Services Office, Inc., 2011.

6.   Includes copyrighted material of Insurance Services Office, Inc. Copyright, Insurance Services Office, Inc., 2011.

9

Workers Compensation and Employers Liability Insurance

Educational Objectives

After learning the content of this assignment, you should be able to:

▷ Describe workers compensation statutes in terms of these common characteristics:

- Basic purpose

- Benefits provided

- Persons and employments covered

▷ Describe workers compensation statutes in terms of these common characteristics:

- Extraterritorial provisions

- Federal jurisdiction

- Methods for meeting employers' obligations

▷ Summarize these sections of the Workers Compensation and Employers Liability Insurance Policy:

- Information Page

- General Section

- Part One—Workers Compensation Insurance

▷ Explain why employers liability insurance is needed and how the Workers Compensation and Employers Liability Insurance Policy addresses this need.

▷ Describe the purpose and operation of Part Three—Other States Insurance in the Workers Compensation and Employers Liability Insurance Policy.

▶▶

9.1

9

Educational Objectives, continued

▷ Describe the need for and the coverage provided by each of the following endorsements:

- Voluntary Compensation and Employers' Liability Coverage Endorsement

- Longshore and Harbor Workers' Compensation Act Coverage Endorsement

▷ Explain how premium bases, classifications, and premium adjustments affect the rating of workers compensation insurance.

▷ Given a case, determine whether the Workers Compensation and Employers Liability Insurance Policy covers a described injury or illness and, if so, what types of benefits or what amount of damages is covered.

Workers Compensation and Employers Liability Insurance

9

WORKERS COMPENSATION STATUTES: PURPOSE, BENEFITS, AND PERSONS COVERED

Insureds with employees that must be covered under state workers compensation statutes need producers, underwriters, claim representatives, and risk management professionals who know the important common characteristics of what causes an employer's loss exposures, what benefits are payable, and who is eligible for payment.

Workers compensation statutes differ by state but share several common characteristics, including these:

- Basic purpose
- Benefits provided
- Persons and employments covered

Basic Purpose

In the United States, before the enactment of workers compensation statutes, workers injured in industrial accidents could, under the common law, sue their employers for damages resulting from the injury. It was up to the employee to establish that the employer was at fault for the injury. The following defenses were among those available to employers:

- The employee contributed to the accident.
- The employee assumed the risk of injury when he or she took the job.
- A fellow worker was responsible for the accident.

It was difficult for employees to overcome these defenses, and the majority of injured workers received no compensation.

To address this problem, individual states enacted workers compensation statutes, starting with New York in 1910 and Wisconsin in 1911. Today, every state, the District of Columbia, Puerto Rico, Guam, the U.S. Virgin Islands, every Canadian province, and some other nations have enacted **workers compensation statutes**. These laws provide no-fault protection by removing the right of employees to sue their employers for injuries covered by the applicable workers compensation statute while obligating employers to compensate injured employees even if employer negligence is not involved. In return for definite payment, the employer's liability is limited (but not eliminated) by

Workers compensation statute
A statute that obligates employers, regardless of fault, to pay specified medical, disability, rehabilitation, and death benefits for their employees' job-related injuries and diseases.

statute. Recovery under the applicable workers compensation law is thus often called the employee's "exclusive remedy" against the employer. The workers compensation system effectively guarantees injured workers prompt payment while reducing costs and court workloads arising out of litigation.

Benefits Provided

Workers compensation statutes provide benefits for medical expenses and wage loss resulting from either occupational injury or **occupational disease**.

Occupational disease

Disease thought to be caused by work or the work environment.

To be covered under a workers compensation statute, an injury or disease must (in most states) arise out of and in the course of employment. That is, the cause of the injury or disease must be related to the employment, and the occurrence must take place while the employee is engaged in work-related activities. For example, the statute would cover an employee who was injured falling from a ladder while changing a light bulb in his office because the injury arose out of and in the course of employment.

Generally, an employee is covered for any work-related injury sustained while at his or her place of employment or while traveling for the employer. Injuries occurring while traveling to or from work at a fixed location are typically not covered by the statute.

All U.S. workers compensation laws also include benefits covering occupational diseases. Most occupational diseases become evident during employment or soon after an employee's exposure to injurious conditions, although for some exposures the disease may be latent for a long time. Consequently, many states provide extended periods of time for the discovery of these slowly developing diseases. Although some states cover only occupational diseases specifically named in the law, the majority provide coverage for all occupational diseases.

Not all diseases contracted in the course of an occupation can be attributed to the work or occupational exposure. For example, the common cold is usually not a covered disease. In general, a cause and effect relationship must exist between the occupation and the disease for coverage to apply.

A typical workers compensation statute imposes absolute liability on employers for the benefits it provides. (Absolute liability is liability imposed without regard to fault.) This allows an employee to be at least partially compensated for expenses and loss of earnings incurred as a result of an occupational injury or disease. The benefits payable under the various state workers compensation laws generally include medical benefits, disability income benefits, rehabilitation benefits, and death benefits. See the exhibit "Workers Compensation Benefits."

Workers Compensation Benefits

Medical Benefits:	Disability Income Benefits:
• Medical • Hospital • Surgical • Related medical care costs, such as physical therapy and prosthetic devices	• Wage loss subject to a waiting period deductible • Payments for scheduled injuries
Rehabilitation Benefits:	**Death Benefits:**
• Medical rehabilitation • Vocational rehabilitation	• Burial expense • Partial replacement of the worker's former weekly wage

[DA07863]

Medical Benefits

In most instances, the workers compensation law provides full and unlimited medical expense benefits for a covered injury or disease. These benefits include medical, hospital, surgical, and other related medical care costs, including physical therapy and prosthetic devices. First-dollar benefits are ordinarily provided; no deductible or coinsurance provisions are imposed on the employee as under most medical insurance plans. Depending on state law, the injured employee may have the right to select his or her own doctor or may be limited to a choice from a list of physicians designated by the employer or its insurer.

Disability Income Benefits

Workers compensation statutes typically use four disability classifications:

- **Temporary partial disability** is a disability caused by a work-related injury or disease that temporarily limits the extent to which an employee can perform job duties for a period of time (such as thirty or sixty days). After that period, the worker is expected to be able to resume all job duties.
- **Temporary total disability** is a disability caused by a work-related injury or disease that temporarily renders an injured employee unable to perform any job duties for a period of time (such as thirty or sixty days). After that period, the worker is expected to be able to resume all job duties.

Temporary partial disability (TPD)

A disability caused by a work-related injury or disease that temporarily limits the extent to which a worker can perform job duties; the worker is eventually able to return to full duties and hours.

Temporary total disability (TTD)

A disability caused by a work-related injury or disease that temporarily renders an injured worker unable to perform any job duties for a period of time.

- Permanent partial disability is a disability caused by a work-related injury or disease that impairs the injured employee's earning capacity for life. The employee is able to work at reduced efficiency.
- Permanent total disability is a disability caused by a work-related injury or disease that renders an injured employee unable to ever return to gainful employment.

Disability income benefits are intended to compensate an injured employee for wage loss in any of these categories. Unlike medical benefits, income benefits are payable subject to a deductible in the form of a waiting period. Disability benefits do not begin until the waiting period has expired. The waiting period generally varies from three to seven days, depending on the state. If disability continues beyond a specified number of days, most laws provide for payment of benefits retroactive to the date of injury.

The benefit is payable weekly and is expressed as a percentage of the employee's average weekly wage at the time of disability. Maximum and minimum weekly benefit amounts vary widely from state to state.

State laws also require compensation for a specific number of weeks for the loss (or loss of use) of specific body parts, such as fingers. These injuries are referred to as "scheduled" injuries because the injuries and corresponding benefits are listed in a document called a schedule. Scheduled injuries do not generally cause permanent total disability, but the resulting permanent impairment is assumed to produce long-term loss of wages. As a result, the benefits for scheduled injuries are payable without regard to actual wage loss. All but the lowest paid or part-time workers generally qualify for the maximum compensation. In most states, the compensation for scheduled injuries is in addition to any other temporary disability benefits payable.

Rehabilitation Benefits

Because rehabilitation of injured workers is a goal of the workers compensation system, most state laws include some rehabilitation benefits. The primary rehabilitation benefit required is the payment of expenses for complete medical treatment and medical rehabilitation. Vocational rehabilitation may also be required by law. Most workers compensation laws provide a maintenance allowance to injured workers during rehabilitation in addition to other compensation benefits.

In addition, insurers provide rehabilitation services extending beyond the requirements of the law. For example, an insurer might include payment of expenses to customize a car or van to accommodate the physical disabilities of an injured worker in order to allow the employee to more easily return to light duty work.

Often, rehabilitation can reduce the cost of a workers compensation claim by shortening the length of time that the injured employee is disabled. Consequently, all parties benefit from rehabilitation. The employer and its insurer often save loss costs, and the injured worker returns to productive employment. Thus, rehabilitation also benefits society as a whole.

Death Benefits

Death benefits include a flat amount for burial expense and partial replacement of the worker's former weekly wage. The burial expense allowance varies among the states. The percentage of wage loss payable also varies by state and depends primarily on the number and types of dependents. Some states provide a maximum benefit expressed as either a total amount or a time period.

Apply Your Knowledge

Sam was employed as a producer at an insurance agency. He was traveling to a prospective customer's office for a sales call when he was involved in an auto accident. Sam was injured in the accident, breaking bones in one foot and fingers on both hands. He was immediately taken to the hospital and treated for his injuries. He had temporary total disability. Because of good medical care, Sam has no residual disability and will be able to resume all of his duties at work, without further treatment, after eight weeks. What workers compensation benefits is Sam eligible for?

Feedback: Sam's hospital, medical, surgical and related medical care costs, such as physical therapy, if needed, will be paid for by his employer's workers compensation insurer. After the waiting period deductible expires, Sam will be paid a percentage of his lost wages, including the wages he lost during the waiting period. Since Sam fully recovered from the accident, his lost wages benefit will end when he returns to work in eight weeks. He will not be paid for any rehabilitation expenses as they were not incurred. Sam, or his estate, will also not receive any death benefits, as he did not die as a result of the accident.

Persons and Employments Covered

Workers compensation statutes apply to virtually all industrial workers and most other kinds of private employment. The statutes of some states exempt employers with fewer than a stipulated number of employees, and many statutes specifically exclude certain employments such as farm labor, domestic workers, and casual employees. (A casual employee is one hired for only a short period, usually to accomplish a particular task.)

Many states provide workers compensation protection for all or certain classes of public employees. Some employees are excluded because alternate plans are provided for them. For example, federal statutes govern the rights of various classes of employees to recover benefits or damages from their employers for occupational injury or disease. Examples of such classes of employees are federal government workers, maritime workers, and interstate railroad workers.

Employees and Independent Contractors

Entitlement to benefits under a workers compensation law depends on whether a person qualifies as an **employee** according to the law.

Employee

A person hired to perform services for another under the direction and control of the other party, called the employer.

Independent contractor

A person (or organization) hired to perform services without being subject to the hirer's direction and control regarding work details.

The distinction between employees and **independent contractors** is not always clear. Unlike employees, independent contractors are not subject to direction and control regarding the details of the work. They agree to perform a task meeting the specifications stipulated in the contract but are free to use their own judgment and methods in performing the task. They may also employ others to perform the task, but they remain responsible under the contract for its completion.

Employment status is a question of fact, not of law. If doubt arises concerning whether an individual is an employee or an independent contractor, a court or an administrative body decides the issue on the basis of the facts. The legislative mandate generally calls for the workers compensation law to be applied liberally. Therefore, the courts have interpreted the definition of an employee broadly to provide protection to those who seek it.

An independent contractor might also employ others. An independent contractor, like all other employers, must provide workers compensation benefits for its employees. In many states, if the contractor does not provide workers compensation insurance, the responsibility and the expense fall on the principal (the firm that uses the contractor's services). Furthermore, if a firm does not have certificates of insurance from the contractors it uses, its workers compensation insurer may require it to pay workers compensation insurance premiums based on the cost of the work sub-contracted. To be certain that the contractor has workers compensation insurance in force, the principal usually requires the contractor to provide a certificate of insurance as evidence of the insurance in force when the certificate was issued.

Leased Employees and Temporary Employees

Many organizations use leased employees, temporary employees, or both. Leased employees differ from temporary employees. Temporary employees are hired for short-term assignments to cope with peak loads or to replace an employee who is on sick leave or vacation. The firm supplying the temporary employee provides workers compensation for temporary employees; the temporary employee is an employee of the providing firm, not the firm that is using his or her services.

In contrast with temporary employees, leased employees have all the outward appearance of regular employees. They work continuously for the same firm and are subject to control by the firm just as they would be if they were its direct employees. Technically, however, they are co-employees of the client company and the leasing contractor, sometimes referred to as a professional employer organization (PEO). Sometimes a firm will transfer its employees to a PEO and then lease them back. The PEO is responsible for all payroll taxes, employee benefits, and workers compensation coverage. Generally, a separate workers compensation policy is written showing the names of the PEO and the client company, although the requirements imposed by law vary from state to state.[1]

WORKERS COMPENSATION STATUTES: EXTRATERRITORIAL PROVISIONS, FEDERAL JURISDICTION, AND METHODS FOR MEETING EMPLOYERS' OBLIGATIONS

In addition to describing the types of benefits covered and the persons and employments eligible, workers compensation statutes address other issues that are vital to understanding workers compensation insurance and handling it correctly.

Three additional common characteristics of workers compensation statutes include these:

- Extraterritorial provisions
- Federal jurisdiction
- Methods for meeting employers' obligations

Extraterritorial Provisions

For some employment-related injuries, the workers compensation statutes of more than one state may apply, depending on the circumstances of employ-ment. Also, many workers compensation statutes provide some coverage for employees who are temporarily working outside the United States.

Application of Laws Out of State

When a worker travels into another state and is injured there, questions may arise as to how to apply the workers compensation laws of the states involved. Most workers compensation laws have extraterritorial provisions dealing with this issue. Extraterritorial provisions provide that employees can receive benefits provided by the law of the state in which they are hired even if the accident occurs in another state.

For example, Jorge, an account executive for an insurance agency in State A, is injured while meeting with an insured in the insured's office in State B. Jorge can collect workers compensation benefits under the State A law. Jorge may also have a right to claim benefits under the State B law instead because he was injured in State B. The determination of which state's law applies depends on the provisions of the laws in question. Typical considerations include these:

- The place and nature of employment
- The place where the employee was hired
- The employee's place of residence
- The state in which the employer is domiciled

The determination can be complicated by the different coverage and benefit provisions found in the various states. For example, a truck driver may live in Massachusetts, work for a trucking firm in Pennsylvania, and drive through several states as part of his or her employment. According to the laws of about half of the states, if the driver is injured, a compensation claim conceivably could be filed in the state where the injury occurred, where the employment principally occurred, or where the employee was hired. Because benefit levels vary from state to state, the employee, when permitted to choose which law will apply, can select the workers compensation law with the most generous benefits.

Apply Your Knowledge

Renee is a claims representative hired and working in North Carolina. Her manager in Florida sends Renee on catastrophe (CAT) duty to an area of Mississippi that has suffered severe winds and hail damage. While inspecting an insured's roof, she slips and falls off the roof, breaking both a leg and an arm. She is unable to return to her work for three months. Which state's workers compensation statute applies to Renee's injuries?

Feedback: Renee will likely have her choice of which state's workers compensation statute she seeks benefits from. She was hired and resides in North Carolina, and her regular place of employment is there. However, the nature of her employment is that she occasionally gets assigned CAT duty in a state other than North Carolina. If the manager that ordered her to Mississippi did so from the state where the insurer is domiciled, Renee could select Florida's workers compensation statute. The fact that the injury occurred in Mississippi also makes Mississippi's workers compensation statute a possibility. In summary, Renee may be able to choose North Carolina's, Florida's, or Mississippi's statute. Her selection could be based on which state provides the most generous benefits for her injuries.

Application of Laws in Foreign Countries

Employees who are temporarily working outside the U.S. are generally covered by the extraterritorial provision of the workers compensation law of the state where they regularly work, provided they have not been out of the U.S.

for longer than the time limit specified in the applicable law. The time limit can be as much as six months in some states but as little as thirty days in others.

In addition to time-limited coverage, another problem for firms with employees outside the country is that workers compensation laws in the U.S. may not provide coverage for repatriation expense or endemic disease. Repatriation expense is the added cost of transporting an ill, injured, or deceased employee back to his or her home area; such transportation can be very costly. Endemic disease refers to a disease that is prevalent in a particular country (for example, malaria in tropical countries).

Many insurers offer foreign voluntary workers compensation coverage either as an endorsement to an insured's workers compensation policy or as part of a separate foreign insurance policy. Foreign voluntary workers compensation coverage provides "home-state" coverage without a time limit for U.S. employees who are working outside the U.S. and also often includes coverage for repatriation expense and endemic disease.

In most countries outside the U.S., the local coverage for occupational injury and disease is very different from that of the U.S. workers compensation system. Only a few countries have workers compensation laws comparable to those found in the U.S. and Canada.

In many countries, employees retain the right to sue their employers. Consequently, employers with employees in these countries need employers liability insurance with a coverage territory encompassing the foreign countries in which the employer operates.

Federal Jurisdiction

Occupational injuries of most maritime workers, employees of interstate railroads, and certain other workers are under the jurisdiction of federal law. Federal jurisdiction over these workers' injuries arises either as a result of specific federal statutes or because the work location comes within the jurisdiction of admiralty (maritime) law.

The **United States Longshore and Harbor Workers' Compensation Act (LHWCA)** provides an exclusive remedy to injured maritime workers (engaged in longshoring or shipbuilding) subject to the act. Like state workers compensation statutes, the LHWCA eliminates the right of injured workers to sue their employers but requires compensation for work-related injuries without regard to fault. Congress has also extended the LHWCA to cover certain categories of government-related employment.

Officers and crew members of vessels are not covered by the LHWCA. However, they have various legal remedies they can pursue for job-related injuries. One of the remedies is commonly known as the **Jones Act**, but is officially named the United States Merchant Marine Act of 1920. Admiralty

United States Longshore and Harbor Workers' Compensation Act (LHWCA)

A federal statute that eliminates the right of most maritime workers (other than crew members of vessels) to sue their employers and, in return, requires such employers to provide injured or ill workers with benefits like those provided by state workers compensation statutes.

Jones Act (United States Merchant Marine Act of 1920)

A federal statute that permits injured members of a vessel's crew (or survivors of a deceased crew member) to sue their employer for damages due to the employer's negligence.

law, the branch of federal law that governs most maritime matters, provides additional remedies to injured crew members, including these:

- A lawsuit against the employer for injury resulting from unseaworthiness of the vessel
- An injured crew member's right to "maintenance" (food and shelter) and "cure" (medical attention), regardless of whether the employer was at fault

Interstate railroad workers, like the officers and crew of vessels, can sue their employers for injuries resulting from employer negligence. This remedy is provided by the Federal Employers Liability Act.

Methods for Meeting Employers' Obligations

Most workers compensation statutes require employers to demonstrate financial ability to pay any claims that may arise. Several methods are available to meet this obligation:

- Voluntary insurance
- Assigned risk plans
- State funds or employers mutual insurance companies
- Qualified self-insurance plans
- Self-insured groups

Not every state allows all of these methods.

Voluntary Insurance

An employer can meet its workers compensation obligations by purchasing insurance from a private insurer licensed to write workers compensation coverage in the state. This insurance market is called voluntary because the insurer is free to select its insureds and voluntarily offers to provide the needed coverage. In return for the premium, the insurer promises to pay the benefits and assume most administrative duties required by law for work-related injuries.

Assigned Risk Plans

Some businesses cannot obtain private insurance in the voluntary market because they do not meet insurers' underwriting criteria. Assigned risk plans exist to make insurance available. An employer rejected by private insurers can apply to the assigned risk plan in the appropriate state to obtain coverage.

In a typical assigned risk plan, the state will "assign" each applicant (rejected first by the voluntary market) to be insured by a private insurer. The private insurers are compelled to accept assigned risk policies in a quantity that is proportionate to their share of the voluntary market. Assigned risk plans are also known as the involuntary market.

State Funds and Employers Mutual Insurance Companies

In approximately one-half of the states in the U.S., state funds provide workers compensation insurance. Territorial funds are in effect in Puerto Rico and the U.S. Virgin Islands. Although controlled by the state or territorial government, these state and territorial funds operate in much the same manner as private insurance companies. The most significant differences are that they accept any good faith applicant for insurance in the state and that no assigned risk plan is necessary. In most jurisdictions, the fund competes with private insurers. In a few other jurisdictions, the state fund is the sole provider of workers compensation coverage. The legislatures in a handful of other states have created employers mutual insurance companies that also accept virtually all applicants but, unlike state funds, are not controlled by the state.

In most states having state funds, such funds are **competitive state funds**. An employer in these states can purchase insurance from either a private insurer or the state fund. In some states, the competitive state fund is the largest writer of workers compensation insurance—sometimes writing more than half of the total premium volume for that line of business in the state.

> **Competitive state fund**
> A state fund that sells workers compensation insurance in competition with private insurers.

Puerto Rico, the U.S. Virgin Islands, and four states (North Dakota, Ohio, Washington, and Wyoming) require all workers compensation insurance to be purchased from the state or territorial fund. Such a fund is known as a **monopolistic state fund (exclusive state fund)**. Workers compensation coverage, but not necessarily employers liability coverage, is available from these funds. Competitive state funds and employers mutual insurance companies usually do provide employers liability coverage.

> **Monopolistic state fund (exclusive state fund)**
> A facility, owned and operated by a state government, that provides workers compensation insurance and that does not permit any other insurers to sell workers compensation insurance in that state.

All Canadian provinces have boards or commissions with complete jurisdiction over workers compensation. These boards are similar in concept and organization to monopolistic state funds in the U.S.

Instead of establishing state funds, the legislatures in a few states have created **employers mutual insurance companies**. (The legislature for each such state creates only a single employers mutual insurance company to operate within that state.) These companies closely resemble any other mutual insurer except that they are typically required by their charters to provide workers compensation insurance to any qualified employer in the state. Unlike state funds, employers mutual insurance companies are not instrumentalities of the state; however, like competitive state funds, they do compete with other insurers. Employers mutual insurance companies are often the largest writers of workers compensation insurance in their states.

> **Employers mutual insurance company**
> A mutual insurer established by a state's legislature to write workers compensation insurance for any qualified employer in the state.

Qualified Self-Insurance Plans

Almost all states allow employers to retain (self-insure) the risk of workers compensation losses if they demonstrate the financial capacity to do so by meeting certain requirements.

To qualify as a self-insurer, an employer must post a surety bond with the workers compensation administrative agency of the state to guarantee the security of benefit payments. In addition, most states require evidence of an ability to administer the benefit payments and services mandated by the law. Self-insurance is usually practical only for employers with a large number of employees in a given state.

An employer that qualifies for self-insurance may decide to purchase excess insurance to cover catastrophic losses. Aggregate excess (also known as stop loss excess insurance) is insurance that covers losses only after the insured has retained a stated amount of aggregate loss during the policy period. For example, if the insurance required a retention of $250,000, the employer would pay losses up to an aggregate amount of $250,000. The insurer would pay any losses above $250,000, up to some stated limit such as $5 million. The amounts of the retention and the insurer's maximum limit are negotiated.

Specific excess insurance

Insurance that covers loss due to a single occurrence only for the amount that exceeds the policy retention.

Specific excess insurance is insurance that covers loss due to a single occurrence only for the amount that exceeds the policy retention. That is, specific excess insurance also requires a retention limit, but the retention is for one loss or all losses from one occurrence. If covered losses from one occurrence exceed the retained limit, the insurer would pay any additional losses from that occurrence, up to the policy limit.

Self-Insured Groups

In some states, employers may join with one another to form self-insured groups (also known as pools or trusts) to provide members with workers compensation insurance. Self-insured groups consist of employers in the same industry that jointly (as a whole) and severally (individually) guarantee payments of workers compensation benefits to the employees of the group's members.

The group processes and pays workers compensation claims on behalf of the participating entities. Frequently, claims processing and administration are outsourced to an unrelated firm called a third-party administrator (TPA).

Because they often deal directly with their members, self-insured groups claim that their costs for selling and servicing the coverage are lower than those of commercial insurers. In addition, in most states, self-insured groups are not covered by state guarantee funds. To increase the comfort level of their members and to avoid catastrophically large losses, self-insured groups generally purchase excess insurance.

WC&EL POLICY—WORKERS COMPENSATION INSURANCE

Workers compensation and employers liability insurance provides essential coverage for employees' bodily injury caused by accident or disease incurred on the job.

The **Workers Compensation and Employers Liability Insurance Policy (WC&EL policy)** was developed by the National Council on Compensation Insurance (NCCI), an insurance advisory organization for insurers that write workers compensation insurance. The WC&EL policy primarily covers an employer's obligation to pay benefits required by workers compensation statutes but also protects the employer against claims or suits for bodily injury to an employee when the workers compensation statute does not eliminate the right to sue the employer.

A complete WC&EL policy consists of an Information Page, a policy form, and any applicable endorsements. These documents are not designed to be included in the ISO commercial package policy format; WC&EL coverage is provided by a separate policy that stands on its own. The standard WC&EL policy form includes a brief General Section and these six parts:

- Part One—Workers Compensation Insurance
- Part Two—Employers Liability Insurance
- Part Three—Other States Insurance
- Part Four—Your Duties If Injury Occurs
- Part Five—Premium
- Part Six—Conditions

Part One—Workers Compensation Insurance, in tandem with the Information Page and definitions provided in the General Section, enables an employer to meet its obligation to pay benefits required by one or more workers compensation statutes.

Workers Compensation and Employers Liability Insurance Policy (WC&EL policy)

The policy used in most states to provide workers compensation and employers liability insurance.

Information Page

The Information Page is equivalent to the declarations page of other policies. It is divided into four major parts, or "items." See the exhibit "WC&EL Information Page."

Item 1 provides essential information about the insured, including name and mailing address, form of ownership (individual, partnership, corporation, or other), and workplace addresses other than personal mailing address.

Item 2 shows the coverage period. Coverage begins and ends at 12:01 a.m. at the address of the insured given in Item 1.

WC&EL Information Page

WORKERS COMPENSATION AND EMPLOYERS LIABILITY INSURANCE POLICY

INFORMATION PAGE

Insurer:

```
┌─────────────────────────────────────────────────┐
│              P O L I C Y   N O .                  │
│  | | | | | | | | | | | | | | | | | | | | | |     │
└─────────────────────────────────────────────────┘
```

1. The Insured: AMR Corporation   ___ Individual   ___ Partnership
    Mailing address: 2000 Industrial Highway   X Corporation or   _____
                       Workingtown, PA 19000

    Other workplaces not shown above:

2. The policy period is from   10/1/20X1   to   10/1/20X2   at the insured's mailing address.

3. A. Workers Compensation Insurance: Part One of the policy applies to the Workers Compensation Law of the states
        listed here: PA

    B. Employers Liability Insurance: Part Two of the policy applies to work in each state listed in Item 3.A. The limits of
        our liability under Part Two are:

        Bodily Injury by Accident $ 100,000   each accident
        Bodily Injury by Disease $ 500,000   policy limit
        Bodily Injury by Disease $ 100,000   each employee

    C. Other States Insurance: Part Three of the policy applies to the states, if any, listed here:

        All except those listed in Item 3.A and ND, OH, WA, and, WY

    D. This policy includes these endorsements and schedules:

        See Schedule

4. The premium for this policy will be determined by our Manuals of Rules, Classifications, Rates and Rating Plans.
    All information required below is subject to verification and change by audit.

Classifications	Code No.	Premium Basis Total Estimated Annual Remuneration	Rate Per $100 of Remuneration	Estimated Annual Premium
Sheet Metal Shop	0454	300,000	11.53	34,590
Clerical Office	0953	275,000	.49	1,348
		Experience Modification of 1.382 Applied		13,728
		Estimated Premium Discount		(4,869)
		Total Estimated Annual Premium $		44,797

Minimum Premium $ 1,273   Expense Constant $ 140

Countersigned by _____ A. M. Abel _____
                                  (authorized representative)

WC 00 00 01 A

Item 3 summarizes coverage provided by the policy. Item 3.A states that Part One—Workers Compensation Insurance applies to the workers compensation law of the state or states listed in that item. This space should list all states in which the insured has operations and the insurer is licensed to provide coverage. Item 3.B shows the limits of liability that apply to Part II—Employers Liability Coverage for bodily injury by accident and disease. Item 3.C indicates that Part III—Other States Insurance applies to any additional states listed under that item. Item 3.D can be filled in with a list of all endorsements and schedules attached to the policy at inception. In some cases, the endorsements are listed in a separate schedule attached to the policy.

Item 4 shows information necessary to calculate the estimated policy premium, including a description of the classification(s) assigned to the insured's business. This description and the corresponding code numbers are taken from the appropriate workers compensation manual. Another column contains the insured's estimate of what the remuneration (payroll) will be for the period covered by the policy. The estimated payroll is shown beside each classification.

The next column shows the rate applicable to each classification. Usually the rate is expressed in dollars of premium per $100 of payroll. The last column shows the estimated premium determined by multiplying the estimated payroll by the rate for each classification.

General Section

The General Section explains the nature of the policy and defines important terms. The first paragraph explains that the policy is a contract and that the parties are "you" (the insured) and "we" (the insurer). The insured is the employer named in Item 1 of the Information Page. The policy states if that employer is a partnership, coverage applies to the partners only in their capacity as employer of that partnership's employees.

The General Section defines "workers compensation law" to mean "the workers or workmen's compensation law and occupational disease law of each state or territory named in Item 3.A of the Information Page." Any amendments during the policy period are included, but provisions of a statute that relate to nonoccupational disability benefits are not included within this definition. Moreover, the definition is limited to state laws. The Longshore and Harbor Workers' Compensation Act (LHWCA) and other federal laws are not included unless the policy is modified by endorsement to include such laws.

The term "state" means any of the fifty states or the District of Columbia. Covered locations are defined to include all workplaces listed on the Information Page and all of the insured's workplaces in states listed in Item 3.A, unless other insurance or self-insurance applies.

Part One—Workers Compensation Insurance

The coverage provided by Part One obligates the insurer to pay all compensation and other benefits required of the insured by the workers compensation law or occupational disease law of any state listed in Item 3.A of the Information Page. The employer automatically receives coverage for all benefits required by that state's workers compensation law for all locations, operations, and employees designated by the law. The policy applies to all operations of the employer except those otherwise insured or specifically excluded by endorsement.

The coverage applies to bodily injury by accident and disease. The accident must occur during the policy period, and the last exposure to disease in the employment of the insured must occur during the policy period.

According to the policy, the insurer will pay benefits required by the workers compensation law. The policy shows no dollar limit for these benefits, so any applicable limits would relate to the law itself. Part One of the policy contains no exclusions.

The insurer has the right and duty to defend the insured against claims, proceedings, or suits seeking benefits payable by the policy. The insurer also agrees to pay additional costs, such as for investigating a claim and handling litigation costs.

For example, an employee of the insured makes a claim for workers compensation benefits, but the insurer denies coverage because it believes the employee's injury was a preexisting condition that did not arise out of employment by the insured. If the employee then sues the employer for workers compensation benefits, the insurer will pay the insured's defense costs.

The policy further provides that the insured will reimburse the insurer for any penalties required under a workers compensation law because of the employer's (1) willful misconduct, (2) knowing employment of anyone illegally, (3) failure to comply with health and safety laws and regulations, or (4) discrimination against employees who claim workers compensation benefits.

When the insurer pays compensation or employers liability benefits on behalf of an insured, any right of recovery the insured or the injured employee may have against a third party becomes the right of the insurer.

The policy also recognizes the legal requirements that directly obligate the insurer to pay workers compensation benefits to any injured employee or, in the event of death, to the employee's dependents. Because the contract is primarily intended to benefit employees and their dependents, these individuals have a direct right of action against the insurer.

For the employee's protection, the policy provides that obligations of the insurer will not be affected by failure of the employer to comply with policy requirements.

All workers compensation laws covered by the policy become part of the insurance contract just as if they were written into the policy, and employees have the right to compensation as defined by those laws. If the policy and applicable workers compensation laws conflict, the policy will automatically conform to the law.

WC&EL POLICY—EMPLOYERS LIABILITY INSURANCE

Employers liability insurance protects employers against liability claims by employees for occupational injuries that are not covered by the state's workers compensation statute.

The Workers Compensation and Employers Liability Insurance (WC&EL) Policy is the policy used in most states to provide workers compensation and employers liability insurance. Part Two of the policy, which provides employers liability coverage, is structured like a traditional liability policy, containing an insuring agreement, exclusions, and other provisions. In contrast with Part One—Workers Compensation Insurance, which covers an employer's liability under workers compensation statutes for occupational injury to employees, Part Two—Employers Liability Insurance covers an employer against liability for an employee's occupational injury or disease that is not covered by a workers compensation statute.

Employers Liability Insuring Agreement

The insurer agrees to pay damages that the insured becomes legally obligated to pay because of bodily injury to an employee. The bodily injury must be caused by accident or disease and arise out of and in the course of the employee's employment. The insurer also agrees to defend the insured against claims or suits seeking covered damages.

The extensive coverage provided by workers compensation laws is theoretically regarded as the exclusive remedy for work-related injuries. Therefore, some employers question their need for employers liability insurance. However, depending on the laws of the particular state, an employer can still be held legally liable as the result of employee injuries, as in these examples:

- Third-party claims (also known as third-party-over claims)—An employee of the insured sues a third party (such as a machine manufacturer) for an occupational injury, and the third party then sues the employer. The third party's suit might allege, for example, that the employer was negligent in maintaining the defective machine and that the employer must therefore indemnify the manufacturer for all damages the manufacturer had to pay to the employee.

- Claim for care and loss of services—The spouse or another family member of an injured employee sues the employer for loss of companionship or services (such as housekeeping or yard work that the employee would otherwise have performed) resulting from the injury. Many states restrict or prohibit such suits.

The insuring agreement for Part Two also requires that the employment out of which the injury arises be necessary or incidental to the insured's work in a state or territory listed in Item 3.A of the Information Page. This provision is not a requirement that the injury must occur in one of the states or territories listed. For example, an employee might be injured after driving into an unlisted state to buy supplies for work being performed in a listed state. Even though the injury occurred outside the listed state, the injury still arose out of employment that was necessary or incidental to the insured's work in a listed state.

The same coverage triggers that apply to workers compensation coverage also apply to employers liability coverage:

- For bodily injury by accident, the policy that is in effect when the injury occurs is the policy that applies.
- For bodily injury by disease, the policy that is in effect on the employee's last day of last exposure to the conditions causing or aggravating the injury is the policy that applies.

Employers Liability Exclusions

Like most other liability policies, employers liability coverage is subject to exclusions that prevent overlapping coverage with other forms of insurance and that eliminate coverage not intended by the insurer.

Statutory Obligations

In keeping with the basic purpose of employers liability coverage, several exclusions are aimed at eliminating coverage for claims that would be covered under various statutes, including these:

- Any workers compensation, occupational disease, unemployment compensation, or disability benefits law
- The United States Longshore and Harbor Workers' Compensation Act (LHWCA)
- The Federal Employers Liability Act
- Damages payable under the Migrant and Seasonal Agricultural Worker Protection Act
- Any other federal workers compensation or occupational disease law

Also excluded is bodily injury to a master (captain) or member of the crew of any vessel. Masters and crew members of vessels are not eligible for LHWCA benefits but can pursue other legal remedies.

Various endorsements are available for deleting or modifying most of the preceding exclusions in order to extend the policy to cover those liabilities. A shipowner's liability for crew injuries, although insurable by endorsement to the WC&EL policy, is usually covered under the shipowner's protection and indemnity policy.

Injury Outside the United States or Canada

Employers liability coverage does not apply to bodily injury that occurs outside the United States, its territories or possessions, and Canada. However, this exclusion does not apply to injury to a resident or citizen of the U.S. or Canada who is temporarily outside those places.

Liability Assumed Under Contract

Employers liability coverage does not apply to liability assumed under contract—even if the insured has assumed another party's liability for injury to the insured's own employee. The Commercial General Liability (CGL) Coverage Form, by way of an exception to the employers liability exclusion in that form, covers the insured against liability assumed under an insured contract for injury to an employee of the insured. Otherwise, the CGL form excludes liability for injury to an employee of the insured.

Employment Practices

Employers liability insurance also does not apply to damages arising out of employment practices, including (but not limited to) demotion, evaluation, harassment, discrimination, and termination. Insurers are being presented with claims that are caused by employment practices but have an element of bodily injury. For example, an employee may have been sexually harassed and, as a result, suffers from debilitating headaches.

Other Exclusions

Employers liability insurance also does not apply to any of these:

- Punitive damages for injury or death of any illegally employed person
- Bodily injury to employees employed in violation of the law with the knowledge of the insured or any executive officers of the insured
- Bodily injury intentionally caused by the insured
- Fines or penalties imposed for violation of federal or state law

Limits of Liability

Unlike workers compensation coverage, employers liability coverage is subject to monetary limits of liability stated in the policy. These are the three limits that apply to employers liability coverage:

- The bodily injury by accident limit is the most that the insurer will pay for bodily injury resulting from any one accident, regardless of the number of employees injured.
- The bodily injury by disease—policy limit is the most that the insurer will pay for bodily injury by disease, regardless of the number of employees who sustain disease.
- The bodily injury by disease—each employee limit is the most that the insurer will pay for bodily injury by disease to any one employee.

Defense costs, as well as supplementary payments, are covered in addition to the limits of liability. Supplementary payments include these costs:

- Expenses the insurer incurs
- Cost of bail bonds
- Cost of bonds to release attachments
- Reasonable expenses incurred by the insured at the insurer's request to assist the insurer in the defense of a claim
- Court costs taxed against the insured in a suit

As with other liability policies, the insurer has no duty to pay defense costs or supplementary payments after it has paid damages equaling the applicable limit of insurance.

Apply Your Knowledge

Rhonda is an employee working on an assembly line of a hand-tool manufacturer. On the job, she was using a hammer that was made by her employer when the head of the hammer came loose and hit her in the face, injuring her eye. Explain what remedies Rhonda has against her employer and how her employer can insure against each remedy.

Feedback: Rhonda has two remedies. One is to assert a workers compensation claim and accept benefits from her employer's workers compensation insurer. Her employer can insure against this remedy with Part One—Workers Compensation Insurance, which covers an employer's liability under workers compensation statutes for occupational injury to employees. Rhonda's second remedy is to assert a legal liability claim against her employer for manufacturing a defective product that caused her injuries. Her employer can insure against this remedy with Part Two—Employers Liability Insurance, which covers an employer against liability for an employee's occupational injury or disease that is not covered by a workers compensation statute. So, Rhonda can either collect benefits for job-related injuries under workers compensation or sue her employer as the producer of the defective product.

WC&EL POLICY—OTHER STATES INSURANCE

It is vital that an employer's workers compensation and employers liability coverage be able to expand along with an employer's operations to new states.

Employers need additional workers compensation and employers liability coverage if they expand their operations into states not listed in Item 3.A of the Information Page when the Workers Compensation and Employers Liability Insurance (WC&EL) Policy is issued or renewed. The mechanism for extending workers compensation insurance to cover such operations is known as other states insurance, which is incorporated within the standard WC&EL policy as Part Three.

If coverage applies to a state designated in Item 3.C and the insured begins operations in that state, the policy provides the same coverage as if that state were listed in Item 3.A. The policy requires the insured to "Tell us at once if you begin work in any state listed in Item 3.C of the Information Page."

If the insured has operations in a particular state on the effective date of the policy but that state is not listed in Item 3.A, the insured must notify the insurer within thirty days or else no coverage will apply for that state. Thus, when operations are known to exist in a particular state, that state should be listed in Item 3.A. When operations do not currently take place in additional states but could be extended into those states, those states should be listed in Item 3.C. States in which the insurer is not licensed to write workers compensation insurance (including those that have monopolistic state funds) should not be included for either item.

If an insurer is licensed to write workers compensation insurance in all states, the wording used in Item 3.C often reads: "All states except those listed in Item 3.A and ND, OH, WA, and WY." This protects the insured if it commences operations in any state other than those listed in Item 3.A, which are already covered, or in any state other than the four monopolistic fund states, where it would be illegal for the insurer to provide workers compensation insurance. Insurers will also exclude states in which they are not licensed or in which they do not wish to provide coverage for underwriting reasons.

If the insured anticipates operating in a state with a monopolistic workers compensation fund, the insured should obtain workers compensation insurance from the appropriate state agency. Because the workers compensation policies issued by some monopolistic state funds do not include employers liability insurance, many employers buy a type of employers liability insurance

Stop gap coverage

Coverage for employers liability that private insurers provide to employers operating in a monopolistic fund state that does not include such insurance in its workers compensation policies.

called **stop gap coverage**. This coverage is often provided by the same insurer that provides the insured's general liability insurance.

Apply Your Knowledge

Just for You (JFY) produces handbags from recycled materials such as vintage dresses, coats, and quilts. The business began in the owner's basement in Iowa. As demand grew, manufacturing locations were added in Kansas and South Dakota. JFY plans to expand into Nevada and Washington (a monopolistic state) in the next six to twelve months. It will be sending employees to those states regularly and for extended periods to do market surveys, lease property, and set up production. JFY's insurer is licensed in all states except the monopolistic states. What does JFY need to do to have workers compensation coverage in place in the states where it currently operates and where it plans to operate?

Feedback: If JFY has operations in a particular state on the effective date of its WC&EL policy, but the state is not listed in Item 3.A, JFY must notify the insurer within thirty days or else no coverage will apply for that state. So, when operations are known to exist in particular states—in this case, Iowa, Kansas, and South Dakota—those states should be listed in Item 3.A.

When operations do not currently take place in a particular state but could be extended into that state—such as, in this case, Nevada (but not Washington, as it has a monopolistic state fund)—that state should be listed in Item 3.C. States in which the insurer is not licensed to write workers compensation insurance (including those that have monopolistic state funds) should not be included for either item.

Because JFY anticipates operating in Washington, which has a monopolistic workers compensation fund, it should obtain workers compensation insurance from the appropriate state agency once it begins operations there. JFY may also consider purchasing stopgap insurance for its employers liability exposure in Washington.

Because JFY's insurer is licensed to write workers compensation insurance in all states, the wording in Item 3.C will likely read: "All states except those listed in Item 3.A and ND, OH, WA, and WY." This protects the insured if it commences operations in any state other than those listed in Item 3.A.

WORKERS COMPENSATION AND EMPLOYERS LIABILITY INSURANCE POLICY— ENDORSEMENTS

Despite the flexibility built into the standard WC&EL policy, a number of situations require modification of standard policy provisions by adding an appropriate endorsement to the policy.

Common endorsements to the WC&EL policy include voluntary compensation coverage (providing workers compensation benefits for employees not subject to a workers compensation law) and LHWCA coverage (covering an employer's obligations under the LHWCA).

Voluntary Compensation and Employers Liability Coverage Endorsement

The workers compensation laws of most states exempt some types of employment from statutory workers compensation benefits. The most commonly exempted occupations are farm labor, domestic employment, and casual labor. In some cases, the law does not apply to employers with fewer than a certain minimum number of employees. The workers compensation laws of some states do not apply to partners, sole proprietors, or executive officers. Even when exempt persons are not entitled to workers compensation benefits by law, benefits may be extended to them by endorsement.

The **Voluntary Compensation and Employers Liability Endorsement** amends the standard WC&EL policy to cover employees who are not subject to a workers compensation statute. The additional coverage, called "voluntary compensation," does not make employees subject to the workers compensation law, but it obligates the insurer to pay, on behalf of the insured, an amount equal to the compensation benefits that would be payable to such employees if they were subject to the workers compensation law designated in the endorsement.

The voluntary compensation endorsement states that if an employee entitled to payment under the endorsement brings a suit under the common law, the coverage provided by the endorsement reverts to employers liability insurance. The insurer will defend the insured against the employee's suit and pay any settlement awarded, subject to the stipulated limits of liability.

Voluntary Compensation and Employers Liability Coverage Endorsement
Endorsement that amends the WC&EL policy to cover employees who are not subject to a workers compensation statute.

LHWCA Coverage Endorsement

The LHWCA follows the same principles as state workers compensation laws. In some circumstances, an employer may be simultaneously subject to both the LHWCA and the state workers compensation law. Although both of these exposures may be insured, they must be covered and rated separately.

United States Longshore and Harbor Workers' Compensation Act Endorsement

An endorsement that amends the Workers Compensation and Employers Liability Insurance Policy to cover the insured's obligations under the U.S. Longshore and Harbor Workers' Compensation Act.

Coverage can be provided by endorsing the WC&EL policy with the **United States Longshore and Harbor Workers' Compensation Act Endorsement**, which amends the WC&EL policy to cover the insured's obligations under the LHWCA. The endorsement amends the definition of workers compensation law to include the LHWCA with respect to operations in any state designated in the endorsement's schedule. (In practice, many WC&EL insurers are unwilling to add LHWCA coverage because of the unfavorable loss experience associated with the LHWCA.)

RATING WORKERS COMPENSATION INSURANCE

Properly determining the estimated annual premium for workers compensation coverage is essential to ensuring its affordability while also being adequate for the risk assumed by the insurer.

Workers compensation insurance covers losses resulting from the work-related injuries or diseases of employees as determined by statute. The premium for that coverage should reflect the exposure to such losses. The exposure varies considerably according to the size of the employer's work force and the degree of hazard in the work performed. Workers compensation premiums reflect these two factors because the premium depends on the amount of the employer's payroll (premium basis) and the type of business (classification) involved.

Most states require insurers to belong to an approved advisory organization in order to write workers compensation and employers liability insurance. An advisory organization gathers statistics for workers compensation (measuring premiums and losses by classification) in those states. The designated organization files with the supervisory authority the manuals for classifications, rules, rates (or loss costs, depending on the state), rating plans, and policy forms on behalf of its members. The National Council on Compensation Insurance (NCCI) serves as the approved advisory organization for workers compensation insurers in most states.

Several states have independent rating bureaus for workers compensation insurance, some of which use the services of NCCI. Other states make their own rates and issue their own rules and manuals. However, the procedures generally resemble NCCI's.

Classifications

Rates for workers compensation insurance vary considerably according to the classification of workers. The class rating system serves to identify groups of similar employments, in terms of risk of injury or disease, whose experience is then combined for the purpose of establishing rates. To achieve this result, however, both premiums and losses must be accurately and consistently assigned to the proper classes. Any business may involve many different operations in widely varying combinations, and some of these operations may be extremely hazardous, while others are not.

The classification section of the workers compensation manual alphabetically lists several hundred classifications. Other than the broad "exception" classifications (such as code 8810, clerical employees), each one describes a particular business. The insurer, with the insured's assistance, must determine the basic classification that best describes the insured's business within the state so that its premium and loss statistics can be pooled with those of all similar businesses.

A governing classification is one that best describes an insured's activities. With only a few exceptions, all of the insured's employees at a single location are assigned one governing classification. For example, a furniture manufacturer and an auto repair shop may each employ painters as part of their operations. To compute the workers compensation premium, the payroll for furniture painters is assigned to the furniture manufacturing classification, and the payroll for auto body painters is assigned to the auto body repair shop classification.

The payroll for certain employees is rated using classifications that are separate from the governing classification. These classifications, called standard exception classifications, apply to these categories of employees:

- Clerical office employees and drafting employees (employees who create technical drawings or plans for use in production or construction), provided they work in an area physically separated from other operations
- Telecommuting clerical and drafting employees
- Salespersons, collectors, or messengers
- Drivers, chauffeurs, and their helpers

The payrolls for employees in these classifications are shown separately on the policy and take the rates applying to the standard exception classification, not the rate for the governing classification. For example, the exhibit shows part of the Information Page of the Workers Compensation and Employers Liability (WC&EL) Policy for an insured with a governing classification of Sheet Metal Shop and a standard exception classification of Clerical Office. See the exhibit "WC&EL Information Page."

Premium Base

With only a few exceptions, the premium base for workers compensation insurance is remuneration (that is, payroll). Payroll serves as an effective premium base because it varies directly with the exposure covered by the insurance, it is relatively easy to determine and verify from available records, and it is not readily subject to manipulation by the insured.

A business obtaining workers compensation insurance may not know how many employees it will have during the coming year. The policy, however,

WC&EL Information Page

WORKERS COMPENSATION AND EMPLOYERS LIABILITY INSURANCE POLICY

INFORMATION PAGE

4.   The premium for this policy will be determined by our Manuals of Rules, Classifications, Rates and Rating Plans. All information required below is subject to verification and change by audit.

Classifications	Code No.	Premium Basis Total Estimated Annual Remuneration	Rate Per $100 of Remuneration	Estimated Annual Premium
Sheet Metal Shop	0454	300,000	11.53	34,590
Clerical Office	0953	275,000	.49	1,348
		Experience Modification of 1.382 Applied		13,728
		Estimated Premium Discount		(4,869)
		Total Estimated Annual Premium $		44,797

Minimum Premium $ 1,273   **Expense Constant $**   140

Countersigned by _____ A. M. Abel _____
                                  (authorized representative)

WC 00 00 01 A

bases the premium on the manual rate for the applicable classification per $100 of payroll for the year. The insured pays an estimated premium based on an estimate of the annual payroll at the inception of the policy. An audit of the actual payroll after the policy expiration allows the insurer to calculate the final earned premium.

As a simple example of calculating the premium, assume an employer has total remuneration (payroll) of $476,800. That amount divided by $100 equals 4,768 units. The number of units is the exposure. The rate multiplied by the exposure equals the amount of premium. So if the rate is $0.25 per $100 of payroll and it is multiplied by the exposure of 4,768 units, the result is the amount of premium, which is $1,192.

Audits

The premium shown on the Information Page is an estimated premium. The final premium is determined by audit. The Audit provision in Part Five—Premium of the WC&EL policy explains the insurer's right to examine and audit the insured's books and records at any time during the policy period and within three years after expiration to the extent that such books and records relate to the policy. The insured must keep records of information needed to compute the policy premium and provide such records to the insurer when requested.

Premium Adjustments

The premium, determined by applying the rate to the exposure (payroll) for each classification, can be modified by any of several adjustments. See the exhibit "WC&EL Premium Adjustments."

WC&EL Premium Adjustments

- Experience rating
- Retrospective rating
- Premium discount
- Merit or schedule rating factors

- Rate deviations
- Expense constant
- Deductible plans
- Dividend plans

[DA02656]

Experience Rating

An experience rating plan increases or reduces the premium for a future period based on the insured's own loss experience for a period in the recent past. The past period is usually the three-year period that began four years before policy inception.

Rating rules provide that insureds whose workers compensation premiums have reached certain levels are subject to experience rating modification. The experience rating computation produces an **experience modification**, or mod, which serves as a rate multiplier. If the mod is less than 1.00 as a result of the insured's low level of losses, the premium is reduced. If the mod is greater than 1.00 as a result of the insured's high level of losses, the premium is increased.

Experience modification
A rate multiplier derived from the experience rating computation.

For example, suppose that the basic premium calculation for one insured's WC&EL policy is $50,000. Suppose also that this insured has an experience modification factor of 1.15. The premium to be charged is calculated as $50,000 × 1.15 = $57,500.

The average premium required to qualify for experience rating varies by state but generally ranges from $2,500 to $5,000 per year. Experience rating provides insureds with an incentive to implement risk control measures that reduce workplace accidents.

Retrospective Rating

Retrospective rating plan

A rating plan that adjusts the insured's premium for the current policy period based on the insured's loss experience during the current period; paid losses or incurred losses may be used to determine loss experience.

A **retrospective rating plan** increases or reduces an insured's premium for a policy period based on the insured's own losses during the same period. The insured pays an estimated premium at the beginning of the period and receives either a refund or a bill for an additional premium after the end of the period, depending on the losses during the period (as well as a final audit of payroll exposures). A formula for calculating the retrospective premium adjustment, subject to minimum and maximum premiums, is written into the policy at its inception.

Premium Discount

Many of the expenses of providing workers compensation insurance do not increase proportionately with increases in premium. For example, the costs of policy issuance and premium collection generally do not increase with the size of the premium. Furthermore, the percentage paid to producers as a commission is usually reduced as the premium increases. In recognition of these lowered expenses, the premium discount plan provides an increasing credit for premiums in excess of a certain minimum.

Merit or Schedule Rating Factors

In many states, the premium can also be modified by a merit or schedule rating factor to give the insured credit for conditions that are more favorable than those normally expected, such as superior housekeeping (standards that foster workplace safety), excellent employee training, and on-site medical facilities.

Rate Deviations

In some states, insurers are permitted to apply a rate deviation factor (for example, 10 percent) to the premium as calculated by the rating manual. Insurers generally reserve these credits for better risks, although competitive pressures sometimes result in average risks receiving a rate deviation.

Expense Constant

An expense constant is a flat charge designed to cover administrative expenses, such as those for policy issuance and record keeping that are common to all policies. An expense constant is applied regardless of the size of the policy premium. Not every state calls for application of expense constants.

Deductible Plans

In almost all states that do not have monopolistic state funds, an insured can reduce its premium by selecting a deductible plan. The deductible applies to both medical and disability income claims on a per claim basis. The greater the deductible, the larger the premium credit.

A **large deductible plan** allows the insured to self-insure most of its workers compensation claims without establishing a qualifying self-insurance plan. Large deductible plans greatly reduce the premium and are available in most states. The insurer does all the administrative work connected with workers compensation claims, and the insured reimburses the insurer for claim payments up to the deductible amount per occurrence.

Large deductible plan

An insurance policy with a per occurrence or per accident deductible of $100,000 or more.

Dividend Plans

For policies written on a dividend plan, the cost of the insurance can be reduced by dividends declared by the insurer. Dividends are, essentially, a return to the insured of a portion of the premiums paid for an expiring policy term.

Two general types of dividend plans are available: a flat-dividend plan and a sliding-scale dividend plan. Under a flat-dividend plan, all eligible policies receive the same percentage of their premium as a dividend regardless of their individual loss experience. Under a sliding-scale dividend plan, the size of the dividend varies with the insured's own experience; the lower the insured's loss ratio, the higher the dividend percentage.

Insurers that offer dividend plans generally make them available to insureds with good safety records and at least a certain minimum premium size. In discussing dividend plans with insureds, insurers should point out that dividends cannot be guaranteed. Dividends are paid after expiration of the policy and then only at the rate declared by the insurer's board of directors.

Apply Your Knowledge

Roland is a roofing contractor who employs twelve roofers and two clerical workers. Total estimated annual remuneration for his roofers is $500,000. Remuneration for his clerical workers is $80,000. The rate per $100 of remuneration for his roofers is $9.00. The rate for his clerical workers is $0.30. Roland has an effective worker safety program and has had favorable loss experience for the last several years. As a result, he has an experience modification of 0.90. Because of his substantial payroll, he is entitled to a 10 percent estimated premium discount. What is Roland's estimated annual premium for his workers compensation policy?

Feedback: See the exhibit "Calculating the Estimated Annual Premium of Roland's Workers Compensation Policy."

Calculating the Estimated Annual Premium of Roland's Workers Compensation Policy

Classifications	Premium Basis	Rate Per $100 of Remuneration	Estimated Annual Premium
	Total Estimated Annual Remuneration		
Roofing Installation	$500,000	$9.00	$45,000
Clerical Office	$80,000	$0.30	$240
		Experience Modification of 0.90 Applied ($45,240 × 0.90 = $40,716. Then $45,240 − $40,716 = $4,524)	($4,524)
		Estimated Premium Discount of 10 Percent ($45,240 − $4,524 = $40,716. Then 10% of $40,716 = $4,072)	($4,072)
		Total Estimated Annual Premium	$36,644

[DA07897]

DETERMINING WHETHER THE WC&EL POLICY COVERS A CLAIM

Knowing how to apply the Workers Compensation and Employers Liability Insurance Policy (WC&EL policy) to the facts of a case is an important skill. This case will help you make the transition from knowing policy language to applying policy language to losses and determining whether coverage applies.

Case Facts

Helpful Medical Devices (HMD), based in Arizona, manufactures medical equipment. In July 20X1, HMD began staffing an office in Virginia to serve the expanding number of customers in the state. HMD hired Fran in Virginia as a technician to train customers in their offices on how to properly use the HMD equipment they purchased.

In September 20X1, Fran was at a customer's office in Virginia. While acting within the course and scope of her employment with HMD, she attempted to demonstrate how to clean a heavy piece of equipment. However, the cleaning solution she was using caused the equipment to slip out of her hands. It landed on her foot and crushed several bones. She was immediately taken to a hospital. She required surgery, hospital care, prescription drugs, and physical therapy to regain 90 percent of her foot's function, but the other 10 percent was permanently lost. After four months, she returned to work for light duty. Fran chose to file for workers compensation benefits under the Virginia statute, after which HMD promptly provided notice of Fran's injury to its insurer and cooperated in the insurer's investigation of the claim.

HMD is insured under a WC&EL policy with an effective date of February 1, 20X1. At that time, Arizona was the only state listed in Item 3.A of HMD's Information Page. HMD's insurer is licensed to write workers compensation insurance in all states except those with monopolistic state funds. Item 3.C on the Information Page of HMD's policy reads: "All except those listed in Item 3.A and ND, OH, WA and WY." HMD did not notify its insurer that it had begun staffing its office in Virginia until Fran had her accident in September 20X1.

In this case-based activity, consider only the information supported by the facts of the case and any reference materials.

Necessary Reference Materials

Relevant coverage material can be found in these forms:

- The WC&EL Information Page
- The WC&EL policy form

In investigating Fran's claim, HMD's insurer obtained Fran's medical and rehabilitation records, as well as documentation of her lost wages.

Overview of Steps

When examining the policy forms to determine whether coverage applies to Fran's claim, you can apply the four steps of the DICE method. Doing this involves analyzing the policy declarations, insuring agreement, conditions, and exclusions and determining whether any information found at each step precludes coverage at the time of Fran's injury. You should also examine other categories of policy provisions, such as the insured's duties; general provisions; endorsements (if applicable); and terms defined in the policy in relation to the declarations, insuring agreement, conditions, and exclusions.

Next, the insurer must determine the amounts payable for Fran's claim under HMD's WC&EL policy and workers compensation law. It must also determine whether more than one policy provides coverage for the same loss.

Determination of Coverage

Application of the four DICE steps to the case facts for each of the losses follows.

DICE Analysis Step 1: Declarations

The first DICE step is to review the declarations page, referred to as the Information Page in WC&EL policies, to ascertain that HMD is the insured and that Fran's injury occurred during the policy period. See the exhibit "WC&EL Information Page."

WC&EL Information Page

WORKERS COMPENSATION AND EMPLOYERS LIABILITY INSURANCE POLICY

INFORMATION PAGE

Insurer:

P O L I C Y   N O .

1. **The Insured:** HMD Corporation
    Mailing address: 2000 Medical Highway
    Goodtown, AZ

    ___ Individual   ___ Partnership
    X Corporation or _____

    Other workplaces not shown above:

2. **The policy period is from** 02/1/20X1 **to** 02/1/20X2 **at the insured's mailing address.**

3. A. **Workers Compensation Insurance:** Part One of the policy applies to the Workers Compensation Law of the states listed here: AZ

    B. **Employers Liability Insurance:** Part Two of the policy applies to work in each state listed in Item 3.A. The limits of our liability under Part Two are:

Bodily Injury by Accident	$ 100,000	each accident
Bodily Injury by Disease	$ 500,000	policy limit
Bodily Injury by Disease	$ 100,000	each employee

    C. **Other States Insurance:** Part Three of the policy applies to the states, if any, listed here:

    All except those listed in Item 3.A and ND, OH, WA, and WY

    D. **This policy includes these endorsements and schedules:**

    See Schedule

WC 00 00 01 A

[DA07916]

Item 1 of the Information Page confirms that HMD Corporation is the insured. Item 2 shows the policy period as beginning on February 1, 20X1, and ending on February 1, 20X2; therefore, Fran's accident, which occurred in September 20X1, occurred during the policy period.

DICE Analysis Step 2: Insuring Agreement

The second DICE step is to review the insuring agreement to determine whether it is applicable to the described claim. The coverage provided by Part One—Workers Compensation Insurance obligates HMD's insurer to pay all compensation and other benefits required of HMD by the workers compensation law or occupational disease law of the state listed in Item 3.A of the Information Page. The insured automatically receives coverage for all benefits required by that state's workers compensation law for all locations, operations, and employees designated by the law. However, Fran has made a claim with HMD for benefits payable under the workers compensation statute of Virginia, which is not listed as one of the states whose law applies.

Knowledge to Action

Virginia is not listed in Item 3.A of HMD's Information Page. How does this affect the benefits payable to Fran?

Feedback: The fact that Virginia is omitted from Item 3.A will not prevent HMD's policy from covering HMD's obligation to pay Virginia workers compensation benefits to Fran. Part Three—Other States Insurance covers HMD's obligations to pay benefits under the Virginia workers compensation statute if these requirements are met:

• Virginia is one of the states listed in Item 3.C of the Information Page.

• HMD began its work in Virginia after the effective date of the policy and is not otherwise insured or self-insured for this work.

The first requirement is met because Item 3.C of HMD's Information Page includes all states except Arizona and the four states with monopolistic state funds (which do not include Virginia). The second requirement is met because HMD began staffing its Virginia office in July 20X1, and the effective date of its policy was February 1, 20X1. Because the two requirements are met, Part Three of the policy states that all provisions of the policy apply as though Virginia was listed in Item 3.A of HMD's Information Page.

DICE Analysis Step 3: Conditions

The third DICE step is to review the policy conditions to determine whether they preclude coverage at the time of the loss. HMD promptly notified its insurer of Fran's injury and cooperated in the insurer's investigation of the claim, which fulfilled one of the conditions of the policy. However, Part Three—Other States Insurance required HMD to tell its insurer at once if it began working in any state listed in Item 3.C. Virginia was included in the description in Item 3.C, and HMD began working in Virginia in July 20X1. Because HMD did not notify its insurer of its new office until Fran had her accident in September 20X1, HMD did not strictly comply with this policy requirement. Despite this noncompliance, for the employee's protection, the WC&EL policy is usually interpreted so as not to relieve the insurer of its obligation to pay benefits even though the employer may have failed to comply strictly with policy requirements.

DICE Analysis Step 4: Exclusions

The fourth DICE step is to review the policy exclusions to determine whether they exclude or limit coverage of the claim. Part One—Workers Compensation Insurance of the policy contains no exclusions.

Determination of Amounts Payable

Now that you have completed the DICE analysis, the amounts payable can be determined. According to the policy, the insurer will pay the types and amounts of benefits required by the applicable workers compensation law. The policy shows no dollar limit for these benefits, so any applicable limits on the insurer's obligation to pay benefits would need to be imposed by the law itself.

Knowledge to Action

Workers compensation statutes typically use four disability classifications:

- Temporary partial disability
- Temporary total disability
- Permanent partial disability
- Permanent total disability

What was Fran's disability classification before she returned to work?

Feedback: During the four months Fran was unable to work, her disability would be classified as temporary total disability. Because Fran was not able to perform any of the duties of her job during this period, she was totally disabled. However, her total disability was only temporary, as evidenced by the fact that she was eventually able to return to work.

What was Fran's disability classification after she returned to work?

Feedback: After Fran returned to work, her disability would be classified as permanent partial disability because she will never regain 100 percent functionality of her foot. However, because she can still perform some of her duties, her permanent disability is only partial, not total.

What types of benefits would be payable to Fran under a typical workers compensation statute?

Feedback: The workers compensation benefits payable to Fran include medical benefits, medical and vocational rehabilitation benefits, and disability income benefits. The medical benefits will pay an unlimited amount for her surgery, hospital care, and prescription drugs. The medical and vocational rehabilitation benefits will also pay an unlimited amount related to any therapy required to return Fran's physical abilities to as close to what they were before the accident as possible. The disability income benefits are payable to Fran for a percentage of her lost wages, subject to a waiting period. If Fran is unable to return to work for a period that extends beyond the waiting period, the lost wages incurred during the waiting period are also paid. Fran's disability benefits will depend on how her disabilities are classified: Temporary total disability benefits will cover a percentage of her lost wages, and permanent partial disability benefits will bridge the gap between her wages upon her return to work and her previous wages, should her disability result in reassignment to a lower-paying position.

SUMMARY

These are three common characteristics found in workers compensation statutes:

- Their basic purpose, which is to guarantee injured workers prompt payment for occupational injury or disease while reducing costs arising out of litigation
- Benefits provided, which are medical benefits, disability income benefits, death benefits, and rehabilitation benefits
- Persons and employments covered, which include employees (subject to some exceptions) but not independent contractors

These are three common characteristics of workers compensation statutes:

- Extraterritorial provisions—provide benefits for employees injured outside their home state
- Federal jurisdiction—arises either as a result of specific federal statutes or because the work location comes within the jurisdiction of admiralty (maritime) law
- Methods for meeting the employer's obligation—can be met by buying workers compensation insurance from private insurers in the voluntary market, assigned risk plans, or state workers compensation insurance funds or by joining self-insured groups

Workers compensation insurance is mainly provided under a standard form called the Workers Compensation and Employers Liability Insurance Policy (WC&EL policy). Part One—Workers Compensation Insurance, in tandem with the Information Page and General Section, enables employers to comply with state workers compensation statutes.

Part Two of the WC&EL policy provides employers liability coverage, which covers an employer against its liability for occupational injury to employees. Employers liability insurance is structured like a traditional liability policy, containing an insuring agreement, exclusions, and limits of liability.

Part Three—Other States Insurance extends the WC&EL policy to cover obligations under workers compensation laws of states in addition to those listed in Item 3.A of the Information Page. Such additional states, however, must be listed in Item 3.C of the Information Page.

Common endorsements to the WC&EL policy include voluntary compensation coverage (providing workers compensation benefits for employees not subject to a workers compensation law) and LHWCA coverage (covering an employer's obligations under the LHWCA).

Workers compensation premiums reflect the amount of the employer's payroll (exposure) and the type of business (classification) involved. The premium, determined by applying rate times exposure for each classification, can be modified by any of several adjustments. The adjustments include experience rating, retrospective rating, premium discount, merit or schedule rating factors, rate deviations, expense constant, deductible plans, and dividend plans.

You should now be able to apply policy language to workers compensation claims to determine whether a certain claim is covered. Nearly every business with employees needs WC&EL insurance. Understanding the standard WC&EL policy will enable you to determine the appropriate coverage for an insured's needs.

ASSIGNMENT NOTE

1. For more information on PEOs, see The National Association of Professional Employer Organizations' Web site at www.napeo.org (accessed July 24, 2011).

10

Businessowners and Farm Insurance

Educational Objectives

After learning the content of this assignment, you should be able to:

▷ Describe the typical businessowners policy (BOP) in terms of these elements:

- The categories of loss exposures that can be covered by a BOP

- The advantages of the BOP to insurers, producers, and insureds

- Why BOP eligibility rules are necessary

- How the BOP is rated

▷ Contrast the property coverages of a typical businessowners policy with the commercial property coverages available in a commercial package policy.

▷ Contrast the liability coverage of a typical businessowners policy with that of the Commercial General Liability Coverage Form.

▷ Summarize coverages provided by the ISO farm program and how specialty farm coverages help farmers address additional loss exposures.

Businessowners and Farm Insurance

OVERVIEW OF THE BUSINESSOWNERS POLICY

The businessowners policy (BOP) is widely used to insure eligible small to mid-size businesses against most of their property and liability loss exposures.

Both Insurance Services Office, Inc. (ISO) and the American Association of Insurance Services (AAIS) have developed businessowners programs for use by their member insurers. In addition, many insurers use their own independently developed BOP forms. This discussion examines these characteristics shared by most BOPs:

- Loss exposures covered by the BOP
- Advantages of the BOP
- The need for BOP eligibility rules
- Rating the BOP

Loss Exposures Covered by the BOP

BOPs usually cover most of the property and liability loss exposures that can be insured under the various ISO commercial package policy coverage parts. Most BOPs cover these common exposures:

- Buildings
- Business personal property
- Personal property of others
- Business income and extra expense
- Premises and operations liability
- Products and completed operations liability
- Contractual liability
- Personal and advertising injury liability
- Employee dishonesty
- Theft of money and securities
- Forgery and alteration
- Equipment breakdown

The BOP does not provide commercial auto coverage for owned autos. However, hired and nonowned auto coverage, as well as a variety of other coverages, can be added to the BOP by endorsement.

Advantages of the BOP

The manner in which the BOP packages basic coverages and uses simplified rating procedures is similar to that of a homeowners policy and offers advantages to the insurer, the producer, and the insured. Packaging several coverages reduces **adverse selection** and, combined with simplified rating, lowers handling costs for insurers.

Underwriting and processing policies through an automated system rather than through individual underwriting also reduces costs for insurers. The resulting lower premiums and broader coverage enable an insurer and its producers to compete effectively with other insurers and producers. Producers also benefit from the simplified rating procedures when quoting coverage. Insureds gain the convenience and economy of having one policy that meets most of their property and liability insurance needs.

The Need for BOP Eligibility Rules

Every insurer that writes BOPs has eligibility rules limiting its program to applicants for which the BOP approach is designed. These rules are needed because the rating structure of all BOPs contemplates a relatively homogeneous group of small to mid-size insureds. Writing BOP coverage for insureds that do not fall within this group can create a mismatch of premium and exposure.

BOP eligibility rules are based on criteria that relate to business size and complexity of loss exposures. Examples of these criteria are total floor area, building height in stories, annual gross sales, occupancy or business type, and characteristics of the applicant's operations.

Since the first BOP was written in the 1960s, insurers have continually expanded their eligibility rules to remain competitive and to increase or maintain market share. For example, BOP eligibility rules once excluded restaurants and contractors. Most insurers now write BOPs for both, subject to certain size and hazard restrictions required to maintain rating integrity.

Under ISO *Commercial Lines Manual* rules for the BOP, eligible risks, generally, may not exceed 35,000 square feet in total floor area or $6 million in annual gross sales at each location. Furthermore, certain types of businesses are not eligible for the ISO Businessowners Program. Examples of ineligible businesses are automobile-related businesses, bars, financial institutions, general contractors, and buildings occupied in whole or in part for manufacturing.

Insurers that have developed their own businessowners programs may have eligibility rules that are either broader or stricter than ISO's. Because of the variation in businessowners eligibility rules and their ongoing expansion, such rules are not discussed in further detail here.

Adverse selection

In general, the tendency for people with the greatest probability of loss to be the ones most likely to purchase insurance.

Rating the BOP

Rating a BOP is much less complicated than rating comparable coverages in a commercial package policy. BOP property coverage is rated based on the amounts of coverage provided for building and personal property. BOP property rates include loadings (built-in charges) for business income and any additional coverages that are automatically included. As a result, the rates do not have to be computed separately for each of those coverages.

The ISO BOP requires separate liability rating for all classes of business. However, in calculating the BOP liability premiums for most classifications, the liability rate is applied to the property insurance amount rather than to a rating basis such as that used to rate commercial general liability (CGL) coverage. For example, under the ISO BOP, the liability premium for an apartment building is based on the amount of building insurance; under the CGL coverage form, the number of apartment units determines the rate. The AAIS BOP program and most independent insurers use separate liability rating only for certain classes of business.

Most insurers that write BOPs for eligible contractors rate the liability coverage apart from the property coverages by applying a separate liability rate to the insured's payroll, receipts, or number of full- and part-time employees.

Typically, the BOP rater or processor enters some basic data into a computer application, which automatically calculates the premium. BOP rating incorporates these variables:

- Territory. (For example, tornadoes are more frequent in the Midwestern United States; theft losses are higher in metropolitan areas; and so forth.)
- Type of construction. (For example, frame, joisted masonry, or fire resistive.)
- Public fire protection.
- Occupancy of the building.
- Presence of sprinklers.
- Deductible. (The standard deductible for most insurers is $250 or $500 per loss. The deductible can be increased or decreased, with a corresponding premium adjustment.)

If the insured wants increased limits for liability insurance, the rates are increased by appropriate factors. If the insured has purchased optional coverages, the policy premium is increased either by adding a premium charge for each optional coverage requested or by applying an increased rate factor to the insured values.

BUSINESSOWNERS PROPERTY COVERAGE

In most ways, the property coverage in a typical businessowners policy (BOP) is comparable to the commercial property coverages that can be included in a

commercial package policy. For insurance professionals who are already famil-
iar with the commercial property forms, an effective way to learn about BOP
property coverage is to contrast these two types of property coverage.

A typical businessowners policy (BOP) offers most of the options available
under commercial package policies, but some differences exist. Major property
coverage differences between most BOPs and Insurance Services Office, Inc.
(ISO) commercial property coverage forms can be highlighted under these
topics:

• Covered causes of loss and valuation provisions

• No coinsurance

• Shorter list of property not covered

• Automatic seasonal increase provision

• Business income and extra expense coverage included

• Other property coverages

Covered Causes of Loss and Valuation Provisions

The ISO commercial property program offers three causes of loss forms—
basic, broad, and special. Most insurers offer only two versions of the BOP
property coverage—a named perils form, similar to the commercial property
broad form, and a special form. The special form predominates; in fact, some
independent forms offer only the special form, with an endorsement available
to change coverage to named perils.

The standard valuation provision in BOPs is replacement cost, whereas the
standard valuation provision in commercial property policies is actual cash
value. Most insurers offer actual cash value as an option for BOPs, just as
replacement cost is an option in commercial property policies.

No Coinsurance

BOPs were originally written without a coinsurance or another insurance-to-
value requirement in the policy. Insurers relied on producers and underwriters
to be certain that the insured carried insurance equal to full insurable values.
Although coinsurance requirements can be suspended in commercial property
policies by the agreed value option, underwriters are careful in granting that
option. As a result, most commercial property forms (other than BOPs) written for smaller insureds are subject to coinsurance.

Because many insurers felt that BOP insureds were not carrying adequate
amounts of insurance, ISO introduced an insurance-to-value provision in
its BOP forms similar to the insurance-to-value provision in homeowners
policies. To collect full replacement cost, the insured must carry insurance
equal to at least 80 percent of the insurable value of the covered property.
Otherwise, recovery is limited to actual cash value or a proportion of the loss

equal to the amount of insurance carried divided by 80 percent of the insurable value, whichever is greater.

Subsequently, ISO introduced an option to remove the insurance-to-value requirement by endorsement. Although many insurers currently do not include an insurance-to-value provision in their BOPs, its use is becoming more widespread. The American Association of Insurance Services (AAIS) has included an insurance-to-value requirement similar to the ISO provision in its most recent BOP form.

Shorter List of Property Not Covered

In most BOPs, the list of property not covered is considerably shorter than the comparable list of property not covered in the Building and Personal Property Coverage Form (BPP). There are two principal reasons for this difference:

- Some of the "property not covered" exclusions in the BPP are not needed in a BOP because they apply to types of businesses that are not eligible for BOP coverage. For example, wharves or docks are often not excluded in BOPs because the types of insureds eligible for BOP coverage rarely have them.

- Insurers are willing to offer broader coverage because the insureds eligible for a BOP are generally lower-risk, more homogeneous types of businesses. For example, cost of excavations, underground pipes, foundations below the lowest floor, and retaining walls, all of which the BPP excludes, are often not excluded in BOPs.

Automatic Seasonal Increase Provision

Some BOPs provide a novel solution to the problem of fluctuating values. A seasonal increase provision is a provision commonly included in BOPs that addresses fluctuating personal property values by automatically increasing the amount of insurance for certain time periods. A seasonal increase provision functions somewhat like the peak season endorsement, which also provides differing amounts of insurance for certain time periods. However, the seasonal increase provision applies automatically. Provided the insured carries an amount of insurance equal to at least 100 percent of its average monthly personal property value for the twelve months preceding the loss, the business personal property limit will automatically increase by 25 percent.

The seasonal increase provision can be advantageous for an insured whose inventory has increased beyond the personal property limit at the time of a loss. For example, if Bill's Gift Shop carried a $100,000 limit for personal property and had an average monthly personal property value of $100,000 for the twelve months immediately before a loss, it could collect up to $125,000 for the loss. If Bill's Gift Shop carried $95,000 of insurance, or even $99,000, the amount would not be increased. And, of course, if the loss were $150,000, Bill would still be underinsured. Some BOP insurers offer a peak season endorsement in addition to the seasonal increase provision to enable the insured to meet an expected seasonal surge in values that will exceed 25 percent.

Business Income and Extra Expense Coverage Included

One of the distinguishing features of most BOPs is the automatic inclusion of business income and extra expense coverage. In commercial package policies, business income and extra expense coverage is provided by a separate form and is subject to its own underwriting requirements, such as a completed business income worksheet. Insurers seldom require any special underwriting for business income or extra expense coverage in a BOP.

Moreover, business income and extra expense coverage under the BOP is usually not subject to coinsurance, a monthly limitation, or even a total dollar limit. However, most BOPs apply a time limit that is not present in the commercial property business income forms. Under a typical BOP, business income loss and extra expenses are payable for up to twelve consecutive months following the occurrence of the direct physical damage. Some BOPs limit ordinary payroll coverage to ninety days.

Some insurers apply a dollar limit in addition to the twelve-month limitation. For example, some BOPs limit business income and extra expense coverage to an amount equal to 20 percent of the building insurance limit plus 100 percent of the personal property insurance limit. This can be a significant difference from the twelve-month limitation. In one case, an office tenant with a $25,000 personal property insurance limit (and no building coverage) sustained a business income loss in excess of $1 million. Because the loss was incurred in less than twelve months and the tenant's BOP business income coverage did not have a dollar limit, its insurer paid over $1 million. Under the alternative approach just described, payment would have been limited to $25,000. However, insurers that use this approach may offer the option to remove the dollar limitation for an increase in premium.

At one time, most BOP insurers did not offer business income coverage for dependent property exposures. However, dependent property coverage can be important, for example, to a small business located in a shopping mall if the business depends on one or more large "anchor stores" to draw customers to the insured's store. ISO, AAIS, and many independent insurers now offer this coverage either as an option or as part of their standard form. Under this coverage, the insurer will pay for a business income loss sustained because of physical loss or damage by a covered cause of loss at the premises of a dependent property. Some insurers offer all business income and extra expense coverage only as an option, not as part of their standard BOP form.

Other Property Coverages

To reduce complexity and to minimize the number of policies required, many coverages that would require separate policies or separate coverage parts in the commercial package program are either included as part of the BOP or available as options. The trend has been for an ever-increasing number of coverages and endorsements to be included in BOP programs. Although this trend conflicts with the goal of simplification, it makes the BOP policy suitable for a growing number of insureds. However, not all insurers offer all options, and certain insureds cannot find the exact coverage combination that they would like in any insurer's BOP. See the exhibit "Property Coverages Available in BOPs."

Property Coverages Available in BOPs

- Employee dishonesty
- Money and securities, when special-form property coverage applies; or burglary and robbery, when named-perils property coverage applies
- Forgery
- Interior and exterior glass (if not included as part of the building and personal property coverage)
- Outdoor signs
- Mechanical breakdown
- Money orders and counterfeit money
- Computer coverage
- Accounts receivable
- Valuable papers and records

[DA02603]

The limits for these coverages are often quite low, with minimal or no options for higher limits. The coverages also may not be as broad as those available in the commercial package program or in separate policies. However, they generally satisfy the needs of most small businesses.

Some coverage options are almost never offered under BOPs because they are not needed by the small businesses for which BOPs are designed or because they require individualized underwriting attention.

BUSINESSOWNERS LIABILITY COVERAGE

The liability coverage provided by a typical businessowners policy (BOP) closely resembles the coverage provided by the occurrence version of the

Insurance Services Office, Inc. (ISO) Commercial General Liability (CGL) Coverage Form: both supply coverage for bodily injury and property damage liability, personal and advertising injury liability, and medical payments.

Some noteworthy differences between typical BOP liability coverage and the CGL coverage form can be described under these topics:

- Limits of insurance
- Professional liability
- Hired and nonowned autos liability coverage
- Employee benefits liability and employment practices liability
- Liability coverage options generally not available in BOPs

Limits of Insurance

The types of limits (such as each occurrence, general aggregate, and products/completed operations aggregate) applicable to BOP liability coverage are generally similar to those of the CGL policy. One exception is that BOP policies typically offer insureds fewer choices regarding limit amounts, and the minimum liability limit is higher in a BOP than in the ISO CGL coverage form. BOP maximum liability limits also are more restrictive—few insurers offer per occurrence limits that exceed $2 million. In many BOPs, the general aggregate limit is fixed at twice the each occurrence limit, and the products/completed operations aggregate equals the each occurrence limit.

Professional Liability

BOP liability coverage is generally subject to an exclusion eliminating coverage for bodily injury or property damage resulting from the rendering of or failure to render any professional service. Similarly, when a CGL policy is issued to a provider of professional services—such as a physician, accountant, or engineer—the ISO *Commercial Lines Manual* requires a professional liability exclusion to be added to the policy. However, some BOPs automatically provide professional liability coverage for retail drugstores by including an exception for such stores in the professional liability exclusion.

A more significant difference between BOP's professional liability coverage and CGL's is the availability of optional professional liability coverage endorsements for use with BOP liability coverage. In many cases, BOPs can be endorsed to cover the professional liability exposures of specified insureds, such as pharmacies, barber shops, beauty shops, veterinary clinics, funeral homes, optical and hearing aid stores, and print shops. No counterparts to these endorsements exist within the CGL policy. Unless insured by a BOP, an insured desiring one of these coverages must purchase a separate professional liability policy or an independently filed package policy designed for a particular profession.

Hired and Nonowned Autos Liability

Hired and nonowned autos liability coverage, like that provided by using symbols 8 and 9 of the Business Auto Coverage Form, is usually offered by BOPs, either as part of the form or by endorsement. For an insured that owns no automobiles, the availability of hired and nonowned autos coverage under the BOP eliminates the need to obtain a separate business auto policy. This is a major advantage for smaller insureds. Those who do not own any autos often overlook the need for, or cannot obtain, a separate policy covering hired and nonowned autos liability. Yet, almost every business at some time or another uses rented, leased, borrowed, or employee-owned autos.

Employee Benefits Liability and Employment Practices Liability

Both ISO and the American Association of Insurance Services (AAIS) offer BOP endorsements that add employee benefits liability coverage and employment practices liability coverage. These cost-effective options enable smaller insureds to avoid the higher minimum premiums that usually apply to stand-alone policies. However, some stand-alone policies offer broader coverage than the ISO or AAIS endorsements. As with all BOP options, some insurers may not offer these options despite subscribing to the ISO or AAIS BOP programs.

Liability Coverage Options Generally Not Available in BOPs

As with some property coverage options, certain liability coverage options are not part of most BOP programs because the insureds that need them generally do not qualify for BOPs. For example, claims-made liability coverage is not available in BOPs; it is usually reserved for liability exposures that need special underwriting and are therefore not suitable for BOP programs.

FARM INSURANCE

Some farms or ranches are operated by families and include both a residence and farm-related structures such as barns or silos. Other farms are operated by agribusiness corporations and are worked by employees who may or may not live on the farm property.

To accommodate both family farms and commercial farm operations, the Insurance Services Office, Inc. (ISO) farm program uses a modular approach in providing farm insurance coverage. When the insured is a family operation, a form covering residential property loss exposures is included with forms to cover the farm property loss exposures. For agribusiness operations, the Farm Dwelling form can be omitted if no residential buildings are insured.

Specialty farm coverage can be used to meet the needs of customers that are not included within the ISO farm program.

ISO Farm Program

The ISO farm program includes various forms and endorsements that can be combined in either a separate farm policy or a commercial package policy.

The Farm Dwellings, Appurtenant Structures and Household Personal Property Coverage Form contains four coverages, which are comparable in most respects to Coverages A through D of homeowners policies. See the exhibit "Farm Property—Farm Dwellings, Appurtenant Structure and Household Personal Property Coverage Form."

Farm Property—Farm Dwellings, Appurtenant Structure and Household Personal Property Coverage Form

Coverage A—Dwellings

Coverage B—Other Private Structures Appurtenant to Dwellings

Coverage C—Household Personal Property

Coverage D—Loss of Use

Coverage B excludes structures, other than private garages, that the named insured uses principally for farming purposes. Similarly, Coverage C insures only household personal property and excludes farm personal property other than office fixtures, furniture, and office equipment. Loss or damage to trees, plants, or other types of crops grown for farming purposes are excluded.

Includes copyrighted material of Insurance Services Office, Inc., with its permission. Copyright, ISO Properties, Inc., 2002. [DA07711]

The Farm Property—Farm Personal Property Coverage Form contains two coverages:

*   Coverage E—Scheduled Farm Personal Property
*   Coverage F—Unscheduled Farm Personal Property

The insured can choose either or both of these coverages. Coverage E applies to only those classes of farm personal property for which a specific limit of insurance is shown in the Declarations page. The types of property that can be insured under Coverage E include farm products, materials, and supplies; farm equipment; various types of livestock; and several other classes of farm personal property. In addition to insuring specified classes of farm personal property, Coverage E can also be used to cover individually scheduled items of farm personal property, such as a particular tractor or combine owned by the insured. Coverage restrictions and sublimits apply to some of the eligible classes of property.

Coverage F insures unscheduled farm personal property under a single limit. To discourage underinsurance, Coverage F is subject to an 80 percent coinsurance requirement. Coverage F excludes an extensive list of property, such as household personal property, animals other than livestock, racehorses or show horses, certain crops and poultry, and vehicles primarily designed and licensed for road use.

The Farm Property—Barns, Outbuildings, and Other Farm Structures Coverage Form, Coverage G is used to insure all types of farm buildings and structures other than the dwelling and private garages.

Three levels of covered causes of loss can be purchased under the ISO farm program: Basic, Broad, and Special. All the policy provisions for these three levels of coverage are contained in the Causes of Loss Form—Farm Property. The insurer marks the declarations page accordingly to indicate which level of coverage applies.

The basic causes of loss in the farm policy are the same as those found in the commercial property Causes of Loss—Basic Form, plus four additional perils: theft, collision, earthquake (covering livestock only), and flood (livestock only). The collision peril has three aspects: collision damage to covered farm machinery; death of covered livestock resulting from contact with vehicles; and collision damage to other farm personal property. The earthquake and flood perils apply only to loss (by death) of covered livestock.

The broad causes of loss in the ISO farm program include all the basic causes of loss, plus all other named perils included in the commercial property causes-of-loss broad form and the homeowners Broad Form. Death of livestock resulting from some additional perils is also covered. These additional perils are electrocution, drowning, accidental shooting, attacks by dogs or wild animals, and accidents in loading or unloading.

The special causes of loss coverage corresponds to the coverage provided by the homeowners Special Form and the commercial property Causes of Loss—Special Form. Most of the exclusions of the farm coverage form are identical to, or closely resemble, the exclusions and limitations found in the commercial property Special Form. However, some are modified either to address the particular loss exposures of farms or to emulate homeowners Special Form coverage. Livestock, poultry, and many other types of farm products are not eligible for farm Special Form coverage under ISO manual rules.

Apply Your Knowledge

Which one of the following Farm Property Coverage Parts would be appropriate for covering specified classes of farm personal property?

a. Coverage A
b. Coverage G
c. Coverage E
d. Coverage C

Feedback: c. Coverage E provides coverage for a specified class of farm personal property such as farm products, materials, and supplies; farm equipment; various types of livestock; and several other classes of farm personal property.

Specialty Farm Coverages

Standard farm policies do not cover some loss exposures for which farmers frequently need coverage. Examples of the specialty coverages that can meet farmers' needs are crop-hail insurance, federal crop insurance, and animal mortality insurance.

Private insurers offer a traditional form of crop insurance called crop-hail insurance. Crop-hail policies cover crop loss resulting from hail and are frequently extended to cover additional perils such as fire, windstorm accompanying hail, damage caused by livestock, and vehicles. Such policies may also cover harvested crops against named perils while being transported to the first place of storage.

Various crop insurance programs are also available from the Federal Crop Insurance Corporation (FCIC), a governmental insurer subject to the Risk Management Agency (RMA), a division of the United States Department of Agriculture. One of FCIC's crop insurance plans is Multiple Peril Crop Insurance (MPCI) which insures farmers against unexpected production losses from natural causes, including drought, excessive moisture, hail, wind, flood, hurricanes, tornadoes, and lightning. MPCI policies do not cover losses resulting from neglect, poor farming practices, or theft. These programs are marketed and serviced by participating private insurers but are reinsured by the federal government.

The livestock coverage provided by most farm policies is not adequate for some farmers and ranchers. In addition, nonfarmers often own valuable animals that they would like to insure for their full value. Farm policies normally cover loss of livestock only by specified causes, such as electrocution, accidental shooting, or drowning. Owners of high-valued animals often want to insure against loss of their animals by any fortuitous cause, including illness or disease.

One example of livestock coverage designed to meet special needs is animal mortality insurance. Animal mortality insurance is essentially term life insurance on animals. This type of insurance may be purchased to cover farm animals such as valuable horses, registered cattle, or calves being grown and exhibited under sponsorship of a club (such as 4-H). Animal mortality insurance is also purchased by owners of racehorses, show dogs, circus animals, and laboratory animals. Animal mortality insurance generally covers against loss of the insured animal by death resulting from accident, injury, sickness, or disease, or by theft, subject to exclusions.

SUMMARY

The businessowners policy (BOP) is designed to insure eligible small to mid-size businesses. Common exposures generally included in the BOP are buildings, business personal property, personal property of others, business income and extra expense, premises and operations liability, and several others. With its package approach and simplified rating procedures, the BOP can meet the needs of insurers, producers, and policyholders.

These are the main differences between BOP property coverage and the ISO commercial property coverage forms:

- Covered causes of loss in the BOP are usually offered on either a broad form or special form basis.
- Replacement cost is the standard BOP valuation provision.
- Some BOPs have no coinsurance, and others have insurance-to-value requirements other than coinsurance.
- BOP property not covered provisions list fewer items.
- BOPs contain automatic seasonal increase provisions.
- BOP business income and extra expense coverage is automatically included, often with no dollar limit.

The liability coverage included in a typical BOP closely resembles but does not mirror coverage provided by the occurrence version of the CGL coverage form. Insureds have fewer choices regarding limit amounts, and the minimum liability limit is usually higher for the BOP. Also, optional professional liability endorsements are available for the BOP, so separate policies are not required for qualifying insureds. Further, hired and nonowned autos liability coverage is usually offered by BOPs, and some programs offer BOP endorsements for employee benefits liability coverage and employment practices liability. Finally, eligibility requirements for the BOP preclude some coverage options that are available for the CGL.

Insurance coverage for farm operations can be provided under the ISO farm program, which uses a combination of forms to provide coverage that meets the need of different types of farm operations. Specialty farm coverages can be used for loss exposures that are not fully covered or are excluded in the ISO farm program.

11

Specialty Coverages

Educational Objectives

After learning the content of this assignment, you should be able to:

▷ Describe commercial excess liability insurance and commercial umbrella liability insurance in terms of these characteristics:

- The three basic types of commercial excess liability insurance

- The provisions commonly found in commercial umbrella liability policies that distinguish them from other types of commercial liability policies

▷ Describe professional liability insurance and management liability insurance in terms of these aspects:

- How they differ from each other

- How they differ from commercial general liability policies

- The common types of professional and management liability policies

▷ Describe the purpose and characteristics of each of these types of environmental insurance policies:

- Site-specific environmental impairment liability (EIL) policies

- Underground storage tank compliance policies

- Remediation stop-loss policies

- Contractors pollution liability policies

- Environmental professional errors and omissions liability policies

▷ Describe aircraft insurance in terms of these characteristics:

- The purpose-of-use categories that insurers use to classify aircraft

- The coverages that can be included in an aircraft policy

▷ Describe the types of losses that can be covered by each of the insuring agreements generally available in cyber risk insurance policies.

▶▶

11

▷ Explain how an organization domiciled in the United States can insure foreign loss exposures that would not be covered under standard property and liability insurance policies.

▷ Summarize the purpose and provisions of the terrorism endorsements developed by Insurance Services Office, Inc., and the National Council on Compensation Insurance, Inc.

▷ Summarize the guarantee provided by the particular types of surety bonds within the following bond classifications:

- Contract bonds

- License and permit bonds

- Public official bonds

- Court bonds

- Miscellaneous bonds

Specialty Coverages

COMMERCIAL EXCESS AND UMBRELLA LIABILITY INSURANCE

Commercial excess and umbrella liability insurance is necessary because many insureds have liability loss exposures larger than the limits available under their commercial general liability, commercial auto, and other liability policies.

Two types of coverage that organizations buy principally to extend the limits of their commercial general liability (CGL), commercial auto, and other primary liability policies are excess liability insurance and umbrella liability insurance. An **excess liability policy** covers liability claims in excess of the limits of an underlying policy or a stated retention amount. An **umbrella liability policy** provides excess coverage over several primary policies and may also provide coverage not available in the underlying policies, subject to a self-insured retention.

Commercial Excess Liability Insurance

An excess liability policy may take any of the following three basic forms:

- A "following form" subject to the same terms as the underlying policy
- A self-contained policy subject to its own terms only
- A combination of the first two types

A following-form excess policy covers a liability loss that exceeds the underlying limits only if the loss is covered by the underlying insurance. To illustrate, assume that an insured has an underlying liability policy with an each occurrence limit of $1,000,000 and a following-form excess policy with an each occurrence limit of $1,000,000. If a claimant obtains a judgment of $1,250,000 against the insured for bodily injury covered by the underlying policy, the underlying policy will pay the each occurrence limit of $1,000,000, and the excess policy will pay the remaining $250,000. See the exhibit "Application of Primary and Excess Liability Policies."

A self-contained excess policy applies to a loss that exceeds the underlying limits only if the loss is also covered under the terms of the excess policy. For example, an excess policy may not cover injury within the products-completed operations hazard, even though the underlying policy does. In such a case, the excess policy would not pay for a products liability claim, even

Excess liability policy
A policy that covers liability claims in excess of the limits of an underlying policy or a stated retention amount.

Umbrella liability policy
A liability policy that provides excess coverage above underlying policies and may also provide coverage not available in the underlying policies, subject to a self-insured retention.

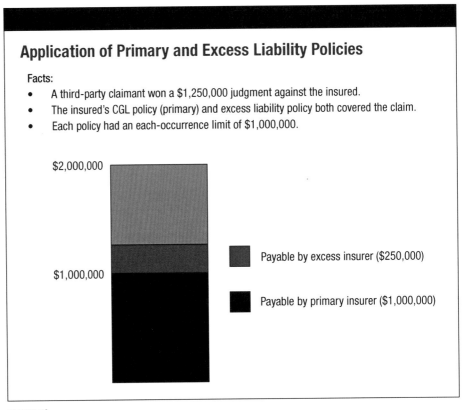

Application of Primary and Excess Liability Policies

Facts:
- A third-party claimant won a $1,250,000 judgment against the insured.
- The insured's CGL policy (primary) and excess liability policy both covered the claim.
- Each policy had an each-occurrence limit of $1,000,000.

$2,000,000

$1,000,000

■ Payable by excess insurer ($250,000)

■ Payable by primary insurer ($1,000,000)

[DA02676]

though the claim was covered by the underlying policy and exceeded the each occurrence limit of the underlying policy. Alternatively, an excess policy may combine both of these approaches by incorporating the provisions of the underlying policy and then modifying those provisions with additional conditions or exclusions in the excess policy.

Commercial Umbrella Liability Insurance

The term "umbrella liability" is generally used to describe a type of excess insurance that is broader than ordinary excess liability policies. Although ordinary excess policies may apply in excess of one or more underlying policies, an umbrella liability policy almost always provides excess coverage over several primary policies, such as CGL, auto liability, and employers liability.

An umbrella liability policy can perform three functions. Like an ordinary excess liability policy, it provides additional limits above the each occurrence limits of the insured's primary policies and takes the place of the primary insurance when primary aggregate limits are reduced or exhausted. In addition, it may cover some claims that are not covered by the insured's primary policies.

When they were first introduced, the distinguishing feature of umbrella liability policies was broader coverage, in at least some respects, than that of the underlying policies. More recently, there has been a reduction in the scope of coverage in typical umbrella policies so that most umbrella policies are not much broader than the primary policies and may even contain more restrictive exclusions than those found in the primary policies.

Umbrella policies contain certain provisions that distinguish them from other types of commercial liability policies and that examples of such provisions are discussed under the headings that follow.

Drop-Down Coverage

Drop-down coverage is provided by many umbrella liability policies for (1) claims that are not covered by an underlying policy because the underlying policy's aggregate limits have been depleted and (2) claims for which the underlying policies do not provide any coverage, regardless of aggregate limits.

To illustrate the first function of drop-down coverage, which may also be performed by an ordinary excess policy, assume that a manufacturer has these occurrence-basis policies:

• A CGL policy with an each occurrence limit of $1 million and a products-completed operations aggregate limit of $2 million

• An umbrella policy with an each occurrence limit of $5 million and an aggregate limit of $5 million

During one policy period, the primary CGL insurer pays products liability claims totaling $2 million, exhausting the aggregate limit. If the insured is sued by a consumer who alleges he was injured by the insured's product during the same policy period, the umbrella policy will "drop down" to defend the insured and/or pay damages (subject to the umbrella policy's limits) as if the umbrella policy were primary insurance. If subsequent products liability claims are made against the insured for injury that allegedly occurred during the policy period, the umbrella policy will defend or pay those claims also. The umbrella insurer's obligation to defend and pay ceases when its limits are exhausted.

As an example of the second aspect of drop-down coverage, assume that a manufacturer has a CGL policy and an umbrella liability policy. A products liability suit is brought against the manufacturer in a country not included in the CGL coverage territory. Because the CGL policy covers products liability only if the suit is first made in the United States or Canada, the CGL policy does not apply in this case. However, if the umbrella policy does not contain the same territorial restriction on products suits, it will drop down and handle the claim as though it were the primary policy.

When a claim covered by the umbrella policy is not covered at all by any primary policy, the drop-down coverage is usually subject to a **self-insured retention (SIR)**. If the SIR shown in the umbrella policy is $25,000, for example, the umbrella policy will pay the part of the claim that exceeds $25,000, subject to the applicable limits of insurance. Retentions vary in

Self-insured retention (SIR)

An amount that is deducted from claims that are payable under an umbrella liability policy and that are not covered at all by any primary policy.

amount, from as low as $500 for small businesses to $1,000,000 or more for large businesses. See the exhibit "Application of Umbrella Policy to a Claim Not Covered by Primary Policy."

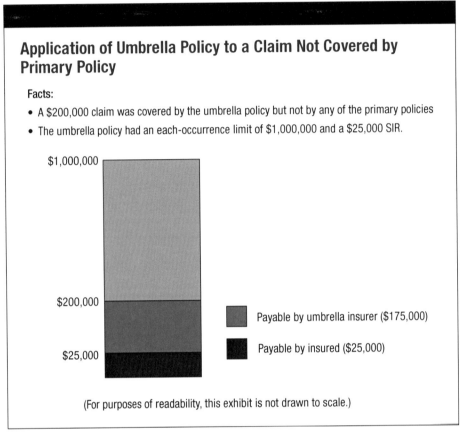

[DA02677]

Required Underlying Coverages

Each insurer writing umbrella liability policies has its own requirements for the types and amounts of underlying insurance that the insured must have. For example, an umbrella insurer might require the insured to have these primary coverages and limits:

Commercial General Liability

- $1,000,000 each occurrence
- $2,000,000 general aggregate
- $2,000,000 products and completed operations aggregate

Business Auto Liability

- $1,000,000 combined single limit

Employers Liability

- $100,000 bodily injury each accident
- $100,000 bodily injury by disease each employee
- $500,000 disease aggregate

The umbrella limits apply in full in excess of each of the underlying coverages. Thus, if an insured with these underlying limits also carried a $10,000,000 umbrella policy, the total coverage available for one occurrence covered by the CGL policy and the umbrella would be $11,000,000 ($1,000,000 primary plus $10,000,000 umbrella). The exhibit illustrates the interaction of the primary and umbrella limits. See the exhibit "Interaction of Umbrella and Primary Liability Limits."

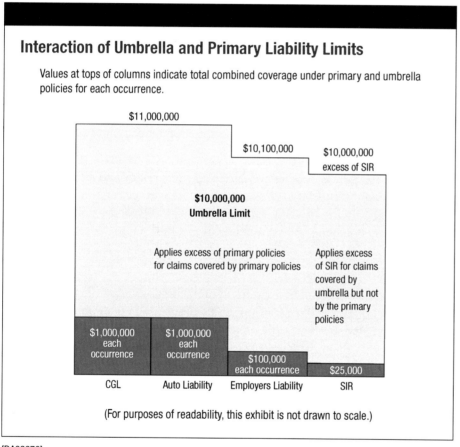

Interaction of Umbrella and Primary Liability Limits

Values at tops of columns indicate total combined coverage under primary and umbrella policies for each occurrence.

$11,000,000

$10,100,000

$10,000,000 excess of SIR

$10,000,000 Umbrella Limit

Applies excess of primary policies for claims covered by primary policies

Applies excess of SIR for claims covered by umbrella but not by the primary policies

$1,000,000 each occurrence

$1,000,000 each occurrence

$100,000 each occurrence

$25,000

CGL   Auto Liability   Employers Liability   SIR

(For purposes of readability, this exhibit is not drawn to scale.)

[DA02678]

Aggregate Limits

The previous example ignores any aggregate limit in the umbrella policy. Almost all umbrella policies contain aggregate limits that operate like those in the primary insurance. In some cases, the aggregate limit applies to all claims under the umbrella; in other cases, the aggregate limit applies only to coverages that are subject to an aggregate in the underlying policies.

If the umbrella policy in the previous example included an aggregate limit, then the total available insurance would be reduced by payments on previous claims payable by the umbrella policy. For example, assume that the umbrella policy described in the example had a $10,000,000 each occurrence limit and a $10,000,000 aggregate limit. Assuming also that no other claims had been paid by either policy, paying a $3,000,000 premises liability claim ($1,000,000 by the primary policy and $2,000,000 by the umbrella), would leave $9,000,000 available for the next covered claim—$1,000,000 (the balance of the underlying aggregate) from the primary policy and $8,000,000 (the balance of the umbrella aggregate) from the umbrella.

Insuring Agreement

Many umbrella liability policies contain one comprehensive insuring agreement instead of several specific ones. A common approach is for the insurer to promise to pay the amount in excess of the underlying limit that the insured becomes legally obligated to pay as damages for bodily injury, property damage, personal injury, or advertising injury arising out of an occurrence to which the policy applies, subject to the umbrella policy's limit.

Other umbrella policies use two insuring agreements, often referred to as "A" and "B." In effect, these policies combine an excess policy and an umbrella policy in one policy. Insuring agreement A is an excess coverage applying over the underlying policies. Insuring agreement B applies to occurrences for which coverage is available under the umbrella but not in the underlying policies.

Exclusions

Although the exclusions contained in umbrella policies resemble those found in underlying policies, some variation usually exists. When an umbrella policy provides broadened coverage, it is typically achieved by using exclusions in the umbrella policy that have narrower application than the exclusions in the underlying policies. To illustrate, an umbrella policy might contain a watercraft exclusion that does not apply to any watercraft, owned or nonowned, less than fifty feet long. Because the watercraft exclusion of the underlying CGL coverage form does not apply only to nonowned watercraft less than twenty-six feet long, the umbrella policy will provide drop-down coverage for owned boats less than fifty feet long and for nonowned boats between twenty-six and fifty feet long.

Another possibility is that the umbrella policy contains an exclusion that does not exist in any of the underlying policies and may provide narrower coverage than the underlying insurance for the particular exposure. For example, the umbrella policy may exclude claims for bodily injury arising from exposure to lead even though no such exclusion appears in the primary policy.

Conditions

Noteworthy differences between the general conditions of primary liability policies and umbrella policies concern maintenance of underlying insurance and the coverage territory.

The maintenance of underlying insurance conditions obligates the insured to maintain all required underlying coverages in full force and effect during the policy period. The insured further agrees to notify the insurer promptly if any underlying policy is changed or replaced by a policy issued by another insurer. If the underlying insurance is not maintained, the umbrella policy will apply as though the underlying insurance had been maintained. That is, a claim that would have been covered by an underlying policy, had it been kept in force, will only be covered for the amount that exceeds the limit of the under-lying policy. The umbrella policy will not drop down to pay claims that would have been covered by the required underlying policy.

Most umbrella policies provide worldwide coverage, in contrast with the more limited coverage territories ordinarily found in primary policies. However, some umbrella policies require that suit be brought in the U.S. or Canada for coverage to apply.

PROFESSIONAL LIABILITY AND MANAGEMENT LIABILITY INSURANCE

Professional liability insurance and management liability insurance are similar in that they cover a variety of claims—often for large amounts of damages—that are usually not covered by more common coverages such as commercial general liability (CGL) or business auto liability.

Before examining specific types of professional liability insurance and manage-ment liability insurance, it is important to understand the distinction between the two types of insurance, why they are needed, and how they differ, in general, from other types of commercial liability insurance.

Distinguishing Between Professional and Management Liability

The word "profession" has historically been associated with occupations referred to as the learned professions—law, medicine, education, and the clergy—and, more recently, such others as engineers and architects. It would therefore seem logical that the term "professional liability insurance" refers to liability insurance for people in those professions.

However, as new liability exposures have evolved, **professional liability insur-ance** has become available for more than just the traditional professions. These additional occupations range from analytical chemists to veterinarians,

Professional liability insurance

Insurance that covers persons engaged in various occupations against liability resulting from their rendering or failing to render professional services.

all of which entail liability for the failure to use the degree of skill expected of a person in their particular field.

Professional liability is also known as malpractice or errors and omissions (E&O) liability. "Malpractice" is the term commonly used to describe liability associated with occupations that involve contact with the human body, ranging from beauticians to physicians. "Errors and omissions" is the term more likely to be used to describe professional liability for occupations such as accounting, insurance, law, and engineering.

Although sometimes included in the definition of professional liability insurance, coverages such as directors and officers liability, employment practices liability, and fiduciary liability are now commonly called **management liability insurance**.

Management liability is distinguished from professional liability in that it is less about individuals in occupations rendering or failing to render professional services and more about the wrongful acts of an organization or of individuals in their roles managing the operations of an organization.

Professional and Management Liability Contrasted With CGL

The CGL coverage form does not include a professional liability exclusion, so many professional liability exposures would be covered unless an exclusion endorsement is attached to the policy. Because professional liability requires different underwriting, rating, and claim handling skills, most insurers do not want to provide it as part of CGL coverage. Accordingly, for several professional classifications, insurers routinely attach a professional liability exclusion that eliminates coverage for bodily injury, property damage, or personal and advertising injury resulting from the rendering or failure to render any professional services listed in the endorsement.

Professional liability and management liability policies differ from the CGL coverage form and other standard liability policies in these important ways:

- Claims-made trigger
- Consent to settle
- Duty to defend and selection of defense counsel
- Deductibles

Claims-Made Trigger

Although Insurance Services Office, Inc. (ISO), maintains a claims-made CGL form, it is seldom used. Most businesses are insured under the occurrence version of the CGL. In contrast, most professional liability policies and management liability policies have a claims-made coverage trigger instead of an occurrence coverage trigger.

Management liability insurance

Insurance that covers organizations and in some cases their directors, officers, and other employees against liability claims for damages resulting from various wrongful acts that are not covered under other commercial liability policies; common examples are directors and officers liability insurance, employment practices liability insurance, employee benefits liability insurance, and fiduciary liability insurance.

The reason for using a claims-made policy is that professional and management liability claims are sometimes not settled until long after the policy has expired. With a claims-made policy, the policy in effect when the claim is first made against the insured is the policy that covers the claim. In contrast, a liability policy with an occurrence trigger can cover a claim that is made many years after the policy has expired, as long as the injury occurred during the policy period. Insurers prefer to cover claims under current policies rather than under policies that expired many years previously.

Key features of claims-made policies include retroactive dates and extended reporting periods. If a claims-made policy has a **retroactive date**, it is shown on the declarations page. If a claims-made policy has no retroactive date, the policy will cover claims first made during the policy period, regardless of when the injury, damage, or other insured event occurred. An **extended reporting period (ERP)** extends the period in which a claim may be made.

Some claims-made professional and management liability policies have a built-in ERP that applies automatically, for no additional premium. Typically, this basic ERP only lasts for thirty to sixty days. Some claims-made policies allow the insured to request a longer ERP in exchange for an additional premium. Typically, these supplemental ERPs last for one to three years. Some insurers provide longer ERPs.

Consent to Settle

The CGL policy provides that the insurer may, at its discretion, settle any claim or suit. The insured is seldom involved in that decision and has no policy-given right to prevent a settlement that the insurer wants to make. In contrast, because professional or business reputations may be at stake in claims under professional liability and management liability policies, the insured frequently is given the right to participate in the decision to settle a claim in such policies.

The policy may provide that the insurer cannot settle a claim without the insured's consent. If the insured does not consent to settlement, the insurer, at its expense, must then (unless the policy provides otherwise) continue to defend the insured and pay any judgment that the court awards.

More typically, professional liability and management liability policies provide that if the insured does not agree to a proposed settlement, the insured must take over the defense and pay any further defense expenses as well as the amount of any judgment or settlement that exceeds the amount for which the insurer could have settled the claim. This provision is sometimes informally referred to as a "hammer clause," because it usually compels the insured to agree to the settlement proposed by the insurer.

Retroactive date

The date on or after which the injury, damage, or other insured event must occur in order to be covered in a claims-made liability policy.

Extended reporting period (ERP)

An additional period (also called a "tail") following the expiration of a claims-made policy, during which the expired policy will cover claims first made for injury or damage that occurred on or after the policy's retroactive date (if any) and before policy expiration.

Duty to Defend and Selection of Defense Counsel

Professional liability and management liability policies can provide defense coverage in the same manner as the CGL policy, in which the insurer has the duty to defend the insured against claims that fall within the scope of the policy's coverage. The insurer selects and pays the attorneys that defend the insured.

In contrast, some professional liability policies provide defense cost reimbursement coverage requiring that the insurer reimburse the insured for defense expenses covered by the policy. Under such policies, the insured usually has the right to select counsel, sometimes subject to the insurer's approval. Some professional liability and management liability policies give the insured the option to assume the defense even though the policy otherwise provides that the insurer shall have the duty to defend.

A further difference is that the cost of defense under professional liability and management liability policies is often paid within (not in addition to) the limit of insurance. Under standard CGL policies, defense costs are paid in addition to the policy limits, until the policy limits are depleted by settlements or court awards.

Deductibles

Most small to mid-size organizations have CGL coverage with no deductible. In contrast, professional liability and management liability policies are usually subject to a deductible. Most insurers have mandatory minimum deductibles for their various classes of professional liability and management liability policies.

Professional Liability Policies

Because the liability exposures of one profession (such as medicine) may differ considerably from the liability exposures of another profession (such as engineering), insurers use different policies to insure each. In many cases, a particular type of professional liability insurance is written only by the insurers that specialize in it. Specialization allows insurers to develop the skills required to successfully underwrite profession-specific risks and to handle claims that differ from the more common types. Professional liability insurance is usually written on forms independently developed by individual insurers, rather than on standard forms.

Certain exclusions are common to most professional liability policies. For example, most policies exclude contractual liability; punitive damages; and the insured's dishonest, criminal, or malicious acts. Professional liability policies for some occupations contain specialized exclusions. For example, insurance agents' and brokers' E&O policies may exclude liability for claims based on the insolvency of an insurer.

To illustrate the diversity of exposures and coverages in the professional liability field, the following sections describe physicians professional liability policies and insurance agents and brokers E&O liability policies.

Physicians Professional Liability Policies

A physician's professional liability usually arises from improper performance in the practice of the profession that results in injury. For example, the failure to properly diagnose a disease and improper performance of a surgical procedure, such as leaving a surgical instrument in a patient following surgery, can cause injury and result in liability.

Physicians can also be held liable for administrative errors or omissions connected with their medical practice. For example, a physician who serves on a hospital's accreditation committee may be held liable for injury resulting from improperly refusing hospital staff privileges to another physician.

The insuring agreement in a typical physicians professional liability policy covers damages for injury resulting from the rendering of or failing to render professional services by the insured or by anyone else for whose acts the insured is legally responsible (such as a nurse working under the insured's supervision). The insuring agreement also covers liability arising out of the insured's service on a formal accreditation board.

The meaning of "injury" as used in such policies is very broad. Therefore, the damages that the insurer will pay on behalf of the insured are not restricted to those for bodily injury or property damage. Damages for emotional or mental injury, libel, slander, defamation, invasion of privacy, and similar offenses are generally covered by physicians professional liability policies unless specifically excluded.

Insurance Agents and Brokers E&O Liability Policies

Examples of the errors or omissions for which insurance agents or brokers have been held liable to their customers are failure to properly advise a customer regarding his or her insurance needs, failure to obtain insurance for a customer in a timely manner after agreeing to do so, failure to renew a policy at expiration without giving prior notice to the customer, and failure to properly advise the customer regarding appropriate limits.

Insurance producers can also become liable to the insurers they represent. For example, an agency that binds coverage that the insurer has not authorized the agency to bind can be held liable to the insurer if any claims are made under the coverage. An agent may be sued for failure to cancel a policy as instructed by the insurer if a loss occurs that would not have been covered had the agent acted properly.

A typical insurance agents and brokers E&O policy agrees to "pay on behalf of the Insured damages that the Insured becomes legally obligated to pay because of claims made against the Insured for wrongful acts arising out of the performance of professional services for others."[1]

Management Liability Policies

Three main types of management liability insurance are directors and officers liability, employment practices liability, and fiduciary liability.

Directors and Officers Liability Policies

Many organizations have a board of directors or trustees and a staff of officers. Directors are selected by the owners to make strategic decisions regarding the organization. Officers, generally selected by the board of directors, are drawn from the organization's top management.

Some lawsuits arising from securities fraud have resulted in enormous judgments against corporations and their directors and officers, several in excess of $1 billion. Smaller organizations are not generally subject to such large claims, but the individuals who serve as the directors and officers of a corporation can be sued, as individuals, for breach of their corporate duties.

In recognition of the potentially devastating liability exposure faced by individual directors and officers, corporations usually agree to indemnify their directors and officers for the costs resulting from suits against them. The laws of several states permit or even require corporations to provide such indemnification to their directors and officers. Therefore, the directors and officers liability exposure affects both individual directors and officers and the corporation itself. Many corporations protect themselves and their directors and officers against this exposure by purchasing **directors and officers (D&O) liability insurance**. Traditionally, D&O policies contain these two insuring agreements:

> **Directors and officers (D&O) liability insurance**
>
> Insurance that covers a corporation's directors and officers against liability for their wrongful acts covered by the policy and also covers the sums that the insured corporation is required or permitted by law to pay to the directors and officers as indemnification.

- Coverage A—Covers the directors and officers of the insured corporation for their personal liability as directors or officers that results from a "wrongful act." Wrongful act is typically defined to include any breach of duty, neglect, error, misstatement, misleading statement, omission, or other act done or wrongfully attempted by the directors or officers.

- Coverage B—Often referred to as company reimbursement coverage, it covers the sums that the insured corporation is required or permitted by law to pay to the directors and officers as indemnification for suits alleging wrongful acts by directors or officers.

> **Entity coverage**
>
> Coverage extension of D&O liability policies for claims made directly against a corporation (the "entity") for wrongful acts covered by the policy.

In addition, most D&O insurers now include an insuring agreement, often called Coverage C, for **entity coverage**, which covers claims made directly against a corporation (the entity) for wrongful acts. Because the corporation is often named as a defendant in a lawsuit alleging wrongful acts by the directors and officers, entity coverage can be a worthwhile extension of the D&O policy. However, entity coverage presents disadvantages for directors and officers because it requires them to share the limits of insurance with the corporation.

Employment Practices Liability Policies

The growth of federal and state legislation dealing with employment discrimination and sexual harassment, the changing legal views on wrongful termination, and the increasing tendency of aggrieved parties to turn to the courts for settlement of such disputes have caused insurers to specifically exclude coverage for such employment-related claims from CGL policies. To fill this gap in coverage, insurers offer **employment practices liability (EPL) insurance**, The definition of insured in an EPL policy usually includes the corporation; its directors and officers; its employees; and its former directors, officers, and employees. In some policies, coverage for employees applies only to managerial or supervisory employees.

Employment practices liability (EPL) insurance

Insurance that covers an organization, its directors and officers, and its employees against claims alleging damages because of wrongful employment practices such as sexual harassment, wrongful termination, and unlawful discrimination.

 Reality Check

Landmark EPL Case

Companies, their risk managers, and employment practices liability (EPL) insurers are captivated by the May 19, 2010, jury verdict in the case of *Velez v. Novartis Pharmaceuticals Corp.* This class action suit was filed by female employees of a subsidiary of Novartis AG. The plaintiffs alleged that they were subjected to gender discrimination in their sales positions by being paid less than male employees, pregnant women were subjected to adverse employment decisions, complaints of sexual harassment were ignored, and less qualified male employees were promoted over qualified women. The jury awarded $250 million in punitive damages, which was the largest punitive damages award made up to that time in an employment discrimination case.

Marsh Inc., "FINPRO Focus—Novartis $250 Million Punitive Damages Award: Why Employment Practices Liability Insurance Matters," FINPRO Practice, June 2010, http://documents.marsh.com/documents/employmentpracticesliabilityarticle.pdf (accessed August 9, 2011). [DA07910]

Fiduciary Liability Policies

The Employee Retirement Income Security Act (ERISA) is the most comprehensive statute regarding employee benefits. Among other things, ERISA imposes specific duties on all employee benefit plan "fiduciaries." ERISA defines a fiduciary as practically anyone whose role in employee benefits involves discretionary control or judgment in the design, administration, funding, or management of a benefit plan.

Those who meet the ERISA definition of a fiduciary can be held personally liable for the full amount of any loss resulting from a breach of their statutory duties. Moreover, the employer of the fiduciary can be held liable for the loss. Because of the broad interpretation of fiduciaries under ERISA, the principal and key employees of a firm are usually exposed to liability as fiduciaries.

Fiduciaries can be sued if they breach fiduciary duties involving discretionary judgment. An example of a duty involving discretionary judgment is using due care in investing funds accumulated for an employee retirement income plan. If the plan's fiduciaries make negligent investment decisions and thus cause financial harm to the plan's participants, the participants can sue the fiduciaries.

Fiduciary liability insurance covers this exposure. Even when the duty to select investments has been delegated to others, such as in a mutual fund or brokerage firm, the fiduciaries may be responsible for the errors or negligence of the investment managers. Fiduciary liability policies also usually include coverage for administrative errors in the same manner as the **employee benefits liability insurance** typically added by endorsement to a corporation's CGL policy.

ENVIRONMENTAL INSURANCE

An organization may be able to obtain coverage for environmental exposures through endorsements to its existing property and liability policies. When the coverage provided by these endorsements is inadequate, it may need to purchase separate environmental insurance policies.

Because exclusions and coverage gaps in primary commercial coverage forms such as the Commercial General Liability (CGL) Coverage Form can leave organizations vulnerable to losses related to environmental exposures, separate policies have emerged to address them. Environmental insurance policies are not standardized, and competing policy forms commonly have significant coverage differences. Additionally, different policy forms can be substantially modified by endorsement or combined to provide packages of different types of environmental insurance that share a common policy limit. Some environmental coverages are available only as part of specialty insurance packages.

There are many different types of environmental insurance policies. Five of the more common types include these:

- Site-specific environmental impairment liability
- Underground storage tank compliance
- Remediation stop-loss
- Contractors pollution liability
- Environmental professional errors and omissions (E&O) liability

Fiduciary liability insurance

Insurance that covers the fiduciaries of an employee benefit plan against liability claims alleging breach of their fiduciary duties involving discretionary judgment.

Employee benefits liability insurance

Insurance that covers an employer against liability claims alleging improper advice or other errors or omissions committed while administering the employer's employee benefit plans.

Site-Specific Environmental Impairment Liability Policies

Site-specific environmental impairment liability (EIL) policies are commonly sold to factories, waste disposal sites, golf courses, farms, municipalities, warehouses, and oil refineries. Coverage enhancements allow policyholders to purchase protection against the costs of on-site cleanup, claims arising from releases from third-party disposal sites, and claims arising from preexisting pollution at insured sites.

The insuring agreement in a typical site-specific EIL policy obligates the insurer to pay on behalf of the insured a loss, in excess of any deductible, for bodily injury, property damage, cleanup costs, and defense expenses. The loss must result from pollution conditions that exist beyond the boundaries of the site(s) listed in the policy declarations. However, on-site cleanup is commonly added by endorsement to the policy.

The policy definitions of bodily injury and property damage are typically the same as those in other liability insurance policies, with two notable qualifications. The first is that for the environmental coverage to apply, the bodily injury or property damage must result from pollutants emanating from an insured site. The second qualification is that physical injury or actual exposure to pollutants is required in some of the policy forms to trigger coverage for bodily injury claims. These two requirements can substantially restrict coverage under a site-specific EIL policy for claims alleging "cancer phobia" or similar fears of future disease or injury.

The definition of the term "loss" often includes the cost to defend against pollution claims within the scope of the policy. The term "cleanup costs" may appear as a separate coverage term, or it may be included within the definition of property damage. The policies sold by different insurers may contain differing definitions of cleanup costs. Most of the definitions include, as a minimum, expenses the insured incurs in the removal or remediation of soil, surface water, groundwater, or other contamination in response to a covered pollution liability loss.

Site-specific EIL policies respond to loss arising from "pollution conditions." The definition of pollution conditions follows the definition of pollutants in ISO pollution exclusions found in general liability, auto liability, and other liability insurance policies.

Site-specific EIL policies provide coverage on a claims-made basis. In most respects, the policies operate like other forms of claims-made insurance. See the exhibit "Typical Exclusions of Site-Specific EIL Policies."

Site-specific EIL policies are typically subject to a per-loss limit of liability, which is the most that the insurer will pay for bodily injury, property damage, cleanup costs, and defense expenses resulting from each release of pollutants. EIL policies also typically contain an aggregate limit of liability. The inclusion

Site-specific environmental impairment liability (EIL) policy

An insurance policy that covers third-party claims arising from either sudden or gradual releases of pollutants from specified locations.

Typical Exclusions of Site-Specific EIL Policies

Name of Exclusion:	Comment (if any):
Known preexisting conditions	The purpose of this exclusion is to eliminate coverage in situations in which the purchaser of the policy knew of an impending claim that would be covered under the policy.
Deliberate noncompliance with environmental laws	
Punitive damages	
Sold or leased premises	EIL policies commonly exclude coverage for an insured location that the insured has sold or leased to others.
Nuclear liability	
Acid rain	Because the damage caused by acid rain can be widespread and can occur at considerable distances from the source of emissions, underwriters are reluctant to delete this exclusion from EIL policies unless the insured does not operate the type of equipment that can cause acid rain.
War	
Contractual liability	
Damage to the insured site	EIL policies traditionally contain exclusions that eliminate coverage for releases of contaminants that do not migrate beyond the boundaries of the insured site. It is also common for EIL policies to specifically exclude on-site cleanup expenses. However, this practice is changing, and EIL policies that cover first-party exposures (on-site cleanup) are now available.
Products and completed operations	Site-specific EIL policies commonly exclude the insured's liability for products and completed operations because standard CGL policies generally cover the insured's liability for products and completed operations.
Workers compensation and employers liability	
Transportation loss exposures	Site-specific EIL policies ordinarily exclude liability arising out of the ownership, maintenance, operation, use, loading, or unloading of any automobile, aircraft, watercraft, or railcar.
Terrorism	EIL policies may or may not include terrorism exclusions.

[DA07911]

Underground storage tank (UST) compliance policy

An insurance policy that provides proof of financial responsibility under governmental regulations that apply to the owners and operators of underground storage tanks containing fuels or other hazardous materials.

of defense expenses within EIL policy limits is an important difference from the CGL policy.

Underground Storage Tank Compliance Policies

The Resource Conservation and Recovery Act (RCRA) requires owners or operators of underground storage tanks to demonstrate proof of their ability to pay claims resulting from the release of fuels or hazardous materials from the tanks. This can be accomplished through the purchase of an **underground storage tank (UST) compliance policy**. UST compliance policies, which vary by insurer, have a site-specific EIL policy as their core coverage. Most UST compliance policies are worded to provide the full financial responsibility compliance required by federal regulations.

Additional policy provisions include a separate limit for defense costs, usually equal to 25 percent of the policy limit. In contrast, an ordinary EIL policy includes defense costs within the limit of liability. The UST compliance policy also adds a sixty-day notice of nonrenewal and an automatic extended reporting period provision. These two provisions assure regulators that UST compliance policies comply with the minimum proof of financial responsibility requirements of RCRA or the applicable state regulations.

RCRA further requires the owners or operators of underground storage tanks to provide evidence of financial responsibility for specified limits. For most tank owners, the required limit of insurance is $1 million per claim. Larger retailers of petroleum products may be required to provide evidence of $2 million of financial responsibility per claim.

Remediation Stop-Loss Policies

Designed to facilitate real estate sales, **remediation stop-loss policies** (also known as cost cap policies) are principally used when a property is known to be contaminated but the cost of remediation is uncertain. A large discrepancy often exists between the low and high estimates of cleanup costs for a contaminated property, making it difficult for buyers and sellers of property to establish the sale price. Remediation stop-loss policies are used to close the gap between these estimates by insuring remediation costs that exceed the projected or anticipated cleanup costs. Such policies provide first-party coverage; third-party coverage is often provided as part of an overall insurance package by adding an EIL coverage form to the transaction.

> Remediation stop-loss policy (cost cap policy)
>
> An insurance policy purchased to insure remediation costs that exceed the projected or anticipated costs of performing an environmental cleanup of a specific location that is being sold.

Remediation stop-loss policies typically agree to pay, on behalf of the named insured, the expenses (in excess of the deductible) that the insured incurs in completing an approved remedial action work plan at a specified location. A claim under the policy is defined as "written notice to the insured that the remediation costs incurred at the project have exceeded the costs contained within the scope of work." The description of the "scope of work," which is different in each policy, is usually expressed in an endorsement to the policy.

Remediation stop-loss policies typically contain relatively few exclusions because they are written on a first-party coverage basis. As with other types of environmental insurance, these policies are written as manuscript forms, without standard terms or conditions. Some of the exclusions commonly found in remediation stop-loss policies are willful noncompliance with environmental regulations, bodily injury, contractual liability, and war.

☑ **Reality Check**

Using Remediation Stop-Loss Coverage

This scenario, although hypothetical, shows how remediation stop-loss coverage facilitates the sale of real estate known to be polluted.

ALB Investments, a real estate investor, wishes to sell, as is, a parcel of land that was once used as a service station and is known to be polluted with gasoline and motor oil. The potential buyer is concerned that environmental remediation costs will exceed an estimate provided by ALB's environmental consultant. The sale has reached an impasse because of the differing estimates of remediation costs.

ALB can obtain a remediation stop-loss policy to guarantee the buyer that remediation costs will not exceed a predetermined amount. Eliminating the uncertainty about remediation costs should enable ALB and the buyer to agree on a sale price.

[DA07912]

Contractors Pollution Liability Policies

Contractors pollution liability (CPL) policy

An insurance policy that covers the pollution-related loss exposures of a contractor.

Contractors pollution liability (CPL) policies address the environmental insurance needs of contractors performing environmental remediation services on contaminated sites. In addition, a wide range of contractors, from general contractors to construction managers, purchase this coverage because of the far-reaching pollution exclusion in the CGL policy.

Because CPL policies are modeled after site-specific EIL policies, many of their policy terms and conditions are similar. Both provide coverage for bodily injury, property damage, cleanup costs, and defense costs. However, many of the features of the site-specific EIL policy had to be modified to address contractors' insurance needs. The site-specific EIL policy is written on a designated premises basis, whereas the CPL policy is designed to cover a contractor's operations and activities at project sites and to cover the contractor's completed operations and contractual liability exposures. Unlike site-specific EIL policies, CPL policies provide coverage for loss arising from the described operations of the named insured.

The insured operations are described in the application for insurance. Because the application becomes part of the insurance policy, failure to accurately describe the insured operations on the application or in the policy may result in deficient coverage.

CPL policies are available with either a claims-made or an occurrence coverage trigger. A CPL policy may contain most of the exclusions of site-specific EIL policies. However, a CPL policy ordinarily omits certain exclusions of site-specific EIL policies so that the CPL policy will cover completed operations, damage to the insured site, and the cost of remediating the job site for a loss created by the contractor's operations. In addition to containing the exclusions commonly found in site-specific EIL policies, CPL policies often exclude these exposures:

- Asbestos abatement operations
- Radioactive matter
- Claims arising out of the insured's products
- Damage to sites owned by or leased to the insured
- Professional liability

However, these exposures can often be covered by endorsement to the contractor's CPL policy. With regard to radioactive matter, the contractor's CPL policy can provide coverage for low-level radioactive exposures but not for risks associated with high-level materials used for weapons or fuel rods in nuclear power reactors.

Environmental Professional E&O Liability Policies

Environmental professional E&O liability policies contain insuring agreements that resemble the coverage grants of traditional engineers professional liability policies and do not contain pollution exclusions. A wide range of professional environmental services vendors who face potential liability from professional errors, acts, or omissions purchase these policies, including environmental engineers, testing labs, tank testers, and environmental consultants. Environmental professional E&O liability policies, like most other professional liability policies, are written on a claims-made basis, usually subject to a retroactive date and a substantial deductible.

Exclusions in environmental professional E&O liability insurance policies differ by insurer. The insured-versus-insured exclusion eliminates coverage for claims in which one insured sues another insured for damages arising out of a professional error, act, or omission. Most professional liability underwriters believe that such suits are a business risk that should be assumed by the affiliated entities and therefore should not be insured. The contractual liability exclusion addresses a similar business risk issue. Other exclusions in environmental professional E&O insurance include nuclear risks, warranties and guarantees, and fiduciary liability.

☑ **Reality Check**

Noteworthy Pollution Liability Verdict

In 2008, the United States Supreme Court upheld a pollution verdict of more than $20.7 million against Continental Carbon Co. and its parent company, China Synthetic Rubber Corp. Four years earlier, a jury ruled in favor of the plaintiffs, the city of Columbus, Georgia; a local boat dealer; and a homeowner. The jury found that the defendants had dumped carbon black into the air, which drifted across a river and damaged the plaintiffs' property. The jury's award allocated $3.2 million for compensatory damages and $17.5 million for punitive damages. It was the award of punitive damages that the defendants had fought on appeal.[2]

[DA07914]

AIRCRAFT INSURANCE

Aircraft insurance performs many of the same essential functions as auto insurance, such as protecting owners from the financial impact of liability and physical damage claims.

Aircraft insurance is purchased by a broad spectrum of insureds, ranging from individuals who own and operate small planes for pleasure to major airline companies that own and operate large fleets of aircraft. The purpose-of-use categories that insurers use to classify aircraft risks, shown in the exhibit, demonstrate the diverse risks covered by aircraft insurance. See the exhibit "Purpose of Use Categories."

Aircraft insurance is a specialized form of coverage with no standard policy. A few insurers write aircraft insurance on their own, but most aircraft insurance is provided by a pool of insurers or by underwriters in the London market.

Aircraft insurance in some ways resembles auto insurance in that its policies are divided into liability and physical damage sections. A fundamental difference between auto insurance and aircraft insurance, however, is that pilots of insured aircraft must meet strict qualifications: They must hold both the appropriate license and current medical certification from the Federal Aviation Administration (FAA) and are often required to have at least a specified number of hours of experience as the pilot-in-command of the type of aircraft insured.

In addition, except for policies covering airlines, aircraft policies cover only the plane or planes specifically described in the policy. Aircraft insurance policies written for general aviation risks (all classes of aircraft shown in the exhibit other than airliners and military aircraft) usually have no counterpart to the "any auto" coverage provided by symbol 1 of the Business Auto Coverage Form.

Aircraft insurance

Insurance that covers liability due to the insured's ownership, maintenance, or use of aircraft; physical damage to aircraft owned or used by the insured; and other aircraft loss exposures.

Purpose of Use Categories

Category	Description
Airline	Scheduled international, national, and regional airlines
Business and Pleasure	Individually owned aircraft used for owner's personal purposes with no charge made or direct profit derived from the aircraft's use
Industrial Aid	Corporate-owned aircraft used for transporting employees, associates, and executives and flown by professional pilots
Commercial Use	Charter operators, air taxi operators, and other profit-seeking operators
Special Use	Crop dusting, banner towing, law enforcement, pipeline patrol, hunting, and so forth
Instruction and Rental	Flight schools that instruct potential pilots and rent aircraft to students for solo-flight experience
Sales Demonstration	Dealers and brokers who demonstrate planes to potential buyers for no charge other than expense reimbursement

[DA02686]

An aircraft policy can include aircraft liability coverage, aircraft hull (physical damage) coverage, and other aircraft coverages. Other aircraft coverages can include medical payments coverage, passenger voluntary settlement coverage, and nonowned aircraft liability coverage.

Aircraft Liability Coverage

Aircraft liability coverage protects the insured against third-party claims for bodily injury and property damage resulting from the ownership, maintenance, or use of insured aircraft. A combined single limit applies to all third-party claims, except in cases in which insurers impose a sublimit on claims by passengers.

For example, the policy may be written for a $1 million per occurrence limit for bodily injury and property damage, or a $1 million per occurrence limit with a sublimit of $100,000 per passenger seat. As with auto liability insurance, aircraft liability coverage is usually not subject to an aggregate limit. Higher limits of liability may be available by increasing the primary liability limit; however, umbrella or excess liability coverage for aircraft is not always available. Private aircraft owners often have difficulty obtaining adequate liability limits.

Aircraft liability coverage typically contains these exclusions:

- Intentional injury, except to prevent interference with safe operations.
- Liability assumed under contract. However, some policies cover liability assumed under incidental contracts, such as a contract for use of an airport.
- Bodily injury to an employee of the insured.
- Obligations under workers compensation or similar laws.
- Claims caused by war, strikes, riots, labor disturbances, terrorism, sabotage, hijacking, or unlawful seizures.
- Damage to property owned, leased, occupied, controlled, or under the care of the insured. However, some policies provide basic limits of coverage for passengers' baggage or for damage to hangars leased by the insured.
- Claims by one employee against another, referred to as the fellow-employee exclusion. The policies used by some insurers do not contain this exclusion, and others will remove it by endorsement when requested by the insured and agreed to by the underwriter.

Various provisions are included in, or can be added to, aircraft policies to cover the insured's potential liability arising out of aircraft not specifically described in the policy. Such provisions can cover newly acquired aircraft; temporary substitute aircraft; and other aircraft not owned, leased, or regularly used by the insured.

Aircraft Hull Coverage

Because marine insurance practices and policy language played a prominent role in drafting early aircraft policies, the term "hull" is widely used to refer to physical damage coverage for aircraft. The two most common aircraft hull coverages are "all risks—ground and flight" and "all risks—not in motion."

All risks—ground and flight, the broader of the two, covers the insured plane whether it is in flight or on the ground at the time of the loss.

All risks—not in motion covers the insured plane only when it is on the ground and not moving under its own power. Thus, coverage applies while the plane is being towed, because it is not moving under its own power. Coverage does not apply, however, while the plane is taxiing, because the plane is moving under its own power.

Aircraft hull coverage is typically subject to only a few exclusions. The exclusion of claims caused by war, strikes, riots, and similar perils noted in connection with aircraft liability also applies to aircraft hull coverage. Most of the remaining exclusions applicable to aircraft hull coverage are comparable to auto physical damage exclusions, such as losses due to wear and tear, mechanical breakdown, and tire damage. Some aircraft policies exclude losses on any aircraft whose FAA Airworthiness Certificate has become void or has been restricted.

Hull insurance on smaller aircraft is usually subject to a dollar deductible, either for a flat amount (such as $1,000) or for a stated percentage (such as 10 percent) of the plane's value. Some policies are written with a specified dollar deductible for ground coverage and a percentage deductible when the aircraft is in flight. Larger multi-engine aircraft are sometimes insured with no deductible because deductibles do not eliminate many claims; the cost to repair even minor damage to such planes can amount to thousands of dollars.

Other Aircraft Coverages

Aircraft liability insurance is often supplemented by medical payments coverage, passenger voluntary settlement coverage, and nonowned aircraft liability coverage. The first two coverages provide a way to make prompt payments to injured persons and perhaps avoid more costly liability claims.

Aircraft medical payments coverage is similar to the medical payments coverage available in auto policies. The coverage pays, regardless of the insured's legal liability, for reasonable medical or funeral expenses incurred by occupants of the insured aircraft.

Passenger voluntary settlement coverage, also known as admitted liability coverage, is unique to aircraft insurance and is normally available for industrial aid aircraft. The coverage provides scheduled benefits if a passenger suffers death, dismemberment, or loss of sight. For benefits to become payable, both of these actions must be taken:

•   The insured must ask the insurer to pay.

•   The claimant must release the insured from liability for all bodily injury caused by the accident.

Nonowned aircraft liability coverage is designed for firms that have employees or other agents who use airplanes in the firm's business. For example, a sales representative might pilot his or her own plane or a chartered plane to make calls on customers. The employer would need this coverage just as it would need nonowned auto liability coverage if the salesperson used his or her own auto.

The coverage is available on a stand-alone basis for firms that have no other aircraft exposure. It is also purchased as part of an aircraft liability policy to provide coverage for substitute or rented aircraft.

☑ Reality Check

Why Aviation Risks Are Often Judgment Rated

In the United States in 2008, there were approximately 228,000 aircraft in general aviation. In contrast, there were approximately 137 million passenger cars.[3] These numbers help to explain why aviation insurers do not, for certain risk classifications, have a sufficiently large number of exposure units to permit the development of credible statistics on which actuarially sound rates can be based. Therefore, like marine insurers, aviation insurers must rely to a large extent on judgment in determining rates.

[DA07917]

CYBER RISK INSURANCE

Cyber risk insurance emerged as a specialized product category to meet the need for coverage that was not provided by traditional policies. Specialized cyber insurers, as well as traditional insurers, offer a variety of cyber risk insurance policies that can be customized to meet an organization's specific cyber risk loss exposures.

The high-tech risk posed to organizations that conduct their operations electronically and/or digitally is commonly known as "cyber risk." Additional terms for this type of risk and related loss exposures include e-commerce, cyber liability, Internet liability, cyber coverage (or insurance), and cyber security. Cyber risk is a generic term that is generally accepted as the insurance industry standard. It includes property, net income, and liability loss exposures.

Traditional commercial property and liability policies either exclude cyber risk loss exposures or provide limited coverage that is inadequate for most organizations. Meanwhile, the use of technology and related loss exposures continue to increase and create demand for insurance coverage.

The specific provisions of cyber risk insurance policies differ by insurer. Insurers typically offer policies containing first-party-only coverage (property and theft), third-party-only coverage (liability), or both in a combination policy format. Because first-party cyber risk losses can be difficult to assess and quantify, policies that offer first-party coverages have not been as widely available as those that include third-party coverages. Some insurers offer combination property and liability policies. Combination policies in particular allow insurers and organizations to match coverage with cyber risk loss exposures. Insurance and risk management professionals should understand the general aspects of cyber risk policies, including insuring agreements, coverage triggers, exclusions, limits of insurance, and coverage territory.

The cyber risk coverage needs of organizations are as variable as the available coverage options. Therefore, some insurers allow their customers to supplement a basic product with the insuring agreements that are appropriate for them, while others allow for full policy customization using insuring agreements. Other insurers offer a standard package of insuring agreements or "modular policies" that include a particular range of coverage options. The names of insuring agreements can vary from insurer to insurer. For example, "digital asset" coverage with one insurer may be known as "electronic data" coverage with another insurer.

The varieties of cyber risk coverage are evolving as rapidly as the technology that has made it necessary. This discussion provides a general description of the insuring agreements commonly found in cyber risk policies to reveal the various types of losses that cyber risk policies can cover.

Electronic Data Protection

An electronic data protection insuring agreement typically provides coverage for costs to recover or restore electronic data that have been altered, destroyed, deleted, or damaged. For instance, a computer virus attack can damage an insured's software and corrupt its associated data, requiring the insured to purchase and install replacement software and restore corrupted data.

Cyber Extortion

A cyber extortion insuring agreement provides coverage for expenses related to computer network kidnap and/or ransom events. For example, a hacker may covertly penetrate an organization's computer network and threaten to reveal specific details regarding the attack's execution unless the organization capitulates to his or her demands.

Cyber Crime

A cyber crime insuring agreement covers theft of money and securities and, depending on the insurer's form, **intangible property**. Cyber crime losses typically result from computer attacks or computer fraud. For example, a cyber criminal could gain unauthorized access to an insured's computer network and, through fraudulent billing, divert funds from the insured's cash accounts.

Intangible property
Property that has no physical form.

Notification or Remediation

A notification or remediation insuring agreement provides coverage for expenses related to crisis management during and after a cyber risk loss (typically related to a security breach). Coverage can include crisis management-related expenses such as costs to notify customers of a security breach and costs to develop and execute a public relations campaign to manage any negative publicity surrounding the breach and to maintain the insured's reputation.

Business Interruption

A business interruption insuring agreement provides coverage for loss of business income, loss of contingent business income, and payment of extra expenses incurred as a consequence of a business interruption or suspension of the insured's computer system (or dependent system) due to cyber risk loss. Depending on the insuring agreement offered by the insurer, in some cases only business income coverage (without extra expense coverage) is provided. For example, if an online retailer's Web site is forced offline for several days during a peak sales period because of a **denial-of-service attack**, the business interruption insuring agreement can compensate the retailer for loss of business income.

Network Security Liability

A network security liability insuring agreement provides coverage for liability arising from security breaches to an insured's computer network. Examples of sources of network security liability losses include a situation in which a cyber criminal attempts to gain access to the insured's network for personal financial gain, a random **malware** transmission, and a denial-of-service attack. Resulting liability losses can include, for example, damage to customers' data, customers' loss of use of services, and misappropriation of funds from customer accounts.

Denial-of-service attack

An attempt to overwhelm a computer system or network with excessive communications in order to deny users access.

Malware

Malicious software, such as a virus, that is transmitted from one computer to another to exploit system vulnerabilities in the targeted computer.

☑ Reality Check

Cost of Data Breach

The cost of a data breach at an organization, whether or not the breach results in theft or damage, can be significant because of compliance with requirements to notify customers of the breach and other regulatory requirements. Even if no customer business is lost as a result of the notifications, the cost of the notifications and assistance to customers, such as monitoring their credit reports, can pose a risk to the bottom line of an organization.

For example, as a result of a 2007 data breach at TJX Companies, the company paid, in addition to other large losses, $9.75 million to settle claims from forty-one state attorneys general relating to TJX's failure to adequately safeguard customers' financial information.

"Attorney General Martha Coakley Announces Multi-State Settlement with the TJX Companies, Inc., Over Massive Data Breach," Office of the Attorney General, Commonwealth of Massachusetts, June 23, 2009, www.mass.gov/?pageID=cagopressrelease&L=1&L0=Home&sid=Cago&b=pressrelease&f=2009_06_23_tjx_settlement&csid=Cago (accessed August 8, 2011). [DA07915]

Privacy Liability

A privacy liability insuring agreement provides coverage for liability arising from unauthorized disclosure or use of the private information of others or, depending on the insuring agreement, liability arising out of an insured's failure to comply with privacy provisions contained in laws such as the Health Insurance Portability and Accountability Act (HIPAA), the Gramm-Leach-Bliley Act (GLBA), or any anti-identity theft legislation. Actions typically are generated by a network security breach or unauthorized access to or use of information. For example, a bank employee could gain unauthorized access to the bank's customer database and obtain customers' Social Security numbers, generating a privacy liability. The employee could also reveal the Social Security numbers and other personal customer information to an accomplice, who could use the information to commit identity theft.

Electronic Media Liability

An electronic media liability insuring agreement provides coverage for liability arising from the insured's electronic content. Depending on the insuring agreement, the coverage can include e-mail communications; Web site content; and message board or discussion forum content that results in actual or alleged acts of defamation, disparagement, libel, slander, or false advertising. Electronic media liability also can be categorized as errors and omissions in the written or spoken word resulting in claims alleging financial loss or damage. For example, a company may post advertising on its Web site that makes certain claims about its product that are subsequently proved to be greatly exaggerated or simply untrue. In such a case, a competitor or customer can sue the company for false advertising under its electronic media liability coverage.

Technology Errors and Omissions Liability

A technology errors and omissions liability insuring agreement provides coverage for liability arising from any negligent act, error, or omission relating to an insured's products or services provided to others. For example, an information technology (IT) consultant may recommend that a customer test its network after performing a software update. The customer runs the test and the computer network crashes, causing the customer's business operations to be interrupted for a week. If the customer sued the consultant for loss of business income and recovery costs, the consultant could be protected against this suit by technology errors and omissions liability coverage. Depending on the insuring agreement, the coverage can also apply to employees of the insured's independent contractors.

Intellectual Property Liability

Infringement

The unauthorized use of an individual's intellectual property.

An intellectual property liability insuring agreement provides an insured with coverage for any copyright, trade secrets, trademark, or patent **infringement** claims arising out of the use of the insured's protected ideas or works (or infringing on the protected ideas or works of another). For example, a Web site offers copyright-protected films for viewing and downloading, for a fee. If some of the films are not yet authorized for release by the film studios who own their distribution rights, the Web site owner may be sued for copyright infringement.

Terrorism Coverage

Cyber risk policies, like most other commercial insurance policies, are subject to the Terrorism Risk Insurance Act (TRIA) of 2002, as amended in 2005 and 2007. Therefore, an insurer writing cyber risk coverage must include coverage against "certified acts of terrorism" as defined in TRIA, unless the insured declines the coverage. TRIA does not prohibit the insurer from excluding terroristic acts other than "certified acts of terrorism."

INSURING FOREIGN OPERATIONS

Commercial insurance policies, with only a few exceptions, restrict coverage to the United States, its territories and possessions, and Canada. Despite these exceptions, standard policies leave insureds with foreign operations exposed to potentially serious coverage gaps.

Organizations that operate outside the coverage territory, as defined in standard commercial policies, need insurance for their foreign exposures. The coverages are similar to those provided by standard policies, although some coverages are unique to foreign exposures.

At one time, small to mid-sized businesses in the U.S. did not have to concern themselves with foreign exposures, because they seldom had any foreign operations. Now, even relatively small organizations frequently do business around the world. See the exhibit "Examples of Foreign Loss Exposures."

To meet the needs of organizations with foreign loss exposures, a number of insurers offer a variety of specialized coverages, including these:

- Foreign property and business income insurance
- Foreign liability insurance
- Foreign supplemental and excess auto insurance
- Foreign voluntary workers compensation and employers liability insurance
- Foreign crime, including kidnap and ransom insurance
- Political risk insurance to provide protection against seizure of assets, currency inconvertibility, and interference with contractual performance

Examples of Foreign Loss Exposures

- Fred, a sales representative for Computer Facilitators, Inc. (CFI), was at the end of a six-month assignment in Europe when he injured a client by dropping his laptop computer on the client's foot. If the client sues for his injuries, CFI's CGL policy will not provide coverage, because Fred has been away from his home base within the covered territory for more than a "short time."

- Pierre, scalded while using a Hot Tub, Ltd. (HTL) product in his home in Paris, obtained a judgment against HTL in France and then commenced a court action in the United States to collect the judgment. HTL's CGL insurer would not provide coverage because the original suit was not brought in the covered territory.

- Sue, an employee of Superior Engineering, Inc. (SPI), rented a car in a country where auto liability insurance does not apply to claims made by passengers. Sue had an auto accident resulting in injuries to her passengers, and the car rental company's insurance did not cover either Sue's legal expenses to defend against the passengers' suit or pay the damages they were awarded. SPI's business auto policy would not cover the claims because the accident occurred outside the covered territory.

- Elaine, an employee of Management Consultants (MC), contracted malaria while on temporary assignment in Southeast Asia for MC. The workers compensation law of Elaine's home state did not cover the expense of treating malaria contracted overseas, and consequently, MC's workers compensation policy did not cover the expense.

- Ed, the CEO of an American corporation, was kidnapped and held for ransom while attending a conference in Europe. Although Ed's company had a crime insurance policy that included extortion, the extortion coverage did not apply because the kidnapping occurred outside the policy territory, which was limited to the U.S., Puerto Rico, and Canada.

[DA02687]

These coverages are similar to their domestic counterparts, although some are unique to foreign situations. For example, foreign voluntary workers compensation policies often include coverage for transportation expense to return disabled or deceased employees to the U.S. (repatriation expense). Foreign voluntary workers compensation policies also can provide coverage for endemic diseases, which are diseases that are generally associated with a specific geographic region (such as malaria). There are no standard forms for these coverages. Each insurer in this specialized market develops its own wordings.

Multinational enterprises with worldwide production and marketing facilities present a different problem. In many cases, the law of a particular nation requires that coverage for properties in that nation be purchased from insurers licensed to engage in the insurance business in that nation. Such insurers are known as admitted insurers, and the coverage they provide is known as admitted coverage. In addition, facility managers in foreign countries may want to maintain good relations with the local business community even when they are not compelled by law to purchase admitted coverage. However, the admitted coverages available in many countries do not meet the needs of multinational enterprises.

To solve this problem, a multinational enterprise can purchase admitted coverages and combine them with a difference in conditions (DIC) policy written to wrap around the admitted coverages, thereby maintaining uniform coverage for all the insured's locations. In some cases, a global insurance program is purchased centrally from an insurer that can provide admitted coverage worldwide, either through its own subsidiaries or insurers with which it has reciprocal arrangements.

TERRORISM ENDORSEMENTS FOR COMMERCIAL PROPERTY AND LIABILITY FORMS

Insurance advisory organizations have developed various endorsements to help insurers provide coverage for terrorism-related losses in accordance with federal law.

Under the Terrorism Risk Insurance Act (TRIA), the federal government shares the financial responsibility for terrorism losses with the insurance industry (through federal reinsurance). Insurers that write the lines of business subject to TRIA are required to make coverage available for certified acts of terrorism on the same terms and conditions as coverages that apply to nonterrorism events.

To help insurers comply with TRIA, Insurance Services Office, Inc. (ISO) has developed multiple versions of specific types of terrorism endorsements to complement various commercial coverage forms. The National Council on Compensation Insurance (NCCI) offers endorsements that address TRIA-related issues in workers compensation policies. ISO and NCCI also have developed endorsements specifically for states that have special provisions that affect terrorism coverages.

Disclosure Endorsements

When insurers extend an offer to purchase insurance or to renew a policy, and at the time of purchase, TRIA requires them to inform policyholders about the costs and limitations of terrorism coverage through these three required disclosures:

- The portion of the policy premium that is attributed to certified acts of terrorism—Additionally, insurers must list (in an endorsement or in the policy declarations) the coverages to which that premium applies.
- The federal share of compensation for certified acts of terrorism under the program—After the insurer's deductible is met, the federal share is 85 percent of losses attributed to certified acts up to the program cap.
- The amount of the program cap ($100 billion)—This disclosure must explain that if the program cap is exceeded, the amount of coverage for certified losses may be reduced at the discretion of the Secretary of the Treasury.

ISO has developed disclosure endorsements applicable to the ISO lines of business to which TRIA coverage applies, and NCCI has developed disclosure endorsements for workers compensation. For the ISO lines of business, policyholders can decline certified acts of terrorism coverage, in which case other options may be offered by endorsement at the insurer's discretion.

Cap Endorsements

TRIA places a $100 billion program cap on annual aggregate insured losses paid by the federal government and all insurers for certified acts of terrorism. When a policyholder accepts certified acts of terrorism coverage, the ISO *Commercial Lines Manual* requires the insurer to attach a cap endorsement developed for the specific line of business and coverage provided.

This endorsement clearly describes certified acts of terrorism as defined in TRIA (as do most of the other terrorism endorsements) and informs the policyholder that the insurer's responsibility to pay losses for certified acts of terrorism will end if the program cap is reached. Additionally, the endorsement states that if the cap is exceeded, the Secretary of the Treasury will mandate calculation of pro rata shares of insured losses below the cap, which could reduce the policyholder's coverage. The program cap does not apply to any acts of terrorism that are not certified acts of terrorism.

Certified Acts Exclusion Endorsements

ISO's certified acts exclusion endorsements exclude coverage for certified acts of terrorism when the insured has declined the insurer's offer of TRIA coverage. These endorsements may be attached for each line of business and coverage to which TRIA applies. Acts of terrorism that are not certified under the federal program are not excluded by this endorsement; however, coverage of such acts would be subject to other exclusions or limitations in the policy.

Some states require that any policy insuring property loss caused by fire provide coverage that is at least equal to the coverage provided under a Standard

Fire Policy (SFP). In these states, fire losses caused by terrorist action cannot be excluded. Certified acts exclusion endorsements contain an exception for these "SFP" states indicating that coverage is not excluded for direct loss or damage by fire to covered property when the fire results from a certified act of terrorism. The exception further states that these fire losses are limited by the program cap.

This SFP exception and its related schedule are for property coverages and are not included in certified acts exclusion endorsements developed for liability (only) policies.

NBCR Exclusion Endorsements

TRIA does not mandate coverage for losses from terrorist attacks that use nuclear, biological, chemical, or radiological materials (NBCR acts of terrorism) when such coverage is not provided in the base policy. Therefore, ISO has developed endorsements for excluding losses caused directly or indirectly by NBCR acts. These endorsements may be offered, at the insurer's option, only when the insured initially rejects certified acts of terrorism coverage.

Limitations Endorsements

If a policyholder initially declines certified acts of terrorism coverage, the insurer may offer more limited terrorism coverage amounts in return for a reduced premium. An insurer may accomplish this by writing the coverage for a sublimit that is lower than the limit applicable to other exposures. Such a sublimit could apply to a subsequent certified act of terrorism that occurs within an annual policy period if the limits are not exhausted by the prior act of terrorism. ISO has developed limitations endorsements for certified acts of terrorism that include a schedule of sublimits that apply to each coverage form, coverage part, or policy to which the endorsement is attached.

Aggregate Limit Endorsements

Aggregate limit TRIA endorsements are available for use with certain commercial liability coverage forms. These endorsements limit the insurer's exposure and provide limited liability coverage for certified acts for a reduced premium. The insurer may offer the aggregate limit endorsements only when the insured initially rejects certified acts of terrorism coverage.

When used with commercial general liability and farm liability coverage forms, the Certified Acts of Terrorism Aggregate Limit applies to bodily injury, property damage, personal and advertising injury, and medical payments arising out of certified acts of terrorism. When used with the Products/Completed Operations Liability Coverage Form, the limit applies to bodily injury and property damage only.

When applicable to a particular policy, the Certified Acts of Terrorism Aggregate Limit is subject to the policy's general aggregate and products/completed operations aggregate limit. Other policy limits, such as the each occurrence limit, continue to apply (to damages arising out of a certified act of terrorism) if and to the extent that the Certified Acts of Terrorism Aggregate Limit specified in the endorsement is not exhausted.

Punitive Damages Exclusion Endorsements

Insurers providing liability coverage for certified acts of terrorism may wish to exclude payment for terrorism-related punitive damages that result from civil actions. ISO has developed punitive damages exclusion endorsements for liability coverages when state laws permit such exclusions. These endorsements exclude coverage for punitive damages awarded against a policyholder that arise directly or indirectly out of certified acts of terrorism as defined by TRIA.

Other Acts Exclusion Endorsements

ISO also makes endorsements available for excluding acts of terrorism other than TRIA-certified acts of terrorism. These endorsements allow insurers to exclude noncertified acts of terrorism occurring outside the United States (including its territories and possessions and Puerto Rico). These endorsements are available only for use with commercial liability coverages, because those coverages insure some exposures outside the jurisdictional boundaries of TRIA.

These endorsements exclude other acts of terrorism committed outside the U.S. only when one or more of these situations exist:

- The total of all damages (including business interruption) to all types of property from terrorism exceeds $25 million (in U.S. dollars).
- Fifty or more people sustain serious physical injury or death.
- The act of terrorism involves the use, release, or escape of nuclear materials or results in nuclear reaction, radiation, or radioactive contamination.
- The act of terrorism is carried out by means of the dispersal or application of pathogenic or poisonous biological or chemical materials.
- Pathogenic or poisonous biological or chemical materials are released when one purpose of the terrorist act appears to be the release of such materials.

Auto Coverage Endorsements

TRIA does not apply to auto insurance, regardless of whether coverage is provided in a primary auto liability coverage form (such as the Business Auto Coverage Form) or included along with other liability coverages in a commercial umbrella or excess liability policy. (ISO has made terrorism exclusions available for use with primary commercial auto coverage forms, although these exclusions are not specifically related to TRIA.)

With respect to the ISO Commercial Liability Umbrella Coverage Part or Commercial Excess Liability Coverage Part, ISO has developed terrorism-related endorsements that address auto liability coverage. The basic purpose of these endorsements is to either cover or exclude acts of terrorism with respect to auto liability exposures, regardless of whether coverage for terrorism is provided or excluded for exposures other than auto.

Workers Compensation Endorsements

Workers compensation insurance is subject to TRIA. Therefore, insurers must include coverage for certified acts of terrorism in any workers compensation policies they write. Moreover, state workers compensation statutes prohibit insurers from excluding or limiting coverage for acts of terrorism (whether certified or not). Therefore, few terrorism-related endorsements are needed for workers compensation policies.

NCCI has developed endorsements to help insurers comply with the TRIA disclosure requirements and to inform policyholders about premiums related to acts of terrorism. The Terrorism Risk Insurance Program Reauthorization Act Endorsement defines certified acts of terrorism and discloses the portion of workers compensation premium that is attributed to certified acts, the federal share of compensation for certified acts under the program, and the amount of the program cap ($100 billion). In contrast to the ISO disclosure endorsements, this workers compensation endorsement states that an insured loss means any loss resulting from an act of terrorism, including an act of war, for purposes of workers compensation. This endorsement also describes the insurer's deductible under the program (20 percent of direct premium earned during the prior year).

TYPES OF SURETY BONDS

Many types of surety bonds are needed to address a variety of surety bonding needs.

Surety bonds may be designed to comply not only with various contractual arrangements that arise between a **principal** and an **obligee**, but also with various legal and statutory requirements.

Suretyship is usually conducted by insurers. Because surety bonds are used to provide a wide range of guarantees, many types exist. They fall into these categories:

- Contract bonds
- License and permit bonds
- Public official bonds

Obligee

The party to a surety bond that receives the surety's guarantee that the principal will fulfill an obligation or perform as promised.

Principal

The party to a surety bond whose obligation or performance the surety guarantees.

Suretyship

The obligation of one entity to answer for the debt, default, or miscarriage of performance of duties by another entity.

- Court bonds
- Miscellaneous bonds

Contract Bonds

Contract bonds are often required of an individual or organization (the principal) that is contractually obligated to perform work or a service for another individual or organization (the obligee). They serve two broad purposes:

- The **surety**'s willingness to furnish the bond is evidence that, in the surety's judgment, the principal is qualified to fulfill the terms of the contract.
- The surety guarantees that, even if the principal defaults, the obligations of the contract will be performed, or the surety will indemnify the obligee.

Contract bonds are frequently required by law; therefore, obligees are often government entities. However, private entities can also be obligees in such contracts. See the exhibit "Relationship Between Parties in a Contract Bond."

Contract bond

A surety bond guaranteeing the fulfillment of obligations under construction contracts or other types of contracts.

Surety

The party (usually an insurer) to a surety bond that guarantees to the obligee that the principal will fulfill an obligation or perform as required by the underlying contract, permit, or law.

Relationship Between Parties in a Contract Bond

Owner, a fast-food chain, wants to build a new outlet and engages Contractor to construct a building. The building contract between Owner and Contractor can be illustrated in this way:

Contractor ████████████████████████ Owner

Building Contract

Owner wants assurance that if Contractor defaults, Owner will not lose money and the project will be completed as per agreement. Contractor goes to Surety to obtain a guarantee that will satisfy Owner. The three-party contractual situation, or surety bond, can be illustrated in this manner:

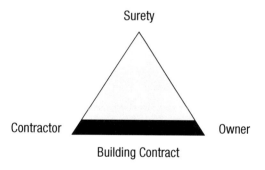

[DA07774]

Contract bonds fall into several categories, each with unique characteristics:

Bid bond

A contract bond guaranteeing that a contractor bidding on a construction or supply contract will enter into the contract and will provide a performance bond if the bid is accepted.

Performance bond

A contract bond guaranteeing that a contractor's work will be completed according to plans and specifications.

Payment bond

A contract bond guaranteeing that the project will be free of liens.

Maintenance bond

A contract bond guaranteeing that the work will be free from defects in materials and workmanship for a specified period after the project is completed.

- **Bid bond**—The obligee is usually the owner of a proposed construction project, although in some cases it may be a general contractor. If the principal (the bidder) fails to fulfill this obligation, the surety will pay the obligee the difference between the amount of the principal's bid and the bid finally accepted, plus any additional expenses incurred because of the contractor's default.

- **Performance bond**—The surety typically has several options if the principal has defaulted, including completing the contract using either the existing contractor or a replacement, having the obligee arrange for completion of the work and reimbursing the obligee for the additional costs, or paying damages. The surety has the right to seek reimbursement from the principal for any payments.

- **Payment bond**—This payment guarantee, also known as a labor and materials payment bond, is usually included in the contractor's performance bond but could be issued in a separate bond. It offers payment protection vital to private project owners because labor and material suppliers who go uncompensated can usually apply a mechanic's lien to the property. When a lien is placed on property, the owner does not have clear title to the property until all debts are settled.

- **Maintenance bond**—Some performance bonds automatically include this coverage without an additional charge for one year.

Contract bonds are also used to secure a variety of contracts other than construction contracts, such as those that deal with mechanical equipment rental with or without operators, transportation of school children, snow and garbage removal, or street cleaning.

License and Permit Bonds

Cities, states, and other political subdivisions often require persons or organizations wanting to engage in a particular business or trade, such as auto dealers, liquor stores, or building contractors, to obtain a license. Similarly, a person or an organization wanting to exercise a particular privilege in connection with its business may be required to obtain a permit. Examples of activities that may require permits include food handling and use and disposal of chemicals that may cause pollution.

License and permit bonds vary in what they guarantee. Some bonds guarantee compliance with laws that apply to the licensed activity; some additionally guarantee the payment of damages to anyone who suffers a loss resulting from noncompliance with those laws.

Other such bonds apply to specific activities. For example, merchandising and dealer bonds guarantee that the principal will conduct merchandising activities according to law and account for any funds held in trust. Reclamation and environmental protection bonds guarantee that, after operations are complete, the principal will restore land to its original state and will clean up polluting spills or runoff.

Public Official Bonds

Certain types of public officials are required by law to have bonds that protect the public against the officials' failure to perform their duties faithfully and honestly. Officials required to obtain such **public official bonds** are those whose duties involve the handling of public funds, the seizure and disposition of property, the arrest or detention of persons, or any other duties that could result in violation of the rights of others. Among the public officials required to be bonded are treasurers, tax collectors, sheriffs and deputies, police officers, judges and court clerks, notaries public, insurance commissioners, and bank examiners.

Public official bond

A commercial surety bond guaranteeing that a public official will perform his or her duties faithfully and honestly.

Court Bonds

Court bonds are often required by courts in connection with lawsuits. For example, if a defendant wants to appeal a court decision, the defendant must provide an appeal bond guaranteeing that the judgment will be paid if the appeal is unsuccessful.

Court bonds are also required in connection with disputes over the ownership of personal property. For example, Sean and Amy disagree about which one of them owns property in Sean's possession. Amy asks a court to compel Sean to return the property. The court will likely require both Sean and Amy to post court bonds until the case is decided. Sean's bond will guarantee that he will turn the property over to Amy if the case is decided in her favor. Amy's bond will guarantee that she will pay Sean any damages resulting from this action if it is decided in Sean's favor.

Court bonds also include fiduciary bonds, which guarantee the performance of persons appointed by a court to administer the property or interests of others. Principals of fiduciary bonds can include court-appointed guardians of minors or others, executors or administrators of estates, and receivers or trustees in bankruptcy proceedings.

Court bonds

A classification of surety bonds guaranteeing that a person or an organization will faithfully perform certain duties prescribed by law or by a court or will demonstrate financial responsibility for the benefit of another until the final outcome of a court's decision.

Miscellaneous Bonds

Miscellaneous bonds are those that do not fit under other surety bond categories. These bonds often support private relationships and unique business needs. These examples illustrate the use of miscellaneous bonds:

- Lost securities bonds guarantee that an entity that issues replacements for lost securities will be indemnified for any financial loss that results from the duplication of the securities.
- Hazardous waste removal bonds guarantee federal or state governments that owners or operators of hazardous waste facilities will comply with laws for closure and post-closure care of the facilities.
- Credit enhancement financial guaranty bonds guarantee governmental entities that investors will be paid promised interest and that principal will be returned at maturity of debt instruments.

Apply Your Knowledge

Which type of bond (contract, license and permit, public official, court, or miscellaneous) may apply to each of the following scenarios?

a. A nuclear power plant stores spent nuclear fuel on its property.

b. A landscape designer is hired to landscape a housing development.

c. After Howard dies without a will, his nephew Sebastian is appointed to administer his estate.

d. A civic organization applies to the city for permission to stage a public fireworks display.

e. Marilyn is appointed treasurer of a school district.

Feedback: a. Miscellaneous (hazardous waste removal) bond; b. contract bond; c. court (fiduciary) bond; d. licensing and permit bond; and e. public official bond.

SUMMARY

Commercial excess and umbrella liability policies provide additional limits above the limits of an insured's primary policies and take the place of the primary insurance when primary aggregate limits are reduced or exhausted. In addition, umbrella policies may drop down to cover some claims that are not covered by the insured's primary policies. Features of umbrella policies that distinguish them from other types of commercial liability policies include self-insured retentions; required underlying coverages; and their insuring agreements, exclusions, and conditions.

Professional liability insurance and management liability insurance differ from each other. They also differ from CGL insurance in terms of claims-made trigger, consent to settle, duty to defend, selection of defense counsel, and deductibles. Specific types of professional and management liability policies include physicians professional liability, insurance agents and brokers E&O liability, directors and officers liability, employment practices liability, and fiduciary liability.

These are five of the more common types of environmental insurance policies:

- Site-specific environmental impairment liability policies, which cover third-party claims arising from releases of pollutants beyond the boundaries of the site(s) listed in the policy declarations

- Underground storage tank compliance policies, which are typically used to provide proof of financial responsibility of owners and operators of underground fuel tanks

- Remediation stop-loss policies, which guarantee buyers of specified locations that remediation costs will not exceed a predetermined amount

- Contractors pollution liability policies, which cover the pollution-related loss exposures of contractors performing environmental remediation services on contaminated sites

- Environmental professional E&O liability policies, which cover engineers' professional liability without a pollution exclusion

The principal coverages available in an aircraft policy include aircraft liability coverage, usually written on a combined single limit per occurrence basis, and aircraft hull (physical damage) coverage, written on either an "all risks—ground and flight" or an "all risks—not in motion" basis. Other coverages available in an aircraft policy include medical payments coverage, passenger voluntary settlement coverage, and nonowned aircraft liability coverage.

The insuring agreements generally available in cyber risk insurance policies include these:

- Electronic data protection
- Cyber extortion
- Cyber crime
- Notification or remediation
- Business interruption
- Network security liability
- Privacy liability
- Electronic media liability
- Technology errors and omissions liability
- Intellectual property liability
- Terrorism coverage

Commercial insurance policies, with only a few exceptions, restrict coverage to the United States, its territories and possessions, and Canada. Despite these exceptions, standard policies leave insureds with foreign operations exposed to potentially serious coverage gaps.

ISO and NCCI have developed numerous versions of terrorism endorsements to complement the various coverage forms filed by these organizations. General categories include disclosure, cap, certified acts exclusion, NBCR exclusion, limitations, aggregate limit, punitive damages exclusion, other acts exclusion, auto coverage, and workers compensation endorsements. These endorsements help insurers comply with TRIA and effectively serve their policyholders' needs.

Surety bonds may be designed to comply not only with various contractual arrangements that arise between a principal and an obligee, but also with various legal and statutory requirements. Most surety bonds fall into these categories: contract bonds, license and permit bonds, public official bonds, court bonds, and miscellaneous bonds.

ASSIGNMENT NOTES

1. International Risk Management Institute, Inc., "Professional Liability Insurance," vol. II, Exhibit XV.E.1, June 2003 (accessed August 16, 2011).

2. Continental Carbon Co. and China Synthetic Rubber Corp. v. Action Marine, Inc., et al., www.appellate.net/briefs/CCC_Petition_Certiorari.pdf (accessed August 10, 2011).

3. Research and Innovative Technology Administration, Bureau of Transportation Statistics, "Number of U.S. Aircraft, Vehicles, Vessels, and Other Conveyances," www.bts.gov/publications/national_transportation_statistics/html/table_01_11.html (accessed August 7, 2011).

Index

Page numbers in boldface refer to pages where the word or phrase is defined.